Financial Risk Management in Banking

As risk-taking is an essential part of the banking industry, banks must practise efficient risk management to ensure survival in uncertain financial climates. Banking operations are specifically affected by fluctuations in interest rates which cause financial imbalance; thus, banks are now required to put in place an effective management structure that incorporates risk management efficiency measures that help mitigate the wide range of risks they face.

In this book, the authors have developed a new modelling approach to determine banks' financial risk management by offering detailed insights into the integrated approach of dollar-offset ratio and Data Envelopment Analysis (DEA), based on derivatives usage. It further analyses the efficiency measurement under stochastic DEA approaches, namely (i) Bootstrap DEA (BDEA), (ii) Sensitivity Analysis and (iii) Chance-Constrained DEA (CCDEA). As demonstrated in the modelling exercise, this integrated approach can be applied to other cases that require risk management efficiency measurement strategies.

Additionally, this is the first book to comprehensively review the derivative markets of both the developed and developing countries in the Asia-Pacific region, by examining the differences of risk management efficiency of the banking institutions in these countries.

Based on this measurement approach, strategies are provided for banks to improve their strategic risk management practices, as well as to reduce the impacts from external risks, such as changes in interest rates and exchange rates. Furthermore, this book will help banks to keep abreast of recent developments in the field of efficiency studies in management accounting, specifically in relation to hedge accounting, used by banks in the Asia-Pacific region.

Shahsuzan Zakaria, PhD, is an Assistant Professor at the Faculty of Business and Management, Universiti Teknologi MARA (UiTM), Kelantan, Malaysia.

Sardar M. N. Islam, PhD, is currently a Professor of Economic Studies (and has also been a Professor of Business, Economics and Finance (2007–2017)) at Victoria University, Melbourne, Australia.

Banking, Money and International Finance

For more information about this the series, please visit www.routledge.com/series/BMIF

Financial Risk Management in Banking

Evidence from Asia Pacific

**Shahsuzan Zakaria and
Sardar M. N. Islam**

Routledge
Taylor & Francis Group

LONDON AND NEW YORK

First published 2019
by Routledge
2 Park Square, Milton Park, Abingdon, Oxon OX14 4RN

and by Routledge
605 Third Avenue, New York, NY 10017

First issued in paperback 2021

Routledge is an imprint of the Taylor & Francis Group, an informa business

British Library Cataloguing-in-Publication Data
A catalogue record for this book is available from the British Library

Library of Congress Cataloging-in-Publication Data
A catalog record has been requested for this book

ISBN 13: 978-0-367-78423-2 (pbk)
ISBN 13: 978-1-138-38827-7 (hbk)

Typeset in Times New Roman
by codeMantra

Contents

List of figures

List of tables

List of abbreviations

AAS	Australian Accounting Standard
AFMA	Australian Financial Markets Association
APRA	Australian Prudential Regulation Authority
ARM	Adjustable Rate Mortgage
ATM	Automated Teller Machines
BCC	Banker-Charnes-Cooper
BCHB	Bumiputra-Commerce Holding Berhad
BDEA	Bootstrap DEA
BIS	Bank for International Settlements
BMDB	Bursa Malaysia Derivative Berhad
BMDC	Bursa Malaysia Derivatives Clearing
BOD	Board of Directors
CAMELS	Capital Adequacy, Assets, Management Capability, Earnings, Liquidity and Sensitivity
CAPM	Capital Asset Pricing Model
CCDEA	Chanced-Constrained DEA
CCR	Charnes-Cooper-Rhodes
CLN	Credit-Linked Notes
COGS	Cost of Goods Sold
CRS	Constant Return to Scale
CRSTE	Constant Return to Scale Technical Efficiency
CTA	Commodities Trading Act
CTC	Commodities Trading Commission
DEA	Data Envelopment Analysis
DEAP	Data Envelopment Analysis Program
DFA	Distribution Free Approach
DGP	Data-Generating Process
DMA	Direct Market Access
DMU	Decision-Making Unit
DRS	Decreasing Returns to Scale
DV	Dependent Variable
EM	Emerging Market
EMEs	Emerging Market Economies

ERM	Enterprise Risk Management
FASB	Financial Accounting Standards Board
FDH	Free Disposal Hull
FI	Fixed-Income
FIA	Futures Industry Act
FRA	Forward Rate Agreement
FSMP	Financial Sector Master Plan
FX	Foreign Exchange
GDP	Gross Domestic Product
GRV	Gross Replacement Value
IAS	International Accounting Standard
IASB	International Accounting Standard Board
IFC	International Finance Corporations
IRS	Increasing Returns to Scale
ISDA	International Swap Dealers Association
IV	Independent Variable
K–S	The Kolmogorov–Smirnov
LLR	Loan-Loss Reserves
LP	Linear Programming
MBS	Mortgage-Backed Security
MLP	Multi-Criteria Linear Programming
MPI	Malmquist Productivity Index
MWW	The Mann–Whitney–Wilcoxon
MYR	Malaysian Ringgit
NDEA	Network Data Envelopment Analysis
NPL	Non-Performing Loans
NPV	Net Replacement Value
O/N	Overnight Tenor
OLS	Ordinary Least Square
OTC	Over the Counter
OTE	Overall Technical Efficiency
PIM-DEA	Performance Improvement Management Software
P&L	Profit and Loss
PLL	Provision for Loan Losses
PTE	Pure Technical Efficiency
RFS	Relative Financial Strengths
RMB	Renminbi Business
ROE	Return on Equity
RVR	Regression Variability Reduction
SC	Securities Commission
SCA	Securities Commission Act
SD	Standard Deviation
SDEA	Stochastic DEA
SE	Scale Efficiency
SFA	Stochastic Frontier Approach

SFAS	Statement of Financial Accounting Standards
SPDEA	Stochastic Programming DEA
SPSS	Statistical Package for the Social Sciences
SRO	Self-Regulatory Organisation
ST	Static Trade-Off Theory
STIR	Short-Term Interest Rate
TE	Technical Efficiency
TFA	Thick Frontier Approach
THB	Thailand Bath
TIE	Times Interest Earned
UK	United Kingdom
USA	United States of America
USD	American Dollar
US GAAP	United States Generally Accepted Accounting Prsinciples
VaR	Value at Risk
VRS	Variable Returns to Scale
VRR	Volatility Risk Reduction
VRSTE	Variable Return to Scale Technical Efficiency
WTO	World Trade Organisation
WWTPs	Wastewater Treatment Plants

Preface and summary

Research background, research gap, motivation and contributions

As risk-taking is an essential part of the banking industry, it is important for banks to practise efficient risk management to ensure survival in uncertain climates, such as the one that occurred during the Asian Financial Crisis of 1997. Due to banking operations-specific susceptibility to fluctuations in interest rates that can cause financial imbalances, banks are now required to ensure an effective management structure that incorporates risk management efficiency measures that help mitigate the wide range of risks they may face in place. Such efficient risk management measures are vital in building robust and sound financial systems.

Since a sophisticated approach to risk management is required to face the challenging domestic and international environments, measurement and analysis of risk management efficiency have become the key for the survival of all banking activities. However, while the literature has recorded some measures for assessing efficiency, there are no specific methods identified for measuring risk management efficiency. This study proposes a new method for measuring risk management efficiency by integrating two elements: (i) a non-parametric approach known as Data Envelopment Analysis (DEA) and (ii) a Dollar-Offset Ratio (DOR) method of hedge effectiveness tests. By integrating these two approaches, risk management efficiency of banks can be appropriately analysed to determine the effect of financial derivatives on the risk management efficiency of banks.

This study provides a new approach to measuring levels of risk management efficiency in banks by offering a more detailed insight into the integrated approach of DOR and DEA, based on derivatives usage. Measurement of risk management efficiency contributes to the strengthening of the efficiency levels of banking risk management and the ability to achieve sound risk management in banking operations. The integrated approach is then able to explore the impact of derivative usage on banks' risk management efficiency. As demonstrated in the modelling exercise, this integrated approach can be applied to other cases requiring strategies to the measurement of risk management efficiency. Additionally, this study is the first attempt to comprehensively review the derivative markets of both the developed and developing countries in the Asia-Pacific region by examining the differences of risk management efficiency of banking institutions in these countries.

The research objectives

The main objective of this research is to develop a new method that measures risk management efficiency in banks based on the integration of a DOR of hedge accounting effectiveness tests and DEA through the usage of derivatives. The integration of DOR and DEA establishes the role of derivatives, as well as shows the impact of derivatives in measuring the risk management efficiency of banks. This study contributes to the risk management literature pertaining to the use of hedge accounting effectiveness based on a DEA approach to analyse the risk management efficiency level of banks in two different markets (the developing and developed countries). This study further analyses the efficiency measurement under stochastic DEA approaches, namely (i) Bootstrap DEA (BDEA), (ii) Sensitivity Analysis and (iii) Chance-Constrained DEA (CCDEA). Finally, risk management and derivative policies are formulated which may help in improving banks' risk management practices in both the developed and developing countries.

Research design, methodology and model

A new approach based on a quantitative research methodology is proposed and developed in this study using the two elements, namely (1) DOR and (2) DEA. This approach is supported by the fundamental ratio concept applied in both the methods. However, since the measurement of hedge effectiveness by the DOR is not driven by risk management issues, the two elements are integrated as a justification for defining input and output variables for risk management efficiency analysis. The selection of input and output parameters is based on an intermediation approach and is established through a dollar-offset formulation. The input parameter is known as the hedging instrument, while the outputs are derived from the hedge items through the usage of derivatives. The input variable is 'interest rate swaps', and the output variables include (a) 'mortgage, corporate and commercial loans', and (b) 'customer deposits'. This study reappraises risk management efficiency by using observations from a sample of 21 commercial banks from nine Asia-Pacific countries for the period from 2007 to 2012. The data are collected from the Bankscope database and the respective banks' financial reports. The model also examines the parameters under uncertainty to ensure that the results are useful from the practical viewpoint. Stochastic DEA approaches are used to incorporate the uncertainty issues to obtain robust, reliable and accurate results.

Results, discussion and implications

This study has performed three key analyses which are presented in three different chapters. First, in Chapter 3, an empirical illustration of the DOR calculation based on the relationship between the hedging instrument and the hedged items has been applied to four Australian banks and four Malaysian banks, selected to respectively represent banks in the developed and developing countries in the Asia-Pacific region. Banks using the DOR analysis value occurring in the range of 80–125% are considered as effective. The results showed that Bank 4 (CB4) was highly effective, with a DOR analysis value of 116%.

Second, in Chapter 4, a DEA approach has been applied to produce risk management efficiency scores over the period from 2007 to 2012. Based on a six-year analysis, banks in Australia and Japan were found to be more efficient when compared to banks from other countries in the Asia-Pacific region. Generally, banks in the developed countries have been found to have more systematic risk management strategies, particularly in using the derivative instrument. However, the robustness assessed by a DEA-based test found no significant differences between banks in the developed and developing countries within the Asia-Pacific region. Surprisingly, the results indicated that the Malaysian banks have superseded a few banks from the developed financial market. As a matter of fact, banks in the developing countries exhibited better scale performance when compared to banks in the developed countries.

Third, in Chapter 5, three different stochastic analyses were performed. In the first analysis presented in Part A, a BDEA approach to measure efficiency produced reliable and robust results. An analysis of risk management efficiency indicated an estimated efficiency bias corrected, which highlighted noise in data and sampling errors, thus improving the deterministic DEA estimation. The BDEA efficiency analysis clearly indicated its ability to reduce bias and noise in the data with better estimations than could be found using more simple approaches. In Part B, a sensitivity analysis demonstrated the influence of changing percentages in the parameters. With different stipulated changes, efficiency results of Decision-Making Units (DMUs) were affected. Lastly, in Part C, the CCDEA approach assumed uncertainty in the output parameters. This approach produced more convincing results when it assumed the probability of a 95% chance that all banks could achieve efficiency levels of 100% in risk management. Using the CCDEA approach, almost all banks in this study achieved better risk management efficiency scores than they could using the traditional form of DEA. The results of the efficiency difference tests between CCDEA and DEA, and CCDEA and BDEA, showed significant differences.

This study has several implications regarding the need for risk management efficiency measurement that integrates a DOR with the DEA method. Based on this integrated approach, a mechanism for developing a new approach that includes contextual as well as methodological elements is set out. Based on this measurement approach, strategies are provided for banks to improve their strategic risk management practices, as well as reduce the impacts from external risks, such as changes in interest rates and exchange rates. Furthermore, as risk management strategies based on derivative usages continue to be important business tools for banks to manage their risk management activities, they are expected to improve their risk management policies by helping banks to keep abreast of recent developments in the field of efficiency studies in management accounting, specifically in hedge accounting used by banks in the Asia-Pacific region.

Conclusion

The limitations of this study are as follows: (1) limited access to data and information pertaining to derivative instruments usage in banks has led to a small sample size, (2) other parametric or non-parametric approaches have not been considered when measuring the risk management efficiency in banks, (3) other stochastic approaches to DEA measurement were not used and (4) the analysis was limited to one type of financial derivative instrument in order to show the direct relationships between the hedging instrument and hedged items.

In conclusion, this study found that the new risk management efficiency measures based on an integrated approach to DEA and on the DOR provide a new approach to risk management efficiency measurements. The introduction of a DEA approach to hedge effectiveness testing is proposed as an alternative for measuring effectiveness in order to strengthen the hedge effectiveness test in hedge accounting. It is expected that these integrated measures would permit researchers and practitioners to be more expansive and ambitious in their use of these important elements. Lastly, the findings of this study will hopefully encourage new and even more exciting applications of DEA in the area of accounting, particularly in hedge accounting.

Acknowledgements

Editorial and proof-reading assistance was received in preparing this book. Some materials of this book are adopted from the following articles:

Shahsuzan Zakaria and Sardar M. N. Islam, (2019), Risk management efficiency measures and analysis: a combined dollar-offset ratio and data envelopment analysis based modelling approach and its implications, *article submitted to a journal.*

Shahsuzan Zakaria and Sardar M. N. Islam, (2019), Risk management efficiency measurement and analysis under uncertainty: an approach based on dollar-offset ratio and stochastic data envelopment analysis, *article submitted to a journal.*

Shahsuzan Zakaria Sardar M. N. Islam, and Murali Sambasivan, (2019), An integrated DEA and hedge accounting approach for risk management efficiency measurement: evidence from derivative markets in Asia-Pacific banks, *article submitted to a journal.*

Shahsuzan Zakaria and Sardar M. N. Islam, (2019), Risk management efficiency analysis in banks using data envelopment analysis (DEA) approach based on hedge accounting: perspectives and implications, *article submitted to a journal.*

1 Introduction

1.1 Background of the study

Firms and businesses operate in a constantly changing and risky environment that is unpredictable, volatile and complex. Efficient risk management strategies that are effective in terms of costs and resources are becoming increasingly important to the success of any business (Lam 2014; Power 2004), with the measurement and analysis of risk management efficiency being crucial for the survival of all business activities, both domestically and internationally. In spite of the availability of guidelines for firms to make financial decisions, Scholtens and Wensveen (2000) maintain that the most important rationale for financial risk management is to protect company balance sheets against severe monetary losses. These include operational cash flows against serious financial market uncertainties such as credit risks-and interest, as well as exchange rate fluctuations. For instance, in the United States of America (USA), the traditional business of banks has declined dramatically, and commercial banks have turned their main activities to fee-producing businesses, with the charging of fees as their main source of profit (Li and Yu 2010; Allen and Santomero 2001).

This new direction in the financial market has led firms to materialise various risk management strategies including insurance, derivative usage and diversification. These strategies are designed to achieve effective corporate risk management. Nowadays, derivatives, as a risk hedging tool, have become prominent particularly in financial institutions. Technological advances in financial innovation together with the creation of financial derivatives have served as risk reduction tools for managers of financial institutions in many developed countries. These scenarios encourage firms to position their businesses and improve their efficiency in risk management. Hence, the quantification of efficiency in risk management will assist in value creation and prevent the occurrence of any adverse events that might not have been properly considered in the relevant business scenario. In times of uncertainty and global economic turmoil, the role of risk management as a leverage for business management and operations becomes more crucial (Grote 2015; Schroeck 2002). The context of risk management, with clearly defined objectives by corporate management, becomes a key tool for supporting decision-making processes at strategic and tactical levels. The same concept applies to banking operations where risk arises from inaccurate business decisions. Therefore, appropriate risk management efficiency measurements in banks can substantially contribute to the implementation of activities, which are aimed at reducing possible future liabilities. Pastor (1999) points out that risk management efficiency measures are important for avoiding poor risk management and increased competition in financial markets. Thus, as far as the risk management of a firm is concerned, it is essential to develop a new method for measuring risk management efficiency. This implies the necessity of having robust measurements of risk management in financial institutions.

Furthermore, the findings of limited studies have demonstrated the impact of derivatives usage in risk management efficiency of financial institutions using a good measurement approach. For example, Rivas et al. (2006) found no clear implications of derivative items on the efficiency of banks' risk management. In addition, their discussions on the use of a Data Envelopment Analysis (DEA) approach failed to examine the technical aspects and roles of derivatives in controlling market risk and measuring risk management efficiency using derivatives-based inputs and outputs. These two points are of particular interest in commercial banks in relation to the efficiency of risk management in developing and emerging market economies (EMEs), particularly in the Asia-Pacific region (Au Yong et al. 2009). More importantly, when firms or banks are tied up with a derivative instrument transaction, they cannot escape from the concept of hedge accounting and hedge effectiveness. Therefore, an investigation into a hedge effectiveness test used in hedge accounting for risk management efficiency is needed. Furthermore, the assessment of financial risk in banks from fluctuations in interest rates through hedging by accounting treatment has implications whereby an accounting risk can create unreliable information.

This study fills the above research gap through an empirical investigation and analysis of banks' risk management efficiency based on the usage of derivative instruments in developed and developing financial markets in the Asia-Pacific region. The measurement and development of a model for financial risk management efficiency measures in banks was carried out using an integration of dollar-offset ratio and DEA approach. Other hedging effectiveness tests were not included, as these methods may have added difficulties in appropriately matching with the fundamental concept of a DEA approach. Moreover, as the use of a six-year data test would yield a better and more accurate dataset, the measurement of relative risk management efficiency involved 21 commercial banks covering the period from 2007 to 2012. The 21 banks selected are from Asia-Pacific countries, of which 6 are developed countries (Australia, Hong Kong, Japan, New Zealand, Singapore and Taiwan) and 3 are developing countries (Malaysia, the Philippines and Thailand). The period from 2007 to 2012 will also reflect a fair view of the institutions' overall performance during the financial crisis. In particular, this study seeks to address the following questions:

1   What is the need and significance of risk management efficiency measures and analysis?
2   How can the impact of derivatives be shown through hedge effectiveness in order to measure the efficiency of risk management in banks?
3   How can risk management efficiency be operationalised using a DEA that incorporates hedge accounting based on a hedge effectiveness test?
4   Are derivatives more efficient in managing risk in developed countries in comparison with developing countries in the Asia-Pacific region?
5   Does modelling risk (uncertainty or risk in modelling) in the measurement of risk management efficiency influence banks' risk management efficiency and its measurements? If yes, how and why?
6   How do deterministic and stochastic efficiency scores influence banks' risk management and derivative policies in developed and developing countries?

This chapter is structured as follows: Section 1.2 presents the general concept of risk in the banking environment. Section 1.3 presents the overview of the general risk management perspective, and Section 1.4 discusses efficiency in risk management and its measurement. It explains the hedge accounting used to measure efficiency in risk management via hedge effectiveness analysis, and compares the dollar-offset ratio with other tests. In this section, the integrated approach used in this book to measure banks' risk management efficiency incorporating DEA method in hedge accounting is presented. Section 1.5 emphasises the relationship between derivatives usage and risk management in commercial banks. Section 1.6 reviews the use of derivative instruments in emerging (developing) markets. Section 1.7 discusses the limitations of existing literature and the motivations for this study. The objectives of this study are stated in Section 1.8, while Section 1.9 presents the research design and planning which consists of the conceptual framework, methodology and empirical framework in the research approach, methodologies of efficiency evaluation, research phase and the proposed DEA approach to hedge accounting. Section 1.10 highlights the contribution and significance of the study (in both academic and practical applications), and lastly, Section 1.11 outlines the organisation of this book.

1.2   Risk

Risk in banking organisations refers to uncertainties resulting in adverse impacts on profitability that can lead to outright losses. According to Omar et al. (2014), McNeil et al. (2010) and Bessis (2002), the concept of risk in a banking environment has shifted from the traditional qualitative risk assessment to quantitative management. Evolution of risk practices, supervisory systems and regulatory incentives have changed the definition of risk. Due to the uncertainties of global market forces and financial movements, there is now an increased potential for an adverse effect on banks' profitability. Therefore, the ability of banks to manage risk directly impacts on their financial performance. For instance, due to the outbreak of the Asian financial crisis, lending growth had been curtailed and tight credit standards imposed. These actions had been taken in order to avoid debt crises that could reduce banks' profits.

As shown by Bessis (2002), credit and interest rates are the two main risks faced by banks. Both types of risk are potentially major sources of losses, and either one may cause clients to fail to comply with their obligations to repay debts and interest charged. Other types of risk faced by banks include liquidity, operational, foreign exchange (FX) and the country in which the banks operate. Because banks understand the adverse impact of risk and the importance of downsizing risk, they tend to focus risk management and strategies by identifying the key drivers that determine and control risk, particularly in terms of financial loss (Kupper 2000).

1.3 Risk management

In most financial institutions, risks are actively managed, and by utilising a variety of financial instruments, traders and risk managers are capable of protecting asset value and firms' financial performance (Ong 2006). Gup and Kolari (2005) noted that futures, options and swaps are the three most common financial instruments used by multinational transaction companies to reduce market risks. The use of these instruments guides banks in the effective and efficient management of risk at all levels in uncertain markets.

1.4 Efficiency in risk management and its measurement

Measurement of a financial risk management tool is essential to ensure its efficiency in contributing to risk management for corporate resilience. According to Fernando and Nimal (2014), efficiency and risk management are basic requirements for measuring risk management efficiency of banks as a decision-making unit (DMU). Despite increasing global market uncertainties, both strategic and operational practices need risk management efficiency measurements to achieve efficiency levels.

1.4.1 Hedge accounting used to measure efficiency in risk management via hedge effectiveness analysis – comparison of dollar-offset ratio with other effectiveness tests

In accordance with International Accounting Standards (IAS 39), companies should perform retrospective and prospective assessments to ensure that as in the past reporting periods, the relationship between hedging instruments and hedged items will remain effective in the future as well.

Hedge effectiveness is usually measured by using a number of specific methods including critical analysis (critical terms), correlation analysis and dollar-offset (ratio analysis). Under retrospective hedge effectiveness, Charnes et al. (2003) agree that the dollar-offset ratio is the most effective measure for hedge effectiveness testing. Here, the degree of confidence for hedge effectiveness (highly effective) is considered to be within the range of 80–125%. The effectiveness range shows a direct comparison between the hedging instrument and hedged item, and if the measure falls outside this range, companies should reconsider their derivative hedge strategy.

Compared to the application of other hedge effectiveness tests (Chapter 3, Section 3.3.1), the assessment of hedge effectiveness using dollar-offset ratio is much simpler (Hailer and Rump 2005; Finnerty and Grant 2003). This is because regression and statistical analyses require appropriate interpretations and understandings of statistical inferences, whereas the dollar-offset ratio allows a more direct analysis of price levels rather than changes in prices where both are exhibiting highly correlated price changes.[1] In this case, the dollar-offset method is significantly capable of measuring the effectiveness of a hedging instrument and hedged item, and hence can be used as a basis for testing a firm's risk management efficiency. The dollar-offset ratio is also preferable to regression analysis (Kawaller 2002), another method commonly used to determine the behaviour of the hedging relationship based on historical market rates through the linear equation.

Using the dollar-offset ratio approach, hedge effectiveness is able to determine whether changes in the fair value of the hedging instrument and hedged items attributable to a particular risk (e.g. interest rate risk or FX risk) have been highly correlated in the past, thus helping to ascertain whether the relationship will have a high degree of correlation in the future. Conversely, by using the more lengthy regression analysis, the R-squared value is lowered, with the likelihood of failure in the effectiveness test on hedging being increased due to the value of R-squared not being reliable. For this reason, further analysis using F-statistic and t-statistic is needed to determine whether the regression is statistically significant or otherwise, in determining the level of hedging effectiveness.

Another test is the volatility risk reduction (VRR) method[2] used to analyse effectiveness of the hedge structure by comparing the position of the hedging instrument and hedged item with the risk of the hedged item. Ramirez (2007, 25) documents that VRR approach comparatively investigates "how small the combined position of risk is relative to the hedged item risk". However, Finnerty and Grant (2003) warn that firms using the VRR method need to be aware that this test statistic is highly sensitive to observations and reflects overly small changes in value.

In comparing the dollar-offset ratio with other available methods, despite the superiority of the former, McCarroll and Khatri (2014) and Bunea-Bontaş (2012) argue that it is inappropriate due to its limited range of 80–125%, which fails to show adequate relationships between risk management and firm performance. As a result, they found that there have been many arbitrary discontinuations in hedging. In addition, many investors have had difficulties in understanding the outcome of effectiveness testing, particularly due to the unpredictable results when using the limited percentage range as a requirement of effectiveness assessment. This is because investment decisions are difficult when these measurements have been unable to prove the effectiveness of using hedging instruments to reduce the presence of risk in the hedged item. Referring to the IFRS (International Financial Reporting Standards) Financial Instruments (replacement of IAS 39) Phase III, the Hedge Accounting Exposure Draft and Comment Letters of February 2010, Seerden (2010) highlights the difficulty of determining relationships between hedge effectiveness and risk management. He recommends that hedging principles need to be developed based on the effectiveness assessments, but with closer relationships to risk management activities in order to achieve an offsetting concept in fair value that fits accounting purposes.

1.4.2 Integrated approach using hedge accounting and DEA

In measuring banks' risk management efficiency, this study proposes to integrate the dollar-offset ratio hedge accounting concept with the nonparametric approach (DEA) that has been used extensively to measure firm performance (efficiency). Due to the limitations of the simple ratio analysis applied in the dollar-offset ratio, DEA is incorporated to accomplish an advanced analysis of the impact of hedging instrument usage on the hedged item. This approach is particularly seen in the banking sector where performance takes into account the hedging instrument (interest rate swap) and the hedged item implication.

The dollar-offset ratio has been chosen as the most suitable method for the hedge effectiveness test in this book due to its theoretical links with the evaluation of efficiency when using a DEA approach that considers multiple outputs to the input ratio. This method is expected to be extremely useful in adequately measuring the risk profile of the traditional performance of banks in the Asia-Pacific region (Greuning and Bratanovic 1999), particularly when the ratio analysis is used with a large number of different units of analysis. In this way, DEA will be able to assign mathematical weights to all inputs and outputs in which "ratio analysis relies on the preferences of policy makers in assigning weights" (Nyhan and Martin 1999, 354), while making simultaneous comparisons of multiple dependent performance measures including output, outcome and quality.

1.5 Derivatives and its relationship with risk management in commercial banks

The use of financial instruments or derivatives as risk management weapons to draw inference on the current situation warrants that firms achieve competitive advantage (Triantis 2000; Clarke and Varma 1999).

As derivatives are extensively traded in developed markets and experience a larger trading volume, they serve the valuable purpose of hedging risk in the spot market (Rao 2012) and providing a means for managing financial risk (Chance and Brooks 2009). Chance and Brooks (2009) show that by using derivatives as protective strategies, individuals and companies can transfer not only risk from one party to another, but can also protect their investment portfolios against market turmoil and downsizing losses. Thus, derivatives should be viewed primarily as instruments for transferring risk (hedging strategy).

Previous studies have revealed a positive relationship between a firm's hedging strategy and its value (Brown et al. 2006; Allayannis and Weston 2001). Allayannis and Weston (2001) found that the impact of derivative usage on a firm's FX exposures can lead to an average increase of 4.87% in firm value. In addition, firms with higher growth aspirations are shown to have used derivatives as a hedging strategy, which is consistent with financial flexibility in the firm's value creation (Léautier 2007).

From an international perspective, most banks are active users of derivatives (Shiu and Moles 2010; Chamberlain et al. 1997). Since the mid-1980s, derivative instruments have become an increasingly important part of the product set used by depository institutions, especially in relation to managing their interest rate risk exposures (Brewer et al. 2001). As interest rates have become more volatile, depository institutions have recognised the importance of derivatives, particularly interest rate futures and interest rate swaps, in reducing risk and achieving acceptable financial performance. Moreover, Adkins et al. (2007) argued that higher investment allocation is channelled to derivative instruments because management has been persuaded on the effectiveness of derivatives in reducing interest rate and FX risk. According to Smith and Stulz (1985), banks use derivative instruments for hedging purposes. Fok et al. (1997) argue that there are three major benefits of using derivatives, namely reduced taxes under a progressive tax schedule, reduced expected cost of financial distress (Borokhovich et al. 2004) and reduced agency cost problems. Smith and Stulz (1985) first developed financial distress arguments for derivative usage in hedging, claiming that hedging can reduce the volatility of a firm's value by reducing the likelihood of costly financial distress, and thus increase the expected value of the firm. They argue that the greater the probability of distress or distress-induced costs, the greater will be the firm's benefits of hedging through reduced expected costs. Additionally, Sinkey and Carter (2001) contend that the larger the debt relative to the firm's value, the higher the probability of bankruptcy, and the higher the likelihood that a bank will use derivatives to hedge.

Minton et al. (2009) and Sinkey and Carter (2001) contend that affluent banks have access to the resources necessary for actively hedging risks using derivatives. Banks can use derivatives in both an end-user and dealer capacity. As end-users, banks use derivatives to hedge exposure to interest rates, FX and credit risk. Sinkey and Carter (2001) demonstrated that using derivatives to hedge can reduce financial distress costs, reduce expected taxes and agency costs, and achieve higher profits. As dealers, banks' derivative activities can increase their non-interest income, as well as enhance bank-customer relationships (DeYoung 2010; Sinkey and Carter 1997).

In addition, using derivatives for hedging purposes can help alleviate the incentive and monitoring problems caused by managerial risk aversion (Whidbee and Wohar 1999; Carter and Sinkey 1998; Weinberger et al. 1995). In addition, if derivatives are employed primarily for hedging purposes, they can be used as a means of reducing agency cost arising from wealth transfer from bondholders to shareholders. Since banks can use derivatives to hedge, they can reduce the volatility of their cash flow and pay out greater levels of income in the form of dividends, while ensuring that they have sufficient cash for debt payments.

1.6 Usage of derivative instruments and their relationships in emerging market economies (developing country markets)

Derivative instruments have been used internationally in both developing and developed financial markets. However, the derivatives market in EMEs remains relatively small compared to those in advanced economies. For instance, according to Rahman and Hassan (2011) and Mihaljek and Packer (2010), the average daily turnover of derivatives in 33 EMEs (including Malaysia, the Philippines and Thailand), for which data are available, was USD 1.2 trillion in April 2010 (6.2% of their combined Gross Domestic Product (GDP)), compared to USD 13.8 trillion in advanced economies (36% of those economies' GDP). Though small, Mihaljek and Packer (2010) found that derivatives markets in EMEs have expanded rapidly, and the turnover of derivatives trading has been growing faster in emerging markets than in developed countries. The average daily turnover increased by 300% from 2001 to 2007, and another 25% in the following three years despite the 2008–2009 economic crisis. This is higher than the growth of turnover in advanced economies (250% from 2001 to 2007, and 22% in the following three years).

In EMEs, derivatives are traded in almost equal proportions over the counter (OTC) and on exchanges. For comparison, in developed economies, almost two-thirds of derivatives are traded on exchanges, with 38% being OTC. In EME markets, derivatives are primarily used to hedge or speculate on the exchange rate, and to a lesser extent, equity market risk. FX derivatives account for 50% of total turnover in emerging markets, equity-linked derivatives for 30% and interest rate derivatives for the remaining percentage of the total turnover. On the other hand, derivatives in advanced economies are used by and large to trade interest rate risk (77% of total turnover), with the FX and equity-related derivatives receiving less focus. These differences are due to the relatively limited concerns about exchange rate risk in developed markets compared to that in emerging markets. However, according to

Guay et al. (2008), in order to achieve efficiency in derivatives markets, firms should consider continuous trading across time zones. Besides resulting in better market efficiency, continuous trading can benefit local firms. Thus, efficiency is also important for gaining competitive advantage when trading with other countries in the same time zone.

1.7 Limitations of existing literature and motivation for the study

In the context of measurement of risk management efficiency, methodologically there is an absence in the literature of attempts to test the use of DEA to ascertain banks' risk management efficiency in relation to its derivative instruments. This study uses a different type of input and output compared to the traditional input and output used in measuring bank efficiency. Previous studies only measure a bank's efficiency without addressing different purposes and therefore find no clear evidence of risk management implications. It may have been more fruitful if these studies had been based on the actual derivative financial instruments used by banks to demonstrate their direct effect on risk management efficiency. This is because input and output determination in these studies was not based on the use of derivative instruments (e.g. interest rate swaps) that correspond with the affected hedged items. In addition, most efficiency studies made little attempt to analyse the risk management efficiency of banks, even though it can be measured by using a frontier analysis approach and by measuring risk management efficiency in the same way as measuring the overall performance of firms (Cummins 1999).

In the dollar-offset ratio of a hedge effectiveness test, besides its failure to address the risk management of banks, the ratio analysis concept seems to offer a separate tool for measuring hedge effectiveness using derivative instruments. Therefore, as suggested by Halkos and Salamouris (2004), Thanassoulis et al. (1996) and Smith (1990), DEA is found to be suitable for setting targets so that units can become more efficient. Hence, integration of the dollar-offset ratio in hedge effectiveness and DEA can provide useful information on the performance of banks' risk management efficiency. In this way, the hedging instruments and hedged item's relationship can be developed to measure the effectiveness of derivatives' usage in the risk management of banks. As this risk management measurement issue based on a derivative instrument has not been explored in prior literature, an injection of new knowledge will assist in simulating an analytical integration of hedge accounting and efficiency measurements to determine risk management efficiency in banks.

As there is no study on the relationships between derivatives' usage and a banks' risk management efficiency in two different financial markets, there is a major limitation in the existing literature. This is because most evidence is limited to individual countries with no studies examining and comparing this issue in developed and emerging countries. Although Prevost et al. (2000) have compared the derivatives usage and financial risk management in small and large economies, they have not done so in different financial markets of developing countries that have experienced robust economic growth (e.g. Malaysia and the Philippines). Most literature focusses on the developed countries, especially on the USA. Hence, there is a need to compare derivatives usage and its impacts on efficiency levels across developed and developing countries. Rivas et al. (2006) analysed bank efficiency but they have not isolated the derivative types used by commercial banks. Therefore, there is a need to redefine the derivative instruments and test the relationships between derivatives usage and banks' risk management efficiency. Besides, there is limited investigation into the impact of derivatives' usage on a commercial banks' performance, with most studies focussing on its impact on non-financial companies; excluding commercial banks among the firms exposed to high external risks of interest rate and FX (Mulugetta and Hadjinikolov 2004). In short, there is a need to confirm whether derivatives usage leads to improvements in the efficiency of banks in both the developed and developing markets.

Due to the issue of uncertainty in traditional DEA estimation, there is a need for an investigation using an extended DEA under an uncertainty environment. However, this issue receives less attention in efficiency studies under the optimisation approach. Most of the efficiency measurements using the traditional DEA approach include studies that involved risk indicators. Therefore, it is pivotal for this study to investigate derivatives usage for risk management efficiency measurements using the appropriate approach to provide meaningful practical results. However, this requires a fresh approach using a decision model to operationalise derivatives usage in a way that suits real practice in the Asia-Pacific financial sector.

The above limitations in the existing literature on the use of derivative instruments and risk management using a DEA approach justify the present study, which combines multiple areas to allow for accurate and precise practices in measuring risk management efficiency in commercial banks that are influenced by both the developed and developing financial markets. In short, this study specifically aims at addressing research gaps identified in the literature on risk management efficiency measures based on derivatives usage.

1.8 Research objectives

The banking sector is continuously struggling to maintain its best risk management efficiency levels. As stated in the previous sections, hedge accounting effectiveness is essential for banks' risk management efficiency levels. The six principal objectives of this study are as follows:

1   To highlight the need for and significance of risk management efficiency measures and analysis;

2   To argue that hedge effectiveness which shows the impact of derivatives through the input (hedging instrument) and output (hedge item) ratio can be adopted as a measure of efficiency of risk management in banks;

3   To propose a new approach on the measurement and analysis of risk management efficiency through the operationalisation of a DEA model based on hedge accounting (hedge effectiveness test), with application to the banking sector;

4   To analyse from the results of DEA the relative impacts of derivative instruments used as a hedging strategy on banks' risk management efficiency, and compare risk management efficiency among banks in the developed and developing countries within the Asia-Pacific region;

5   To evaluate the influence of uncertainty (risk) issues in the modelling measurement (DEA) of risk management efficiency to determine its influence on banks' risk management efficiency measurements under uncertainty and

6   To formulate risk management and derivative policies through the DEA-based risk management and analysis for banks in the Asia-Pacific region that will help improve the banks' risk management practices by comparing banks in the developed and developing countries. This will help provide insight into risk management and measurements, managerial accounting practices and perspectives, integrating approaches of DEA with dollar-offset ratio, risk management efficiency measurement from the perspective of banks in the developed and developing countries, stochastic efficiency analysis, efficiency differences between deterministic and stochastic approaches, and other related implications.

In summary, this study aims at developing risk management efficiency measures by integrating hedge effectiveness (dollar-offset ratio) and non-parametric approach (DEA) to provide the possibility for financial institutions, specifically commercial banks to improve their risk management efficiency measurements and practices based on both hedging instruments and the hedged items.

1.9 Research design and planning

1.9.1 Conceptual framework

In accordance with the existing literature, the integration of two theoretical approaches, namely finance theory and efficiency theory, provides a significant contribution to the banking industry. Although to date, there has been no absolute model for measuring risk management efficiency based on the usage of derivative instruments and items, and their effect on the efficiency of risk management in banks, the framework adapted from Mulugetta and Hadjinikolov (2004) and Rivas et al. (2006) provides the path for this study. This path will help develop a new approach to measuring risk management efficiency in the banking industry, and its use of derivatives to improve risk management efficiency. Conceptually, this study will show how the integrated approaches of a DEA and a dollar-offset ratio, with derivative instruments and its relationship with hedge items, can positively influence banks' risk management efficiency level.

In order to measure risk management efficiency in banks, input and output variables need to be determined using a DEA. However, unlike the applications of DEA in the production field, where inputs and outputs are tangible elements, the choice of inputs and outputs for the present study is not straightforward when dealing with hedge accounting items and risk management. This situation has been demonstrated by Sufian and Haron (2009) when determining inputs and outputs using DEA applications that combine the use of market data including risk and profit in the stock market. Nevertheless, in a multiple criteria decision-making framework based on the hedge effectiveness concept, it is logical to consider inputs as certain amounts of hedging derivatives that are allocated by commercial banks to attain risk management sustainability, and outputs as hedged items measured in accordance with a financial derivative instrument. This study will measure the efficiency of banks' risk management by incorporating the use of derivative financial instruments in order to avoid the aggressive market risk and performance of banks.

In agreement with Berger and Humphrey (1997), the determination of inputs and outputs in this study is based on an intermediation approach. However, the determination of inputs and outputs needs to be viewed in the context of their relationship with risk management. Hence, in assessing the efficiency of derivatives and risk management, this study will examine the elements in a specific order considering interest rate swaps as the input, and customer deposits together with mortgage, corporate and commercial loans as the outputs. The determination of input and output variables is based on the hedge effectiveness test of the dollar-offset ratio in hedge accounting, which explains the relationship between the hedging instrument and hedged items. In banks, hedged items are affected by the use of a derivative instrument (hedging instrument), as reported in asset and liability management items. To integrate a derivative instrument in hedge effectiveness of the dollar-offset ratio with the measurement of risk management efficiency, a DEA approach is used to measure banks' risk management efficiency levels using a hedging instrument.

However, although DEA can be interpreted as a maximum likelihood efficiency estimator, an upward bias analysis in the sample can lead to inaccurate and less reliable results. It is also essential to address an uncertain climate in the banking industry. Therefore, the risk management efficiency study is further measured and tested by engaging stochastic optimisation approaches including Bootstrap DEA (BDEA), the Sensitivity Analysis, and Chance-Constrained DEA (CCDEA) to provide meaningful and robust results that contribute to sound banking practices (Figure 1.1).

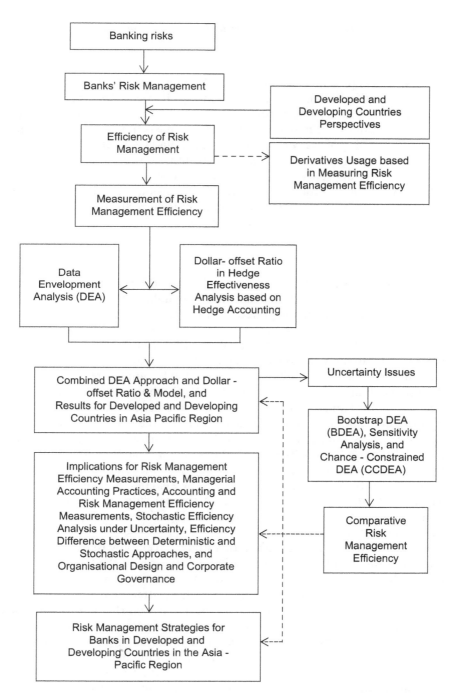

Figure 1.1 Conceptual Framework of an Integrated Approach based on DEA and Dollar-Offset Ratio for Risk Management Efficiency Measures.

1.9.2 Research methodology and empirical framework for the study

1.9.2.1 Research approach

The research approach in this applied study emphasises the deductive orientation to identify and measure the relationships between the concept of risk and banks' risk management performance. By looking at the nature of the investigation into risk management efficiency measures in banks through the understanding of the concept of derivatives and hedge effectiveness, it is deemed that *Analytical* and *Predictive is* the most appropriate combination for the research approach in this study. The integrated measure of the DEA and the dollar-offset ratio explores the risk management efficiency based on the usage of derivative instruments and its efficiency, thus highlighting its role as a management tool for mitigating risk.

1.9.2.2 Research design

The research design will be carried out using DEA mathematical programming techniques and models, where the dollar-offset ratio of hedge effectiveness test will be integrated with the DEA. The input and output variables will be determined from the usage of financial derivatives. For the purpose of analysis, samples of 21 banks in nine Asia-Pacific countries will be selected based on specific criteria and the availability of data. Almost all banking data used will be based on the banks' annual reports and the Bankscope database of Bureau van Dijk. Bankscope contains a standardised format for banks' financial statements, and hence cross-country comparisons are valid. For a comprehensive analysis, the banks are involved in derivative transactions and disclosed their derivative instruments in their financial reports from 2007 until 2012 (six years). The 21 samples selected for this study will comprise commercial banks in nine Asia-Pacific countries including Australia, Hong Kong, Japan, New Zealand, Singapore, Taiwan, Malaysia, Thailand and the Philippines. A six-year data test will be used for accuracy and because it will allow the screening of the overall performance during the recent financial crisis.

Besides a classic DEA approach, this study will employ BDEA to ensure more accurate results by compensating weaknesses in the classical DEA approach, which includes noise in data and sampling error measurement issues in analysis. A sensitivity analysis will be attempted to observe the variation in parameters, and how this will impact on the performance of risk management efficiency of banks in the Asia-Pacific region. Lastly, CCDEA will be applied to further address the issue of parameter uncertainty in the context of derivatives usage in banking operations, by modifying the DEA model itself. For this purpose, the CCDEA will address the issue of uncertainty in banks while focussing on the uncertainty of the parameters.

1.9.2.3 Research phases

This research consists of three phases, namely conceptualisation, research design and analysis. First, this study formulates the research problem and research questions, and sets the boundaries and objectives of the study. The research problem begins with the phenomenon of risk and its relationships with banks' risk management. After considering the related literature, this study formulates a primary research question by focussing on the measurement and analysis of the risk management efficiency approach by involving the usage of a derivative instrument as the risk management tool for banks.

In this sense, the study has set the boundaries within which risk management efficiency is measured and analysed using an integrated DEA and dollar-offset ratio approach based on financial derivatives. Currently, there are no specific measures in risk management efficiency in the efficiency literature. Moreover, the previous literature has shown that the extent to which the usage of a derivative instrument can affect risk management efficiency levels of banks has not been extensively examined. The discussion on hedge accounting tests and its treatment, which has been evaluated using the hedge effectiveness test principle, is important to evaluate the efficiency levels of risk management in banks.

Current materials related to the research problem were reviewed for a comprehensive investigation to develop the research framework. A comparative analysis of hedge effectiveness tests is reviewed where the dollar-offset ratio analysis can be integrated with the DEA approach, with both techniques sharing similar ratio principles. The DEA is proposed to enhance the risk management efficiency measures based on the derivative usage. Simultaneously, this study focusses on the specific form of derivative instrument used by commercial banks, and its relationship with hedge effectiveness testing in the hedge accounting treatment. The analysis of risk management efficiency also includes uncertainty (risk) issues related to DEA measurement, business environments and derivatives usage, thus allowing for more precise research questions and objectives to be determined for investigation.

Following this, the concept of risk and nature of risk management strategy in banks with the involvement of financial derivative instruments is explored and identified in all the selected banks in the Asia-Pacific region. The study then investigated whether a derivative instrument, through the analysis in the dollar-offset ratio as a test in hedge effectiveness, can result in effective risk management efficiency, particularly as a banking tool to mitigate risk, in this case interest rate risk. With the vital issue of whether a dollar-offset ratio can effectively influence banks' risk management efficiency, this study posits that the existing test is less effective in explaining the risk management efficiency measurement based on financial derivatives. For this reason, DEA is introduced to develop a good measure for risk management efficiency that may also help to highlight the role of derivatives. In order to determine the best approach, both parametric and non-parametric approaches were compared to find the best efficiency measurement technique to be used in this study. This comparison provides a justification of the methodology chosen: a non-parametric approach. DEA was chosen due to its strength and ability in measuring efficiency performance in banks. Both the dollar-offset ratio and DEA approaches were chosen based on their fundamental ability to perform within the ratio concepts. These concepts then become the basic theoretical approach for performing efficiency analyses, where the hedging instrument and hedged items were transformed to a DEA formulation.

The research procedures began with an empirical test for dollar-offset ratio analysis to determine the levels of effectiveness when using a hedging instrument (derivative instrument) and hedged items. Here, the level of effectiveness was categorised within the specific range from 80% to 125%. Analysis values falling within this range were considered as delivering an effective usage of derivatives. To match the input and output variables in an efficiency study, this research conducted an investigation based on the hedging instrument and hedged items relationships in a hedge effectiveness test. The input was selected from the hedging instrument (interest rate swap), and the outputs were (i) mortgage, corporate and commercial loans and (ii) customer deposits which have been derived from the hedged items based on the intermediation approach used in DEA efficiency studies. This information was then transferred to the DEA test for measuring efficiency levels of risk management in banks. The data were obtained from the banks' financial reports on derivatives used for hedging purposes in order to determine the banks' efficiency scores. Lastly, to solve the issue of noise in data and sampling errors that have been ignored in the traditional DEA measurements, as well as in derivatives trading and the market, an efficiency analysis was then performed using BDEA, a sensitivity analysis and CCDEA. From these, new risk management efficiency scores were deduced, which produced more accurate, robust and reliable results that could not be achieved using the traditional DEA approach.

1.9.2.4 Empirical framework

The empirical framework of risk management efficiency measures using derivative instruments to test the performance of banks' risk management efficiency in this study has been adopted from the frameworks presented by Rivas et al. (2006), Chernenko and Faulkender (2008), and Balakrishnan (2009). These authors believe that it is essential that banks monitor and manage their risk management in a systematic manner, taking into account the various risks involved in their areas, especially interest rate risk.

As discussed in Section 1.4, the relationships between the hedging instrument and hedged items, and interest rate swaps were used as the input for this study. This derivative instrument is used by a wide range of commercial banks for various reasons, namely: (i) to obtain lower cost funding, (ii) to hedge interest rate exposure, (iii) to obtain higher yielding investment assets and (iv) to take speculative positions in relation to future movements in interest rates. However, outputs were selected based on the hedged item that corresponds with the selected input, while being associated with the banks' risk management functions. This is due to the growing importance of new derivative products and markets characterising their role as a facilitator of risk transfer. Based on this relationship, (i) mortgage, corporate and commercial loans and (ii) customer deposits were chosen to analyse banks' risk management efficiency. Based on available literature and the support of expert opinion, this book uses a correlation test and non-parametric analysis (DEA) to determine the relationship between the inputs and outputs. The level of risk management efficiency proposed to provide for a better risk management policy for banks in the developed and developing countries was then ranked within the Asia-Pacific region.

1.9.2.5 Methodological approach – DEA

Many methodological approaches, parametric and non-parametric, have been proposed and used for efficiency measurement levels in banks. However, the application of DEA approach has been chosen based on several advantages which have been indicated in previous studies. The advantages of using DEA in measuring relative risk management efficiency of DMU are as follows: (i) this approach makes no assumptions about the functional form that links its inputs to outputs; (ii) it seeks a set of weights to maximise the technical efficiency; (iii) it performs better as a tool for estimating empirical production functions; (iv) it can guide the management to improvise on inefficient projects or DMUs by identifying a number of benchmark efficient units that are used as reference sets; and (v) it can be used to deal with multiple inputs and outputs with different measurement units, and can handle multiple inputs and outputs simultaneously, as well as it does not impose any functional form specification on the production function and it assumes no random errors. In addition, this approach is found to be successful and most widely used methodology for measuring efficiency levels (Feruś 2014; Zhang et al. 2014; Athanassopoulos and Curram 1996).

1.9.3 Modelling scheme: a new DEA modelling approach for financial risk management efficiency measures

Pursuant to the brief discussion above, the modelling scheme of this study shown in Figure 1.2 adopts the DEA approach as an efficiency measure for financial risk management efficiency. As far as the literature is concerned, since no specific application of this approach for financial risk management efficiency measures has been found, an example of its application is needed. Furthermore, in relation to financial risk management, the literature shows that the derivative instrument has received less attention in investigating the impact of its usage in analysing banks' risk management efficiencies. Indeed, results of this investigation may assist in reducing the long-standing controversy about how the usage of derivative instruments impacts on firm performance.

In measuring risk management efficiency based on the derivative instrument, derivatives and hedge effectiveness are closely related to each other, particularly in effectiveness tests (as discussed in Chapters 2 and 3). Based on the hedging instrument (derivative) and its impacts on the hedged items, an effectiveness test can evaluate and decide whether hedging relationships should be terminated or not. What is not yet clear is the impact that hedging instruments have on risk management. This indicates the need to understand the various perceptions on the derivative instrument existing in hedge effectiveness (hedge accounting rule), and to determine the extent to which the derivative can affect risk management efficiency levels.

In reviewing the weaknesses found in using hedge effectiveness measures, DEA has been found to be suitable for enhancing the efficiency analysis in this study. Using hedge effectiveness measurement, input and output variables can be derived for DEA. Thus, the integration of the two quantitative measures (DEA method and dollar-offset ratio of hedge effectiveness tests) provides an exciting opportunity to advance the knowledge of financial risk management efficiency measures. The proposed modelling scheme is shown in Figure 1.2.

1.10 Contribution and significance of the study

1.10.1 Contribution to knowledge

This particular study is the first to provide risk management efficiency measures by integrating hedge effectiveness test of the dollar-offset ratio and DEA approach based on the usage of financial derivative in measuring risk management efficiency in banks. The inputs were derived from the hedging instrument (derivative financial instruments) and outputs were based on the hedged item that corresponds with the derivative instrument usage. The input and output variables are directly related to each other. The study on the hedge accounting concept and its application to risk management efficiency measurement is relatively new. This hedge accounting practice can be used as a strategy to manage risk in the accounting contexts which will directly assess the effects on the hedged item.

At the methodological level, not only the application of hedge accounting in risk management measurement using DEA contributes to the development of DEA and efficiency literature, but also its rigorous and systematic operational approach has strengthened both hedge accounting and efficiency estimation concepts. The introduction of the DEA approach in hedge accounting, a technically sophisticated method, will contribute to the knowledge gap particularly within the derivatives efficiency study framework. The

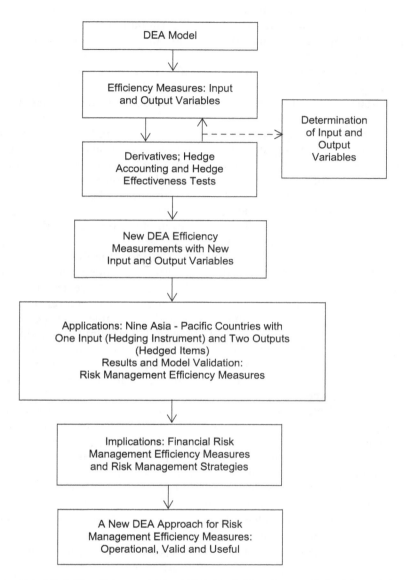

Figure 1.2 Modelling Scheme: A New DEA Modelling Approach for Financial Risk Management.

method chosen can be applied consistently to all similar hedging relation-ships (other hedging derivatives such as futures and cross-currency interest rate swap and related hedged items). Therefore, DEA is a different method that can be used to justify explicitly the effectiveness of instruments used, as well as to measure the performance of risk management in banks. This demonstrates that the measurement of risk management in banks based on hedge accounting and hedge effectiveness formulation is an accurate, valid and reliable approach because the items are measured in accordance with IAS 39 requirements and associated with the rules of the thumb according to the DEA. Consequently, the study will expand the existing methods of measuring the effectiveness of hedging. On a wider scope, after investigating the issue in this study, the researcher concluded that the implementation of the DEA method is very limited in the field of accounting. Almost all previous researchers evaluated bank efficiency using DEA by directly determining the input and output, either through a production or intermediation approach. In short, this study aimed to improve the measurement methods and procedures of banks' risk management based on hedging derivatives and strengthening the structure of hedge accounting. The research contributes to the consolidation of these two important areas within the scope of the banks' risk management. This integration of various fields will broaden the knowledge in the academic world.

This is the only study which explicitly considers the differences in the economic and institutional variations between developed and developing markets within the same region. It is the first attempt to review derivative markets in the developed and emerging economies on a comprehensive basis. The picture of derivatives markets in EMEs available from the existing literature is highly fragmented. Most of the evidence is limited to individual countries, types of derivatives or specific episodes of market development, without a thorough comparison with the developed derivatives market. Furthermore, even though the countries are located within the same region, a comparison between the two markets is vital since there is a difference in the market indicators such as price stabilisation, features of market architecture, order flow and trade execution, the role of information, market-making mechanisms, and the control and enforcement function. Therefore, discussing the implications for financial derivatives and financial management in commercial banks in both markets provides a new insight theoretically compared to previous studies where the researcher believed that market differences can contribute to the efficiency of risk management in commercial banks. The evidence is also important as it indicates the stage of development of derivative markets in the nine countries analysed.

As far as the literature is concerned, this is the first study involving an efficiency measurement approach and derivatives for comparative analysis of the risk management efficiency approaches or modelling, and risk management strategies. This study can give more realistic perspectives on measuring risk management efficiency using derivatives in banks in developed and developing countries in the Asia-Pacific region. Furthermore this study also makes a methodological contribution through the application of BDEA to reduce noise in the data and solve sampling error problems due to the small sample size. From the combination and comparison of the two approaches under DEA, this study will provide more accurate and realistic implication of the Asia-Pacific banks' risk management strategies.

In short, the originality of this study is an integration of the dollar-offset ratio of hedge effectiveness test which consists of hedging instruments and the hedged items in the banking sector, with the DEA risk management efficiency analysis. This new measurement, for the first time, provides thorough analysis in investigating hedging practices in commercial banks that combines a non-parametric approach, which leads to better risk management accounting method (risk governance) and better management (reducing) of an accounting risk. The proposed study makes an original contribution to the literature since it is the first comprehensive investigation into the comparative roles of derivatives and risk management efficiency in banks, and attempts to synthesise this study using a DEA comparing both the developed and emerging financial markets within the Asia-Pacific region.

1.10.2 Contribution to practice

The phenomenal growth in the turnover of derivative instruments has made them important in the financial sector. For financial institutions exposed to various external risks such as interest rate risk and market volatility, derivative usage is believed to be able to reduce the impact of market volatility, as well as providing an edge in banking risk management. When banks are able to absorb market obscurity, it can directly and positively affect their financial performance. However, to what extent will derivative usage, as a risk management tool, contribute to the efficiency of risk management in banks? This phenomenal growth needs to be studied carefully, as derivative markets, though relatively new, are growing fast.

The literature on banks' efficiency and risk management is relatively quiescent in respect to derivative activity. Past studies have particularly examined the efficiency of banks efficiency in general, without focussing on how derivatives and their relationship with risk management can affect the level of bank efficiency. The contribution of derivative instruments has been neglected and has received little attention by researchers on banks' risk management efficiency, even though this instrument can determine the future of financial institutions. This study attempts to fill this gap. Furthermore, the significance of this includes providing a framework for better risk management control, further research in the area of risk management in other financial sectors and recommendations into risk management control across the global network, to avoid a solvency crisis, as well as to understand how derivatives interact with the performance of banks to hedge unfavourable events. Derivatives will continue to be an important business tool for managing an entity's risk management activity. Their significance is expected to increase with the development of new products and techniques that refine and improve on the risk management policy, and keeping abreast of recent

developments in the field of efficiency studies within the context of management accounting and hedge accounting.

1.11 Book structure

Chapter 1 has set the stage by highlighting the need to determine the relevance of incorporating hedge accounting and the risk management
efficiency of DEA banks. It has also provided a justification for the consideration of hedge accounting in the banking practice. The chapter has set out
the motivation underlying the study from which the research questions were
deduced. It has also provided an overview of the research design followed by
the chosen methodology to be used to realise the research objectives of the
study. Finally, the research contributions have been explicitly stated from
both the academic and practical perspectives.

Chapter 2 provides the background and overview of the study, the concept of banking risks, risk management and the measurement of the risk
management efficiency of banks and its relationship with the use of derivatives. A significant consideration of risk management under uncertainties
will be explored since derivatives are used as a hedging tool for risk and
uncertainties. This chapter also introduces the differences in derivatives usage in commercial banks in the developing and developed financial market.
Finance theory will be discussed to highlight the role of derivative instruments in both financial markets and the existence of a gap in the literature
will also be discussed. This chapter provides a review of efficiency theories
and evidence of banking efficiency studies conducted in developing and developed countries, and the rest of the world. However, no claim is made
that it covers all extant studies. This chapter also discusses the DEA theory
and highlights some methodological issues in adapting this approach for
the measurement of risk management efficiency. The rationale for their inclusion is provided, particularly as to why this investigation is regarded as
interdisciplinary in nature.

The next three chapters (Chapters 3, 4 and 5) will discuss different scopes
and issues. However, the issues in each chapter will be integrated based on
the criticism and comments established at the end and beginning of the
chapter. By focussing on the findings and implications of the issues discussed, this study will be more focussed and the central analysis achieved.
Chapter 3 presents the risk management efficiency analysis and discussions
on finance theory and its relations to the need for financial derivatives usage
as a hedging tool. This novel application concentrates on hedge accounting
as a measure of efficiency in risk management by investigating the hedge
effectiveness test methods from the perspective of commercial banks. The
reasons for choosing the dollar-offset ratio hedge effectiveness test will be
highlighted, besides providing the empirical evidence of its calculation. Following from that, policy and theoretical implications will be discussed. The
last part of the chapter presents the conclusions.

In Chapter 4, a criticism of the hedge effectiveness test (dollar-offset ratio analysis) is discussed. This chapter reviews the usage of derivative instruments as a tool for mitigating risk in the context of bank's risk management efficiency study. Its application for measuring efficiency of risk management in banks is highlighted. Furthermore, the details of DEA methodology as well as the reason for choosing this approach instead of other approaches, either parametric or non-parametric, are explained. A choice of its orientation and, input and output variables have been evaluated. Applying a hedging instrument as an input and the hedged items as an output variable, the result will be generated and the implication in the developing and developed countries within the Asia-Pacific region can be seen when the chapter highlights the implications of the efficiency level of banks' risk management. In a nutshell, this chapter highlights the impact on the risk management policy based on the usage of derivative instruments. The model aims at encouraging policy makers to monitor and examine their level of efficiency to improve banks' overall performance.

Chapter 5 presents the weaknesses in 'deterministic' DEA measurement particularly on the upward bias (Ozcan 2014; Simar et al. 2014) which ignore the uncertainty issues in the context of noise in data, small sample (sampling error) and probability. These weaknesses are dealt with by using the extension of the classical DEA approach known as BDEA, the Sensitivity Analysis and CCDEA. This chapter addresses the importance of the assumptions of uncertainty issues in uncertain climate and shows how risk management efficiency results will change. These three approaches are formulated to suit the purpose of this study to achieve accurate, robust and reliable results, and the objective to provide comparative discussion on the traditional DEA results, implications and conclusion.

Lastly, Chapter 6 summarises and brings together the implications, recommendations and suggestion for future research.

Notes

1 Regression analysis has been discussed in detail by Wallace (2003) and Castelino (2000).
2 The VRR method for hedge effectiveness testing was invented by Andrew Kalotay Incorporation and implemented in a leading telecommunications company. This method has also been accepted for use in the Big-5 accounting firm. Telekom Italia Company is also among the few entities adopting this approach (Kalotay and Abreo 2001).

2 Literature review – relationship between derivatives and risk management and the concept of risk management efficiency and its measurement

2.1 Introduction

The primary objective of this study is to measure the efficiency of risk management in commercial banks through an integrated measurement of dollar-offset ratio and Data Envelopment Analysis (DEA), based on the usage of derivative instruments. This chapter provides an overview of banks' risk management strategies, using financial instruments in the developed and developing economies. This study is interdisciplinary, which involves the measurement of efficiency of derivative instruments, considering the need for efficient risk management. The research gaps are identified based on the arguments of risk management efficiency measurement in banking institutions, using financial derivative instruments.

The initial part of this chapter (Section 2.2) will discuss the concept of risks including financial and market risks. Based on the understanding that banks deal with risky conditions, Section 2.2.1 highlights the different types of risk, particularly interest rate risk since it is considered to represent the biggest source of risk for commercial banks. Section 2.3 discusses the concept of banks' risk management measurements with emphasis on the usage of derivative financial instruments in managing risk. In general, the relationship between derivatives and risk management is discussed in Section 2.4. Section 2.5 discusses the perspective in depth by explaining the relationship between derivatives and risk efficiency. Section 2.6 reviews the impact of derivatives usage on risk management strategy in the developing and developed countries. A theoretical perspective of derivatives and risk management efficiency is being discussed in Section 2.7. Analysis of risk indicators and strategies is discussed in Section 2.8, while Section 2.9 overviews banks' derivatives activities in both the developing and advanced economies of nine selected countries in the Asia-Pacific region. Section 2.10 presents the DEA theory, and Section 2.11 lists some methodological issues in adapting DEA for this purpose. Section 2.12 discusses the stochastic measurements to undertake risk management efficiency measures. Section 2.13 looks into the limitations of existing literature and the motivation of this study. The discussion in this chapter becomes the introductory analytical framework for evaluating risk management efficiency level in banks. Finally, Section 2.14 summarises the chapter.

2.2 The concept of banking risks

Generally, the concept of risk refers to the potential of losses resulting from a specific action or activity. Bartesaghi et al. (2012, 2) define risk as the "intersection between the achievement of instrumentally constructed means to goals and the likelihood of failure and negative outcomes". In the banking sector, uncertainty has an important role in the recovery of loans and capital, which constitutes the basic part of the asset and liability management of commercial banks.

2.2.1 *Uncertainty in banking risks management*

A bank is defined as an organisation that is empowered with cash and receives demand deposits of money and grants them as loans to different categories of borrowers or third parties, as well as investing in securities (Hubbard et al. 2002; Kashyap et al. 2002).

Banks deal with risky conditions as they are constantly exposed to uncertainties which may adversely affect their profitability (Bessis 2011; McNeil et al. 2010; Kupper 2000). For example, changes in interest rate can significantly alter a bank's profitability and the market value of its equity. In the banking environment, risk often refers to the impact of market focussing on the changes in the macro effects or volatility of market value, also known as the financial risk (Bessis 2011; Kupper 2000). Managers seek to balance the risk inherent in investments against the potential for profits (Bartesaghi et al. 2012).

In the banking atmosphere, interest rate risk is often referred to as a negative impact of the economics of banking and on financial statements through assets and liabilities (Scannella and Bennardo 2013; Hassan and Bashir 2003), and it can be substantial (Bank for International Settlements (BIS) 2003). This justifies a focus on analysis which highlights the importance of interest rate risk for this research. Most scholars believe that interest rate risk has an impact on the overall earnings and can create outright losses threatening the financial stability of institutions (Drehmann et al. 2008; Fraser et al. 2002; Saunders and Schumacher 2000; Madura and Zarruk 1995). Therefore, risk management policies and procedures that limit and control interest rate risk are crucial in the risk management of banks (Greuning and Bratanovic 1999).

2.2.1.1 *Interest rate risk*

Although there are many types of major risks including credit risk and liquidity risk, faced by banks, in considering the financial environment, this review will focus on interest rate risks which will appear repeatedly throughout the literature review (e.g. Delis and Kouretas 2011; Maddaloni and Peydró 2011; Elsinger et al. 2006; Brewer et al. 2001; Hirtle 1997). This emphasis is imperative since interest rate is non-diversifiable and banks naturally are repositories of interest rate risk (Gorton and Rosen 1995). Literally, this type of risk is related to a decline in earnings due to the movements of interest rates and also connected to potential movements in the volatility of bond yields (Viceira 2012; Jorion 2003). In an open market, the volatility of bond prices moves inversely with interest rates. This relationship is depicted by the formula used for fixed-income (FI) securities valuation, as shown below:

$$P = \sum_{t=1}^{T} \frac{c^t}{(1+y)^t} \tag{2.1}$$

where P represents the price of a bond, c^t is for cash flows generated by the security in time 't', while y stands for a discounting factor appropriate for the 't' period. The market price P of a bond with a given coupon is determined by demand and supply on the bond market. Bonds issued by a state treasury are considered to carry no risk assuming that risk-free interest rates are the only factor affecting the bond price. The above formula also relates to the concept of 'time value of money', which refers to the basic method of discounted cash flows valuation. The concept of 'discounted back to the present' has been explained by Fabozzi and Mann (2005).[1] As depicted in Equation 2.1, the discount factors (y) used for valuation of bonds depend on the level of market interest rate for tenure 't', where banks quote different interest rates based on how long the market participants would borrow money or agree to give money to the bank. The tenure begins from day one (overnight, or O/N tenure), up to several years. For the interest rate with tenure of less than or equal to one year, it belongs to the money market which falls into the short-term financial market (≤1 year), and if the tenure is for more than one year (>1 year), it belongs to the capital market (long-term financial market).

From an accounting perspective, most of the banks' financial statements and cost items are interest-rate driven. If interest rates rise, the increase in the cost of funds reflects more rapidly compared to the yield on assets. This circumstance reduces the value of banks' earnings (net income). If the pressure on interest rates is not strategically controlled, an increase in interest rates would have a relatively more dramatic effect on a firm's financial viability, consequently profits and shareholder value will erode (Dhanani et al. 2005). Historically, increasing exposure with regard to interest rate shock has de-capitalised the saving and loan industry. As the banking crisis has shown, Herring (1998) discovered that interest rate shock had distressed most players in the industry. In 1979, most of the banks and savings and loan industries took no account of the influence and impact on the balance sheet of changing market values in response to rising interest rates. In this regard, no reserve was created as a measure to face fluctuations in interest rates. During the 1970s, interest rates were very volatile and accelerated. At this point, most saving and loan industries suffered as interest rates showed no sign of retracement. As a result of this uncertainty, the senior managers were actively engaged in the measurement and assessment of risk exposures.

Banks use different objective risk measurement techniques to evaluate the effects of the different interest rate phenomena on the various types of interest rate risks they are exposed to. Kohn (2010, 8) is concerned that interest rates may affect the safety and performance of institutions, and propounded different types of risks as depicted below:

> … basic re-pricing mismatches that are most sensitive to changes in the level of rates; exposures to different yield curve shifts, twist, and slopes; basic risks, which arise from the re-pricing differences in instruments with similar maturities; and the risks that both explicit and embedded interest rate options can pose to the performance and safety and soundness of an institution.

Such risks illustrate the seriousness of interest rate movements in threatening market transactions. Evidently, financial institutions must understand the shape and movement of the risks and how to control and minimise those risks. For example, Yong et al. (2009) and Saunders and Cornett (2007) documented the evidence of banks having a great market risk profile. Banks consider derivative instruments as quality risk management tools and relevant to discovering the relationship between derivatives usage and risk reduction. A bank is a major consumer of financial derivatives to reduce systematic risk. As reported by Chaudhry et al. (2000), the association between different foreign currency derivatives (forwards, futures, options and swaps) and banks' risk is measured by systematic risk. The findings show that derivative elements are used primarily for hedging and consequently proven to be sound risk management tools.

The variable rate loan is also among the complex indexations influenced by the market interest rates. Variable rate is interest rate that is being changed periodically using some market reference rate that a borrower has to pay on their loan based on the interest rate movements (Lange 2007). In the event of a decline in the underlying index, the borrower's interest payments are also low, and vice versa. When interest rates rise, banks will lend less and thus reduce bank profits, (*Interest = Debt Outstanding × Interest Rate × Time Overdue*). For instance, if many loans are issued in adjustable rate mortgage (ARM) and a higher rate caused homeowners to default, banks will have less profits from repayment and will incur higher costs related to asset forfeiture. With the influence of inflation rate, it is not easy to discover the trend of interest rate movement. In conclusion, it can be stated that banks are institutions trading in risks. With various forms of risk faced, undoubtedly banks should hedge their interest from the financial risk exposure.

2.3 Banks' risk management efficiency measurements and the use of derivatives

2.3.1 Definition, principle and concept

Fundamentally, risk management can be defined as the process of identifying, quantifying and managing the risks that an organisation faces. Collier (2009) raises more dynamic purposes related to the risk management and enterprise risk management (ERM). The relationship between risk management and ERM must include concrete strategies and organisational goals. Risk management should be a culture in the overall structure of an organisation which considers risks as opportunities as much as threats. It has been a matter of continuing concern for most firms since the fall of the Bretton Wood System in the 1970s. The Institute of Risk Management (2002) indicates that risk faced by an organisation can result from both external and internal factors, which include financial, strategic, hazardous and operational risks. Some risks have both external and internal drives (e.g. employees, supply chains, products and services, and the integration of mergers and acquisitions). In relation to financial risks, companies are exposed to various types of risks that can affect their expected returns (Kempf et al. 2014; Kim et al. 1993). Interest rate risks, foreign exchange (FX) risks and credit risks are associated with the economic environment (market risk), where their changes affect all companies. An internal control strategy will not effectively manage these risks.

From the financial perspective, risk management refers to the process of analysing risk exposure and attempting to minimise it through various means including diversification such as hedging, leverage and others. To reduce the risks of interest and currency rates, different measures have been introduced to measure risk management effectiveness and risk exposure, whether by subjective or quantitative forms (Barrieu and Scandolo 2015; Morgan and Small 1992; Kaplan and Garrick 1981). From the quantitative perspective, it is typically concerned with portfolios volatility (portfolio variance), diversifications, capital asset pricing models (CAPM) and hedging (McNeil et al. 2005). Early risk management literature also focussed on efforts to minimise the variance of stock return through the CAPM (Fama 1980; Lintner 1965; Sharpe 1964). The CAPM model suggests that individual investors should hold a diversified portfolio to reduce the unsystematic risk associated with each stock. However, theoretically, the CAPM measurement is less conclusive in explaining the risk management effort based on risk and return relationships. From the perspective of homogeneous beliefs, Kassi et al. (2019) states that undiversified risks in financial markets can cause the market to underperform at different times; thus, the measurement may be less accurate simply because of economic changes or unfavourable market events.

At this point, Collier (2009) contended that although these methods are accepted and adopted in measuring the risk in the banking industry, it is difficult to quantify the risk using quantitative techniques without balancing them with more subjective judgements of operational risk and the concept of risk management. Firms can also measure their value at risk (VaR) through models developed internally or by a standardised approach using a risk-weighted process developed by the Basel Committee on Bank Supervision. Thus, the modest way of measuring risk exposure is to look at the historical data and examine the methods that have used firm value and earnings as a function of pre-specified risk.

The common strategies of hedging (eliminate or reduce) risks include insurance or derivatives. Since firms are not associated with nationalisation, risk can be managed using derivatives to reduce and share risk among firms (Ehrhardt and Brigham 2011; Collier 2009). The action, also known as a "reduced form" in nature, is taken by transferring a portion of the risk through portfolio diversification or hedging to third parties. Hedging protects assets against unfavourable movements in FX and interest rate fluctuation where hedging strategy will move the financial and economic risk within financial markets. Banks are working to fully institute a comprehensive risk management policy, and most banks are finding it increasingly difficult to mitigate risk, especially in the post-global financial crisis scenario (Siregar et al. 2011). Banks are struggling to ensure that their specific business decisions are consistent with their risk appetite and offer the best solutions to reduce uncertainties (Kupper 2000). Some researchers (Abdel-Khalik 2013; Fratzscher 2006; Bodnar and Gebhardt 1999) believe that financial derivatives have become invaluable tools for risk management. Historical records show that in the past decade, established firms which were considered as regular users of financial derivatives have made considerable progress in measuring the risks of derivatives portfolios (Stulz 2003). The VaR approach, which is one of the popular approaches in measuring risks of derivatives portfolio, may not always work well. Stulz (2003) provides an example whereby during the Russian crisis, banks exceeded their VaRs more than they theoretically should have. It thus highlights the limitation of VaR measurements in setting-up firms trading and hedging strategies in order to achieve risk management objectives. This study observes that for risk management purposes, the measurements have to encompass the entire impact either on return density or efficiency level. Thus, firms can see a range of risk management behaviours in order to facilitate derivatives usage. Collectively, from the literature search for this study, it appears that there are no existing known measures of efficiency for risk management. What have been discussed in the literature are the measures for risk, but not for risk management efficiency. Therefore, this justifies the necessity for risk management efficiency measurements to be established, by developing a measure for risk management efficiency. From here, the derivatives usage strategy used by firms can be measured, so that their influence on risk management efficiency can be determined.

In the literature, when new derivatives users implement a derivatives strategy, it has been associated with the financial derivatives function used as hedging tools on the firm's assets and to reduce financial distress costs (Bartram et al. 2009; Borokhovich et al. 2004). Recommending the use of derivatives for hedging purposes, Guay (1999) found that the taking of a derivatives position is associated with the reduction of a firm's risk. Research on new derivatives users shows that they experience a significant impact in reduction in stock return volatility as well as interest rate and FX exposures from using derivatives. Several researchers such as Borokhovich et al. (2004), Smith and Stulz (1985) and Fok et al. (1997) have argued that hedging can not only reduce the present value of expected tax liabilities but also decrease the expected cost of financial distress and agency cost problems. As derivatives are primarily employed for hedging purposes, they can be used as a means of reducing agency cost arising from wealth transfer from bondholders to shareholders. Since banks can use derivatives as a hedging instrument, they can reduce the volatility of their cash flow and pay out greater level of income in the form of dividends to ensure that bondholders have sufficient cash for debt payments.

In hedge accounting, derivatives usage whether for hedging or trading purposes follows the International Accounting Standard (IAS 39) which requires hedging strategies to test the effectiveness of the hedging instrument and the hedged item with a measurement that was originally introduced by Ederington (1979). The purpose is to measure the risk reduction effect of a futures market. Even though the measurement of risk reduction is often the most challenging part of the whole process (Ramirez 2008; Finnerty and Grant 2003), such a measure can test the effectiveness of the hedging item to show how risks are offset by changes in the fair value or cash flows of the hedging instruments.

2.3.1.1 Efficiency in risk management

Risk management, with clear objectives defined by the corporate management and formulated in business terms, becomes a decision supporting tool at strategic level. Appropriate risk management strategies contribute substantially to the accomplishment of actions aimed at reducing possible future losses or liabilities. Stulz (2008) establishes that efficient risk management does not necessarily guarantee success. A major loss could occur if the top management takes higher risks in expectation of higher returns. Consequently, this implies an investment theory that risk lovers are willing to accept higher risk for a higher return. Higher earnings depend on choices made by those management teams who are entrusted to determine the firm's appetite.

According to Collier et al. (2006), consistent with current trends, risk is considered in a systematic way in organisations. Since risk assessments are being used in decision-making, companies have a sophisticated approach to their risk management practices. For instance, in VaR models, volatility assessment and derivatives contracts are among the sophisticated models used to achieve efficient risk management, due to the unknown or market risk. The technical and specific techniques to deal with known and unknown risks are important for risk management people or managers to select the most appropriate risk handling options. Conrow (2003) mentions that risk handling options include assumptions, avoidance, control and transfer. All of these elements are crucial to ensuring that risk management can complement the objectives of the organisations. One of the reasons for the failure of risk management highlighted by Stulz (2008) is the failure to monitor and manage risk. Stulz (2008) asserts that identifying the nature of the risk and hedge method will significantly contribute to the bottom line of an organisation. The strategy of managing the chosen risk will determine the level of impact of the market risk on the organisation.

2.3.2 Derivative instruments: definitions and concepts

The definition of derivatives is well developed in literature. Rubinstein (1999) defines derivative as a contract between two parties that specifies the conditions (in particular, dates and the resulting values of underlying variables) under which payments or payoffs are to be made between the parties. According to Bajo et al. (2014) and Sheedy and McCracken (1997), derivatives are mainly based on financial products, such as interest rate securities, FX and company shares, and their value responds to price changes in these products. Derivatives contracts include forwards, futures, options and swaps. As end users, both non-financial and financial firms use derivatives either to hedge against the unexpected changes in FX rates, interest rates or commodity prices, or speculate on the future movements of the economic variables (DeYoung 2010; Sinkey and Carter 2000). Mallin et al. (2001), Phillips (1995) and Froot et al. (1994) proved that companies use derivatives contracts to hedge interest rate and foreign currency exposure by more than 90% and 75%, respectively.

2.3.2.1 Foreign currency derivatives

Futures contract, forward contracts, swaps and options are among the derivatives instruments, being used by firms to manage their exposures to FX risks (e.g. Jones 2014; Otieno 2013). Each of these instruments is applied differently in each firm's situation. It sometimes depends on the effect of unexpected changes in interest rates or FX rates, coupled with the influence of the size of the firms (Boukrami 2002; Kim and Koppenhaver 1992). The effectiveness of these techniques has received much attention by many researchers, particularly forward contracts and currency futures contracts (Bergendahl and Sjögren 2013; Castelino 1992; Herbst et al. 1985).

According to Chance and Brooks (2009), a forward contract is an agreement between two parties (buyer and seller) to purchase and sell something of a specific quantity at a later date at a price agreed upon today. Forward contracts are normally traded with maturities of up to one, three or six months. However, they can also be taken out for up to five years. In dealing with a number of risks, a forward contract is essential for treasures to exercise caution. The forward rate is not reflected purely by the strength or weakness of a currency, but also allows for differences in interest rates. This phenomenon may move the forward rates more dramatically than spot rates. Consequently, it will expose firms to more risks such as counter party risk and settlement risk. Since the two parties in a forward contract incur the obligation to ultimately buy and sell the goods, this contract contains considerable risk. Generally, it has a symmetric payoff, whereas the gain when the value of the underlying asset moves in one direction is equal to the loss when the value of the asset moves by the same amount in the opposite direction (Heston and Nandi 2000). The forward market is very much more important to many industries and is dominated by large institutions such as banks and corporations since it is now easier to enter into forward contracts and is extremely useful as they facilitate the understanding of futures contracts (Chance and Brooks 2009).

Entering into a futures contract is another technique which a company might use in order to reduce the risk of FX volatility (Chance and Brooks 2015; Jorion 1995). This contract possesses several similar characteristics to forward contracts since both involve the agreement of buying and selling currency at a future date. The difference in the profits or losses from holding futures contracts are paid each day subject to a daily settlement procedure by a clearinghouse, while in forward contracts, they are realised and transferred only when a contract expires (Ali et al. 2006). Futures market is one of the most important ways to hedge risky assets. In a long hedge futures contract, a firm will be protected against a rise in a foreign currency value and vice versa if the firm takes out a short hedge futures contract. A daily fluctuation of futures prices and the contract between buyers and sellers attempting to profit from these price movements lowers the risk of transacting in the underlying goods.

Based on empirical evidence of the currency futures usage, many found that this instrument received less attention among companies. Khoury and Chanf (1993) have confirmed that currency futures were the least used method by most companies both non-financial and financial. The main deterrents impeding the usage of this instrument include high administrative costs, opportunity for continuous arbitrage activities that stem from convergence mismatch, margin requirements and inflexibility in contract sizes. This study also found that forwards are the main instruments used in managing largely transaction exposure and anticipated cash flows or economic exposures, while futures are the instruments least used in managing both exposures (Wang 2015; Mallin et al. 2001). Wang (2015) and Mallin et al. (2001) believe that currency futures are not used in the majority of developed countries such as the UK, Japan, Australia and the United States of

America (USA) since they are not available on their exchanges. Bartram et al. (2003) statistically figured out that for currency risk, forwards (used by 35% of firms) are the most commonly used instrument, while swap (11.0%) and options (9.6%) are much less common. They found that almost no firms (1.1%) use FX futures contracts. The above reasons justified the small percentage shown.

Like futures and forwards, option is also a contract that involves the underlying instrument and market. However, options differ from forward contracts as holding an option gives the holder the right, but not the obligation, to purchase or sell an asset at a specified price agreed upon today. Currency options have become popular in protecting the company from adverse movements in exchange rates, while protecting the companies' ability to gain from favourable fluctuations in exchange rates (Hull 2009, 2012). In call options, this hedging protects hedgers against the falling in price, resulting in fulfilling the expectation of the underlying currency to appreciate in value. The holder of a call option can profit if prices rise. Conversely, if the price decreases, the option holder will simply not exercise the option.

According to Chance and Brooks (2009), currency swap is a transaction in which two parties agree to make payments between one another in different currencies. This instrument is becoming very popular and has become one of the largest financial derivative markets in the world, materialised as an instrument to manage FX risk exposure. Fundamentally, this instrument is used when companies operate in one currency but need to borrow in another type of currency. Géczy et al. (1997) find that currency swaps are used in firms with tighter financial constraints and greater growth opportunities. Approximately, 41% of the firms that have potential exposure to foreign currency risk from foreign operations, and high concentration of foreign competitors, are more likely to use currency derivatives. If the company participates in a currency swap, the principle and interest amount will be received in its own currency, thereby partially offsetting its payments on its debt, and it will be able to make payments in the other desired currency. This will reduce the exchange rate risk exposure through the reduction in borrowing costs, thereupon enabling contracting parties to achieve a competitive advantage (Diamond 1984).

2.3.2.2 Interest rate derivatives

Interest rates are used for discounting as well as for defining the payoff for some interest rate derivative products, depending on future interest rates (Hull 2009; Stulz 2003). The same derivative products can be used to manage interest rate risks, i.e. forwards, futures, options and swaps with the most popular being interest rate swaps (Bartram et al. 2003; Mallin et al. 2001; Allen and Santomero 1998).

A forward rate agreement (FRA) is a forward contract on an interest rate. The agreement will determine the rates to be used along with the notional principal and a termination date. It gives the buyer of the FRA the right to lock in an interest rate for a desired term that begins on a future date. It is an inter-bank traded contract whereby if interest rates fall below the agreed limit, the buyer will pay the seller the differential interest expense on the notional principal. On the contrary, when the interest rate scales up above the agreed limit, the seller will pay the buyer the increased interest expense (Miltersen et al. 2012). FRAs are used to manage and cover short-term interest rate (STIR) risks and protect against the risk of unfavourable interest rate movements. In a financial market, there is a risk if interest rates rise. If it seems likely, the interest rate will rise beyond the FRA rate, then buying an FRA allows the firm to lock in their short-term financing cost for the period up to the settlement date. In contrast to currency forward contracts, FRAs are the least used derivatives to manage interest rate exposures due to the currencies available and limited maturities (Mallin et al. 2001).

Interest rate futures are widely used by treasurers and corporate financial managers of non-financial companies (Chernenko and Faulkender 2012; Géczy et al. 2007). It is a financial derivative based on the underlying security which explains a debt obligation that moves in value as interest rates change. Most companies use them because of their simplicity and standardised nature of interest rate exposures (Li and Marinč 2014; Purnanandam 2007). However, a vast majority of financial institutions were reluctant to use this instrument for various reasons, ranging from management reluctance, lack of knowledge of the futures markets and a perception that these markets were extremely risky (Shanker 1996). Buying the instrument allows the buyer to lock in a future investment rate. In a situation where the interest rates rise, the buyer obliges to pay the seller of the futures contract an amount equal to the profit expected when investing at a higher rate against the rate mentioned in the futures contract. On the contrary, when interest rates fall, the seller will pay off the buyer for the poorer interest rate when the futures contract expires (Chance and Brooks 2009; Phillips 1995). Interest rate options are similar to FRA. However, they provide an optional right to receive one interest rate and pay another instead of being obliged to receive one interest rate and pay another. According to Phillips (1995), interest rate options are as popular to use as interest rate swaps compared to other interest rate derivatives.

Interest rate swap is used as a tool to protect against the unfavourable movement of interest rates. It allows a company to change its fixed rate debt to floating rate debt or vice versa without prior re-negotiation of the underlying loan agreement (Chernenko and Faulkender 2012; Ali et al. 2006). In the agreement, the counterparties to the swap agree to exchange interest payments on specific dates based on a predetermined formula. Interest rate swaps are widely used in commercial banks, investment banks, non-financial institutions, insurance companies, investment vehicles and trusts. For commercial banks, they are likely to consequently receive fewer funding constraints and enjoy greater funding flexibility (Brewer et al. 2014). Interest rate swaps are also popularly used among companies in order to obtain lower cost funding, hedge interest rate exposure, or obtain higher yielding investment assets, and to implement overall asset or liability management strategies (Balakrishnan 2009; Kim and Koppenhaver 1992). Bartram et al. (2003) found that swaps are the most common instruments used by firms in managing interest rate risk and limiting a company's exposure to interest rate fluctuations, and thus, they reduce risk. From a sample of 7,292 non-financial firms in the USA, about 28.8% use swaps in managing interest rate risk.

2.4 Derivatives and risk management

Today, financial derivatives have become invaluable tools for risk management. Chernenko and Faulkender (2012) and Bodnar and Gebhardt (1999) have reported that most managers of firms have positive attitudes towards derivatives usage and recognise them as an important tool for managing risk. However, derivatives usage also poses dangers to the stability of financial markets and have been called potential "weapons of mass destruction" (Fratzscher 2006). Technically, there is a dispute over the role of derivative instruments to reduce the level of firm risk when derivatives trading involve a private contract between banks or other sophisticated investors. As a result, it is hard to know the total volume of derivatives outstanding that will lead to an economic recession as that exemplified by the Cyprus case. However, firms will use derivative instruments as a form of protection against future changes, such as changes in interest rates, stock prices, commodity prices, fluctuation in FX currencies and even the weather.

Derivatives have been widely studied by researchers, with the focus being on whether firms use derivatives for speculation or for hedging purposes to maximise shareholders' wealth and hedging their financial risk (Velasco 2014; Chernenko and Faulkender 2012; Zenios 2007; Collins and Fabozzi 1999). Abdel-Khalik (2013) and Hull (2012) suggested that risk management for banks can be done by using hedging practice, which mitigates unexpected losses due to market exposures such as rate and price fluctuations. Grant and Marshall (1997) concluded that large UK companies use derivative instruments with the intent to manage and reduce the risk of FX and interest rates. Bartram et al. (2009) and Ahmed et al. (1997) found strong evidence that derivatives are used for the purpose of risk management rather than for speculation. For instance, firms that use interest rate derivatives will gain higher leverage and firms that use FX derivatives will have higher proportions of income or sales, and acquire higher amounts of foreign assets. Based on a survey in 1995, Bodnar and Gebhardt (1999) found that firms in the USA and Germany primarily use derivatives to manage risk from fluctuations in market prices. They believed that the size of the firms influenced the decision to use derivatives. For example, most of the large firms believe that the usage of derivatives would have a greater impact on their financial risk performance.

Derivatives can also reduce exposure to risk. According to Ahmed et al. (1997), derivatives users reduce risk exposure more than the non-users. Market risk will certainly affect a company's financial performance and could cause the risk of bankruptcy. Smith and Stulz (1985) developed financial distress arguments for derivatives usage for hedging purposes and claim that hedging reduces the volatility of firm value. This has been realised by reducing the likelihood of costly financial distress (Borokhovich et al. 2004) and thus increasing the expected value of the firm. The greater the probability of distress or hardship is due to cost, the greater the firms will benefit from hedging through the reduction in the expected costs. Additionally, Sinkey and Carter (2000) argue that the larger the amount of debt relative to the firms' value, the higher the probability of insolvency, and the higher the likelihood that banks will use derivatives to hedge. In short, Chance and Brooks (2010) and Saunders and Cornett (2007) stressed that hedging is a specific example of managing risk and part of an overall process in risk management.

2.5 Relationship between derivatives and risk efficiency

It has been found that recently, firms are actively using futures, forwards, options and swaps and routinely addressing market, operational, legal and credit risk in their more traditional activities. In a complex market environment, sound risk management practices are important elements in meeting these challenges.

Consistent with the use of derivatives for hedging purposes, Guay (1999) found that the initiation of taking a derivatives position is associated with a firm's risk reduction. Surveys on new derivatives users show that they experience a significant reduction in stock return volatility as well as interest rate and FX exposures. Derivatives programs implemented by new derivatives users function as hedging tools on a firm's assets and reduce financial distress costs. According to Fehle and Tsyplakov (2005), efficiency of risk management must involve an element of the impact of risk management on firm value, the volatility of the equity and credit spread. When companies use risk management tools like derivatives contracts, 'value creation' occurs when lower volatility increases the firms' ability to pursue investment opportunities and decisions (Lin et al. 2008).

In addition, Léautier (2007) agrees that to a certain extent, an increase in the usage of derivatives contracts for hedging purposes will reduce the cost of capital and in some cases, hedging has a significant impact on the performance ratio (fair value) and cash flow volatility. For instance, hedging the interest rate risk can significantly reduce the cash flow volatility for a commercial bank. In banks, derivatives are primarily used for the purpose of hedging risk exposure. Hedging potentially influences risk and managerial incentives to increase firm value by reducing cash flow uncertainties, and concurrently increases the sales level. Denis (2011) and Whidbee and

Wohar (1999) found that cash flow uncertainty results in a value-reducing investment strategy by firms. Firms tend to neglect good investments when the cash flow is low.

On the contrary, not all firms experience growth in value even if a derivatives program is implemented. Derivative instruments usage may not provide a positive impact on a firm's decision to achieve effective risk management. The reason for this, according to Smith and Stulz (1985), is that use of derivatives does not totally depend on firm value, but is linked to the relationship between the manager's wealth and firm value. If the manager's wealth is a concave function of firm value, firms tend to hedge as much as possible because firm value leads to higher wealth creation. Otherwise, if managers are risk averse, they will not hedge and this goes against the risk-reduction benefits of hedging and when a significant share of a firm's wealth is tied to its stock, the preference is for lower volatility (Léautier 2007; Whidbee and Wohar 1999). The ability of derivatives contracts on risk management can be explained by the risk management theory.[2] This theory believes that derivatives securities can hedge firms that are exposed to market risk and contributes to positive implications on volatility in earnings, cash flows and firm value. In addition, Khor (2001) agreed that there could be positive spill-over effects of the derivative markets in terms of better risk management. Improvements in risk management techniques if used first in derivative trading may improve the management of risks in other, more traditional businesses taking deposits and lending by banks, purchasing and financing of securities positions by securities firms, or treasury management by corporations. Moreover, the advances in risk management will enhance the stability and profitability of the institutions.

To shed light on this, the study argues that the use of derivative instruments would be interpreted as contributing to better and efficient portfolio management where their use enables positive implications for investment strategies. Their use will contribute to better economic spending and more readily without any corresponding significant increases in investment risks. Even though Fong et al. (2005) found that the use of derivatives has a trivial impact on fund returns, they believe that it provides significant protection from risks.

2.6 Impact of derivatives usage on risk management strategy

There have been extensive studies in emerging markets (EM) focussing on various financial fields such as equity markets, corporate finance, the degree of financial developments, international finance corporations (IFC), financial crisis and investments (Kearney 2012; Siregar et al. 2011). Studies on derivatives have also been wide-ranging in the field of financial research in EM. The role of derivatives contract is important and continues to grow as fast as in the developed financial market.

According to Aysun and Guldi (2011), derivatives market volume has dramatically increased in EM in comparison to advanced economies. The paper empirically reveals that from 1998 to 2007, the volume of daily derivatives market transactions increased by 115.6% in EM economies, while only 29.9% in advanced economies. The huge difference underscores the importance of investigating the role played by derivative instruments in a firm's capability in managing risk. On the contrary, Mihaljek and Packer (2010) found that the average daily turnover of derivatives in 33 emerging market economies (EMEs) was $1.2 trillion in 2010, compared to $13.8 trillion in advanced economies. The phenomenon shows that the structure and size of the derivatives markets in EMEs are relatively small compared to advanced markets.

However, a study by Sundaram (2013) shows that the EM derivatives usage grew a bit faster over the period from 2001 to 2010, registering a growth of 300%, compared to 250% for the advanced economies. This is supported by Ahmad and Haris (2012) who noted rapid growth in the development of the derivatives market in the Asia-Pacific region. In a Futures Industry Association Survey, Acworth (2011) reported that the Asia-Pacific region has over-taken North America as the world's biggest derivatives market, accounting for 39% of the global total, compared to 33% for the latter. Moreover, in terms of the risk traded, there is a sharp difference in both markets. In advanced financial markets, 77% of the total derivatives turnover is accounted for by interest-rate derivatives, while 50% is in currency derivatives contracts and interest rate derivatives are relatively new and unimportant in EM. The figure shows that exchange rate risk has become a major concern in EM (Sundaram 2013). However, in the Asia-Pacific region's banks, Balakrishnan (2009) and Yong et al. (2009) suggest that derivative activities have a significant relationship to banks' interest rate exposure and the usage of interest rate swap influences the loans and advances portfolio, and asset performance.

According to Rao (2012), financial derivatives serve a useful purpose in fulfilling risk management objectives. Risks from traditional instruments can be efficiently managed independently. Through derivatives, both financial and non-financial firms can save costs and increase returns. As for non-financial firms, they can use various strategies in risk management. Despite that fact, Beatty (1999) suggests that these firms have an alternative to use interest rate swaps since the firms are more exposed to interest rate exposure. Through derivative instruments, these firms could directly obtain that desired type of debt, either variable or fixed.

Pramborg (2005) compared risk management practices and FX swaps between Korean and Swedish non-financial firms. Both countries use derivative instruments to deal with FX risk. Nevertheless, the objective of hedging is different. Korean firms use derivative instruments to minimise fluctuations in cash flow, while Swedish non-financial firms concentrate more on minimising earning volatility and protecting the balance sheet. Comparatively, the use of derivative proportion among non-financial firms in Korea is lower than in Swedish firms due to immature derivatives markets.

Milos Sprcic (2007) explored the differences between financial risk management practices in Croatian and Slovenian companies using derivative types. Three hypotheses (company size, leverage and investment opportunities) were tested to show the relationship with derivatives used. In Slovenian companies, the result shows that the decision to use derivative instruments only depend on the size of the firm as a significant correlation was proven. Regarding the risk management instruments in managing currency risk, companies in Slovenia prefer to use currency forward (about 32%), followed by currency swap (of 17%), since their major trade partners are Italy, France, Austria and Germany, where the majority of transactions are denominated by one currency. On the other hand, all the hypotheses are insignificant to the derivatives usage due to fewer derivatives structures as compared to Slovenian non-financial companies. However, regarding the interest rate risk in markets, forward contracts and swaps are becoming more important derivative instruments in risk management strategies.

The importance of derivatives usage in risk management strategies was also studied by Batten and Hettihewa (2007) using Australian firms as samples. They found that the use of swaps and options were more popular in managing risk among Australian firms, specifically for the larger and more internationally exposed firms. Derivative instruments were believed to enhance firm value. The results are consistent with the findings by Nguyen and Faff (2002). In Germany, 88% of the firms indicated that they do use derivative instruments in transferring the complex environmental risk (Fatemi and Glaum 2000). The survey results show that 89% were used for hedging purposes. The complex nature of the changes in FX risk and interest rate risk and the value of firm have increased the usage of derivatives. However, interest rate exposures have received little attention and are not regularly assessed by German firms.

An international comparative study on the issue of derivatives and risk management practices was conducted by Jalilvand et al. (2000), in which they distinguished the managers' perspective on the ability of derivatives in providing systematic risk management in Canada, the USA and Europe. Based on the study, most of the companies do not have an integration between derivative roles and risk management policy, as well as the company's strategic plan. Also, Canadian risk managers are less likely to know the function of derivatives as compared to American and European risk managers. However, 35% of users stated that derivative instruments and risk management policy do not affect corporate financing decisions. Management does not see the use of derivative to be important in the overall financial structure of the company. Overall, the use of derivative products is more widespread in Canada.

2.7 Derivatives and risk management efficiency: theoretical perspectives

Smith and Stulz (1985) and Froot et al. (1993) state that corporate risk management theory suggests that firms are more likely to manage financial risks such as interest rate and exchange rate risks with derivatives. Servaes et al.

(2009) emphasise that the corporate risk management functions are largely viewed as a set of approaches, measurements and procedures by which managers identify the classes and levels of risk exposures faced by their companies. From there, the companies choose which exposures to bear and which to transfer to others, through a variety of risk management techniques, including insurance purchases and derivatives. These techniques verify risk management measures to provide strong evidence in the function of mitigating the risk (hedging perspectives). Allayannis et al. (2003) state that the theory, studied by various scholars from a variety of theoretical perspectives, has resulted in a number of competing theories, whereby several scholars have attempted to find support for differing theories of corporate financial risk management. According to Klimczak (2007, 2008), there are three major corporate risk management theories which would provide a strong statement of their verification status. The first is finance theory that has extended the risk management concept. The second is the relationship between the managers and the shareholders' expectation (agency theory), and the third is a discussion on how one group of shareholders can affect the firm's performance (freeman's stakeholder theory).

2.7.1 Finance/financial theory (financial economics approach)

The financial economic approach was built upon the classic Modigliani-Miller paradigm published in a seminal paper in 1958, which specified the conditions for the diversion of the financial structure for corporate value. Initially, Modigliani and Miller (1958) argue that capital structure or leverage is irrelevant because the value of the firm is influenced by how the firm is financed and does not affect the firm's earnings power. This paradigm formed the basis of modern thinking on capital structure that eventually extended the concept of risk management. This approach stipulates that hedging fluctuations in cash flow could be reflected in lower volatility of the firm. The rationale for corporate risk management has been inferred from the irrelevance of conditions and includes higher debt capacity (Modigliani and Miller 1963).

The capital structure is irrelevant if a fixed investment policy is adopted on a regular basis with no contract or tax costs. The argument entails that if a firm chooses to hedge policy changes, investors who hold claims issued by the firm can change their holdings of risky assets to offset any change in hedging policy, leaving the distribution of their future wealth unaffected. Smith and Stulz (1985) argue that when firm value is affected by hedging policy, firms will also enjoy the benefit of a reduction in tax charges under a progressive tax schedule structure (tax rises with income), better investment value, and aligning the interest of managers and owners of the firms. These advantages provide opportunities for firms to take a position in the derivatives (forward, futures or options) markets. The theory, however, is less credible since it does not consider the risk elements that will affect the firm's entire financial performance, nor does it consider that the mixed evidence is affected by hedging policy. The classical corporate finance theory also indicates that firm value is not affected by the usage of derivatives. Hence, Froot et al. (1993) believe that finance theory provides less guidance to a hedging strategy and Stulz theory is a straightforward prediction on the derivatives instruments, as it believes that it will provide an advantage to the firms, and that managers face significant costs when trading in hedging contracts for their own account. This extreme forecast does not limit the derivatives allocation which seems to suggest that managers can hedge as much as possible. Graham and Rogers (2002) found that there is no impact of derivatives usage on the tax function, contrary to firm size and financial distress that may be affected in times of crisis (Bartram et al. 2009). However, the usage of derivatives by banks that act as financial intermediaries benefits them because of their comparative advantage as delegated monitors (Brewer et al. 2000; Diamond 1984).

The ability of a firms' financial performance to influence the labour market's perception will change the manager's opinion that will directly influence any hedging activities, based on asymmetric information (Breeden and Viswanathan 1998; Géczy et al. 1997; DeMarzo and Duffie 1995). When managers have superior knowledge as compared to shareholders regarding the nature of the firm's various market exposures such as interest rate risk and FX risk, it can result in an imbalance of power that causes transaction to go awry, a kind of market failure in the worst-case scenario. Uncertainty about the quality of management will affect the interests of shareholders, which is certainly correlated with firm value. However, DaDalt et al. (2002) argue that through hedging, managers can reduce the "noisiness" in earnings contributed by environmental factors such as interest rates and exchange rate uncertainties. The research hypothesis shows that derivatives usage is associated with a reduction in the level of information asymmetry between managers and outsiders (shareholders), especially on the accuracy of the analysts' forecasts. With respect to the findings, the use of derivatives is able to shrink the information asymmetry problem and eventually make a significant impact on the expansion of the high cash flow and profitability. In this regard, Jensen and Meckling (1976) and Huang and Song (2006) also linked the increase of cash flow to debt. These authors found that debts can be used as a tool to ensure that the managers give preference to wealth creation for the equity-holders. In the finance world, a firm can gain extra finance through debt creation and issuing of shares.

Despite that fact, Stulz (1990) states that debt payment decreases the opportunity for generating profits and leads to potential bankruptcy costs and agency costs. Thus, a firm with less debt structure has more prospects for investment and has more liquidity as compared to other active companies. Costs and benefits of alternative sources "traded off" until the marginal cost of equity is equal to the marginal cost of debt, resulting in an optimal capital structure, and maximising the value of the firm. On the one hand, Jensen

(1986) pointed out that it has a leverage effect and a function to reduce an agency cost of free cash flows and embeds a solvency risk. Therefore,

> the firm is supposed to substitute debt with equity, or equity with debt, until the value of the firm is maximised, and the firm will refuse to buy equity unless the firm has exhausted its 'debt capacity', that is, unless the firm has issued debt so much already that it will face substantial additional costs in issuing more.
>
> (Myers 1984, 4)

The debt-equity trade-off, also known as the *static trade-off theory*, implies that a firm is moving towards at target. The *static trade-off theory* argues that firms in a stable (static) position will adjust their current level of gearing to achieve a target level. The value of the firm is not optimal if the position is above debt ratio. This shows that financial pressures and agency costs outweigh the benefits derived from debt, thus lowering the level of debt. On the other hand, if the position is below the target debt ratio, the firm value can still increase because the marginal value of debt ratio exceeds the costs related to the use of debt, and firms increase their debt. Positions above or below target debt indicate a significant association with the firms' risk management. Firms can make quick decisions to mitigate the risk level. However, their debt base approach is judged to be less "transparent" because external investors cannot accurately distinguish and estimate the really risky firms. Accordingly, such firms should hedge more than other firms in order to reduce asymmetry costs, especially commercial banks that are less transparent as compared to firms in other industries. Therefore, banks should hedge more (and publicly disclose risk management activities), so that the costs associated with information asymmetry can be reduced (Knill et al. 2006; Merton and Perold 1993).

In the world of *pecking order theory*, firms will always take into account external financing needs with debt as long as it is not constrained by debt capacity. However, firms need to be careful because of the potential financial risks as it affects the Times Interest Earned (TIE) ratio, which carries special importance in the eyes of investors (Besley and Brigham 2007).[3]

De Jong et al. (2011) have taken into account these two theories by taking a firm's debt capacity into account as well. This figure shows whether the *pecking order theory* and the *static trade-off theory* predict a debt or equity issue, or repurchase for different positions of the debt ratio. The two theories contradict each other when firms are not constrained in their issuing of investment-grade debt. When the firms are above their debt capacity, they possibly face a choice between debt or equity. Otherwise, in order to achieve financing surplus, repurchase equity and debt is to be considered.

However, this prediction does not explain the role of retained earnings in this financing structure, since retained earnings will affect the firm's average, even if the firm does not repurchase or issue any securities. The role of retained earnings is part of the financial behaviour that affects the capital

structure of the firm, which has an impact on the overall financial performance. Myers (1984) argued that the *static trade-off theory* is weak because
it is unable to explain the firm's financing behaviour, and fails to identify
the company's performance when it is organising its financial structure
(Jahanzeb 2013; Huang and Ritter 2009). However, both theories provide a
synergistically powerful combination which shows a strategic technique as a
guide to strategic financing methods for the managers to avoid poor financial
performance. This phenomenon has been supported by Frank and Goyal
(2007), Fama and French (2002), Myers (1984) and Myers and Majluf (1984)
when they stated that firms with positive net present value will finance new
investments first using internal funds, and if not, the firm will finance with
secured debt before risk debt, then with equity. However, evidence to support
the prediction of the financial theory approach to a firm's risk management
is still needed (Klimczak 2008, 2007). However, various studies provide evidence of the benefits specified by the theory. Jin and Jorion (2006) accepted
that risk management does lead to lower variability of firm value. Nguyen
and Faff (2002) positively verified that the leverage (financial distress costs),
firm size and liquidity are powerful determinants of the extent to which a firm
will use derivatives in risk management and in managerial decision-making.

The above discussion suggests that financial economic theory offers new
insights into the determinants of risk management and its relations to the
usage of derivative instruments and firm value. Undeniably, the direct relevance of this will affect the efficiency of risk management and the overall
performance of the firm (Rivas et. al 2006). Whether the capital structure
can be explained by financial economic theory, pecking order theory or
static trade-off theory is still unresolved, especially in the absence of the
role of capital structure, firm value, risk management and elements of systematic and unsystematic risks. The main essence of the underlying theories
of capital structure is still of paramount interest to shareholders or, perhaps,
the stakeholders, in creating value for the firm and serve as a guide to risk
management and on how to avoid dangers for the company.

From the finance theory (Klimzack 2008, 2007; Rivas et al. 2006; Smith
and Stulz 1985; Mayer and Smith 1982), these influencing factors have been
addressed in derivatives and firm performance studies in different contexts.
The theory, however, has so far, not been well regarded for investigating a
firm's risk management efficiency. Therefore, the present study strives to
investigate how the use of derivatives increases banks' risk management efficiency, and relates the above theory base to investigate the effects of using
derivative based instruments for driving input and output to measure risk
management efficiency.

2.7.2 *Agency theory*

After discussing the relevant theories of capital structure from a risk management perspective, this section will discuss agency theory by extending
the analysis of the firm to include the separation of managerial motivation,

ownership and control. The separation is one of the basic tenets of a free-market society because it allows for specialisation (Lambert 2001). This theory distinguishes the parties who have enough wealth but lack the skills to run a firm, and the parties who may lack the wealth but have the skills to generate the highest income for the firm. However, when ownership and control are separated, agency costs arise. These problems arise in firms because corporate decisions are made by agents (managers) on behalf of the principals (firm's capital suppliers). However, agency costs also have a role in a firm. For instance, Jensen and Meckling (1976) and López de Silanes et al. (1999) highlighted the role of agency cost in affecting the firm value in developing financial markets through different types of agency costs in a financial market including bonding costs, residual costs and monitoring costs. These costs are for the purposes of handling processes to ensure that the firm value can be increased simultaneously in providing returns to the principal. Furthermore, as the firm is operationalised under a legal fiction, where conflicting objectives of individuals are brought into equilibrium within a framework of contractual relationships, the contractual relationship must be well integrated between all parties, not only with the employees, but also with the suppliers, customers and creditors.

In the field of firms' risk management, Smith and Stulz (1985) believe that agency theory has influenced managerial attitudes towards risk-taking and hedging. In reality, shareholders select the management compensation package in order to increase the value of the firm and also to increase managers' expected utility. Managers' expected utility depends on the distribution of firms reward (payoffs), where hedging will change the expectations of payoffs, thus changing the managers' expected utility. In the event that managers do not dare to take risks, firms will hedge portfolios merely from the creation of cash-in or cash-out. Since the principals are either risk averse or risk neutral, Weston and Copeland (1992) pointed out that they have either constant or decreasing marginal utility ($U' \leq 0$), where the marginal utility is affected by the compensation paid, both directly and indirectly to the agent. The impact of the compensation function provides an indirect effect on the action chosen by the manager, which, in turn, affects the distribution of the payoffs. This situation can precipitate the conflict between the principal and the manager because according to the perspective of agency theory, the primary responsibility of the managers towards the principals is to maximise the payoffs. This is supported by the fact that the intention of the contract between principals and managers is that managers are acting in their self-interest and are motivated to maximise the value of the organisation, reducing the agency costs and adopting accounting methods that ultimately reflect their own performance (Deegan and Unerman 2006). This emphasises the role of accounting in reducing the agency cost in a firm effectively through proper accounting systems. If managers are rewarded for their performances such as through accounting profit, they will work to increase profits and this will lead to an increase in a bonus or in remuneration.

Accurate financial reporting will provide a strong foundation in reducing agency problems due to information asymmetries (Healy and Palepu 2001; Jensen and Meckling 1976).

A firm's financial performance should be viewed from a number of approaches and strategies. Whether comparing firms in the same or a different industry, the basis of assessment must be based on empirical evidence of debt and equity structure. For example, bankruptcy (insolvency) ratios are constructed to measure the efficiency of the financial risk management by considering debt to equity, debt to assets, and the ratio of the ability to pay interest. Indirectly, this ratio shows the level of debt controlled by the firm mainly when it receives the effects of uncertain external risk. In research undertaken by Jensen and Meckling (1976), it appears that agency costs associated with debt (paying for legal fees, professional services, trustees' fees and filing fees) consist of three different types of costs, namely monitoring and bonding costs, reorganisation and bankruptcy costs, and opportunity wealth loss affected by debt on the investment decisions of the firm. The classification of costs and debt is seen closer to financial theory. The difference is that the benefit is derived from the value of debt and equity to the company's capital structure, as opposed to debt and equity implications in reducing the agency cost problem. Debt acquired from outside will involve the payment of interest and at the same time to meet the goals of capital contributors (principals). These two sources of capital can be described as 'debt' to the firm as it is necessary to meet the goals of creditors and shareholders. This argument is in line with Tufano (1996) who found that the financial and agency theory has similar predictions. In explaining this issue, the above authors integrate these concepts into the beginnings of a theory of the corporate ownership structure. The paper highlighted three crucial variables not just to determine the relative amounts of equity and debt, but also the fraction of equity held by managers. The variables are as follows: Si, inside equity (held by the manager); So, outside equity (held by anyone outside of the firm); and B, debt (held by anyone outside of the firm). However, the combination of these concepts is not concerned with risk and uncertainty of market conditions in the ownership structure. Since there is an element of equity and debt from the outside, the element of risk and uncertainty need to be taken seriously. For example, a financial institution is an institution that always obtains debt capital and equity financing from external parties. At the same time, systematic risk cannot be controlled and directly affects returns and refunds.

In understanding the focus of agency theory, this study tries to understand the phenomenon of risk and uncertainty affecting the interests of both the principal and the agent. For instance, Demsetz et al. (1997) and Brewer and Saidenberg (1996) found a statistically significant relationship between risk and ownership structure only for banks with a relatively low franchise value. When the franchise value is low, it appears that the ownership structure is used to align managers' risk-taking by the owner, where moral hazard is very closely related to the franchise value. The role of franchise value is to reduce moral hazard by means of reducing risk (bankruptcy costs). When the risk of financial distress (bankruptcy) upturns the value of the franchise, it will reduce value-maximising of choice for both asset risk and leverage. Therefore, if the moral hazard is reduced by the franchise value, banks will be able to reduce the risks that would affect the distribution of income among depositors and shareholders.

On the contrary, the literature suggests that agency theory does not help in identifying the determinants (individual block ownership, debt to equity ratios, equity to asset ratios) of hedging (Klimczak 2007). For instance, studies by Nguyen and Faff (2002) and Géczy et al. (1997) show a negative effect between managerial motivation factors and corporate risk management. Agency theory provides a weak support for hedging in response to a mismatch between the shareholders' interests and managerial incentives. This argument is supported by the conditions whereby underlying the Modigliani & Miller (MM) propositions, decisions to hedge corporate or firm exposures to exchange rate, interest rate and commodity price risks are completely irrelevant because stockholders already protect themselves against such risks by holding well-diversified portfolios (Madhumathi 2012; Sprčić 2008).

In a nutshell, even though agency theory has little evidence in aligning with derivatives usage, the present study is likely to agree with Nance et al. (1993) and Myers and Smith (1987). Both studies indicate that derivatives usage for hedging purposes can reduce agency costs by aligning the interests of managers and stockholders, and it can also align the interest of bondholders and shareholders. Therefore, since banks can use derivatives to hedge, they can reduce the volatility of their cash flow and thus are able to pay greater levels of income as dividends. Additionally, it can also help to alleviate the incentives and monitoring problems caused by managerial risk aversion (Cartey and Sinkey 1998). This means that agency theory can function in risk management practices by highlighting the usefulness of derivatives hedging strategies for firms. This illustrates that risk management can reduce agency costs based on derivatives usage, particularly for hedging purposes (Klimzack 2007; Deegan and Unerman 2006; Nace et al. 1993; Myers and Smith 1987; Smith and Stulz 1985).

In summary, this study could align the relationship between agency theory and risk management involving the usage of derivatives. As also being explained by Rivas et al. (2006), the strategy of using financial derivatives can influence firm value as well as efficiency of the firm.

2.7.3 Freeman's stakeholder theory

Research into risk management also discusses stakeholder theory in relation to firm value. This theory was originally developed by Freeman (1984) as a managerial instrument. This theory implies that stakeholders as a group of individuals can affect or be affected by the activities of the firm. Hence, stakeholder theory focusses clearly on the equilibrium of stakeholders as key determinants of corporate policies. In the context of risk management, Cornell and Shapiro (1987) pointed out that risk management is an extension of the theory that implies employment contracts, including sales and financing. From this perspective, the claimant of the firm goes beyond the external stakeholders such as bondholders and shareholders, which also include internal stakeholders (customers, suppliers, suppliers of complementary products and services, employees and distributors). In this context, the claims from stakeholders will have implications on the financial structure and firm value. Therefore, adequate attention in the financial literature has been given to differentiate between implicit and explicit demands of stakeholders.

In addition, Cornell and Shapiro (1987) stated that if only explicit claims are considered, it does not affect monetary or financial policy for most firms as explicit claims were made generally senior to those bondholders and stockholders. The authors consider the implications of the claim have very little impact on the probability of financial stress and can be considered to be risk-free. This statement received strong support when Titman (1984) and Chung and Smith (1987) investigated manager and stakeholder relations in the context of a bankruptcy model which had proven that the explicit claims from stakeholders did not influence the risk of bankruptcy. They were convinced that only implicit claims are highly sensitive to the firm's financial distress. Conversely, this argument failed to state claim details that emphasises the concept of transparency and accuracy, since it might influence the firm's financial performance. The conclusion is of a general nature to set aside ethical aspects of offense in a lawsuit. Offense and this doubt must be factors in determining the validity of claims, because the offense did not just come from implicit claims. Even though Freeman (1994) has touched on the issue of mixes in business and morality, the ethical issue is not considered even though it has an important role in enhancing a firm's performance.

Contrary to the explicit claims, Klimczak (2007) believes that the value of implicit claims is highly sensitive to the expected costs of financial distress and failure. The implicit claims held by stakeholders correlate with uncertainty issues since firm value is sensitive to information about the firm's financial condition (Cornell and Shapiro 1987). Based on the empirical observations, this theory receives inadequate supporting evidence in the financial risk management literature. Judge (2006) investigated the relationship between financial distress hypothesis with stakeholder theory and agency theory and proved that risk management instruments do not provide a strong relationship with stakeholder theory. Agency theory is more comprehensive in determining risk management strategies for managers.

In conclusion, even though stakeholder theory has already transformed the field of strategic and risk management (Laplume et al. 2008), the stakeholder entity still does not prove its role in influencing a firm's behaviour towards risk management strategy.

2.8 Analysis of risk indicators and risk management strategies in banking firms

Risk-averse banks may choose to fund a loan with a higher ratio of financial capital to deposits than a risk-neutral bank. Financial capital is normally more expensive than deposits. Many banks have resorted risks after facing a steady rise in bad loans. This situation may cause one to conclude that banks' risk averse nature may produce an inefficient output (Sun and Chang 2011). This conclusion may be less accurate as each bank's approach to risk (risk preferences) is different. Factors such as the deterioration in asset quality and the macroeconomic environments (effects of interest rate fluctuation, annual real GDP growth, governmental regulations, etc.) supervened to added risk aversion in the banking sector. Internal factors also influence risk-taking behaviour. García-Marco and Robles-Fernández (2008) found that return on equity (ROE) has significantly affected the performance of financial institutions. In fact, its impact is significantly greater in large financial institutions. The implications for risk preference are influenced by the internal and external environments of the banks. Hence, in order to control the different risk preferences, particularly in raising financial capital, Mester (1996) suggests that the level of financial capital be included in the cost function associated with banks' action or a certain level of their output. Past research has extended the cost function model that incorporates measures of the quality of bank output that can influence the banks' cost.

An investigation on the connection between risks and bank efficiency has received popular attention among researchers. Chang (1999) measured the technical efficiency (TE) of the major financial institutions in Taiwan that incorporate three risk indicators, namely (1) total allowances for loan losses, (2) amount of non-performing loans (*NPL*) and (3) risky assets. In this case, risk has been treated as a joint indicator but "undesirable" output to test the significance of risk adjustment. The result supports the idea that incorporating risk as a result of an undesirable output has contributed to a significant impact on the ranking of a banks' efficiency performance. Different risk indicators were used by Pasiouras (2008) to evaluate the efficiency of Greek commercial banks over the period from 2000 to 2004. Net interest income and loan loss provisions (valuation reserve) have been used as risk elements in the banking industry. These two inputs are well connected to a bank's risks and might affect the bank's performance due to market risk evaluation. From the analysis, the study found that an inclusion of these inputs increases the efficiency scores. However, the analysis is not comprehensive, and an in-depth analysis of how market risk influences net interest income is not studied. According to Maudos and Fernandez de Guevara (2004), market interest rates have caused the changes in interest income, interest expense and net interest income. The percentage change in the net interest income is influenced by interest rate fluctuations, including those resulting from the inflation rate. Interest rate risks will be set as a reference to determine the variable rate loans, which will have significant impacts on the sensitivity of the interest income (Corvoisier and Gropp 2002; Bessis 2002; Uzzi 1999).

Several studies had focussed on the relationship between banks' efficiency and risk, and had divided them into internal and external environment risk effects. For instance, Altunbas et al. (2000) investigated the impact of internal risk and quality factors on Japanese banks' cost efficiency considering a liquidity ratio and financial capital to control risk. The study estimated a cost function that controls for risks and quality factors using three risk variables, namely non-performing loans-to-total loans ratio (*NPL/TL*), liquid assets-to-total assets ratio and financial capital. By using the stochastic frontier estimation, the authors compare the performance of the efficiency scale before and after risk factors and quality are taken into account. As a result, when risk factors are involved, the majority of Japanese banks experience diseconomies of scale, which appear to get larger by the asset size. However, this result is in contrast with that of previous studies. For example, McAllister and McManus (1993) concluded that the efficiency score resulted to be less sensitive to the inclusion of risk variables. This evidence is supported by Clark (1996, 342) when he states that "the inference that some banks may be concentrating too heavily on reducing their production cost efficiency ratios without paying sufficient attention to the impact of their decisions on other attributes such as risk, which are reflected in economic costs". Risk assessment on the impact of cost efficiency was shown by Girardone et al. (2004) when the inclusion of risk variables reduced the significant impact of the economic scale estimates in Italian banks. Considering the level of capital and loan losses as an argument in the cost function context to control for default risks, the authors stress that the higher cost efficiency of the banks is correlated with better credit risk evaluation. Risks appear to have relevance to the estimation of economies of scale, and there are also significant differences in the characteristics of high performing banks. However, Pastor (1998) stressed that the cost function is unable to capture the effect of loan losses, asset prices and asset quality on liabilities and therefore on efficiency. Loans taken by risky borrowers will set high interest rates, and simultaneously affect the price of the asset. Depositors who put money in the banks also expect to have a risk premium that will directly affect the liability price (Hughes and Mester 1993).

Murinde and Zhao (2009) and Pasiouras (2008) highlight the impact of credit risk on the efficiency of banks by assessing the provision for loan losses (*PLL*) as an additional input. The result found that when *PLL* is considered (model 3 and model 4 in intermediation and profit-oriented approach), the overall mean technical efficiency increases by 1.5%. Thus, credit risk appears to influence and have some impact on the efficiency scores. The result indicates that failure to adequately account for risk factors can have a significant impact on relative efficiency scores, and the finding in this regard is consistent with previous studies by Drake et al. (2006), Drake and

Hall (2003), Pastor (1998) and Charnes et al. (1990). These studies indicate that the efficiency of banks is controlled by risk, since the management of loan and loan growth are influenced by internal factors. Soedarmono et al. (2012) assert that bank market structure, quality of institutions and economic development are interrelated and are capable of affecting the relationship between the provision of non-discretionary and bank loan growth. The evidence from the incorporation of the actual changes in the ratio of non-performing loans to total loans $(DNPL)$, $NPL = \left(NPL_{i,\,t+1} - NPL_{i,t} \right)$ has shown a positive effect on loan provision since the provision is used to cover the expected credit risks. This is consistent with the previous study which stated that a sound provisioning system is essential in avoiding credit risk (Berger and Udell 2004; Cavallo and Majnoni 2002). In a more recent study on German banks, Altunbas et al. (2007) also show the links between loan-loss reserves *(LLRL)* for banks as an addition to bank-specific variable and interest rate *(INSBOC)* (country-specific) to account for interest rate environment in European banks. Risk is found to be positively related to efficient banks or capital.

Previous studies assessed risks that are directly connected to the structure of banks. However, there are no studies that evaluate the impact of risk control tools used by banks on their level of efficiency and business risk, which is highly sensitive to exchange rate risk and interest rate risk. Therefore, this study considers this issue as highly important to be brought into the context of various countries or regions.

2.9 Background of the case study

2.9.1 *Financial system in Asia-Pacific region*

Theoretical and empirical studies have overwhelmingly shown that a well-functioning financial system is crucial to providing for and sustaining the process of economic development (Levine 2005). The Asia-Pacific economy has attracted economists' interest to examine its phenomenal economic development since the 1960s. Mainstream economists believe that the Asia-Pacific economy development is mainly guided by dynamism in economic growth, diversity in economic structure and heavy dependence on international trade and investment (Do and Levchenko 2007; Kwan 1994). Related to economic development, and particularly the conflict issue, is the design of a well-functioning financial system (Levine 2005). In the Asia-Pacific region, a bank-based financial structure is the fulcrum in the financial system and in the delivery of key financial services. The financial systems of some countries like Japan, Korea, Australia and Malaysia have evolved with the changing world economic trends and are more dynamic in facing market uncertainties (Lynch 1996). However, after the Asian financial crisis in 1997 and 2008, the regional financial markets have not progressed uniformly (Dekle and Lee 2015; Singh 2010).

2.9.2 Banking system

In many countries of the Asia-Pacific region, the financial systems continue to be dominated by banking institutions, with banks still playing a superior role in financing the economy (Singh 2010). As compared to European and US banking institutions, Yong et al. (2014) believe that Asia-Pacific banks' play an important role in economic development, specifically in the developing Asian economies. Their dynamic banking characteristics, ownership structure and financial features have strengthened the Asia-Pacific banking industry, whereas the European financial institutions are in a crisis due to their governance, financial structure and leadership (Institute of Bankers Malaysia (IBBM) 2012). The requirements of European and US banks for mortgage and residential lending are down and have become harder. The ability to rise significantly after the Asian Financial Crisis of 1997 has made the Asia-Pacific banking system better and more resilient. For example, Genay (1998) point outs that Japanese banks have more leverage and have greater equity investments when compared to banks in the USA. Government ownership and financial supervisory system of banks are also more common in the Asia-Pacific region relative to the Europe and the USA (Young et al. 2009; Barth et al. 2001; East Asia Analytical Unit 1999).

In terms of market power, Elzinga and Mills (2011) believe that a firm's price-setting discretion is a better indicator than its ability to sustain monopoly prices. Based on the finding of Elzinga and Mills (2011), Fu et al. (2014) conducted an empirical study on bank competition and financial stability in 14 Asia Pacific countries and found that banks in this region are able to obtain greater discretion in terms of price-setting. Good price discretion boosts banks' profitability and reduces their insolvency risk, in addition to increased banking concentration (product differentiation) (Phillips et al. 2015; Homburg et al. 2012). This situation illustrates that pricing power boosts the capacity in Asia-Pacific banks that serve as "capital buffers". This gives the ability to banks and protects them against liquidity shocks and external macroeconomic risks.

2.9.3 Banks' risk management with derivative activities in Asia-Pacific countries

Financial derivatives are gaining importance in the Asia-Pacific region. Sheedy (1997) believes that Asia-Pacific derivatives market is very different compared to the USA and European markets. This scenario has been supported by Yong et al. (2014) who studied the financial aspects of Asia-Pacific countries, particularly focussing on the determinants of banks' derivative activities that have generally been restrained, as compared to US banks. A study in 2009 clearly shows that the use of financial derivatives plays a significant role in reducing Asia-Pacific banks' STIR exposure (Au Yong et al.

2009). Based on this evolution, a survey of derivative development and activities in both the developed and developing countries in Asia-Pacific markets warrant an exploration.

2.9.3.1 Derivatives market development in Asia-Pacific (developed countries)

2.9.3.1.1 AUSTRALIA

The improvement of derivatives usage in Australia has consistently increased after 1990 (Kent and Debelle 1999). According to Kent and Debelle (1999), a threefold increase was seen due to technological advances that have reduced the cost of storing and processing information. Advances had been made in the development and pricing of complex financial products used for risk management where it was closely related to improvements in information technology as well as more sophisticated integration in finance and mathematical methods.

The Australian over-the-counter (OTC) derivatives market has been growing rapidly in recent decades due to a number of factors. Negotiated tailored contract terms in OTC markets are often more attractive to many market participants than the standardised contracts traded on the traditional exchanges. With less prescriptive regulation of financial intermediaries, more of these trading opportunities have been exploited, which, in turn, has been supported by improvements in participants' operational and risk management capacities.

Referring to the Australian Prudential Regulation Authority (APRA) (2012) data acquired within the Australian market suggest that the majority of OTC derivative positions reported by the six Australian banks are entered by Australian domiciles. Therefore, based on the notional value, it can measure the size of the derivatives market in Australia. By this measure, Ahn et al. (2012) emphasise that Australian banks' OTC derivatives have contributed to the global OTC derivatives contracts that has been growing about six-fold over the last decade, even though the growth had slowed down after the financial crisis in 2008.

According to the BIS (2012), until the end of June 2012, Australian banks have contributed over USD 11 trillion (about 1.7%) of the total global notional amount (USD 40 trillion). This development is in line with the global derivatives growth which shows a drastic improvement between 2006 and 2007 despite the global derivatives market that is highly competitive and that has been determined by customer's (user's) choice and new market entry (Mai 2008). There are plenty of derivatives market entries and three different categories of user's choice: (a) OTC dealers within the OTC segment, (b) choice between the OTC and on-exchange segments for many contract types and (c) choice between different derivatives exchanges, has seen almost all derivatives exchanges across all countries in the world. Consequently, established banks or other financial institutions will act as dealers that play an important role in intermediating these markets.

2.9.3.1.2 HONG KONG

Banks in Hong Kong have developed derivatives and structured products designed to keep up with other banks in the London market. Tokyo is a strong central market and many foreign banks have their equity derivatives team in Hong Kong. According to the Hong Kong Monetary Authority (HKMA) (2010), derivatives activities have brought significant benefits to the commercial community in facilitating and assisting hedging for business planning, and have empowered the financial institutions to offer a progressively wider range of services and greater efficiency in the intermediation process. Besides that, derivatives usage by financial institutions is aimed at exploiting market imperfections and other trading opportunities for their own benefit. The resilience of the activity related to the interest rates may be partly attributed to the element of growth in swaps or other composite products such as structured notes. This was also associated with an aggressive growth in the interest rate swap market that has a positive relationship with the continued development of the Hong Kong dollar bond market.

In a press release by HKMA (2010), the average daily net turnover of OTC interest rate derivatives rose by 6.8% to USD 18.5 billion. The growth was driven by interest rate options and FRA transactions, which increased by 128.7% and 85.8%, respectively. However, Hong Kong dollar denominated interest rate swap contracts fell by 68.4% in 2010 compared to the achievement in 2007. Based on a market survey, the drop was caused by a low interest rate environment prevailing for the Hong Kong dollar since late 2008. This provides less incentive for the pursuance of active management of short term Hong Kong dollar interest rate exposures with interest rate derivatives.

2.9.3.1.3 JAPAN

According to the report by the Bank of Japan in 2003, the notional amount of outstanding derivatives transactions by major Japanese financial institutions by the end of June 2010 was equivalent to USD 38.0 trillion for OTC contracts and USD 3.8 trillion for exchange-traded contracts, respectively, an increase of 10.4% and a decrease of 4.6% from the previous survey as of end-December 2009. A breakdown by the risk categories shows that the amount outstanding of single currency interest rate contracts was USD 33.1 trillion for OTC contracts, representing an increase of 9.5%. That of FX contracts was USD 4.7 trillion, an increase of 16.6%. Equity contracts increased by 19.1% to USD 180.5 billion. Commodity contracts decreased by

0.1% to USD 39.1 billion. A breakdown by instrument types shows that interest rate swaps continued to represent the largest share of OTC contracts, accounting for 72.8%. In terms of exchange-traded contracts, interest rate futures accounted for a dominant share of 81.4%.

From end-December 2009 to end-June 2010, the gross positive and negative market values of OTC derivatives contracts respectively increased by 29.6% to USD 698.2 billion, and by 29.3% to USD 653.8 billion. After taking into account of the bilateral netting agreements, the positive market value was USD 198.4 billion (up 15.6%), and the negative market value was USD 154 billion (up 11.4%). The ratio of the net positive market value to the notional amount outstanding was 0.5%. In regard to the interest rate contracts of OTC derivatives, the US dollar and the Japanese yen taken together continue to be dominant, with a market share of 79.2% of notional amount, as compared to 79.6% at end-December 2009. The Japanese yen accounted for 56.9%, decreasing from 58.8% at end-December 2009. As for FX contracts of OTC derivatives, the US dollar and the Japanese yen taken together accounted for 81.9%, decreasing from 83.9%. Transactions between reporting dealers respectively accounted for 79.9% and 64.2% of notional amount outstanding in OTC interest rate and FX contracts.

Among OTC contracts, interest rate derivatives with remaining maturities of over one year and up to five years continued to occupy the largest share, at 45.5%. With respect to FX derivatives, contracts with remaining maturities of over one year and up to five years continued to be dominant, accounting for 47.3%. The notional amount outstanding of credit default swaps was USD 1,110.4 billion. By counterparty, transactions between reporting dealers continued to be dominant, accounting for 89% of credit default swaps contracts. By remaining maturity, contracts with remaining maturities of over one year and up to five years were dominant at 64.9%, followed by those with remaining maturities of over five years, accounting for 25% of notional amounts outstanding.

2.9.3.1.4 NEW ZEALAND

Before exploring derivatives growth in the New Zealand environment, Berkman and Bradbury (1996) first stated that FX and interest rate volatility in New Zealand is relatively high compared to that in the USA and elsewhere. For instance, the annualised volatility of STIR over one year estimation (January 1993–January 1996) was 5.4% for New Zealand, while for the USA, the estimated volatility was 4.3%, and Japan had the lowest exposure at 3.1%. Thus, New Zealand firms are exposed to several risks, which can be managed by derivative instruments. In 1994, the uses of derivatives have grown drastically after the deregulation of the New Zealand financial market. As of June 1994, the notional amount of the swap held by banking and financial institutions increased by $2.350 million to $39.710 million, an increase of 15.89%; options and futures increased by $22.670 million to $29.106 million;

and future increased from \$53.718 million to \$143.076 million. For comparison, the assets in the balance sheet held by financial institutions increased by 58.78%, from \$61.090 million to \$96.996 million in the same period.

According to Alkebäck and Hagelin (1999), the manufacturing companies are the major contributors to the drastic growth in the derivative market in New Zealand, where these companies have higher derivatives usage than other producers of derivative products such as banks and non-financial companies. Manufacturing firms are more exposed to FX risk due to their involvement in export and import activities. The same scenario exists in Sweden. Even though Sweden market operates in a small open economy, the companies were more exposed to FX risk as compared to firms located in the USA. As a result, the likelihood of manufacturing firms in New Zealand using derivatives to mitigate FX risk is higher than in developed countries like the USA.

2.9.3.1.5 SINGAPORE

As an international financial and trading centre, financial derivatives have also been growing in importance in Singapore with an increasing emphasis on risk management following the financial crisis. Even though the performance of Singapore's financial institutions suffered a slowdown in 2001, the derivatives trading activities grew strongly, benefiting from the more uncertain economic environment. The trading volume reached an all-time record of 31 million contracts, surpassing the previous high in 1998. Record high trading volume was seen in several contracts, in particular the Eurodollar futures, Morgan Stanley Capital International (MSCI) Taiwan Index options and futures and the Singapore dollar Interest Rate futures contract. In contrast, FX activity was submissive, reflecting ongoing consolidation and weak activity in regional currency markets. Nevertheless, Singapore maintained its position as the fourth largest FX centre in the world.

In cross-border derivative activities, Singapore's asset and liability positions in financial derivatives with non-residents increased from 2007 to 2011. As at 2011, Singapore's gross asset position in cross-border derivatives amounted to USD 160 billion, while liabilities totalling USD 100 billion. Both derivative assets and liabilities peaked in 2008 before declining significantly at the end of 2009 during the economic downturn following the global financial crisis. Substantial amounts of underlying securities were written off during the financial crisis, resulting in significant reductions in holdings and unwinding of positions in financial derivatives by both resident and non-resident investors. As the world economy recovered in 2010 amid signs of stabilisation in the global financial system, cross-border investments in derivative assets and liabilities rebounded. Throughout the financial crisis and ensuing global recession, Singapore continued to record net asset positions in cross-border derivatives over the years. The deposit-taking in corporate and banking sectors accounted for the majority of investments in financial derivatives. Resident banks held between 79% and 87% of total cross-border derivative assets, and accounted for 72–84% of total cross-border liabilities from 2007 to 2011. With the exception of sharp declines in 2009 as the Singapore economy went into recession in the midst of continued uncertainties in global financial markets, the stocks of both derivative assets and liabilities in the banking sector have generally been increasing in recent years.

2.9.3.1.6 TAIWAN

Taiwan started financial innovations in its financial market very late. The FX and interest rate derivatives were only launched in 1998 on the Taiwan Futures Exchange. From this period, Taiwanese commercial banks started to have access to locally traded derivatives. Compared to developed markets, the characteristics of the Taiwanese derivative markets include a lack of innovation, products and liquidity. Most of the regulations are designed for a particular product, and there are few systematic regulations. However, regulators are expected to liberalise the market to advance the development of OTC derivatives, including allowing more products, lowering the tax rate and lowering the threshold for market entry.

Taiwan started the Taiwan Dollar (TWD) business in 2013, and many financial institutions are preparing for this business. After the launch of offshore Taiwanese official currency known as TWD, Taiwan plans to develop a TWD derivatives market. Taiwan will also establish a Treasury Markets Association to serve TWD bond and Non-Deliverable Forward (NDF) trading. There is a distinct lack of a commodities market. After becoming a member of WTO, and following the government's removal of price protection, corporations faced a global market, which brought greater price fluctuations. Taiwanese corporations could only seek overseas commodities markets. As regards derivatives usage and banks' competitiveness in 2013, CTBC Bank proved to be the number one bank in Taiwan's derivatives market. Also, with the deregulation of TWD products in Taiwan, CTBC Bank made every effort to provide and develop relevant FX products to satisfy client's needs as the major TWD product provider among Taiwanese banks. The two types of Renminbi Business (RMB)-related derivative transactions include (i) principal-settled and non-principal-settled TWD derivatives involving the TWD exchange rate or interest rate and structured products with a combination of the above and (ii) derivatives and structured products with a link to the People's Republic of China (PRC) stock index or specific shares issued by a Taiwan listed company (Chang 2013). Derivative products are in a better position to offer their TWD derivatives business to investors in Taiwan. In addition, some TWD structured products were offered to local investors through retail banking channels after February 2013, thus further expanding the diversified investment spectrum for Taiwanese investors.

2.9.3.2 *Derivatives market development in Asia-Pacific (emerging countries)*

2.9.3.2.1 MALAYSIA

In Malaysia, derivatives are generally used as hedging instruments and to a limited extent to enhance yield. Derivatives have allowed banking institutions to increase product innovation without losing their ability to manage the increased risks. With the advent of credit derivatives and Basel II proposals, derivatives have been more widely recognised as a risk mitigation technique, which could also economise on capital adequacy requirements. In 2003, it was estimated that the notional value of total outstanding OTC derivatives, comprising interest rate and FX forwards, swaps and options, grew by more than twofold in Malaysia, with MYR171 billion over the last four years. It is important to note that statistics on OTC derivatives are difficult to capture, and that any notional amount is not an accurate reflection of the actual risk exposure to financial institutions. Between 1999 and 2003, it was estimated that the average annual growth in interest rate and FX OTC contracts collectively and, in aggregate, it was about 40%. However, interest rate derivatives have experienced stronger growth given the sensitivity to interest rate changes and the need to manage exposure to fixed and floating rate financial assets.

In the international financial markets, the growth in OTC derivatives has been phenomenal in recent years. The statistics compiled by the BIS indicate that as of the end of June 2003, the total outstanding OTC derivatives in notional amounts were USD 169 trillion (Bank Negara Malaysia 2004). This total figure includes USD 22 trillion of FX contracts, USD 121 trillion of interest rate contracts, principally swaps, USD 2.7 trillion of equity-linked contracts, almost USD 1 trillion of commodity contracts and USD 18 trillion classified as others.

2.9.3.2.2 PHILIPPINES

The notional amount of stand-alone derivatives held by Philippines banks between February 2008 and August 2009 was on average, about P2.3 trillion (USD 50 billion). Embedded financial derivatives (e.g. structured notes) represented about P13 billion (USD 275 million). FX derivatives are the most frequently stand-alone traded instruments, with FX forwards and swaps together constituting two-thirds of all derivative contracts and FX swaps representing about half of the derivatives markets. The majority of derivative transactions are short-term (less than one year).

The most popular structured notes in the Philippines are range-accrual notes, plain vanilla credit-linked notes (CLN) and leveraged CLN. The fact that reference assets on which banks sell protection are usually Philippine government bonds whose risk or return profile is well known by the local banks that speaks of the conservative approach that banks take to structured financial products. Conversely, this approach could create higher systemic risk in the event of fiscal problems, since it would compound bank losses from these products. Moreover, for the seller of the notes, these structures imply a wrong way exposure (i.e. protection is sold on a risk to which the seller is also exposed).

Foreign banks lead the local derivatives activities in the Philippines with their entry because of their expertise in the area and also as a result of the regulations that prescribe different types of licences to participate in this market. Licences depend on the complexity of the products, their terms, and on whether the banks take a position on them or they act on behalf of their clients. No domestic bank has the broadest type of licence (Type 1 or expanded dealer). They either have a Type 2 (limited dealer) or Type 3 (end-user) authority. Most domestic banks' activities are end-users (proprietary trading or hedging exposures) and their counterparties are foreign banks with a presence in the Philippines or offshore international banks. Derivatives expose banks to market and counterparty risks. These can be measured by current exposures (i.e. the current value of the contract) or by potential exposures, given specific scenarios, usually measured by value-at-risk methodologies. Counterparty risk to foreign counterparties through CLN was significantly reduced after the global crisis.

2.9.3.2.3 THAILAND

The Central Bank of Thailand (Bank of Thailand) recognises that derivatives are important for Thai companies, particularly with such a volatile currency and market interest rate uncertainty. Thai derivative volumes are considerably small. According to the Bank of Thailand, in 2009, data show that total outstanding Thai baht interest rate swaps at Thai commercial banks came to USD 67 billion (THB 2,231 billion). This tremendously increased value is described by Thailand's financial policy on derivatives to accommodate derivatives development as one of the risk management tools among others to ensure financial system stability and financial institutions' soundness. The high volatility in baht currency makes it particularly essential for Thai firms and industries to have access to derivatives since the penalty for not hedging a currency exposure can be severe.

For instance, during the financial crisis in 1997, the Bank of Thailand acknowledged that Thailand's managed floating exchange rate was due to the high volatility in exchange and interest rates in the countries with EM. This circumstance has prompted them to aggressively participate in hedging exchange and interest rate risk whereas they realised that derivatives usage for hedging purposes is a necessity for Thai companies to protect themselves against market uncertainties. According to Shamsher and Taufiq (2007), since the 1990s Thailand has become one of the emerging countries that experienced fast growing financial derivative market for interest rates, currencies, futures and options. Financial derivative market process plays an important role for managing systematic risk in the market place. Therefore, the Bank of Thailand estimates that hedging activities must continuously encourage business players to hedge interest and exchange rates. In 2009, the Financial Sector Master Plan Phase II was issued by the Bank of Thailand, which shelters a congregation of issues around Thailand's financial system. Thailand's financial experts believe that with the pledges made by the Bank of Thailand to support the development of credit derivative transactions, as well as to continue encouraging interest rate derivatives, participants should use International Swap Dealers Association (ISDA) market agreements. In relation to formulating the supervisory framework for derivatives business, the Bank of Thailand is guided by the five pillars as follows:

1   Efficient risk management, appropriate to the nature and complexity of the business;
2   Financial and economic stability;
3   Sufficient customer protection;
4   Relevant prudential regulations being in place and
5   Sufficient information for supervisory purposes.

These five pillars or principles also have a significant impact on Thailand's derivatives financial market, which also drive the commercial banks and other type of companies to hedge their market exposures especially for those companies that are involved in foreign transactions. The Bank of Thailand strongly believes that the policy and principles that have been developed in their supervisory and risk management frameworks has provided alternative investment channels for the institutional investors. Therefore, they can further diversify their investment and enhance their investment returns through the flexibility and convenience of their derivative activities (Ritdumrongkul 2011).[4]

2.9.4 Justification for choosing banks in the Asia-Pacific countries

Despite the growing importance of derivatives usage and activities in the Asia-Pacific region (Rahman and Hassan 2011; Au Yong et al. 2009; Marshall 2000), and the development of their financial system and regional economic expansion (Deesomsak et al. 2004; Lynch 1996), the investigation on risk management efficiency in Asian-Pacific banks is necessary. Not only its uniqueness relative to other regions, such as the European region and the USA, enables it to discover important contributions, for the banks, but the results will also strengthen the theories explaining that banks' derivative activities in managing risk are applicable to banks in the Asia-Pacific context. Theories formulated will contribute to the evidence on how derivatives usage for banks operating in the developed and developing markets functions in the operation of risk management within the Asia-Pacific region. In addition, there have been very few studies on efficiency in the Asia-Pacific region so far, but they are increasing.

This study will therefore develop a new conceptual framework for banks' risk management efficiency in nine Asia-Pacific countries that will incorporate interest rate swaps as one of the derivative instruments, particularly known as a hedging instrument in the concept of hedge accounting. This new framework will expedite the risk management strategy in understanding the theories and the macro-hedging process that has been implemented in the commercial banking sectors, as well as understanding how derivative instruments affect the efficiency of banks' risk management in the developed and developing financial markets. Studies on these two groups of countries (the developed and developing countries) are important as, on average, the construction and development of derivatives among them are highly competent (Mihaljek and Packer 2010; Lien and Zhang 2008).With the integrated approach between hedge accounting and DEA, the findings may have important implications for banks in both groups of countries. As such, an investigation on the risk management efficiency in Asian-Pacific banks based on a derivative instrument is justified and warranted.

2.10 Methodology: data envelopment analysis (DEA) theory

The majority of studies on banking efficiency focus on the TE measurement of how well firms actually process inputs to achieve outputs. A survey of the literature suggests that there are two widely used empirical approaches used to evaluate the efficiency of banks, namely parametric (stochastic frontier approach – SFA) and non-parametric approach (DEA). To measure the risk management efficiency of commercial banks, this study employs the DEA approach because of its strength over the parametric SFA. The following subsections elaborate the various aspects and justifications of using DEA for the purpose of risk efficiency analysis of derivatives usage in this study.

2.10.1 Definition of DEA: a deterministic non-parametric method

DEA is a non-parametric mathematical programming model developed by Charnes et al. (1978) for measuring the relative efficiency of a group of entities or decision-making units (DMUs) in their use of multiple inputs to produce multiple outputs in a situation where the form of the production is not known. Under the ingredients of optimisation problems and classification, DEA identifies the best practice performance frontier using a comparable process of transforming inputs into outputs. Theoretically, it expresses the importance of knowing how far firms can be expected to increase their outputs by simply increasing the level of efficiency without increasing any further resources.

A DEA is based on linear programming (LP) making it more powerful in comparison to other productivity management tools (Cooper et al. 2011).

DEA uses actual data to obtain the efficiencies in cases where every boundary of firms in the sample can be measured such that no explicit functional form has to be specified in advance. The production frontier will be generated by a mathematical programming algorithm which also calculates the optimal efficiency score for each DMU. Besides its ability to make no assumptions about the functional form that links inputs to outputs, DEA also seeks a set of weights to maximise the TE (Athanassopoulos and Curram 1996). This model can be constructed to either minimise inputs or to maximise outputs. An input-oriented model aims at minimising the amount of input while maintaining the same output levels, while an output orientation aims at maximising output levels without increasing the use of inputs (Cooper et al. 2000). Beginning with the simple concept of a DEA containing a single input and a single output, efficiency is defined as:

$$\text{Efficiency} = \frac{\text{Output}}{\text{Input}}$$

However, in most cases, managers are often interested in evaluating the efficiency levels of various productions or processes with respect to multiple inputs and outputs. In the real world, organisations operate under the influence of multiple inputs to produce multiple outputs instead of using a single input to produce a single output.

2.10.2 CCR model of DEA

There are a few different DEA models that have been developed for conducting efficiency measurement such as ratio, additive, multiplicative, CCR (Charnes, Cooper, Rhodes) and BCC (Banker, Charnes, Cooper) models. Three types of scores are used in estimates of efficiency originally proposed by Farrell (1957) based on the relative efficiency concepts: (1) TE, (2) Pure Technical Efficiency (PTE) and (3) Scale Efficiency (SE). Charnes et al. (1978) have reproduced Farrell's TE and proposed a model which had an input-orientation and assumed constant return to scale (CRS) known as a CCR (Charnes-Cooper-Rhodes) model, while Banker (1984) introduces a variable return to scale (VRS) approach, which is known as a BCC model (Banker-Charnes-Cooper).

This study focusses on the CCR model developed by Charnes et al. (1978). In this model, the efficiency of a DMU is defined as the ratio of the sum of its weighted outputs to the sum of its weighted inputs. Given the CCR model, where the ratio measure of relative efficiency for DMU_K is given by the following non-convex, nonlinear, fractional programming (2.2) and (2.3):

$$\text{Maximise: } h_p = \frac{\sum_{r=1}^{k} w_r y_{rp}}{\sum_{i=1}^{m} v_i x_{ip}}, \quad p = 1,2 \dots, n \qquad (2.2)$$

Subject to: $\dfrac{\sum_{r=1}^{k} w_r y_{rj}}{\sum_{i=1}^{m} v_i x_{ij}} \leq 1, \quad j = 1, 2 \ldots, n$

$$w_r \geq 0, \qquad\qquad r = 1, 2 \ldots, k$$
$$v_i \geq 0, \qquad\qquad i = 1, 2 \ldots, m \qquad\qquad (2.3)$$

where:

h_p denotes the efficiency score;
y_{rp} denotes the amount for output r from unit p;
x_{ip} denotes the amount for input i utilised by unit p;
y_{rj} denotes the amount for output r from unit j;
x_{ij} refers to the amount for input I utilised by unit j;
w_r is the weight of output r;
v_i denotes the weight of input i;
p denotes the number of optimisations for each $DMUj$ to be evaluated;
n denotes the number of DMUs;
k denotes the number of outputs and
m denotes the number of inputs.

In this model, there are two constraints on assigning weights, where no DMU can get a score more than 1.0 and the weights must be positive and the sum of weights is one. This is the limitation in weight selection for the inputs and outputs. The weights w_r and v_i are determined by x_{ij} and y_{rj} data. The objective function, h_p represents the relative efficiency of DMU_J which ranges j from 1 to n. The x_{ij} and y_{rj} (all positive) are known input and output values of j-th DMU. The efficiency of DMU must not exceed unity (100%). Thus, the DMU is efficient if the score is 1 and inefficient if the score is less than 1. The objective function (2.2) and constraints (2.3) are composed of fractions and need to be transformed into a linear program so that the model can be solved using simple LP such as the simplex method. Ragsdale (2010, 113) noted that "an efficiency rating of 100% does not necessarily mean that a unit is operating in the best possible way". He has suggested that linear combination of efficient units is important as it would result in a composite unit that produces at least as much output using the same or less input than the inefficient unit (DMU).

2.10.3 Advantages and disadvantages of DEA

The advantages of DEA in measuring relative efficiency of DMU are shown below (Emrouznejad et al. 2014; Athanassopoulos and Curram 1996):

1   DEA is a non-parametric model that makes no assumptions about the functional form that links its inputs to outputs.
2   DEA seeks a set of weights to maximise the TE.

3   DEA performs better as a tool for estimating empirical production functions.
4   DEA can guide management to improvise the inefficient projects using the projection suggestions given by the DEA - Solver. For each ineffi-cient activity unit DEA identifies a number of benchmarks or efficient activity units that can be used as reference sets.
5   DEA can handle multiple inputs and outputs simultaneously. DEA can be used to deal with multiple inputs and outputs with different measure-ment units.
6   DEA can be used to deal with multiple inputs and outputs with different measurement units.

However, this approach also has some disadvantages in measuring the rela-tive efficiency of an organisation's projects and programmes as shown below:

1   DEA concept needs the number of DMUs to be equal to the maximum number of multiplications of input and output or three times of the summation of inputs and outputs (Raab and Lichty 2002). Meanwhile, Troutt et al. (1996) suggest that the training data for non-parametric models should be at least ten times the number of input variables. The more the data were trained, the more accurate the Multi-Criteria Linear Programming (MLP) model achieved.
2   DEA model yields inaccurate results if the important inputs and out-puts are ignored or if the selected inputs and outputs are not relevant (Rosmaini 2002).
3   DEA provides only the relative efficiency of DMUs but not an absolute efficiency because DEA concept does not allow for single DMU to be presented only once over time.
4   DEA attempts to compare non-homogenous DMUs and environments which can lead to unfair comparisons and provides a direct impact on the performance of units (Dyson et al. 2001).

2.11 Methodological issues in adapting DEA for risk management measurement

Having provided the conceptual definitions as well as justifications for using DEA for hedge effectiveness test for derivatives (Sections 1.9 and 4.4.2), this section turns to the methodological issues in the use of DEA. In relation to this, this study consequently has followed Arjomandi (2011) to analyse three important methodological issues, namely (1) input-output orientation, (2) CRS vs. VRS and (3) input and output variables.

2.11.1 Input-output orientation

In DEA, two types of models in LP technique can be used, namely the out-put orientation and the input-orientation models. The input-oriented model maximises the proportional reduction in inputs while retaining the same level of outputs; on the other hand, the output-oriented model maximises the proportional expansion in outputs for the same level of inputs. Input-oriented TE focusses on the use of minimum input resources to achieve a given level of output. The model deals with questions relating to the reduction of input quantities without changing the output quantities produced. Meanwhile, the output oriented model focusses on using a given set of inputs to achieve the maximum possible output quantities that can be expanded without altering the input quantities used (Joro and Korhonen 2015; Coelli et al. 2005a).

Technically, relative efficiency of a DMU can be estimated through any of these two models. For instance, Ally (2013) employed an input-oriented DEA to analyse the efficiency of regional and small commercial banks in Tanzania over the period from 2006 to 2012, while some other studies (e.g. Ataullah and Le 2006; Ataullah et al. 2004) have adopted an output-oriented approach or report the results by adopting both orientation (e.g. Beccalli et al. 2006; Casu et al. 2004). Further, a strict choice between input or output approach is not absolutely essential (vital) since the DEA approach does not suffer from statistical problems. Dong (2010) points out that the selection of a suitable orientation is based on the input or output quantities that the managers have more control over. Therefore, if the firms' managers are required to meet market demands, and they can freely adjust input parameters, an input-oriented model is strongly recommended. In contrast, if the firms have a fixed quantity of inputs and the objective is to produce as much output as possible, then an output-oriented model is more appropriate. However, Coelli and Perelman (1999) and Coelli et al. (2005a) mention that the choice of orientation reflects a minor effect on the efficiency scores obtained and not as vital as other econometric approaches since the DEA does not suffer from statistical problems. In addition, Daraio and Simar (2007) and Halkos and Tzeremes (2010) stated that the choice between input and output orientation is based on whether the decision maker controls most the inputs or the outputs. However, an input-oriented model has been employed in most studies to estimate the efficiency of banks because of the assumption that bank managers have more control over inputs (e.g. on operating expenses, employees, etc.) instead of output variables (e.g. profit, loans, etc.).

2.11.2 CRS vs. VRS

There are two types of efficient scale of operations that can be applied in DEA, namely Constant Returns to Scale (CRS) or Variable Returns to Scale (VRS). The CRS assumption is only suitable when all the firms are operating at an optimal scale. However, factors like imperfect competition and market size that may affect income distribution, and international trade constraints, alongside other factors in the banking system may cause a firm not to be operating at its optimal scale. Therefore, Banker et al. (1984) state that in order to comprehend both PTE and SE and yield the score that specifies the overall technical efficiency (OTE) for each firm, VRS assumption is more appropriate. VRS assumption is more appropriate for large samples (Arjomandi 2011), and each unit is compared only against other units of similar size, instead of against all units (Avkiran 1999c). VRS enables PTE by improving the ability of managers to utilise firms' given resources. VRS certainly enables the exploitation of scale economies by operating at a point in which the production frontier exhibits CRS. Due to those advantages, the majority of efficiency studies using DEA are based on the assumption of VRS and has been commonly used since the 1990s (Coelli et al. 1998). In other examples, using the Indian banking industry as a case study, Ataullah et al. (2004) applied DEA method to investigate their TE during the period from 1992 to 1998. In two different panels (Panel 1 and Panel 2), the VRS assumption is selected to examine the implication of loan-based model and the income-based model, respectively. For a loan-based model, on average, public sector banks are more efficient than private banks. However, in some cases, private banks are more efficient (outperformed) than public sector banks, which indicates that private banks effectively generated their earning assets to translate into maximising their income. These results indicate that under the VRS assumption, private banking systems are improving in terms of input management and SE. But recently, the assumption of VRS has been used in specifications because this assumption is more suited to the environment of imperfect competition in which banks operate (Kablan 2007; Grigorian and Manole 2002; Leightner and Lovell 1998).

The CRS assumption is only justifiable when all the DMUs are operating at an optimal scale. Conversely, DMUs in practice might face either economies or diseconomies of scale due to imperfect competition, constraints on finance and so on. In this case, the CCR model will bias the estimation of the TE by confounding scale effects, so Banker (1984) suggests an extension of the CCR model to account for VRS cases.

2.11.3 Input and output variables for DEA model

In a real-world application, an organisation operates with the use of multiple inputs to produce multiple outputs instead of using a single input to produce a single output. The use of multiple inputs and multiple outputs are the main problems for determining the relative efficiency of the organisational units known as DMUs. Morita and Avkiran (2009) argue that the input and output variables directly affect the efficiency score evaluation and the efficiency model will provide inaccurate results if the inputs and outputs chosen are not relevant.

To date, there is considerable disagreement on the choice of banks' inputs and outputs. For instance, there is no consensus on whether deposits should be treated as inputs or outputs (Bogetoft 2012; Holod and Lewis 2011; Jackson and Fethi 2000;). Furthermore, Gregoriou et al. (2005) consider outputs as the effect of processing the inputs, and believe that this assesses how efficiently a company has attained its goals. The selection of input and output may be found, based on production or intermediation approaches to bank behaviour, or based on the expert knowledge on accepted practices (Morita and Avkiran 2009). Moreover, in any decision made, Mokhtar et al. (2006) essentially suggested that it should be subject to the banks' treatment of money received from the depositors and the money that they lent to the creditors.

In relation to this, three distinct approaches are provided in the literature and used for selecting inputs and outputs, namely a production approach, an intermediation approach and a value-added approach. Nevertheless, in banking efficiency studies, Barros et al. (2012), Kasman (2012) and Drake et al. (2009), among others, suggested that the first two approaches are more appropriate since both approaches assume banks as producers and as financial intermediaries where most of the activities consist of turning funds into financing or investments, and reflect banks' goals to maximise profits in an ambiguous environment and dealing with risk.

The production approach views banks as producers who use physical inputs of capital and labour to generate outputs of loan accounts and deposits. Sufian (2010) and Neal (2004) are among the researchers who use this approach. The intermediation approach views banks as intermediaries of financial services that transfer and convert financial assets from a surplus or deficit units. This approach assumes that banks collect deposits from customers, using labour and capital to transfer into loans and other earning assets (Freixas and Rochet 1997; Sealey and Lindley 1977). Within this approach, there are alternative conceptualisations when defining inputs and outputs. Fried et al. (1993) and Kirkwood and Nahm (2006) conceptualised inputs in terms of labour, capital costs and deposits and outputs in terms of financial investments and loans. In another type of intermediation approach, inputs are determined in terms of expenses and outputs in terms of revenue (Paul and Kourouche 2008; Avkiran 1999c; Miller and Noulas 1996; Charnes et al. 1990). The value-added approach is based on the share of value added to identify inputs and outputs for the banking sectors. According to Minh et al. (2012), this approach considers deposits as outputs since they focus on value-addition.

The intermediation approach is based on the theory of financial intermediation proposed by Allen and Santomero (1998). This approach is very popular in DEA efficiency analysis and most widely used in the banking literature (Paradi et al. 2011; Tahir and Bakar 2009; Kwan 2006). Berger and Humphrey (1997) have argued that the intermediation approach is the most appropriate approach since it is inclusive of interest expense as compared to the production approach which is known to have limitation as the latter excludes interest expense, which is considered an important element of banking operations. Thus, in agreement with the study involving risk elements issues, this approach is perhaps appropriate for this study.

Furthermore, in determining input and output parameters, and using DEA as the diagnostic tool, Shimshak et al. (2009) state that it is important to take quality measurement into account in measuring efficiency. They state that it is often a difficult concept to define and can vary considerably based upon the context in which it is to be applied. For instance, there is one aspect that it is essential to recognise in DEA approach that there are conditions in which the quality of output measured does not increase with additional input resources. The same situation exists when qualitative measures are involved in efficiency analysis, whereas the 'antecedent' has been used in evaluating and identifying the input, while "consequences" are referred to determine the output (Manzoni and Islam 2009a, 2009b). It is concluded that input and output can also be determined without the productivity concept.

2.11.4 Verification and validation of the model

Once the model has been formulated and solved, it is important that it is verified and validated before analysing its output. It is to avoid any computational error, thus ensuring the internal consistency of the model. McCarl and Spreen (2011, 1997) mention two general approaches to validity which may be used, namely (i) validity by construct and (ii) validity by results. They believe that validity by construct is most applicable for both predictive and prescriptive models. To ensure verification and validity, the following processes are most applicable:

1   Following the right procedure when developing the model. The model needs to be consistent with the industry, previous research and/or theory. The data also need to be specific based on reasonable scientific estimation or risk management procedure.
2   Ensuring that the results indicate that the model is behaving satisfactorily.
3   Ensuring the constraints are imposed, which restrict the model to realistic solutions.

However, McCarl and Spreen pointed out some limitations when the validity of the model is determined by construct. They believe that as the model is tested, validity is ensured by the results. Some of the processes of validity by results include parameter outcome sets, prediction experiment, change experiment, tracking experiment, etc. Hence, the steps to conduct validation test as suggested by McCarl and Spreen (2011, 1997) are as follows:

1   Alter the model variables, data and equations to reflect the validation experiment;
2   Solve the model(s);
3   Evaluate the solution (to see whether it contains LP problems such as infeasibility, unboundedness, etc.) or it is optimal?

4   If the model has a sufficient degree of association, then conduct a higher validation experiment, or determine the model's validity and process to use it;

5   If the model is not satisfactory, consider whether the data are consistent and correctly calculated, and the objective function is correctly specified and

6   Fix the model. For the procedures of recalculating model parameters, it would be considered as problem-specific.

2.12 Stochastic measurements

In relation to the deterministic DEA discussed above, this approach, however, is unable to be generalised easily. Due to the many uncertainties in the business environment and modelling and analysis of risk management, stochastic measurements need to be considered to undertake an analysis of risk management efficiency measures under uncertainty. By using the stochastic models, the study can provide new insights into the effects of methodological choice on estimated efficiency (detailed discussions will be highlighted in Chapter 5).

2.13 Limitations and motivation

This chapter presents some general conclusions regarding risk management efficiency measurement and derivatives usage in banks.

First, it is imperative to point out that the risk management efficiency based on the derivatives usage has not been measured by a proper approach in any efficiency literature. Therefore, this justifies the necessity for risk management efficiency measurements to be established, by developing a measure for risk management efficiency. From here, the derivatives usage strategy used by firms can be measured, so that their influence in determining risk management efficiency can be determined. Furthermore, through the study, banks are exposed to the risk of volatile markets. Derivatives usage is increasingly popular in reducing the risk faced by banks, proving that this instrument deserves special attention. However, there are a few studies focussing on the effectiveness of using derivative instruments as better risk management. This phenomenon deserves study on the impact of financial instruments usage on banks risk management efficiency perspectives.

Second, until now, the only research documented in the literature is the research by Rivas et al. (2006), who measured the influence of derivatives on banks' efficiency level based on the DEA measurement approach. The derivative variables in that study are not extensively examined in measuring efficiency levels of firms, and this leads to a very general conclusion. Indirectly, the DEA measurement used in the study does not show the relationship between derivatives as a risk management tool, as the main purpose of derivatives usage is for the firm's better risk management strategy and the direct influence of derivatives on its accounting items has not been examined. However, they conclude that derivative instrument usage increases banking efficiency levels.

Third, as far as the literature is concerned, to date, there is no literature that directly compares and assesses the possible influence of using financial derivatives, such as interest rate swaps, for risk management efficiency in commercial banks in the developed and developing financial markets. The impact in different markets plays a pivotal role in view of the risk management efficiency of derivatives usage in banks. Moreover, while some literature has focussed on the derivative activities among banks in European countries, studies of this type are largely absent in the Asia-Pacific region. This is in contrast with the majority of the efficiency studies that focus on the US, European and Latin American banks. Therefore, due to the rapidly increasing derivatives usage in the Asian-Pacific commercial banks, an investigation into this issue is important.

Fourth, since derivatives involve an uncertain environment, the derivative strategy may produce uncertain data that may create noise in the data. This issue received less attention in efficiency measurement studies. The sampling error issue in DMUs also receives little attention in efficiency studies. Furthermore, in the banking environment, banks are unable to escape from an uncertainty environment that may affect their strategy and performance. Therefore, to achieve accuracy, robustness and predictive power in risk management efficiency results, this study will use three stochastic approaches: (i) Bootstrap DEA (BDEA), (ii) Sensitivity Analysis and (iii) Chance-Constrained DEA (CCDEA) to resolve these issues.

To address gaps in the existing literature, a new conceptual framework has been developed and implemented.

2.14 Conclusions

Generally, this chapter addresses the importance of risk management efficiency measurement and analysis to be developed when dealing with the concept of financial derivatives. In the context of the banking industry, which is exposed to different market risks, specific risk management measures evaluate the impact of derivatives usage on risk management efficiency levels. Interest rate risk is one of the main risks faced by banks and its effect on the loans and investment performances. Therefore, the measurement of risk management efficiency based on the derivative instruments is important for better risk management strategies and hedging from severe impacts. Consequently, the measurement improves banking risk management efficiency levels. Therefore, the study proposes the measurement and analysis to directly examine the risk management efficiency levels and provides implications for the use of derivatives in the risk management efficiency performance of banks. At this point, this study proposes and develops another approach to risk management efficiency measurement and analysis based on the integrated approaches of DEA and dollar-offset ratio in hedge accounting as discussed in Chapter 3. Thus, the limitations of the existing literature and the need to further develop the efficiency literature in the developed and developing financial markets are also suggested.

Notes

1 Fabozzi and Mann (2005) describe the method in determining the value of FI securities that lies to the 'time value of money' concept.
2 An example of how risk management is affected by the derivatives contract is shown in Hartford Financial Services Group case, see Brigham and Ehrhardt (2013).
3 Analysis of interest rates and bond valuation is explained in detail.
4 Ritdumrongkul (2011) has shown that the notional amount of derivatives in Thailand is THB 5.5 trillion for 2008 and THB 8.4 trillion in 2010. The majority of derivative activity is concentrated among large-sized banks. The summary of statistics show that derivative activities grew at 76.52% per year where small- and medium-sized banks grew at a higher rate (107.82%) than large-sized banks (72.77%).

3 Risk management efficiency measurement and analysis – an alternative measure based on hedge accounting

3.1 Introduction

As indicated in previous chapters, risk management efficiency measures and analyses can be based on the usage of financial derivatives which are normally used for hedging purposes. As interest rate changes are considered a major source of risk that potentially impact on a banks' risk management efficiency (Acar and Acar 2014), changes in interest rate are important hedging factors (Adcock et al. 2017; Robinson 2014). This study recognises that derivatives and risk management efficiency in commercial banks are not defined according to the importance of hedge effectiveness based on the hedge accounting scope in the developed and developing financial markets, where the size and application of derivative instruments differ. These differences arise due to various legal, political and economic circumstances, as well as the derivative structure and size, market regulation and a country's financial standing (Morgan 2008; Ali et al. 2006). However, due to the high competition in promoting the usage of derivatives in the financial systems of the developed and developing financial markets, a comprehensive comparative study of both derivatives and the financial institutions' risk management efficiency is vital.

The purpose of this chapter is to prepare the foundation for a study to establish an alternative measure for risk management efficiency that will incorporate interest rate swaps as one of the derivative instruments, which is known as a hedging instrument in hedge accounting concept and banks' risk management efficiency. This new framework expedites the risk management strategy in understanding the macro-hedging process that has been implemented in commercial banking sectors where derivative instruments have affected the efficiency of risk management in banks, in both the developed and developing financial markets.

After the introductory section, financial theory and the need for the derivative instruments used are discussed in Section 3.2. Section 3.3 presents the scope of hedge accounting on measuring the efficiency of risk management in banks. It concentrates on the hedge effectiveness test used in hedge accounting and explains the role of derivative instruments (swaps) to hedge risk. Section 3.4 discusses hedge effectiveness tests in hedge accounting in the context of risk management. Later, Section 3.5 develops a framework for the hedge effectiveness test in hedge accounting. Section 3.6 discusses the dollar-offset ratio (DOR) as one of the hedge effectiveness tests through the actual empirical illustration in selected commercial banks in the Asia-Pacific region. Section 3.7 highlights the policy implications when the DOR is used to measure banks' risk management efficiency. Section 3.8 highlights the plausibility of the chosen hedge effectiveness test approach. Finally, Section 3.9 concludes the chapter.

3.2 Financial theory and the need for the use of derivatives as a hedging tool

Globally, about 60% of the established large business firms use derivatives (Lioui and Poncet 2005; El-Masry 2003). As tested in prior research, financial distress (bankruptcy) costs, taxes, underinvestment problem and managerial incentives are the reasons identified in most of the existing theories that describe the incentives for the derivatives used (Borokhovich et al. 2004; Bartram et al. 2003). Modern financial theory suggests that capital market imperfections create incentives for firms (including banks) to use derivatives for hedging purposes. Several authors such as Smith and Stulz (1985) and Fok et al. (1997) argue that hedging can reduce the present value of expected tax liabilities, the expected cost of financial distress and the agency cost problems. As derivatives are employed primarily for hedging purposes, they can be used as a means for reducing agency cost arising from the transfer of wealth from bondholders to shareholders. Since banks can use derivatives to hedge, they can reduce the volatility of their cash flow and pay out a greater level of income in the form of dividends and ensure that the bondholders have sufficient cash for debt payments. Consequently, in the light of corporate risk management theory, firms engaging in derivatives for hedging activities can avoid the cost of financial distress (Borokhovich et al. 2004; Cummins et al. 2001).

Rivas et al. (2006) stress the benefits of using derivatives in the banking sector. They believe that derivatives are optimal for the banking sector and for hedging purposes. Derivatives can reduce agency costs by the efficient alignment of the interests of the managers and stockholders, along with aligning the interests of the bondholders and shareholders. The interaction between the influence of managerial attitudes on risk-taking and hedging also has a basis in agency theory (Wall 1989; Smith and Stulz 1985). Fite and Pfleiderer (1995) embraced this theory, by defining the stance that hedging policy affects the value of corporate organisations. In contrast, this concept has been said to have led to higher risk levels, as large banks, understanding the importance for financial stability, know that in the case of financial difficulty, they will be bailed out to avoid excessive financial instability (Battilossi 2008; Hellmann et al. 2000). In addition, Hentschel and Kothari

(2001) found that the use of derivatives has a relatively less significant effect on the total risk profile of commercial banks.

As such, due to the systemic risk posed by banking, the implicit assurance that they will be bailed out (in most cases) exacerbates the incentives for risk-taking, as shareholders will not bear the majority of the costs in case of failure (Alexander 2006). As such, the concept of shareholder primacy, as promoted by agency theory, may indeed conflict with the role of the banks. As Adams and Mehran (2003) argued, the stakeholders of a bank extend well beyond the shareholders, as the depositors, creditors and the government all have an interest in the well-being of the bank as an integral part of the financial system. Clearly, agency theory focusses on the relationship between the ownership structure assessment and performance management, which involves shareholders' interest (Seifert et al. 2005; Sarkar and Sarkar 2003; Demsetz and Villalonga 2001; Lauterbach and Vaninsky 1999; Cho 1998). The situation is slightly different when a bank aims to boost profits without primarily concentrating on the maximisation of shareholders' wealth. A discussion on risk management should be comprehensive and take into account the strategies a firm employs to reduce risk, particularly when dealing with bankruptcy issues and financial distress.

By taking into account the effects of hedging on the interests of various stakeholder groups, managers have to decide upon the use of hedging instruments. At this point, stakeholder theory suggests that the purpose of a business is to create as much value as possible for stakeholders (Freeman et al. 2004; Edward 1984). Firms should create value, beyond value maximisation as their organisational objective. Seen in this light, long-term risk management strategies driven by financial theory are important in the assessment of the success or failure of an organisation. This indicates that in order to achieve maximum value, firms cannot ignore the interest of its stakeholders. In order to be successful and sustainable over time, executives must keep the interests of customers, employees, communities and shareholders aligned. Banks must learn to lower the risk of financial distress by implementing a hedging strategy and communicating it to their shareholders. Therefore, it can be argued that stakeholder theory provides a new insight into the possible rationale for risk management even though no empirical evidence on this has been tested directly. This theory is indeed closely associated with financial theory, which suggests that capital market imperfections create incentives for firms (including banks) to use derivatives for hedging purposes. Several authors, such as Smith and Stulz (1985) and Fok et al. (1997), maintained that some major benefits will be obtained by using derivatives, such as reducing taxes under a progressive tax schedule, reducing the expected cost of financial distress and reducing agency cost problems. This approach stipulates that hedging leads to lower volatility of cash flow, therefore bringing about higher volatility of firm value. Theoretically, this study demonstrates that financial theory and efficiency theory are interconnected, whereas the creation of financial products such as financial derivatives through financial innovation (also known as a financial engineering) can help banks to achieve better efficiency levels (Rizvi and Khan 2001).

The association between derivatives usage and risk management is of interest to the banking industry because banks are the major users of derivatives (see, e.g., Woods and Marginson 2004; Sinkey and Carter 2001). Banks are active in derivatives as end-users to hedge on-balance sheet risks and as dealers to boost non-interest income. Since derivatives provide a relatively easy and cost effective means for banks to alter their risk profile, regulators and investors are particularly concerned about whether banks use derivatives primarily to reduce risk from other banking activities (i.e. hedging) or for trading purposes to increase income, accompanied by higher levels of risk exposure (i.e. speculating) (Yong et al. 2009).

Today, most large multinational corporations are engaged in some form of volatility management through derivatives, most likely interest rates and foreign exchange rate swaps (92% according to a survey by International Swaps and Derivatives Association – ISDA). Léautier (2007) mentioned that numerous academic studies show that there is a significant change in the use of derivatives compared to their use in the 1980s. The use of derivatives is no longer considered dangerous in a risk management strategy. For instance, to reduce interest rate risk, many researchers believe that firms (including banks) will benefit from the use of interest rate swaps (Harper and Wingender 2000). Phillips (1995) believed that swap dominance as a vehicle for interest rate risk management stands out clearly. Prior to that, Smith et al. (1988) demonstrated a method that financial managers can use in order to swap interest rates, which is to hedge interest rate exposure. It is clearly shown that the issue has significantly touched on reducing interest rate exposure with interest rate swap usage.

Empirical comparisons provided by Samant (1996) show that compared to the non-fixed payers swap users, interest rate swaps have diverging return prospects and have created greater profits, with firms experiencing growth in earnings. Obviously, when a firm is able to reduce the risk, and, at the same time, expects an increase in revenue, it will achieve the concept of competitive advantage (Diamond 1984). Marshall and Bansal (1992) and Bicksler and Chen (2012) argue that the use of interest rate swaps would be beneficial for achieving a competitive advantage between institutions in the same industry, and that even financial institutions can make it an effective tool for managing a variety of underlying risks as recorded on the balance sheet. This phenomenon is consistent with the model of Diamond (1984), where he expects that intermediaries' use of derivatives is able to increase capacity and allow a firm to overtake its competitors.

Regarding hedging and value creation, a few surveys suggest that the use of currency derivatives increases a firm's value. For example, the cross-sectional survey by Allayannis and Weston (2001) of 720 large US non-financial firms between 1990 and 1995 found that firms that use currency derivatives have a higher market valuation relative to the book value of their assets than firms that are not involved in hedging activities. Subsequently, studies found that the use of currency derivatives is associated with higher firm value for industrial firms. These conclusions address the significant relationship between derivative usage and firm value. This result is economically important but puzzling in view of the mixed empirical evidence on hedging theories. Graham and Rogers (2002) argued that derivatives-induced debt capacity increases firm value by 1.1% on average. However, the validity of these results was questioned by Guay and Kothari (2003) who have suggested that the substantial increases in firm value documented in previous studies are either driven by other risk management activities (e.g. operational hedges) that are correlated with derivative use, or that the results are spurious.

Nevertheless, this study shows that firm value is driven by derivatives usage based on some instances in which hedging currencies may in fact increase cash flow volatility. Similarly, many commodity companies have incurred costs in currencies that are positively correlated with commodity prices, and the same scenario occurs in commercial banks. Léautier (2007) empirically found that hedging the interest rate exposure can significantly reduce cash flow volatility for a commercial bank. This effect may be different on cash flow volatility for non-financial firms. Yong et al. (2009) believe that collectively, derivative activities will contribute to better risk management of banks by bringing stronger market discipline, particularly for banks with intensive derivative activities. Financial theory also implies how the use of derivatives affects the cost of the agency. Therefore, by integration, financial theory not only focusses on risk management issues, but also covers all aspects of the firms' operations.

3.3 Hedge accounting as a measure for efficiency in risk management from derivatives usage

This section builds on Section 2.3.1. In order to measure firms' exposure to risk and the impact of derivatives usage on firms, the measurement could assess the effect of the usage on accounting items. At its broadest level, the study can capture the risk exposure by examining how the derivatives used for hedging purposes affect the hedged item. At this point, there are numerous accounting rules governing how firms should report and record interest rate and exchange rate movements corresponding to the derivatives usage and its hedged items in dealing with each type of risk. From an accounting standpoint, with respect to risk of derivative transactions, either for trading or hedging purposes, changes of interest or currency rates are captured to explain the effect of these changes on the current balance sheet and income statement (Maines and McDaniel 2000; Hirst and Hopkins 1998).

Mulugetta and Hadjinikolov (2004) examined the issues surrounding the enactment of the Financial Accounting Statement 133, known as the Statement of Financial Accounting Standards (SFAS 133), in managing risks. In their study, ten major US banks were assessed from 1999 to 2002, and their performance was discussed after new rules were implemented in SFAS 133 in 2001. In general, the most likely impact of SFAS 133 would be positive and complementary to the accounting harmonisation efforts of the International Accounting Standard Board (IASB). In fact, they confidently state that the new rules have forced bank managers to learn more about derivatives and apply this knowledge in the design of new, more efficient assets and liability hedging strategies.

According to Panaretou et al. (2013), the goal of adopting the more comprehensive International Financial Reporting Standards (IFRS) regime in this area is to enhance their use for risk management purposes and transparency in the reporting of derivatives. Firms are now required to measure and disclose derivatives as prescribed by IAS 32 Financial Instruments: Disclosure and Presentation and IAS 39 Financial Instruments – Recognition and Measurement. For instance, in the Australian Accounting Standards Board (AASB) 139 Financial Instruments: Recognition and Measurement, all derivatives are required to be recognised on a balance sheet at fair value and hedge accounting is only available when specific conditions are met. Under the United States Generally Accepted Accounting Principles (US GAAP), the requirements of SFAS 133 Accounting for Derivative Instruments and Hedging Activities, as amended by the SFAS 149 Amendment of Statement 133 on Derivative Instruments and Hedging Activities, are similar to the requirements of AASB 139. However, for the US GAAP purposes, the group considers that without undue cost, it could not substantiate that AASB 139 requirements with respect to cash flow hedges and fair value hedges would satisfy SFAS 133 requirements with respect to such hedges. IAS 32 and IAS 39 imply that although derivative items can be useful tools for managing risks, they can also present risks to the banks.

However, in order for a "hedging relationship" to exist, a hedging instrument and hedged items are required. As stated in paragraph 9 of IAS 39, the hedged item can be

> a firm commitment, an asset, a liability, a net investment in a foreign operation that exposes the entity to the risk of changes in fair value or future cash flows, and has to be designated at the outset as being hedged.

A financial instrument is required to meet eight essential criteria before it can be classified as a hedging instrument. It must be expected to offset changes in the value of the hedged item and it must be with an external party, not the reporting party. These criteria for the classification of derivatives as hedging instruments have implications for risk management practices, as certain derivatives used for hedging will not qualify for hedging accounting (Panaretou et al. 2013).

In the banking sector, Türel and Türel (2014) and Ramirez (2007) pointed out that banks are much more active in applying macro-hedging (i.e. portfolio fair value hedging) in as much as most derivative activities are featured in the trading book at fair value, they still need to pass through the Profit and Loss (P&L) statement. The authors revealed that financial derivatives usually have a strong impact on the income statement of the hedging bank and are useful for banks that use derivatives to hedge against financial risks occurring from their borrowing and lending businesses. In addition, under the new concepts of accounting for financial instruments, which allow certain exceptional accounting treatments for risk management activities which are aimed at minimising the "accounting mismatches" and allow for their transparent presentation in financial statements (Fiechter 2011). Thus, the relationship between the hedging instrument and the hedged items requires investigation to determine how banks may take advantage of hedge accounting, particularly as the activities of universal and commercial banks are usually concentrated on granting loans and taking deposits.

3.3.1 Methods for testing effectiveness

There are several methods for conducting hedge effectiveness analysis. Accordingly, effectiveness will be measured using a number of specific methods, such as critical term analysis, dollar-offset (ratio analysis), correlation or regression analysis, scenario analysis, Volatility Risk Reduction (VRR) method and the short-cut method. According to IAS 39, the effectiveness test requires two isolated categories of testing to be applied: (1) a prospective test and (2) a retrospective test. A prospective test is highly effective during its life while a retrospective test (looking back) refers to the proof of whether the actual hedging relationship was highly effective in the period since the last test was performed. A retrospective test must be completed for each annual financial statement. Guided by this appropriation, the retrospective test is more accurate in assessing the effectiveness of the hedge. Evaluations based on current and past annual or interim financial statements are more realistic. However, both testing categories are significant in evaluating the effectiveness of the hedging relationship.

Nevertheless, no specific standard to determine the best method to test the effectiveness of hedging has been set by the Financial Accounting Standards Board (FASB). Under retrospective hedge effectiveness, Charnes et al. (2003) agree that the DOR (ratio analysis) standard is a widely used reference for hedge effectiveness testing. Charnes et al. (2003) defined this approach as the changes in the value of the hedging instrument divided by the changes in the value of the hedged item over the assessment period, where the changes in the value of derivative instruments effectively offsets the changes in value of

the hedged items. It can be formulated as $-\left(\sum_{i=1}^{n} X_i / \sum_{i=1}^{n} Y_i\right) = 1.0$, where $\sum_{i=1}^{n} X_i$

is the cumulative sum of the periodic changes in the derivative instrument value and $\sum_{i=1}^{n} Y_i$ refers to the cumulative sum of the periodic changes in the value of the hedged item. The degree of confidence for hedge effectiveness (highly effective) is considered to be within the range of 80–125%, where the formal test formulation can be expressed as $0.8 \leq - \left(\sum_{i=1}^{n} X_i / \sum_{i=1}^{n} Y_i \right) \leq 1.25$.

However, according to Althoff and Finnerty (2001), the problem with the DOR test is that it is very sensitive to small changes in the value of the hedged item or the derivative. Thus, sensitivity often caused difficulties in producing effective results, and it is often difficult to consistently achieve high effectiveness from one period to another. Thus, failing the hedge effectiveness test precludes the use of hedge accounting (Kawaller 2002). However, Kawaller (2002) admits that the DOR is the simplest approach to test for hedge effectiveness. This shows that sometimes the direct comparison between the hedging instrument and the hedged item can give false signals that fall outside the range of effectiveness results. The strength of this method is also explained by Wallace (2003), who considers it to be a highly effective method, in which the cumulative is recommended for analysis of the ratio, because a longer period should be more stable compared to a shorter period. Consequently, it may reduce the probability of falling outside the highly effective range, as stated by Choi (2003, 13):

> The application of a regression or other statistical analysis approach to assessing effectiveness is complex. Those methodologies require appropriate interpretation and understanding of statistical inferences. This approach allows regressing on price levels, rather than changes in prices, since one could have highly correlated prices but not highly correlated price changes.[1]

Another commonly used method of showing the relationship between the hedging instrument and hedged item is the regression analysis method, which analyses the behaviour of the hedging relationship based on historical market rates. In this case, the linear equation would be: $Y = \alpha + \beta^* X + \varepsilon$, where X is the change in fair value (or cash flow) of the hedging instrument attributable to the risk to be hedged, Y is the change in fair value (or cash flow) of the hedged item attributable to the risk to be hedged, α represents the intercept, β is the slope of the line and ε is the random error term. Through this equation, hedge effectiveness determines whether the changes in fair value of the hedging instrument and hedged items attributable to a particular risk (e.g. interest rate risk or foreign exchange risk) were highly correlated in the past, thus ascertaining whether the relationship will have a high degree of offset to the changes in fair value of both the hedging instrument and hedged item in the future. According to Kalotay and Abreo (2001, 95), "the changes in value should be roughly offsetting; that is, the slope of the regression line should be close to 1.0". By following the "least squares" method, the value of the X and Y variables determines whether the relationship estimation is the best "fitting" line or vice versa. Through the coefficient of determination (R-squared), it measures the degree of explanatory power between the Independent Variable (IV) and Dependent Variable (DV) in the regression analysis. A 95% R-squared value indicates that 95% of the changes in the DV are explained by changes in the IV (Ramirez 2007). An 80–95% R-squared value indicates a highly effective relationship between the hedging instrument and hedged item. A lower R-squared value indicates that the effectiveness test for hedging has failed. This is because the value of R-squared itself is not a reliable indicator of the effectiveness testing. Therefore, the F-statistic and t-statistic are needed to measure the regression result in order to determine whether or not the relationship between the hedging instrument and hedged item is statistically significant. This means that both the hedging instrument and the hedged item are interconnected in determining the level of hedging effectiveness. However, according to Kalotay and Abreo (2001, 95):

> The Financial Accounting Standards Board (FASB) has provided only broad guidelines to effectiveness testing. Accountants, as examiners of the results, not implementers of tests, are understandably reluctant to pronounce a priori what would be an acceptable test. Instead, clients are often directed to management consultants.

Even though the argument has not been satisfactorily resolved, the above-mentioned method is clearly able to demonstrate the connection and has provided a platform to show the relationship between the hedging instrument and the hedged item. Based on the above argument, this study believes that the level of efficiency of a firm can also be measured by the hedging instrument and the hedged item components.

Similar to the VRR method,[2] which compares the hedge package, it combines the position of the hedging instrument and the hedged item to the risk of the hedged item. Ramirez (2007, 25) documented that the VRR approach investigated "how small the combined position risk is, relative to the hedged item risk". More formally, the volatility reduction is defined as VRR = 1 − [SD (hedged item + hedging instrument) / SD (hedged item)] where SD is the Standard Deviation to be minimised in order to maximise the VRR. The SD will affect the value of the swap that, ultimately, will reflect the maximum volatility reduction (Regression Variability Reduction – RVR). Through the test statistic formulated as follows, VRR compares the SD of the combined position to the SD of the hedged item. Ramirez (2007) also claims that an effectiveness test result of 40% indicates high effectiveness. This percentage is equivalent to a correlation of 80%. However, this output is contradicted by inconsistencies with IAS 39's rule of effectiveness, where the effectiveness benchmark must be within the range of 80%–125%. A score of 80% has been generally accepted as more realistically achieved.

$$VRR \ or \ RVR = 1 - \frac{\sum_{i=1}^{n} -\hat{a} - \hat{b}X_i + Y_i}{\sum_{i=1}^{n} Y_i^2} \qquad (3.1)$$

From the analysis, it is possible to claim that a certain percentage of the bond face value is being hedged. In short, it also shows that the swap instruments provide a relationship in reducing the bond's volatility. On this basis, the usage of interest rate swaps by firms will hedge the issuing of bonds through the VRR approach.

The qualitative methods for assessing hedge effectiveness are critical terms and short-cut methods. For the Critical Terms Match (CTM) method, the hedging instrument must perfectly match all the critical terms of the hedged item. In this study, important business data (the critical terms) of the hedged item and the hedging instrument are matched. If the critical terms matched, the hedging relationship can be justified as highly effective. In the short-cut method, the effectiveness of the hedging instrument to the hedged item can be assessed when certain requirements are met. For instance, if the notional amount, interest period and underlying interest rates in the swap and the hedged item coincide, then the hedge effectiveness test is considered highly effective. However, for the time being, IAS 39 does not allow the use of this method under any circumstances due to several reasons (Ramirez 2007). Current interpretations of Financial Accounting Standards (FAS) 133 would not demonstrate compliance with the short-cut method, and CTM would not result in perfect effectiveness. In this case, Okochi (2007) argues that in either case, these approaches still have to perform the effectiveness test, which will not necessarily be always perfectly effective.

3.3.1.1 Decision to choose DOR

Based on the above discussion and analysis, Hailer and Rump (2005) and Finnerty and Grant (2003) believe that measuring hedge effectiveness using the DOR method is a more straightforward assessment and exempt in terms of risk reduction. They suggest that firms using this method should be aware of the usage of the test statistic since it is sensitive to the observations of small changes in value. This foundation proves that the dollar-offset method is significantly capable of measuring the effectiveness of the hedging instrument and hedged item. Furthermore, the quantitative measurement of this approach is fundamentally based on the ratio analysis concept for the measurement of risk management efficiency. Hence, following the preference test by Ramirez (2007), Hailer and Rump (2005) and Finnerty and Grant (2003), the DOR is chosen as a basis to test the risk management efficiency of firms to highlight the relationship between the hedging instrument and hedged item which can explain the function of derivatives as one of the useful risk management strategies.

3.3.2 Hedge effectiveness analysis based on hedge accounting – variables determination based on the analysis of the relationship between hedging instrument and the hedged item

A hedge is a structured strategy to minimise the risk or uncertain market exposure of another transaction. When firms decide to use derivative instruments, such instruments are classified as a hedging instrument. These groups of financial instruments will change the value of the hedged item, which is associated with the risk being hedged against (Butler 2009; Charnes et al. 2003). On the basis of hedge effectiveness, qualifying for hedge accounting does not imply that the hedging strategy will have no volatility impact on earnings. The effectiveness of hedging depends on the correlation of the hedging instruments and hedged items. If highly effective, the change in the fair value of the hedging instruments is allocated.

In applying hedge accounting, IAS 39 chooses hedging strategies by testing the effectiveness of the hedging instrument and the hedged item. This measurement was originally introduced by Ederington (1979), to measure the risk reduction effect of a futures market. Even though the risk reduction measurement is difficult, it will test the effectiveness of the hedging item, which shows how risks are offset by changes in the fair value or cash flows of the hedging instruments (Loftus et al. 2013; Ramirez 2007). In hedge accounting, Trombley (2003, 35) noted that

> a company must expect that the hedge will be highly effective in offsetting changes in the value of the hedged item or changes in cash flows related to the hedge item and after the hedge is in place, it must be highly effective to continue the use of hedge accounting.

Hence, when a firm is restructured on the ability of derivative instruments, the hedged item exists.

Furthermore, the linkages have been strengthened by the interpretation of both these terms. Landsman (2006) states that the hedged items for the company can be fixed rate loans, inventories or firm commitments. The detailed explanation by Ramirez (2007) classified the hedged items as a recognised asset or a liability, or recognised firm commitment, which refers to a legal agreement for the exchange of a specified quantity of resources at a specified price and on a specified date or future date. An anticipated transaction based on the frequency of similar past transactions can also be included as a hedged item. On a consolidated basis, a net investment in a foreign operation is also a part of the hedged item. These items will accommodate the implications of the use of financial instruments (swap, futures, forward). However, in mitigating only the interest rate risk (macro-hedge), hedge items can be classified as a portion of financial assets or financial liabilities that share the risk of being hedged. Indeed, in a banking transaction, if hedging instruments are interest rate swaps, the hedged items would be bonds or loans (on either side of the balance sheet), which are normally on the asset side (Ramirez, personal communication, December 7, 2012). In other words, it will show the changes in value recorded in an accounting report, either above or below the locked value based on the derivatives rules. This phenomenon is suitable for the method of testing any entity or firm's efficiency level, whereas hedging instruments serve as inputs to control over the hedged items (outputs). If the majority of the efficiency studies used the total labour or number of employees as inputs, which will affect the total assets or net income of the firm, then the hedging instrument also affects the hedged item, hence influencing the risk management efficiency level, and reflects the nature of banks as intermediaries.

In a wider discussion, as the hedging instrument refers to the derivative instrument, losses or gains from re-measuring derivatives at fair value are recognised in P&L. In practice, hedging instruments affect the change in fair value where its usage will offset (wholly or in part) the change in cash flows or fair value of the hedged items. Therefore, the correlation has to be a negative relationship, in which the changes will be offset by an opposite change in the value of the cash flow of the hedging item. However, due to transaction costs, such hedges are hard to observe (Chernenko and Faulkender 2012; Shunko et al. 2010). The transaction costs may involve a default risk during the transaction period, and lead to a loss in the mark-to-market value.

According to Trombley (2003), the purpose of fair value hedge accounting is to hedge risk exposure pertaining to the changes in the fair value of a recognised asset or liability, or an unrecognised firm commitment. On the other hand, Ramirez (2007, 7) clearly mentioned that "only the fair value hedge provides a perfect synchronisation between the hedging instrument and hedge item recognitions". In addition, as stated in IAS 39, the offsetting of risk may reduce the volatility of the P&L. Both changes in the fair value of the hedging instrument and hedged items are presented in the income statement. The changes enable a reduction of the P&L variability, which is able to offset the risk exposure. Kocon (2007) reported that the changes in items and instruments will offset and result in a null net impact on the P&L statement.

Ramirez (2007) highlighted that the most common practice in hedge accounting is to have the effective portion of the hedge to show up in the P&L statement after being recorded in equity. The excluded portion of the hedge is usually recorded in the "other income and expenses" line of the P&L statement.

Due to the use of a fair value hedge in eliminating and reducing the exposure that arises from changes in the fair value of a financial asset or liability for a particular risk, such as interest rate risk, the measurement of the derivative instrument will also be reflected in the performance of a firm's income statement. According to Bessis (2011), the main implication of fair value accounting is that earnings (income) would come from the fluctuation of value, generating volatile P&L. Therefore, the rule applies where derivative instruments are serving as hedges to bank exposure, as most of a bank's derivative activities are featured in the trading book, and as is common with other activities, fair value has to be applied through the P&L statement. Bessis (2011) also states that hedging activity in the banking book is typically devoted to asset-liability management by applying macro-hedging to interest rate bearing assets and micro-hedging of the interest rate risk of issued debt. Also, although there is hedging of the credit risk of assets with credit default swaps, the application of hedge accounting in the banking institution is limited (Ramirez, personal communication, July 29, 2013).

3.3.3 Swaps

Although it is often assumed that fair value is not consistent with the purpose of hedging because no evaluation combines exposure and hedging, a swap is able to manage interest rate risk and limit a company's exposure to interest rate fluctuations, thus reducing the risk. Through swap usage, a firm is able to mitigate its interest rate exposure.

Jagtiani (1996) also provides evidence that bank loans and interest rate swaps are significant. The findings indicate that banks with higher nonperforming loans are more active in swaps as a strategy for reducing risky loans. Essentially, this strategy should help in reducing the risk of loan default. In the banking sector, interest rate swap receipts and payments are recognised within the net interest income, using the effective interest method as interest for the designated hedged item or class of items being hedged over the term of which the swap is effective as a hedge. Similarly, with cross-country swaps, the receipts and payments are also recognised on the same basis as interest rate swaps.

In this case, it is clearly shown that the use of derivative instruments will change in fair value with respect to the risk being hedged. The usage will protect the hedged items against the changes in fair value of financial assets and financial liabilities due to movements in the market interest rates. Among the main purposes of using the interest rate swaps and cross-currency swaps is to hedge against the interest rate risk of subordinate obligations, loans, negotiable instruments of deposits issued and foreign bonds. Therefore, when these instruments are used by banks, their role is to mitigate the risk and provide low volatility in a bank's performance. There are some arguments in relation to a fair value hedge in which the derivative does not cause volatility in the P&L account. This issue is explained by Butler (2009, 69), who emphasised that "under the fair value hedge accounting rules, the company is permitted to change the value of the underlying asset, so as to eliminate the artificial profit". On this basis, the profit is indirectly influenced by the use of derivative instruments. The items that are being hedged will be affected according to the instruments being used. From the basic investigation of this discussion, two components of the hedging instrument and hedged item are used to test the effectiveness of the use of derivatives to protect firms from dealing with market risk. However, their influence in testing the efficiency of a firm is non-existent and there has been limited application in the context of accounting reporting standards.

Under the cash flow hedge accounting rules, a firm may manage its floating interest rate risk by using an interest rate swap to transform a floating-interest rate exposure to a fixed interest rate exposure (McConnell 2014; Kawaller 2007). Cross-currency interest rate swaps may also be used to manage the currency exchange rate risk and floating interest rate. The new rules in IAS 9 require all firms that are involved in derivatives to disclose the two risk mitigating strategies separately, namely interest rate and exchange rate risks.

If the interest rate swap or cross-currency swap qualifies for cash flow hedge accounting, the accounting treatment requires a comparison of the derivative's performance with that of an ideal treatment. In this case, it refers to a hedge that perfectly offsets the effects of the risk (interest rate or exchange rate) that is being hedged. As the objectives of some banks are to swap from floating to fixed (e.g. banks in Thailand), the use of swaps

> reflects the best estimates of the expected future cash flows of the variable cash flows that were designated the hedged item. As such, unless and until any aspects of the hedged item change, this swap will be perfectly effective at offsetting cash flows.
>
> (Kawaller 2007, 16)

Based on the role played by derivatives to impact on the performance of a firm, this phenomenon should be viewed in a more collective and inclusive context so as to form the basis of a firm's risk management. The level of firm efficiency, especially in managing risk, will receive a boost from the use of derivative instruments and hedged items. It also has a direct impact on the cost of taxes and reduces the expected cost of financial distress. Smith and Stulz (1985) and Sinkey and Carter (2001) were convinced that the use of derivatives to hedge the impact of bank efficiency led to a reduction in tax. Moreover, investors can evaluate the capability and strategies of a firm to address the risks and achieve a competitive strategy. Returning to the question posed at the beginning of this study, it is now possible to state that relevant connectivity exists through the use of hedging instruments, and that hedged items correspond to the efficiency evaluation methods through the bank's role in regulating financial activities using an intermediation approach.

3.4 Hedge effectiveness measurements and risk management context

Recent studies have shown that hedge accounting that arises from the use of derivatives does not represent its actual role within a firm's risk management concepts and strategies (Bernhardt et al. 2014; McCarroll and Khatri 2014). This weakness has obstructed the operational efficiency level of firms' risk management processes for some treasurers. This issue has been raised for years, and in November 2013, the IASB (IFRS 9) added a new model in the hedge accounting chapter to enhance and closely align accounting for hedging activities with a greater focus on reflecting a firm's risk management strategies and policies. Hailer and Rump (2005) observed that there are difficulties in choosing an appropriate effectiveness test when the accounting standard specifies an ambiguous approach to selecting the method for assessing hedge effectiveness and links with firms' risk management strategies. Thus, the decision to choose an appropriate approach may be different from one firm to another, which consequently provides a different justification for the use of the hedging instrument as a risk management tool. Therefore, it is not possible to find a simple rule to determine the impact on an organisation's performance of risk management. This argument is in complete agreement with Bernhardt et al. (2014) when they critiqued that hedge effectiveness assessment in hedge accounting is not aligned with a firm's risk management strategies, hence making hedge accounting rules more complicated.

Apart from the lack of quality for an effectiveness measurement, the hedge effectiveness measurements are too complex to collectively discuss the potential impact of derivative instruments use in enhancing the safety and soundness of financial institutions. Therefore, the extension of the traditional ratio analysis which is applied in the DOR in hedge effectiveness test permits the incorporation of the simple ratio dimension of performance, using a DEA approach. It thus supports the implementation of the new hedge accounting model, as McConnell (2014) believes that it will better align and reduce inconsistencies between financial accounting and the economics of the related risk management strategy.

3.5 Framework for hedge effectiveness in hedge accounting

In the banking environment, derivatives are preferred as a hedging tool to mitigate exposure to risk, including interest rate risk. Finance theory explains that derivative activities are used for hedging strategies. To hedge specific types of risks, the management has to designate a hedging relationship that satisfies the accounting definition of derivatives. Due to this requirement, the hedging relationship measurement depends on hedge effectiveness to highlight the offsetting value of the hedged items. The DOR has been chosen as an approach to an effectiveness test comprising the hedging instrument and hedged items. The effectiveness of a hedging strategy reflects the management's intent to use the derivative instrument as a financial risk management tool to actually hedge risk exposure. Hence, the involvement of a bank in financial derivatives provides evidence for measuring whether risk management is successful or vice versa (Figure 3.1).

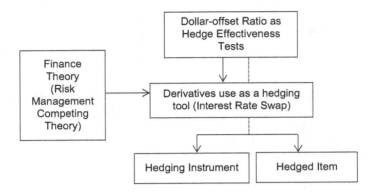

Figure 3.1 Hedge Effectiveness Framework Involving the DOR.

3.6 Empirical illustration of hedge effectiveness test using dollar-offset ratio

The DOR approach is one of the quantitative hedge effectiveness tests that assesses and measures hedge effectiveness for derivative instruments used (hedging instruments) and its impact on items that exposes an entity to the risk of changes in future cash flows or in the fair value, which is designated as being hedged (hedged items) (Clemente 2015; Saxena and Villar 2008). However, other than defining only what is to be done to achieve an accounting outcome, the exposure draft (ED) on hedging tests and measurements in hedge accounting does not precisely define the risk management objective (Ernst & Young's International Financial Reporting Standards Group 2011). According to the report, the sole objective of hedge accounting is to avoid profit or loss volatility. The economic strategy that led to hedging for risk management purposes has not been addressed. Therefore, this study argues that DOR has a similar fundamental approach to mutually integrate the concept of risk management of institutions for risk management purposes. Thus, with a measurement standard of 80%/125% of the cumulative changes in the cash flows or fair value of the hedged item (Swad 1995), the formula for the DOR of a hedge effectiveness test (see Section 3.3) becomes the guideline for assessing the hedge effectiveness of derivative contracts under SFAS 80. This measurement requires the derivative's change in value of the offset to be at least 80% and not more than 125% of the value change of the hedged item.

In the banking sector, this study has found that an interest rate swap is the most useful instrument (Gyntelberg and Upper 2013; Sundaram 2013; Minton et al. 2009), as this tool is able to mitigate and limit the interest rate risk (Section 3.3.2). Items hedged by this instrument include mortgage, corporate and commercial loans, and customer deposits (Ramirez 2007). These items have been determined when banks are engaged in an interest rate swap for various reasons. For instance, banks may have gaps in their balance sheets due to long-term loans such as mortgage loans, loans for company investment and other liabilities consisting of short-term cash deposits including household deposits. These gaps are created when banks are exposed to changes in variable interest rates where loans are at a fixed interest rate (interest received on loans) and variable rates paid on customer deposits. These banks may run into losses when the variable rate paid is higher than the interest received at a fixed rate. Bicksler and Chen (1986) and Kim et al. (1993) noted that to solve the gap issue and reduce variable interest exposure, banks and other financial institutions tend to engage in interest rate swaps that yield floating-rate liabilities and assets for customers, and fixed-rate liabilities and assets for the banks.

To explain this with an example, Table 3.1 provides empirical evidence of interest rate swaps as a hedging instrument, and mortgages, corporate and commercial loans (hedge item 1) and customer deposits (hedge item 2) as hedged items using the dollar-offset method in commercial banks for the year 2007. Out of the 21 banks, only eight commercial banks, comprising four Australian banks (CB1–CB4) and four Malaysian banks (CB14–CB17), respectively, representing the developed and developing countries are chosen for an empirical illustration. These eight commercial banks in the two countries are chosen based on their dramatic derivatives growth when compared to other banks in the developed and developing financial markets.

Table 3.1 shows the measures of the risk management efficiency of the banks which highlights the impact of the accounting (asset-liability) management treatments on each bank's asset-liability management. Based on

Table 3.1 Empirical Illustration of the Hedge Effectiveness Method – DOR for 2007

Banks	Change in Hedging Instrument	Change in the Hedged Item 1	Change in the Hedged Item 2	DOR	Effective (Yes/No)
Australian Banks					
CB1	1,222.55	38,017.8	50,391.2	0.013828343	No
CB2	7,276.31	35,535.5	46,638.5	0.088547594	No
CB3	2,291.72	35,477.2	34,958.8	0.032536203	No
CB4	7,682.73	3,756.7	2,859.9	1.161129583	Yes
Malaysian Banks					
CB14	39,026.56	−19,262.6	9901.3	4.168925256	No
CB15	96,584.97	1,390.6	6,736.2	11.88474799	No
CB16	−9,634.15	1,411.1	4,211.7	1.713407911	No
CB17	105,273.62	952.5	1,929.6	36.52670622	No

the dollar-offset range of effectiveness, the outcome does not show a huge impact on hedge effectiveness (highly effective) since it is out of the range (80%–125%), except for CB4 (116%). This scenario indicates that the hedge is deemed ineffective even though the net change is insignificant compared to the change of the item size. Based on these empirical results, Wilary (2014) argues that not all hedges will be perfect. Based on this premise, FAS Accounting Standards Codification 815 does not specify the precise percentage range that would be considered highly effective under the DOR method. Ramirez (2007) further argues that achieving the range limit when considering hedge effectiveness is in fact unrealistic. Notwithstanding this argument, in practice, he believes that a DOR range of 80%–125% would be considered as highly effective.

Ramirez (2007, 21) provides a solution to eliminate this weakness through "the use of cumulative change, since the hedge inception in fair value for both the hedged item and the hedging instrument". However, due to a direct relationship between the hedging instrument and hedged item, the remedial solution suggested by the author failed to be counted and the direct impact is unresolved. Moreover, in the context of risk management, Ramirez (2007) is unable to emphasise its function as an alternative method or product to manage the interest rate risk. The weakness has been argued by Mann and Sephton (2010), Bodnar and Gebhardt (1999) and Asay et al. (1981), who highlight the conflict among practitioners and users over the issues of choosing a method for testing hedge effectiveness and its range, as well as its relationship with an entity's risk management objectives (Ernst & Young's International Financial Reporting Standards Group 2011). They argue that hedge effectiveness tests including the DOR is neither a sufficient nor necessary condition to highlight the role of derivatives for hedging and risk management purposes. They further concentrate on the ability of the accounting standards that may discourage the use of derivatives by financial institutions to show a true picture of a firm's performance. As a result, these regulatory accounting procedures have stimulated an important discussion regarding their effect on firms' risk management. In addition, as stated in the ED of the ISDA, the hedging relationships should be driven by firms' risk management activities. Measurements without the corresponding risk management can create greater complexity in hedge accounting.

Therefore, to address its role as a risk measurement tool in commercial banks, its measurement must go beyond the measurement of risk management effectiveness, particularly in showing its performance on a yearly basis. The derivative instrument's impact on the level of risk management efficiency indicates its role in delivering a better risk management function. Due to these reasons, it is necessary to consider another measurement with advanced mathematical applications to measure the impact of a derivative instrument on risk management effectiveness.

3.7 Policy and theoretical implications

This study posits that the DOR is a significant tool for measuring the efficiency of risk management in banks, and that this method can be formulated using a non-parametric approach as a powerful and robust technique to measure the efficiency level of institutions (Asmild et al. 2007; Casu and Molyneux 2003; Grosskopf 1996). These integrated approaches can intervene in both accounting and efficiency of risk management in banks. The application of the ratio analysis can clearly measure the direct impact of the derivative instrument usage for risk management efficiency analysis.

In addition, it will strengthen financial and risk management theory with a focus on value creation and risk management effectiveness to increase firm value and shareholder wealth. This assessment is important for the management and other stakeholders who have an interest in the financial performance of banks, particularly investors who are concerned that they may experience significant losses if the bank does not perform well. The failures of inefficiently managed banks certainly pose grave risks for the financial sector at large as well as exert negative external influences on efficient banks. This study also contributes to the practice of risk management professionals to closely consider the evaluation of the hedging instruments and the implications for the hedged items, thus helping them to adequately monitor and control their portfolio, loan and interest rate.

In practice, this study enhances the role of management accountants in managing risk. This is consistent with the findings by Soin (2005), who found that management accountants with skills in analysis of information, systems, performance and strategic management can play a significant role in developing and implementing risk management strategies. Therefore, this analysis provides not only the results of hedge effectiveness in using derivative instruments, but also provides a basis for investigation by accounting managers to precisely monitor risk movement and its impact on the performance of banks in risk management efficiency. In agreement with Abdel-Khalik (2013), the integration between risk management and reporting is considered vital in order to shift and establish an internal regulatory system and the assessment and control of risk. A proper approach in managing interest rate, for instance, can reduce the impact from interest rate sensitivity that can be reflected and influenced by the composition of customer deposits such as sudden withdrawals of large amounts.

In addition, the technique developed for measuring hedge effectiveness helps in decision-making, and in communicating and embedding risk management across the whole banking organisation. Through the existing empirical test, investigation and findings, and not by survey as most research has done, this analysis should be able to provide management accounts the channels within an organisation for linking strategy, risk management and performance measurement by identifying relevant information and issues for management attention. Consequently, the study draws attention to

Harker and Zenios' (2000) argument that very limited research has focussed on strengthening the relationship between risk management and banking performances. Therefore, this study generates the possibilities for the use of hedge accounting techniques to specifically focus on risk management efficiency in the context of banking.

Finally, since hedging activities have been carried out in the scope of a suitable and appropriate risk management policies approved by the Board of Directors (BOD), relevant procedures, systems and controls, and management information and reporting should be in place. Therefore, this investigation can be aligned with the concept of risk profile for the BOD. The reassessing of hedge effectiveness provides a necessary guide to the BOD in tolerating risk.

3.8 Plausibility of the approach

Interpretative arguments were investigated by defining and examining the relationship between the hedging instrument and the hedged items in order to propose a new measurement for analysing the risk management efficiency for banks. After the concept of derivatives in finance theory and their needs for hedging purposes were discussed, this study explored the different approaches that have been used in measuring hedge effectiveness. At this point, the study found that the DOR is regularly used by the banking industry due to its strength in measuring hedge effectiveness. The advantages of the DOR measurement approach as discussed in the literature give a strong justification for further exploration and enhancement of its effectiveness as a measurement using a non-parametric approach. The goal is to improve the hedge effectiveness measurement method, which is most relevant for formulating a risk management strategy in the banking sector based on derivative instruments.

3.9 Conclusion

The ratio analysis of the hedge effectiveness test implements a basic concept of ratio concerning the derivatives and items being hedged. With the function played by derivative instrument to minimise risk, it has been included in the risk management of firms when its usage reflects on the accounting treatment known as hedge accounting. However, the methodology has been unable to measure and represent risk management efficiency based on derivative usage. Therefore, the integration of another approach is needed for measuring risk management efficiency, as will be expounded in the next chapter.

Notes

1 Further analysis of regression analysis has been discussed by Wallace (2003), Choi (2003) and Castelino (2000).
2 The VRR method for hedge effectiveness testing was invented by the Andrew Kalotay Incorporation and has been implemented at a leading telecommunications company. This method has also been accepted by a Big-5 accounting firm. Telekom Italia Company is among the few entities adopting this approach.

4 An alternative methodology for risk management efficiency measurement and analysis using DEA approach with ratio analysis based on hedge accounting

4.1 Introduction

The literature shows that the current hedge effectiveness practice is inadequate in addressing the issue of risk management efficiency measures since the simple ratio concept applied in the dollar-offset ratio (DOR) ignores the context of risk management. This study argues that currently, not only is such an approach scarce, but that it is vital to incorporate it with other approaches for further innovation in measuring risk management efficiency. Therefore, this chapter presents the details of the methodology proposed in this study for incorporating a hedge effectiveness test (DOR) with data envelopment analysis (DEA) to measure risk management efficiency based on derivatives usage.

Theoretical observations and empirical experiments reported in the literature suggest that the DEA approach is capable of simultaneously capturing interactions between multiple parameters (input and output) to represent semantic relationships between the concept of hedge effectiveness and risk management efficiency measurement. The integration of derivative instruments and hedge accounting based on hedge effectiveness contemplation is essential to boost the efficiency of a bank's risk management. DEA can easily allocate efficiency measurements into several components including technical, pure technical and scale efficiencies that are robust enough to satisfactorily exploit the parameters of efficiency analysis for measuring risk management efficiency.

The remainder of this chapter is structured as follows: Section 4.2 presents a review of the methods that can be used for efficiency frontier modelling. Section 4.3 presents a thorough literature review of existing studies on efficiency in the banking sector using these models, and specifically highlighting the gap in literature on risk efficiency measurement, and focussing on financial derivatives. Section 4.4 presents the justifications for the alternative methodology proposed in this study by first presenting a criticism of the DOR analysis and then rationalising the need for adapting the DEA to the DOR before outlining the conceptual framework of DEA/DOR hedge effectiveness test. Section 4.5 presents the mathematical model, descriptive statistics of variables, data sample and statistical tests used in the empirical examination, and Section 4.6 presents the results of the empirical study on the examination of 21 banks. Section 4.7 discusses the verifications and validations of the model, while Section 4.8 elaborates on the implications of the results for using derivatives as a hedging instrument in risk management in the banking sector. Finally, Section 4.9 concludes the chapter.

4.2 Efficiency frontier models/measurement approach (parametric vs. non-parametric approaches)

Inefficient organisations are fraught with failures in their procedures, policies, strategic framework and decision-making. When banks are not efficient, this imperils not only the effectiveness and profitability of their risk management strategy but also their survival in a highly competitive market. Performance efficiency measurements are extremely important for improving or eliminating inefficient operations, as well as for avoiding misleading evaluations of the intrinsic productivity of labour (Luptacik 2010). Farrell (1957, 11) describes the significance of the efficient frontier estimation for modern economic development, thus "the problem of measuring the productivity efficiency of an industry is important to both the economic theorist and the economic policy maker."

There are several techniques used to measure efficiency in financial institutions. The most frequent approaches used by researchers are parametric and non-parametric approaches. Parametric approaches specify the functional form and take into account residual terms in the analysis, while non-parametric approaches do not require prior structural constraints on the specification of the best practice frontier and assume no random error. The main difference between the parametric approach and non-parametric approach is the distribution of the data. Parametric approaches are concerned with the normality of the data distribution before the data can be used to determine efficiency, while non-parametric approaches do not depend on the normality of the data. Parametric approaches consist of three types: Stochastic Frontier Approach (SFA), Distribution Free Approach (DFA) and Thick Frontier Approach (TFA). On the other hand, non-parametric approaches include DEA and Free Disposal Hull (FDH).

4.2.1 Parametric approach for efficiency measurement

i   Stochastic Frontier Approach

The SFA or economic frontier approach was derived from the concept of cost frontier analysis and was first proposed by Aigner et al. (1977). SFA specifies the functional form for the production, cost, profit and revenue that arise from the relationship between inputs, outputs and environmental factors (Berger and Humphrey 1997). SFA allows random errors and gives a composed error model in which inefficiencies are assumed to follow an asymmetric distribution, usually the half-normal, while random errors are assumed to follow a symmetric distribution, usually the standard normal. The inefficiency must have a truncated distribution because inefficiency cannot be negative. This method makes it difficult to separate inefficiency from random error in a composed error framework.

i   Distribution Free Approach

The DFA was introduced by Berger et al. (1993). DFA specifies a functional form for the frontier but separates the inefficiency from the random error in a different way. The DFA assumes that the efficiency of each firm is stable over time, whereas the random error tends to average out to zero over time.

ii   Thick Frontier Approach

The TFA was introduced by Berger and Humphrey (1991). TFA provides the efficiency measure for overall firms and not for individual firms. TFA specifies a functional form as SFA. TFA assumes that the deviation from the predicted performance values within the highest and the lowest performance quartiles of observations represent the random error while deviations in predicted performance between the highest and the lowest quartiles represent inefficiencies (Jondrow et al. 1982). This approach does not specify any assumptions on the distribution of the inefficiencies and random errors.

4.2.2 Non-parametric approach for efficiency measurement

i   Data Envelopment Analysis

The DEA was developed by Charnes et al. (1978). DEA involves the use of linear programming (LP) technique and assumes no random errors. The frontier is identified by the best performance of the data sets that is evaluated (Inman 2004). Each data set is composed of a number of decision-making units (DMUs) that have multiple inputs and multiple outputs. The LP formulation yields a ranking of the different DMUs in the systems in a scale of relative efficiency from the lowest (0%) to the highest (100%).

ii   Free Disposal Hull

The FDH was introduced by Deprins et al. (1984). FDH is a special case of DEA model where the points on lines connecting the DEA vertices are not included in the frontier. FDA gives larger estimates of average efficiency than DEA because the FDH is interior to the DEA frontier.

4.3 Literature review

4.3.1 Studies on measuring the efficiency of banks

The analyses of efficiency in research on banking institutions have given rise to a number of studies centred on cost and/or profit efficiency measurement. Using a single country context (Australian banks), Sathye (2001) calculated X-efficiency (technical efficiency (TE) and allocative efficiency) as well as cost efficiency and found that the efficiency of Australian banks is below the world average efficiency mark, meaning that Australian banks need to reduce their operating expenses by encouraging customers to fully utilise banking technology facilities that have been developed (i.e. internet banking). In another study based in Australia, Avkiran (2004) investigated the efficiency of ten commercial banks and found that the big four Australian banks are technically efficient, while the other six banks are inefficient.

In Turkey, Isik and Hassan (2002), employing the DEA approach, found that the overall cost efficiency of Turkish banks over the period from 1988 to 1996 is 72% (0.72), while 28% of bank resources are wasted during the production of banking services. They also indicate that an increase in the cost of funding and growth in banking business caused lower production efficiencies and found that the main source of cost inefficiency was technical inefficiency rather than allocative inefficiency resulting from poor regulation and management. By utilising DEA window analysis, Webb (2003) studied the relative efficiency levels of seven large retail banks in the UK and found that the mean inefficiency levels are low and the average efficiency trend is deteriorating. In India, Kumar and Gulati (2008) investigated the efficiency of 27 public sector banks in the year 2004/2005, applying DEA to estimate technical, pure and scale efficiency (SE) in the first stage. The empirical results revealed that the average PBSs in the sample operate at 88.5% of overall technical efficiency (OTE) where their inputs could be reduced by 11.5%. Sufian and Majid (2007) evaluated five characteristics of banks, namely size, profitability, capitalisation, provisions to loans and overheads in the Singapore banking sector through two DEA models to analyse efficiency in the pre- and post-merger periods. Overall, the TE levels are higher than Model 1 during the merger period and improved significantly during the post-merger period.

Apart from these single-country studies, many efficiency studies have focussed on comparative analysis of foreign and local banks. Studying the efficiency of commercial banks in Greece, Pasiouras (2008) found that the differences between the efficiency scores are generally small. However, banks that had expanded to the international level experienced improved efficiency levels as compared to those that are locally operated. Most other studies on this topic have also used DEA as a method of analysis. Jemriæ and Vujèiæ (2002) used the DEA to analyse the efficiency of banks in the Croatian banking sector in the period from 1995 to 2000 and found that foreign-owned banks, on average, are more efficient than local banks. The number of employees and fixed assets are also found to be the two major factors that contributed to the inefficiency of local and old banks in Croatia. In a different study, Havrylchyk (2006) employed the DEA method to investigate the cost, allocative, technical, pure technical and SE of the Polish banking industry (foreign and domestic) between 1997 and 2001. Differing from a previous study in Poland by Grigorian and Manole (2002), this study found that across the European Union (European Commission 1997) lower efficiency (90%) was the average. Overall, they found that foreign banks exhibit a higher efficiency level than local banks. In the African continent, Saka et al. (2012) analysed the impact of entry of foreign banks and changes in bank concentration in Ghana through a TE analysis derived from the DEA approach. Surprisingly in this context, the foreign bank efficiency average was 71% (0.71), while the domestic bank efficiency average score was higher at 78% (0.78). They argue that foreign banks have a positive impact on the TE levels of domestic banks and the lower TE of foreign banks signals that local banks have a great potential for competitively beating foreign banks.

Other efficiency measurement studies with DEA have focussed on productivity growth. Drake (2001) used a panel data sample covering nine main UK banks from 1984 to1995 to investigate relative efficiencies within the banking sector and to calculate productivity changes in banks in the UK. The two modified forms of the intermediation and production approaches proposed in two different models showed that in banks in the UK, SE levels are lower than E-efficiencies (pure technical efficiency (PTE) and TE), particularly for the very big and very small-sized banks. Recently, Fethi and Pasiouras (2010) employed a DEA-like Malmquist Index to attain productivity growth. In short, the Malmquist Index measures changes in efficiency relative to a base year to see firms' movement in efficiency. Malmquist productivity analysis suggests that on average, UK banks have indicated productivity increases during the period due to the influence of the elimination of excess capacity in facing competition in the UK financial services industry. Sathye (2002) investigated 17 Australian banks during the period from 1995 to 1999 to calculate productivity change and recommended that fee structures have to be rationalised and operating expenses cut down to avoid unnecessary expenditures.

4.3.2 Research gaps in risk management efficiency measurement of derivatives as hedging instruments

The study of risk management and efficiency using non-parametric approaches has received little attention in banking literature. Only a small number of scholars have considered risk elements in their studies. For example, Pastor (1999), in evaluating the Spanish banking system from 1985 to 1992 shows that the risk management standards and internal management action are improved when the proportion of loans is either increased or decreased under the influence of internal or external factors. Despite this fact, the author fails to discuss the risk management context from the actual bank's risk perspective. External risk elements such as interest rate risk and foreign exchange risk are not considered as the major elements of risk, and the strategy of managing these types of risks is neglected.

Using stochastic frontier analysis (SFA), Kasman and Carvallo (2013) examined 15 Latin American and Caribbean commercial banks to find that on average, the bank in the region could improve its revenue and cost efficiencies by 15% and 25%, respectively. The study included a risk indicator represented by the difference between the average amount that the bank receives from loans and the average rate the bank pays on deposit or borrowings (interest rate spreads). Kasman and Carvallo show that there is a relationship between efficiency scores, revenue and risk, but they do not evaluate risk management indicators except for correlating their environmental effect with their efficiency score.

Studying efficiency in investment banks in G7 countries (Canada, Germany, France, Japan, Italy, the USA and the UK), Radic et al. (2011) examined capital risk, liquidity risk, security risk and insolvency risk to analyse the cost and profit efficiency using the non-parametric SFA method. They found that investment banks with higher liquidity risk (the study used ratio of liquid to total assets (LIQ) as a proxy) are penalised in the case of cost efficiency, but have an advantage in making profits and higher capital levels, leading to greater cost efficiency but reduced profit efficiency. The mixture of the variables used in the study, however, was unable to specify the concrete implications where there is no absolute agreement in entertaining specific risk indicators.

Alam (2012) investigates the impact of loan-loss reserves (LLR) as a bank risk on cost efficiency in 11 emerging countries from 2000 to 2010, using inputs of traditional balance sheet items including labour, physical capital and deposits, while output variables identified are loans and other earning assets. But the determination of inputs and outputs for the efficiency analysis do not directly represent risk management indicators, where the parameters received less risk management focus. Another limitation of the study is that it does not consider the type of risk (market risk) faced by the unit of analysis. In short, the variables do not represent the risk concept in the banking sector and how the selection of the variables reflects certain risk. The study combined overall (systematic and unsystematic) risks which leads to general conclusions and lacks specific resolutions on risk treatment.

Using the DEA approach, Laeven (1999) investigates banks in five East Asian countries (Indonesia, Korea, Malaysia, the Philippines and Thailand) from 1992 until 1996. By considering excessive loan growth as a proxy for bank risk-taking, the study found that it is significantly correlated with an increase in the efficiency level of the banks. Although the study has taken into account the risk profile in the bank efficiency analysis, the measurement still suffers from non-accounting considerations where it only postulates excessive loan growth with less treatment of business mix and correlation with interest rate risk. Sun and Chang (2011) also investigate the cost efficiency for eight Asian country banks. They considered three different risk aspects, namely credit risk, market risk and operational risk. Using a total of eight risk measures, such as interest rate volatility, exchange rate volatility, changes in interest rate, return on asset (ROA), etc., the study concludes that each risk measure has a different effect on banks' cost efficiency levels.

However, the risk management section neglects the major role of risk management tools in managing and reducing these types of risks. The above risk measures also do not consider measuring the actual efficiency scores, yet these measurements are important to assess the operations of the banks that will influence their risk management performance.

In addition to this lack of focus on risk management efficiency measurement studies, there is also a lack of research on the use of interest-based products, such as derivatives, as a tool for risk management. Employing the DEA method and the two-stage approach using Tobit regression, Chang and Chiu (2006) investigate the efficiency index and, credit and market risk effect in 26 Taiwanese banks using Non-Performing Loans (NPLs) to represent the credit risk and Value at Risk (VaR) as a proxy of the market risk. The relative VaRs of different banks using the historical approach has been used. Even if this study incorporates some aspect of risk, they do not incorporate the use of derivatives as a means for mitigating the risks faced by banks. This study admitted that due to problematic regulations and disclosures for financial derivatives in Taiwan, derivative elements have been discarded.

Although loans and non-interest revenue are involved as an output in Chen (2012), the traditional lending activity of banks (total loans) is not helpful as it is a less accurate indicator of measuring true bank efficiency levels. Even if the non-interest revenue is sometimes used as a proxy for off-balance sheet (OBS) item, Boyd and Gertler (1995) and Clark and Siems (2002) highlighted that using these items can have drawbacks for efficiency measurement. For instance, total credit equivalent used as an output may underestimate the level of OBS. Hence, Clark and Siems (2000) instead argue that OBS items, such as derivative instruments, may be used for hedging purposes to highlight balance sheet risks. But they fear that this could possibly motivate distortions in efficiency measurement, and also do not elaborate on the implications of the use of a derivative instrument due to its complicated measurement.

Sherman and Gold (1985) were the first to apply DEA to the banking sector with general inputs and outputs indication. However, Rivas et al. (2006) were the first to raise the issues of the use of derivatives and their impacts on the efficiency in banks. The study used 182 banks from three Latin American countries in 2005 and employed a two-stage[1] approach using DEA and regression analysis. Based on the analysis, the result shows that the size of portfolio loans, total assets and equity ratio has a positive effect on the efficiency of Latin American banks. DEA results indicate that on average, banks that use derivatives are more efficient as compared to banks that do not use derivatives in the three countries. On average, Chilean banks have the highest efficiency mean score followed by Brazilian banks and then by Mexican banks. Rivas et al. (2006) thus provide an important fundamental platform that derivatives increase banking efficiency. However, on the important question of differentiating derivative instruments in measuring efficiency, the authors remained silent.

Some scholars have, however, argued that financial tools that have been used by banks, such as financial derivatives usage, are strong risk controls and are able to maximise firm value, and need to be investigated (e.g. Cebenoyan and Strahan 2004). Ramirez (2007) revealed that derivatives must show a strong impact on a hedging bank's income statement and they are useful for banks in hedging against financial risks arising from their borrowing and lending businesses. There is a need to incorporate interest rate indications to measure actual risk involvement, and accounting data needs to be considered in relation to risk to evaluate bank performance. For instance, the difference between interest rate and currency derivatives, and the difference between forwards, futures, swaps and options, is significant in measuring efficiency in banks. The direct impact of savings and deposits, and of loans to borrowers is expected to be positively related to the use of derivative instruments, hence correlating with banks efficiency levels, as derivative activities mitigate interest rate sensitivity and other types of market risk (Bartram et al. 2009; Zhao and Moser 2009; Fan 2009). To understand the risk factors, it is not sufficient to assess only bank performance and efficiency; it is necessary to extend to the use of the derivative tools as a weapon to mitigate risk. The use of this instrument can positively affect a firm's earnings, the value of the loan and assets, and the absolute value of the firm. No definite conclusion on the efficiency measurement of banks can be made without thoroughly integrating the purpose and the instruments used (Table 4.1).

To summarise, the literature reviewed here shows that many studies have treated the inclusion of risk elements as environment variables for efficiency measurement, but as far as the literature is concerned, no previous studies measure the risk management efficiency based on the actual instrument that is used to manage risk. Further, while some studies do measure the efficiency level based on OBS activities in the specification of their output measurements, these are restricted to non-interest revenues or loans. As far as this review shows, there is no study addressing the risk management efficiency measurements based on financial derivatives as instruments.

In short, the existing literature has found no good measurement approaches (as discussed in Chapter 2) in measuring risk management efficiency using financial derivatives. The existing measurements for parametric and non-parametric approaches used in previous studies do not measure specific risk management efficiency. They do not represent the role of a derivative instrument, and therefore have not received proper evaluation with respect to firms' performance measurements. As discussed in Chapter 3, hedge effectiveness tests do not include a proper discussion on how these instruments address risk management issues. Even though the DOR has been decided as one of the most suitable methods in testing hedge effectiveness, the concept of simple ratio without involving mathematical weights and inconsistencies among tests, therefore, justified that this measurement needs to be improved. The above issues motivate this study to develop a new

Table 4.1 Summary of Findings of Banking Efficiency Studies Incorporating Risk Elements in the Modelling

Author	Country	Years	Approach	Risk Elements (Variable Used)	Main Conclusion
Chan et al. (2014)	East Asian	2001–2008	DEA and Tobit Regression	Insolvency Risk and Interest Rate Sensitivity	Bank insolvency risk shows a positive effect on profit efficiency, while interest rate sensitivity impacts on cost efficiency.
Kasman and Carvallo (2013)	272 Latin American and Caribbean commercial banks	2001–2008	SFA and Granger causality techniques	Loan loss reserves	With an increase of risk and lowered capital, banks have tended to improve cost efficiency.
Alam (2012)	11 Emerging Countries	2000–2010	Seemingly Unrelated Regression (SUR)	Bank Risk (NLTA, LAD, Total Assets, and LLPTAC)	In general, LLR is negatively related to the inefficiency of banks. Bank inefficiency and risk are positively related to conventional banks, while negatively to Islamic banks.
Chen (2012)	Taiwan	1999–2007	Malmquist Productivity Index (MPI)	Capital Adequacy Ratio (CAR) and Reciprocal Capital Adequacy Ratio (RCAR)	Neglecting risk inputs resulted in weak efficiency measurement.
Sun and Chang (2011)	8 Emerging Asian Countries	1999–2008	SFA	Credit risk, Operational Risk and Market Risk	Each risk measure presents a different effect on the cost efficiency of banks.
Radic et al. (2011)	G7 Countries and Switzerland	2001–2007	SFA	Capital Risk, Liquidity Risk, Securities Risk and Insolvency Risk	By including bank-risk-taking factors, it reflects the efficiency level of investment banks (cost efficiency). However, it is significant in generating a bank's profits.

(Continued)

Author	Country	Years	Approach	Risk Elements (Variable Used)	Main Conclusion
Matthews (2012)	Chinese Banks	2007–2008	NDEA	Operational Risk	The risk management practice and risk management organisations provide insights into the risk function in Chinese banks.
Chang and Chiu (2006)	Taiwanese Banks	1996–2000	DEA and Tobit Regression	Credit and Market Risks	Credit and market risk provide no significant difference to the banking efficiency index.
Pastor (1999)	Spanish Banking	1985–1995	DEA	Credit Risk (PLL)	Provision for Loan Loss (PLL) does not indicate a significant impact on a bank's efficiency level based on the evaluation of the bank's internal factors.
Laeven (1999)	East Asian Banks	1992–1996	DEA	Operational Risk (Excessive Loan Growth)	On average, the efficiency of East Asian banks has been influenced by excessive risk-taking. However, the study admits that it is only a rough efficiency estimation using risk indications.

Notes: NLTA: Net Loan to Total Assets, LAD: Liquidity Assets-to-Deposits Ratio, LLPTAC: Loan-loss Provisions to Total Loans, NDEA: Network DEA, PLL: Provision for Loan-Losses.

approach by integrating the DOR with DEA to offer a deeper academic and practical insight into the risk management efficiency measurement and analysis.

4.4 Justification for alternative methodology in the risk management efficiency measurement

This section explains an alternative new method for risk management efficiency measurements by integrating the DOR and the DEA approach prior to undertaking the investigation underlying the concept of ratio analysis that suits both approaches. However, the DEA approach is considered as a better approach for measuring efficiency as it is able to enhance the DOR measurement, thus providing new measures for examining risk management efficiency in banks.

4.4.1 Criticism of dollar-offset ratio analysis in risk efficiency measurement

Abdel-Khalik (2013, 83) argues that "banks have the highest leverage ratio of any industry because the majority of a bank's assets are financed by debt in the form of short-term and long-term deposits." In the event of a fall in interest rates, the banks' financial position can be hampered, as their liabilities are mostly short-term, and the assets have long-term fixed-rate interests. This study posits that a superior model is needed for evaluating the interest rate risk and providing financial strategies to mitigate risk impact on the performance of banks. This model needs to act as a decision support tool to protect the mismatch between interest rate sensitive liabilities and assets for the reduction of impacts from volatility in interest rates, as these rates on a bank's assets are reset more frequently than liabilities. A decision support model should be able to assess the impact of interest rates on risk management as well as prescribe a course of action. The current, traditional ways of assessing the performance of financial institutions use financial ratio analysis for either comparative studies or as basic measurement tools for strategic analysis. Yet, Smith (1990) states the weakness in using the ratio analysis where one denominator and one numerator severely limits its effectiveness and usefulness. Hence, a reasonable question arises as to whether the ratio concept applied in the DOR evaluating comparisons between the hedging instrument and the hedged item can improve banks' levels of risk management efficiency.

Sherman and Gold (1985) argue that ratio measurements do not capture the long-term performance of institutions, and do not explore beyond the available data from an accounting ratio analysis. The ratio should not only provide information about the relationships in historical accounts but also consider the needs of users who are more concerned about both the current information and future expectations. Another argument forwarded by Nyhan (2002) and Nyhan and Martin (1999) state that the ratio analysis concept only depends on the preferences of policymakers in the assignment of weights, which highlights the weaknesses of this concept. For a wider scope of assessment using DOR, Nyhan and Martin (1999) are of the opinion that this method is incapable of being used as a performance measurement on the basis of the decision rule. These authors believed that this approach derives the weights it assigns to each of the provider's input and/or performance variable when the maximum weight is placed on them and the provider compares negatively.

Ratio analysis applied in the DOR does not make use of mathematical programming models to assimilate ratios into a single aggregate measure of efficiency. In particular, ratio analysis does not take into account interactions over the full range of inputs and outputs simultaneously.[2] Its objective is to compare the performance of an institution, either with other institutions or historical performances over a period of time, which becomes difficult when using the DOR as an evaluative tool. It evaluates just a handful of indicators and is unable to influence overall corporate efficiency (Vincová 2005). Furthermore, the use of ratio analysis in a DOR can be considered as a basic technique for measuring performance. Mante (1997) explains this by stating that the performance of units of analysis cannot be determined by an examination of the simple ratio concept, unless the relative importance (weight) of each ratio is specified. Furthermore, unlike DEA, if ratio analysis does not involve mathematical programming to organise the ratios into aggregate measures of efficiency, it will lead to incorrect judgement and misclassifications. This is because it usually provides only partial measures of multiple input and output relationships (Manzoni and Islam 2009b; Halkos and Salamouris 2004; Ludwin and Guthrie 1989).

Further, as the increase in the amount (number) of output is affected by input usage, the problems of weighting and assimilation grow. Hence, the comparative effect of changes in fair values of the hedging instrument over the hedged item may not be determined accurately, and when fair value changes are relatively small, tests may yield ineffective results. Related to the usage of the hedging instrument as a risk management tool, it is not possible to find a simple rule to determine the impact on an organisation's performance of risk management. Apart from the lack of tools for quality assessment and effectiveness (outcomes) measurement, this approach is too complex to collectively discuss the potential impact of derivative instrument usage for enhancing the safety and soundness of financial institutions. Therefore, the extension of the traditional ratio analysis applied in the DOR in hedge effectiveness test is used to permit the incorporation of a simple ratio dimension of performance using the DEA approach.

4.4.2 Justification for adapting DEA with dollar-offset ratio

In recent surveys, there have been developments in measuring the performance levels of financial institutions using a frontier approach. This is undertaken with either non-parametric or parametric frontier analysis, in which both approaches have particular strengths and limitations. A survey by Arjomandi (2011) demonstrates that no consensus has been reached in the literature on any preferred approach to be used to investigate the performance measurement of institutions. However, based on the shared fundamental concept that has been applied in the DOR of hedge effectiveness, a non-parametric DEA model is chosen as a suitable counterpart to the DOR analysis.

Feroz et al. (2003) demonstrate that DEA can augment the traditional ratio analysis concept, as it can consistently and reliably measure managerial and operational efficiency of an institution. Halkos and Salamouris (2004) also concluded that the DEA model is more reliable than other models when correlation among the ratios is low. In testing their null hypothesis of no relationship between DEA and the traditional accounting ratio measurement concept, their results indicate that DEA can provide more reliable information for the firm's analyst than ratio analysis. In sharp contrast to the limitation of a simple ratio analysis concept applied in the DOR, DEA can accomplish an advanced analysis of the impact of hedging instrument use on the hedged item. DEA is particularly useful in assessing the performance of the banking sector as it takes into account the implications of the hedging instrument (interest rate swap) and the hedged item. DEA is also able to make simultaneous comparisons of multiple dependent performance measures of outcome, quality and output, with a new principle for determining weights directly from the data.

According to Manzoni and Islam (2009b) and Thanassoulis et al. (1996), unlike DEA, ratio analysis is not suitable for setting targets to enable units to become more efficient. The main reason is that DEA simultaneously takes into account all the resources and outputs in assessing performance, while ratio analysis relates only one resource to one output at a time. However, they agree that these two methods can support each other in providing useful information on specific aspects of the performance of a unit and can support the communication of DEA results for the measurement of an institution's performance. As Chen and McGinnis (2007) suggested, the bilateral comparison between the relationship knowledge of conventional ratio analysis based on a DEA approach can enhance conventional ratio analysis, particularly in establishing the input-output ratio performance gap.

The integration of a simple ratio and DEA measurement can also provide a more effective way to measure the performance of a unit relative to that of other units. In addition, this study legitimises the use of DEA within the context of risk management efficiency due to its ability to act as a multi-criteria decision analysis technique with the benefit of weightings that can assign ranked positions to the measured units. Provided that the performance indicators of DEA can capture all variables used in its assessment of ratio analysis, these two methods agree reasonably closely on the performance of the units as a whole. As this approach also works well with a small sample size, and as there are only 21 banks from the Asia-Pacific countries in this study that have used derivative instruments (interest rate swap for hedging purposes), DEA has been considered as more suited than other non-parametric approaches for the purposes of this study.

In accordance with the above discussion, the DOR has been chosen as the most suitable method for the hedge effectiveness test, which, theoretically is linked to the efficiency evaluation using a DEA approach. The dollar-offset approach of the effectiveness test is based on a simple ratio analysis, which only provides limited information about effectiveness and/or efficiency (DeLancer 1996) in traditional banking performance analysis to provide an adequate indication of risk (Greuning and Bratanovic 1999), particularly when the DOR analysis is used with a large and varying number of units of analysis. A thorough measurement will occur when DEA is able to assign mathematical weights for all the inputs and outputs determined, in which the ratio analysis relies on the preferences of policymakers in the assigning of weights (Nyhan and Martin 1999). This means that the ratio analysis concept applied as a dollar-offset test and the ability of DEA in measuring a bank's performance need to be integrated as quantitative supervisory tools to examine the effectiveness and efficiency of a bank's risk management.

4.4.3 Modelling scheme of DEA/dollar-offset ratio hedge effectiveness test

The integrated framework of this study aims at incorporating DOR and DEA to support sound decision-making processes in risk management measurement and strategies for achieving the benefits of the risk management practices of banks. The DOR analysis is incapable of analysing the impact on firms' risk management when it does not show the implication of the derivative instrument (hedging instrument) usage on the hedged item (asset and liability management).

According to finance theory, derivative activities are pivotal in the risk management of banks by bringing stronger market disciplines. Therefore, given the weaknesses in the DOR, the DEA model provides an alternative for assessing the effectiveness of a hedging instrument (in this case interest rate swap) and strengthening the hedge effectiveness test. DEA evaluation of a hedge effectiveness test is incorporated with the quantitative measurement of the dollar-offset approach, as this hedge effectiveness test shares a fundamental concept of ratio with this approach. Figure 4.1 shows the DOR process in which its approach is formulated based on the changes in the hedging instrument and the hedged item.

Even though the current quantitative prospective and retrospective hedge effectiveness tests (assessment) within the range of 80–125% will soon be replaced by a new range[3] and expected to be implemented by the International Accounting Standards Board (IASB), this study posits that there is an economic relationship between hedging instruments and the hedged item. Therefore, in order to evaluate the economic performance of firms, results

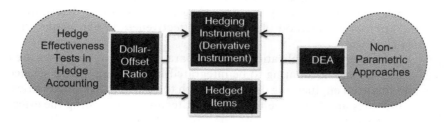

Figure 4.1 Modelling Scheme of DOR and DEA Approach.

produced using the DEA approach can indirectly show the relationship between both the hedging instrument and the hedged item. From the hedge accounting perspective, the 80/125 rule applicable to the hedge effectiveness measurements represents the impact of a hedging instrument on the hedged item, and further enhances the DEA model by incorporating risk management issues. In other words, DEA provides a better methodological and measurement approach in risk management efficiency in solving the derivatives usage measurement in the hedge accounting ratio and highlights the derivatives roles.

In this study, the correlation and coefficient of determination are investigated prior to DEA to strengthen the relationship between the hedging instrument and the hedged item. Here, the hedged items are affected by the use of the hedging instrument with the assumption that these items will yield highly effective results and better risk management implications ranging between 85% and 125%. In the current hedge accounting practices, the effect of interest rates does not dominate the fair value changes in hedging relationships. For instance, the fair value change as interest rate risk tends to be a significant driver of the fair value changes of the hedged item. The hedging ratio in this study refers to the DOR, which should not only be designated based on the quantities of the hedging instrument and the hedged items, but also for risk management purposes (Ernst & Young's International Financial Reporting Standards Group 2011). Even though the derivative hedging instrument could affect profit and loss as a reflection of a firm's equity (Bunea-Bontas et al. 2009), this study focusses on the relationships between the hedging instrument and the hedged item, as this makes the analysis more determined.

The application of DEA essentially makes the following extensions to the existing method for a hedge effectiveness test in the area of hedge accounting by incorporating the following aspects.

1   A comprehensive discussion of the hedge effectiveness test, particularly in the DOR in evaluating the effectiveness of the use of hedging instrument (derivatives) on the hedged items.

2   Expansion of research within the field of both efficiency analysis and hedge accounting by incorporating recent issues of determining the appropriate method of the hedge effectiveness test in banks' risk management.
3   Development and application of a non-parametric approach in the area of finance and accounting to be integrated in the management science and financial engineering disciplines with the following characteristics:
    • provides an alternative measurement technique in testing the effectiveness of derivatives usage, as stressed by Ramirez (2007) on the need for an alternative technique;
    • incorporates interdisciplinary issues into finance and accounting;
    • combines the risk management, finance and efficiency theory in evaluating risk management efficiency in banks;
    • provides a fundamental risk management evaluation in measuring hedge effectiveness; and provides an easier and more operationalised estimation involving financial derivative elements.
4   Provision of a balanced and alternative decision-making framework for commercial banks based on the established methodology using a LP technique (Coelli et al. 2005b).
5   Provision of a basis for banks for their competitiveness level in the global financial market through the efficiency ranking produced by the DEA approach. This helps banks to achieve better strategic planning.

4.5 Mathematical model and statistical tests used in this study

In specifying the model, this study assumes that commercial banks are producers that have full control over most of their financial activities including turning funds into finance or investments, and reflecting the banks' goals of profit maximisation in an ambiguous environment dealing with risk. Due to the growing importance of new financial instruments and markets (swaps) characterised as facilitators of risk transfer (Scholtens and Van Wensveen 2000), the control over derivative transactions for hedging purposes can determine the level of risk management efficiency. The DEA framework used in this study employs: one derivative input of interest rate swaps ($x1$); and two outputs including mortgages, corporate and commercial loans ($y1$), and customer deposits ($y2$). DEA will be used to investigate the relationships between the one input and the two outputs for hedging in risk management by the 21 banks in the Asia-Pacific region, as explained in Figure 4.2.

4.5.1 Input-oriented model

This study uses the assumption of input orientation (input-oriented model) since banks are believed to have better control over their interest rate swaps and can freely adjust the "notional amount" of the derivative instrument (input) that influences their risk management performance. In order to evaluate the input-oriented TE of any firm, this study examines if, and to what

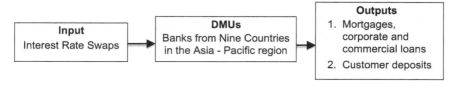

Figure 4.2 DEA Framework of the Study.

extent, it is possible to reduce its input(s) without reducing output(s). In this study, this orientation is quite straightforward due to only one input being involved. However, in the presence of multiple inputs, a relevant question would be whether reducing one input is more important than reducing a number of them. When market prices of inputs are not available, one way to circumvent this problem is to look for an "equi-proportionate" reduction in all inputs. This would amount to scaling down the observed input bundle without altering the input proportions. Therefore, the input-oriented TE of firms t is θ^*, where:

$$\theta^* = min\theta : \left(\theta x^t, y^t\right) \; T^C \tag{4.1}$$

Note that $\left(x^t, \varnothing^* y^t\right) \in T^C$. Hence, $\left(k x^t, k\varnothing^* y^t\right) \in T^C$. Setting $k = \dfrac{1}{\varnothing^*}$, we get $\left(\dfrac{1}{\varnothing^*} x^t, y^t\right) \in T^C$ Under constant return to scale (CRS), $\theta^* = \dfrac{1}{\varnothing^*}$. In this case, the input- and output-oriented TE measures are identical.

In order to specify the mathematical formulation of the input-oriented model, this study assumes that k is the DMU using N input to produce M output, and TE_K is the efficiency score for k_{th} DMU. Inputs are denoted by x_{jk} $(j=1....,n)$ and outputs are denoted by y_{ik} $(j=1....,m)$ for each $DMUk$ $(k=1....K)$. Therefore, the following mathematical programming model is specified in order to measure the TE of each DMU (Coelli et al. 1998).

$$TE = \frac{\sum_{i=i=1}^{m} u_i y_{ik}}{\sum_{j=1}^{n} v_j x_{jk}} \tag{4.2}$$

$$\text{Subject to: } \frac{\sum_{i=i=1}^{m} u_i y_{ik}}{\sum_{j=1}^{n} v_j x_{jk}} \leq 1; r = 1,...k; u_i, v_j \geq 0 \tag{4.3}$$

where y_{ik} is the quantity of the i_{th} outputs which are net income, asset quality ratio and capitalisation produced by the k_{th} DMU, x_{jk} is the quantity of j_{th}

inputs which are the interest rate swaps used by the k_{th} DMU, and u_i and v_j are the output and input weights, respectively.

The above model has a problem of infinite solutions so this study has to impose the constraint $x_{jk} = 1$, which leads to:

$$\min_{\mu,\varphi}(y_{ik}),$$
$$\mu'x_{jk} = 1$$
$$\mu'y_{ik} - \varphi'x_{jk} \leq 0 \ r = 1,\dots k,$$
$$\mu,\varphi \geq 0 \tag{4.4}$$

where the notation is changed from u and v to μ and φ, respectively, in order to reflect transformations. Using the duality in LP, an equivalent envelopment form of this problem can be derived as:

$$\min_{\theta,\lambda}\theta,$$
$$y_{ik} + Y\lambda \geq 0$$
$$\theta X_{jk} - X\lambda \geq 0$$
$$\lambda \geq 0 \tag{4.5}$$

where θ is a scalar representing the value of the efficiency score for the k-th DMU which will range between 0, and 1. λ is a vector of $K \times 1$ constant. This LP needs to be solved K times, once for each DMU in the sample.

4.5.2 Description and definition of the chosen variables

This study uses the intermediation approach originally suggested by Charnes et al. (1990) and later revised by Paul and Kourouche (2008), in which banks are viewed as intermediaries that conceptualise inputs as allocations of a certain amount of funds and outputs in terms of revenue or gain from the amount invested. In this study, the selection of the variables is mainly guided by the associations of the risk management functions of financial intermediaries with the growing importance of the new financial instruments and markets (swaps), which are characterised as facilitators of risk transfer (Scholtens and Van Wensveen 2000). For instance, within the scope of interest rate risk management, Beets (2004) posits that commercial banks have become intermediaries (market makers) for their products, including forward rate agreements to futures contracts, interest rate swaps, and options including caps, collars and floors. Banks will therefore become intermediaries between the long and short positions, taking over the role of clearinghouses, and hedging residual exposure will result from the imbalance between the two opposite sides of a transaction (Brown and Smith 1988). Banks will also adapt contracts to meet the needs of depositors and borrowers, and design contracts that help prevent companies from protecting those who are trying to hedge against falling and rising rates (Brown and Smith 1988). These arguments have been validated by Diamond (1984) and Rajendran (2007) through a model of the intermediary role of banks. They state that derivatives usage and lending activities are complementary activities that can increase the intermediary role of banks. With regard to these dimensions, the role of commercial banks as financial intermediaries has changed. Simultaneously, banks' roles now support financial theories that include the innovative use of derivatives in their operations (Sangha 1995).

Definitions of the variables used in DEA models are based on hedge accounting recognition rules under the cash flow hedges that are associated with risk management indicators. In this study, variables are based on a hedge effectiveness test to show relationships between the hedging instrument and the hedged item. The outputs chosen have been converted by entering an input. As stated in Table 4.2, interest rate swaps $(x1)$ is chosen as an input variable and is measured in terms of the notional value of the interest rate swap. For output variables, the hedged items represent the exposure to variability in a cash flow hedge. In this circumstance, the direct effect associated with interest rate exposure is designated as the hedged items. These maintain and initiate a hedging relationship that allows the hedging instrument to directly correspond with changes in the hedged items. Therefore, two outputs from mortgages, corporate and commercial loans $(y1)$ and customer deposits $(y2)$ are selected. These two outputs are directly influenced by the use of derivative instruments (interest rate swaps), and are most frequently reported in the annual reports (balance sheet) of banks in the Asia-Pacific region.

Referring to Bunea-Bontaş (2009), the derivative hedging instrument could affect the profit and loss as a reflection of a firm's equity. For instance, Balakrishnan (2009) found a significant relationship between loans-to-total asset ratio and the use of interest rate swaps as a hedging tool. Even though this relationship has proven that there is a significant correlation between using derivative financial instruments (in this case the interest rate swaps) and overall financial performance, this study only focusses on the relationship between the hedging instrument and the hedged items rather than the more common strategy of determining inputs and outputs that affect the overall financial statement.

Table 4.2 List of Input and Output Variables

	Parameters	Measurement
Input	Interest rate swaps $(x1)$	The notional value of interest rate swaps
Output	Mortgages, corporate and commercial loans $(y1)$	Total mortgages, corporate and commercial loans
	Customer deposits $(y2)$	Total amount of customer savings

4.5.3 Descriptive statistic of input and output variables

In order to cope with the business environment test concept and following the general acceptance theories and prerequisite conditions of the DEA model, Ueda and Hoshiai (1997) strongly suggest that outputs need to positively correlate with input variables. Hence, this study assesses the relationships between input and output variables using the Pearson's correlation test (Hair 2009) as formulated below:

$$r = \frac{SS_{YY}}{\sqrt{(SS_{XY})(SS_{YY})}} \tag{4.6}$$

Following the descriptive statistic, the correlation coefficient test (r) is performed (Table 4.3). Here, both customer deposits ($y1$) and mortgages, corporate and commercial loans ($y2$) show a positive correlation with interest rate swaps ($x1$). Therefore, both output variables are appropriate to be included in measuring banks' risk management in the performance evaluation model of this study (Table 4.4).

A coefficient of determination is used for satisfactory and robust model that explains the relationships between variables. According to Taylor (1990),[4] although the correlation coefficient is the best known and preferred

Table 4.3 Summary of Descriptive Statistic of Input and Outputs

Variables	Units	Minimum	Maximum	Mean	Std. deviation
Outputs					
Customer deposits	Dollar	0.046	243669	0.0848	0.0332
Mortgages, corporate and commercial loans	Dollar	14.848	2922.070	530.327	716.600
Input					
Interest rate swaps	Dollar	0.011	5.615	1.476	1.916

Note: Figures are presented in USD for nine Asia-Pacific countries over 2007–2012. The minimum value for interest rate swaps is referring to the percentage of London inter-bank offered rate (LIBOR) swaps after the company (bank) finds it advantageous to enter into the swap.

Table 4.4 Correlation of Coefficients between Input and Outputs

Input	Outputs	
	Customer deposits (y1)	*Mortgages, corporate and commercial loans (y2)*
Interest rate swaps ($x1$)	0.730**	0.588*

Note: ***p ≤ 0.001, **p ≤ 0.01, *p ≤ 0.05.

Table 4.5 Correlation of Determination between Input and Output Variables

Input	Outputs	
	Customer deposits (y1)	Mortgages, corporate and commercial loans (y2)
Interest rate swap (x1)	0.533*	0.345*

Note: ***p ≤ 0.001, **p ≤ 0.01, *p ≤ 0.05.

for statistical testing, perhaps the coefficient of determination (r^2) is a more meaningful and more conservative measure of relationships between the two variables. However, even though this test is seldom reported in the statistical analyses of research data, the results for coefficient of determination in this study are presented in Table 4.5.

4.5.4 Decision making units

Using a DEA approach, the minimum number of DMUs in this study is determined by the number of inputs and outputs. Raab and Lichty (2002) suggest that the general rule of thumb to determine the number of DMUs is that this number must be greater than or equal to three times the number of inputs plus outputs. This means that the minimum number of DMUs must be equal to the maximum number of multiplications of the numbers of inputs and outputs, or three times the summation of the number of inputs and outputs. Otherwise, the model losses its discretionary power, $S_S \geq I^*O$ (Cooper et al. 2006; Ramanathan 2003). Cooper et al. (2006) have provided a guideline for calculating the minimum number of DMUs as follows: n is the number of DMU s, m is the number of inputs and s is the number of outputs where

$$n \geq max\{mxs, 3(m+s)\} \tag{4.7}$$

This study evaluates 21 units of DMUs (Banks), with each bank taking a $m(1)$ different input to produce $s(2)$ different outputs in measuring the efficiency of productive units DMUq in order to maximise efficiency rates. The 21 commercial banks from nine Asia-Pacific countries are selected as the data set, covering the period from 2007 to 2012. Three specific selection criteria are used as follows:

1 Homogeneity in the derivative usage based on interest rate swaps as the financial instrument (hedging instrument) and mortgages, corporate and commercial loans, and customer deposits of items being hedged (hedged item);

2   Financial instruments only for hedging purposes and used continuously from 2007 to 2012 and
3   Financial reporting standards of banks needed to comply with hedge accounting requirements. The sample period is restricted to the period of 2007–2012 to ensure that derivative positions are available for the entire sample period. To meet the requirements of a DOR, all data in the current year will be divided by the previous year.

From this, a DEA will be used to evaluate the efficiency of banks' risk management. Using DEA, the linear divisive programming model for this study is developed to fulfil the basic assumption that efficiency rates are not less than 0 and greater than 1, and the weights of output and inputs are greater than zero. Therefore, in order to maximise the efficiency rating θ for commercial banks:

$$\text{Maximise: } h_p = \frac{\sum_{r=1}^{k} w_r y_{rp}}{\sum_{i=1}^{m} v_i x_{ip}}, \; p = 1, 2 \ldots, 21 \tag{4.8}$$

This equation is subject to the constraint that no service unit n (21 banks in this case) can be more than 100% efficient when the same values for w_r, v_r are applied to each unit, which involve two outputs and one input:

$$\text{Subject to: } \frac{\sum_{r=1}^{k} w_r y_{rj}}{\sum_{i=1}^{m} v_i x_{ij}} \leq 1, \; j = 1, 2 \ldots, 21$$

$$w_r \geq 0,_{r=1,2\ldots,2} v_i \geq 0,_{i=1,2\ldots,1} \tag{4.9}$$

4.5.5   Univariate analysis – statistical test based on DEA (efficiency robustness tests)

One of the purposes of tests based on DEA is to address the efficiency comparison within a group (Banker and Natarajan 2011; Charnes et al. 1978). In the case of efficiency comparisons between two groups of DMUs, Banker (1993) builds statistical tests that enable a contrast between two different groups of samples (N1 and N2) to measure whether one is more efficient than the other. To appreciate the effects of TE, PTE and SE, this study will use a DEA-based test to resolve the issue of whether differences in TE, PTE and SE scores in both the developed and developing countries within the Asia-Pacific region are statistically significant.

The four advantages of ranking data in statistical analyses instead of using the original observations include (1) the calculations are simplified; (2) only very general assumptions are made about the kinds of distribution from which observations arise; (3) data available only in ordinal form may be used; and (4) when assumptions of the parametric test procedure are too far from reality, there is a good chance that any differences of real interest will be detected (Banker and Natarajan 2011; Chan and Walmsley 1997).

To test the differences in efficiency levels of banks in developed and developing countries of the Asia-Pacific region (inter-country comparison), this study follows Fadzlan (2010), Isik and Hassan (2002) and others who have performed a series of parametric (*t*-test) and non-parametric including Mann–Whitney and Kolmogorov–Smirnov (K–S) tests. However, as in the current study, these tests yield inconclusive results between parametric and non-parametric tests, so regression analysis is performed to provide more robust results (details in Section 4.6.7).

4.5.5.1 Parametric test

Parametric tests are used to perform means analysis of inefficiency to compare two groups of DMUs. Two common parametric tests are considered, namely (i) OLS regression-based test and (ii) *t*-test.

4.5.5.1.1 OLS REGRESSION

In analysing DMUs, Cummins et al. (1999) applied an OLS regression technique to compare two groups of DMUs. Without considering the error term, the OLS regression yields an estimator of the mean inefficiencies when the logarithm of the inefficiency is regressed on a group dummy variable (Banker et al. 2010). The OLS regression of the inefficiency on a dummy variable z takes a value of 1 if a particular DMU belongs to group 1. Otherwise, it takes a value of 0 (Banker et al. 2010; Cummins et al. 1999).

4.5.5.1.2 T-TEST

Banker et al. (2010) suggest that a *t*-test is appropriate for comparing the mean inefficiencies across two DMU groups. By only looking at a mean value, the reliable difference cannot be ensured. Therefore, a *t*-test (categorised as inferential statistics) needs to be carried out, and this allows inferences about the population to be made beyond the sample of testing. The formula is as follows:

$$t = \frac{\bar{x}_1 - \bar{x}_2}{\sqrt{\frac{s_1^2}{n_1} + \frac{s_2^2}{n_2}}} \qquad (4.10)$$

where $\bar{x}_1$ denotes the mean of the first set of values, $\bar{x}_2$ denotes the mean of the second set of values, s_1 denotes the standard deviation of the first set of values, s_2 denotes the standard deviation of the second set of values,

n_1 denotes the total number of values in the first set and n_2 denotes the total number of values in the second set. The t-test has a corresponding p-value which explains the probability that the pattern in the sample data could be produced by random data. If $p = 0.05$, there is a 5% chance that there is no real difference, if p-value = 0.01 it means there is a 1% chance, while $p = 0.10$ means a 10% chance. In most research, the cut-off point of reliable consideration is when p-value is equal to 0.05 or below (e.g. Hariri and Roberts 2015; Giovanis 2013).

The exact p-value associated with the t-value depends on the sample size. A bigger sample size contributes to easier evaluation to detect significant differences (Kotrlik and Higgins 2001; Wallenstein et al. 1980). Statistical power might not be gathered if a sample size is small (Ellis 2010; Carver 1978). The most common types of t-test are independent-samples tests (between-samples or unpaired-samples t-test), which test the mean for two different groups.

4.5.6.1 Non-parametric tests

Banker et al. (2010) state that a non-parametric test is more suitable and commonly used when certain assumptions about the underlying population (samples) are questionable. In their study, three tests were used which are (i) the median test, (ii) the Mann–Whitney test and (iii) the Kolmogorov–Smirnov (K–S) test.

4.5.6.1.1 MEDIAN TEST

This procedure is appropriate for making inferences about the differences between two location parameters (Daniel 1990). The median test is the simplest and most widely used procedure for testing the null hypothesis of two populations that have the same median (Cabilio and Masaro 1996; Brown and Mood 1951). Gibbons (1985) used the median test for testing the null hypothesis that there is no difference between the medians of two groups of DMUs. By looking only at denotation M_1 and M_2 as the median inefficiency of U_1 and U_2 for group 1 and group 2, respectively, M becomes the median of the combined sample of the two groups. In null hypothesis (H0), the populations represented by the k conditions (e.g. groups or samples) have the same median on the quantitative response variable. The null hypothesis is derived as $H0 = M_1 = M_2 = M$. It is easy to verify that the corresponding estimates $\hat{M}_1$, $\hat{M}_2$, and $\hat{M}$ for $\hat{u}_m (m = 1, 2)$ are also consistent.

4.5.6.1.2 MANN–WHITNEY TEST

The Mann–Whitney test, which is also known as Wilcoxon Rank Sum test, does the same job as a the t-test but can work with ordered-level data or non-normal distributions. This test does not require equal sample sizes like an independent-sample *t*-test, and hence is considered to be one of the most powerful non-parametric tests. Consider two independent samples with size n_k and let y_{ki} be some continuous outcome from the ith subject within the kth group ($1 \leq i \leq nk, k = 12$). Let R_{ki} denote the rank of y_{ki} in the pooled sample. The Wilcoxon rank sum statistic has the following form:

$$W_n = \sum_{i=1}^{n1} R_{1i} \tag{4.11}$$

Note that the sum of the rank scores $W_n = \sum_{j=1}^{n2} R_{1j}$ from the second group may also be used as a statistic. However, since the two sums add up to $\frac{n(n+1)}{2y}(n = n_1 + n_2)$, only one of the sums can be used as a test statistic. This test is often performed as a two-sided test; thus, the research hypothesis indicates that the populations are not equal as opposed to specifying directionality. A one-sided research hypothesis is used if interest lies in detecting a positive or negative shift in one population as compared to another. The procedure for the test involves pooling the observations from the two samples into one combined sample, keeping track of which sample each observation comes from, and then ranking the lowest to the highest from 1 to $n_1 + n_2$.

4.5.6.1.3 KOLMOGOROV–SMIRNOV (K–S) TEST

This test is one of the most useful non-parametric methods. It is used to either compare a sample with a reference probability distribution or to compare two groups of samples. It is able to do this because it is sensitive to differences in both locations (Smirnov 1948). K–S is formulated as:

$$Z = max_j |d_j| \sqrt{\frac{n_{1,f} n_{2,f}}{n_{1,f} + n_{2,f}}} \tag{4.12}$$

The *p*-value is calculated using the Smirnov approximation described in the K–S one-sample test. If $p < \alpha$, the null hypothesis is rejected. Chen et al. (2010) used the *z* test to verify if a significant difference existed between two pairs of project delivery methods.

4.5.6.1.4 KRUSKAL–WALLIS TEST

This non-parametric alternative test is for a situation where all assumptions are not satisfied. It provides a comparison of more than two groups with unequal distribution as well as groups not normally distributed. The three requirements of the Kruskal–Wallis test are: the k samples are random and independent; there are five or more measurements per sample and the probability distributions are continuous.

With the degree of freedom (df) = 0.05, and based on the decision rule stated, the decision for area of rejection or acceptance of the null hypothesis is determined. A test statistic is performed to organise scores by rank using the following formula:

$$H = \frac{12}{N(N+1)} \left(\sum \frac{T_i^2}{n} \right) - 3(N+1) \tag{4.13}$$

4.5.6 Peer units analysis

In establishing the superiority of peer units' performance, Ramanathan (2003) has stated that the analysis of peers is important information in DEA. With the help of the DEA method, the performance assessment for inefficient DMUs can be carried out by comparing them with efficient DMUs (peer efficient units) for having best performance within the same group or another group performing similar functions (Malana and Malano 2006).

Efficient DMUs can be selected by inefficient DMUs as models of best practice, making them a composite DMU instead of using a single DMU as a benchmark. A composite DMU is formed by multiplying the lambda value λ (intensity vector) by the inputs and outputs of the respective efficient DMUs (Banaeian et al. 2011). The summation of all lambda values in a benchmark DMU must equal to 1 (100%). The lambda values are weights to be used as multipliers for the input levels of a reference DMU to indicate the input targets that an inefficient DMU should aim at in order to achieve better efficiency levels (Banaeian et al. 2011).

According to Adler et al. (2002), one of the strategies to rank a DMU is by using a benchmark technique. An efficient DMU is ranked on the basis of counting the number of times it appears in a referent set. Each set is formed by the efficient DMUs that have similar input and output levels to inefficient DMUs. Moreover, the DEA is a valuable benchmarking approach for management that can provide a continuous improvement strategy. For example, the DEA approach can also be used for natural extension of balanced scorecard system for integrating the financial measurement and operation with non-financial operational measures (Avkiran 2000). The current study defines inefficient DMUs as reference set E_0 based on the max-slack solution as obtained by $E_0 = \left\{ j \middle| \lambda_j^* \rangle 0 \right\} (j \in \{1,...,n\})$.

4.5.7 Slacks analysis

Slacks analysis can be undertaken when certain DMUs have been identified as inefficient (<1.000). Coelli et al. (2005) argue that both the Farrell measure of TE and any non-zero input and output slacks should be reported to provide an accurate indication of TE of DMUs. Following this suggestion, Kumar and Gulati (2008) show that the slacks should be elaborated along with the efficiency values. After presenting the leftover portions of inefficient DMUs and proportional reductions in inputs and outputs, the inefficient DMUs should reach *efficient frontiers*. If a DMU cannot reach the efficient target, slacks results need to push the DMU to the frontier (target) (Li et al. 2013; Ozcan 2008).

The slack result frequently occurs in DEA estimation. It is always useful to report when the optimal solution (*radial*) reveals that the excesses in inputs and shortfalls in outputs occur (Daraio and Simar 2007; Tone 2001). Therefore, this analysis is important to discuss both the efficiency and the slacks to unify the objective function θ^* and slacks into a scalar measure (Pastor 1995; Tone 1993). In case of input-oriented model, Avkiran (1999a) and Ozcan (2008) stated that the input-slack represents the input excess, while the output-slack reported the output which is shortfall (under produced). With regard to this issue, this study defines the input excesses as $s^- \in R^m$ and the output shortfalls (shortage) as $s^+ \in R^s$.

4.6 Discussion of results

In contrast to previous studies in DEA, this research first presents the strongly expressed role of derivative instruments used in hedging effectiveness test in banks' risk management efficiency measurements. Using the software package DEAP Version 2.1 by Coelli (1996), the analysis is based on annual data using 2007 as the base year, for estimated efficiency scores in individual banks (Table 4.6).

4.6.1 Superiority of DEA measurement

Table 3.1 is revisited to highlight the superiority of the proposed DEA model over DOR.The DEA results have ranged both Australian and Malaysian banks from 0.895 (89.5%) to 0.957 (95.7%) through the advancement of mathematical programming elements to measure efficiency level of banks based on the usage of derivative instrument. The superiority of DEA model has extended the existing method for a hedge effectiveness test (DOR) in the area of hedge accounting as well as minimising some major issues in hedge effectiveness measurements. By incorporating of advancement ratio concept in DEA approach, this study exhibits that DEA is becoming an appropriate alternative method to measure hedge effectiveness test in banks' risk management, as posited by Ramirez (2007). More importantly, the DEA model has provided an alternative decision-making framework for commercial banks based on the established methodology using a LP technique.

Table 4.6 Efficiency Summary in 2007 and RTS for Commercial Banks in Nine Asia-Pacific Countries

Commercial Banks	OTE Score	OTIE (%)	PTE Score	PTIE (%)	SE Score	SIE (%)	Nature of RTS
Australia							
CB1	0.953	4.7	1.000	0.0	0.953	0.47	DRS
CB2	0.945	5.5	0.995	5.0	0.950	5.0	DRS
CB3	0.947	5.3	0.997	3.0	0.950	5.0	DRS
CB4	0.943	5.7	0.986	1.4	0.956	4.4	DRS
Hong Kong							
CB5	0.943	5.7	0.988	1.2	0.955	4.5	DRS
Japan							
CB6	0.949	5.1	0.992	0.8	0.957	4.3	DRS
CB7	1.000	0.0	1.000	0.0	1.000	0.0	CRS (MPSS)
CB8	0.838	16.2	1.000	0.0	0.838	16.2	DRS
New Zealand							
CB9	0.948	5.2	0.995	5.0	0.953	4.7	DRS
CB10	0.948	5.2	0.994	0.6	0.955	4.5	DRS
CB11	0.911	8.9	0.952	4.8	0.957	4.3	DRS
Singapore							
CB12	0.949	5.1	0.996	0.4	0.953	4.7	DRS
Taiwan							
CB13	0.954	4.6	0.997	0.3	0.957	4.3	DRS
Malaysia							
CB14	0.923	7.7	0.967	3.3	0.955	4.5	DRS
CB15	0.898	10.2	0.946	5.4	0.949	5.1	DRS
CB16	0.957	4.3	1.000	0.0	0.957	4.3	DRS
CB17	0.895	10.5	0.936	06.4	0.957	4.3	DRS
Philippines							
CB18	0.949	5.1	0.992	0.8	0.957	4.3	DRS
Thailand							
CB19	0.949	5.1	0.992	0.8	0.957	4.3	DRS
CB20	0.944	5.6	0.987	1.3	0.957	4.3	DRS
CB21	0.940	6.0	0.982	1.8	0.957	4.3	DRS
Mean	**0.937**		**0.985**		**0.951**		

Note: CB denotes commercial bank. OTE = overall technical efficiency, OTE = pure technical efficiency (PTE) x scale efficiency (SE), OTIE% = overall technical inefficiency = (1-OTE) x100, PTIE% = pure technical inefficiency = (1-PTE) x100, SIE% = scale inefficiency = (1-SE) x100, CRS denotes constant returns to scale. DRS = decreasing returns-to-scale and MPSS = most productive scale size.

4.6.2 Risk management efficiency estimates

By means of an integrated analysis approach between DEA and the DOR, risk management efficiency levels based on derivatives were estimated. Based on the input-oriented approach under the CRS assumption of 2007, Table 4.6 presents the OTE scores of 21 CBs, along with the magnitude of overall technical inefficiency (OTIE). The results indicate that the commercial banking sector of the Asia-Pacific region has been characterised with small asymmetries between banks with regard to OTEs (in percentage terms) that range from 83.8% to 100% – an average OTE of 93.7% (0.937). This implies that on average, these banks could proportionally reduce their input by 6.3% and produce the same amount (proportion) of output. Of the 21 CBs, CB7 from Japan is the only bank found to be technically efficient, since its OTE score of 1.000 achieved the unity SE score, thus operating at its most productive scale size (MPSS). CB7 defines the *best practice* or *efficient frontier* bank in managing both input and output, within the Asia-Pacific region. At MPSS, this bank operates at the minimum point of its long-run average cost curve. This result is consistent with that found by Gulati (2011). For 2007, the remaining 20 banks have OTEs of less than 1.000, which means that they are technically inefficient, thus indicating the presence of marked deviations of the banks from the *best practice* or *efficient frontier* levels.

For the period of 2007, the nature of returns to scale (RTS) indicates that all banks, except CB7, were operating in a region of decreasing returns to scale (DRS) (also known as diseconomies of scale or non-increasing returns-to-scale), implying that they were operating on scales that were too large. Arising from these results, the assumption is that in the Asia-Pacific region, almost all the banks in this study are too large to take full advantage of scale. In agreement, Kumar and Gulati (2008) state that banks included in the DRS region have supra-optimum scale size necessitating reduction of inputs to increase efficiency levels. OTE scores among these inefficient banks range from 0.838 for CB8 (in Japan) to 0.957 for CB 16 (in Malaysia). These findings imply that, respectively, CB8 and CB16 can potentially reduce their input levels of derivatives (for hedging size reductions) by 16.2% and 4.3%, while retaining an unchanged impact on output levels. The same interpretation of OTE scores can be extended to the other remaining inefficient banks in Table 4.6. This study observes that OTIE levels ranged from 4.3% to 16.2% among all the inefficient CBs.

Table 4.7 provides a summary of the OTE of commercial banks in the Asia-Pacific region. Inspection of this table reveals that banks in Malaysia and Australia are the most technically efficient in the sample period of 2007–2012, with the country average efficiency scores of 92.9% and 92.8%, respectively. With average efficiency scores of 92.9%, Malaysian banks compete with other banks in both the developed and developing countries to gain the highest average OTE scores in the region, while commercial banks

Table 4.7 Efficiency Summary in 2007–2012 for Commercial Banks in Nine Asia-Pacific Countries

BANK/COUNTRY	2007	2008	2009	2010	2011	2012	Mean (Country)
	Efficiency Scores						
Australia							
CB1	0.953	1.000	0.835	0.976	0.840	0.991	0.932
CB2	0.945	0.993	0.845	0.985	0.803	1.000	0.929
CB3	0.947	0.993	0.867	0.977	0.809	1.000	0.932
CB4	0.943	0.994	0.827	0.970	0.791	0.996	0.920
							0.928
Hong Kong							
CB5	0.943	0.993	0.825	0.969	0.808	1.000	0.923
Japan							
CB6	0.949	0.960	0.827	0.970	0.799	0.994	0.917
CB7	1.000	1.000	0.843	1.000	0.836	0.974	0.942
CB8	0.838	0.890	0.813	0.954	0.757	0.994	0.874
							0.911
New Zealand							
CB9	0.948	0.993	0.827	0.970	0.817	0.994	0.925
CB10	0.948	0.993	0.827	0.970	0.796	0.993	0.921
CB11	0.911	0.997	0.826	0.970	0.796	0.998	0.916
							0.921
Singapore							
CB12	0.949	0.994	0.827	0.970	0.806	0.996	
Taiwan							
CB13	0.954	0.995	0.822	0.969	0.783	0.984	
Malaysia							
CB14	0.923	0.988	1.000	0.969	1.000	0.974	0.976
CB15	0.898	0.970	0.854	0.970	0.781	0.969	0.907
CB16	0.957	0.990	0.825	0.970	0.803	0.969	0.919
CB17	0.895	1.000	0.824	0.970	0.803	0.986	0.913
							0.929
Philippines							
CB18	0.949	0.993	0.827	0.970	0.795	0.993	0.921
Thailand							
CB19	0.949	0.993	0.827	0.970	0.794	0.994	0.921
CB20	0.944	0.993	0.826	0.969	0.795	0.993	0.920
CB21	0.940	0.993	0.826	0.970	0.795	0.992	0.919
							0.920
Mean (Year)	0.937	0.986	0.839	0.972	0.810	0.990	

in Japan are rated as the worst performers with a mean value of 91.1%. These results may seem counter-intuitive, since economists assume that banks in developed countries should achieve better results.

Interestingly, the mean score of banks in Malaysia, a developing country outperformed that of Australian banks, which are found to be the best among banks in the developed countries. On the whole, this study found that the majority of banks in the sample scored above 90% and close to 100% (1.000). Such a pattern in the results might reflect the relatively small market size of the country and the extent of banking competition in the country. Overall, their average OTE in 2012 was found to be the best compared to all previous years, with 99% scores.

As illustrated in Figure 4.3, it is noticeable from the country average OTE estimates (2007–2012) that Malaysian commercial banks performed better than other banks in the region. Therefore, Malaysian banks were found to be able to gain competitive advantage in future due to their excellent performance in risk management.

4.6.3 *Most productive scale size (MPSS)*

Table 4.8 summarises the MPSS banks that consistently achieved the highest efficiency score (100%) for OTE, PTE and SE, which implies that DMU's production of inputs is minimised per unit of outputs (Wang and Lan 2013; Avkiran 2001; Zhu and Shen 1995).

On the whole, seven banks were operating at MPSS (CB1, CB2, CB3, CB5, CB7, CB14 and CB17). As per 2007 data, only CB7 from Japan (the country achieving lowest mean scores of OTE) had achieved MPSS. This bank was found to be fully technically efficient at the MPSS during the sample period, achieving MPSS three times in 2007, 2008 and 2010, thus dominating as the top performer (best efficiency frontier) for the period of 2007–2012. Three Australian banks also reached MPSS in 2008 (CB1) and in 2012 (CB2 and CB3), which means that all three banks were operating at

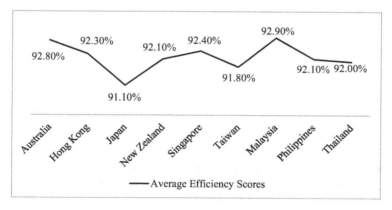

Figure 4.3 Average Efficiency Score for Banks in the Asia-Pacific Region.

Table 4.8 Summary of MPSS, 2007–2012

Country/Bank	MPSS					
	2007	*2008*	*2009*	*2010*	*2011*	*2012*
Australia						
CB1		√				
CB2						√
CB3						√
CB4						
Hong Kong						
CB5						√
Japan						
CB6						
CB7	√	√		√		
CB8						
New Zealand						
CB9						
CB10						
CB11						
Singapore						
CB12						
Taiwan						
CB13						
Malaysia						
CB14			√		√	
CB15						
CB16						
CB17		√				
Philippines						
CB18						
Thailand						
CB19						
CB20						
CB21						

Note: MPSS is indicated by the CRS which produced 1.000 efficiency scores for all OTE, PTE and SE, that is scale elasticity equals 1.

maximum levels in those years as they switched to MPSS. In this context, MPSS results indicate that the risk management divisions in these banks were becoming more skilful and proficient in controlling and managing their interest rate risks. Furthermore, the results could help to determine the procedures and principles of internal supervision, including auditing and controlling activities and risk management systems that banks should establish to monitor and control the interest rate risks they are exposed to. It also helps in risk management issues by (i) defining, (ii) verifying and (iii) assessing interest rate risks that banks are exposed to, through quantitative measurements, thus lending support to equip the staff with better knowledge in risk management.

The developing financial market environment in the Asia-Pacific region yields remarkable efficiency results, with CB14 from Malaysia operating at MPSS levels in 2009 and 2011, and CB17 in 2008. This phenomenon may have been influenced by the Direct Market Access (DMA) for derivatives launched by the government to facilitate sophisticated trading strategies of trade and commerce algorithmic baskets (basket trading). This enabled the Bursa Malaysia (Stock Exchange) Derivatives to obtain reciprocal recognition of change and expand the range of derivatives products. When compared to the Philippines and Thailand, Malaysian banks are more successful in their derivatives strategy.[5] The MPSS banks also do not share a common size, which implies that it is feasible for different banks to reach MPSS at different sizes, depending on their configurations of inputs and outputs. This has been confirmed in several related studies by Paul and Kourouche (2008), Neal (2004), Avkiran (2001) and Avkiran (1999b).

Table 4.9 provides further information on the RTS detailed at individual commercial bank levels. None of the banks were consistently efficient technically for the whole six-year period. Even CB7, the highest achiever, failed to achieve TE in 2009, 2011 and 2012. Another interesting finding from Table 4.9 is the mixed nature of RTS in the years 2007–2012. In 2007, almost all banks from both country groups were operating at DRS, which is above optimal size. These results imply that all CBs, except CB7, could raise their efficiency levels by downsizing both size of the banks and hedging size activities. As stated in Avkiran (2004), a bank that is inefficient in a purely technical (PTE < 1.000) sense can still be rated as operating at CRS, also known as optimal returns to scale (ORS), as long as it is scale efficient (SE = 1.000). This rule applies to the results from 2008, 2009, 2011 and 2012, which show that the majority of banks were operating at the optimal size of CRS. Interest rate swap is used as a function of productivity to increase the performance of both outputs: (i) mortgages, corporate and commercial loans and (ii) customer deposits. This explains why Interest Rate Swap has played a successful role as one of the risk management tools which finally influence the performance of both outputs. These results are similar to that of the study by Avkiran (2004) who also found a mixed nature of RTS for Australian trading banks. Another interesting observation is that in 2010, 20 banks were operating at increasing returns to scale (IRS), indicating that they needed to enlarge their scales of operation to strive for optimal results.

Table 4.9 Nature of RTS for Individual Commercial Banks, 2007–2012

	2007	2008	2009	2010	2011	2012
Australia						
CB1	DRS	CRS	DRS	IRS	DRS	CRS
CB2	DRS	CRS	DRS	IRS	DRS	CRS
CB3	DRS	DRS	DRS	IRS	DRS	CRS
CB4	DRS	CRS	CRS	IRS	CRS	CRS
Hong Kong						
CB5	DRS	CRS	CRS	IRS	DRS	CRS
Japan						
CB6	DRS	IRS	CRS	IRS	DRS	CRS
CB7	CRS	CRS	DRS	CRS	DRS	IRS
CB8	DRS	IRS	DRS	IRS	DRS	CRS
New Zealand						
CB9	DRS	CRS	CRS	IRS	DRS	DRS
CB10	DRS	CRS	CRS	IRS	DRS	CRS
CB11	DRS	CRS	CRS	IRS	CRS	CRS
Singapore						
CB12	DRS	CRS	DRS	IRS	DRS	CRS
Taiwan						
CB13	DRS	CRS	CRS	IRS	CRS	CRS
Malaysia						
CB14	DRS	CRS	CRS	IRS	CRS	CRS
CB15	DRS	CRS	CRS	IRS	CRS	CRS
CB16	DRS	CRS	CRS	IRS	DRS	CRS
CB17	DRS	CRS	CRS	IRS	CRS	CRS
Philippines						
CB18	DRS	CRS	CRS	IRS	CRS	CRS
Thailand						
CB19	DRS	CRS	CRS	IRS	CRS	CRS
CB20	DRS	CRS	CRS	IRS	CRS	CRS
CB21	DRS	CRS	CRS	IRS	CRS	CRS

Notes: IRS = Increasing returns to scale, CRS = Constant returns to scale also known as ORS = Optimal returns to scale, and DRS = Decreasing returns to scale.

4.6.4 Peer analysis

As shown in Table 4.10, in order to be more efficient, each underachieving DMU is recommended to refer to other efficient DMUs, known as peers. The efficient peers can be more than one bank that uses input and efficiency to mitigate risk.

Table 4.10 Peers and Peer Weights

Banks	Variable	Original Value	Radial Movement	Slack Movement	Projected Value	Listing of Peers	Lambda Weight
CB1	Output 1	17.597	0.000	0.000	17.597	CB1	1.000
	Output 2	11.521	0.000	0.000	11.521		
	Input 1	11.576	0.000	0.000	11.576		
CB2	Output 1	17.596	0.000	0.000	17.596	CB16	0.062
	Output 2	11.483	0.000	0.000	11.483	CB1	0.938
	Input 1	11.631	−0.062	0.000	11.569	CB7	0.000
CB3	Output 1	17.596	0.000	0.000	17.596	CB1	0.728
	Output 2	11.355	0.000	0.000	11.355	CB8	0.004
	Input 1	11.586	−0.033	0.000	11.533	CB16	0.268
CB4	Output 1	17.596	0.000	0.000	17.596	CB8	0.001
	Output 2	10.883	0.000	0.025	10.908	CB16	0.999
	Input 1	11.635	−0.164	0.000	11.470		
CB5	Output 1	17.596	0.000	0.000	17.596	CB16	0.850
	Output 2	11.000	0.000	0.000	11.000	CB1	0.150
	Input 1	11.629	−0.144	0.000	11.484	CB7	0.000
CB6	Output 1	17.596	0.000	0.000	17.596	CB16	1.000
	Output 2	10.848	0.000	0.060	10.908	CB7	0.000
	Input 1	11.564	−0.096	0.000	11.468		
CB7	Output 1	16.903	0.000	0.000	16.903	CB7	1.000
	Output 2	11.010	0.000	0.000	11.010		
	Input 1	10.537	0.000	0.000	10.537		
CB8	Output 1	17.640	0.000	0.000	17.640	CB8	1.000
	Output 2	10.980	0.000	0.000	10.980		
	Input 1	13.130	0.000	0.000	13.130		
CB9	Output 1	17.597	0.000	0.000	17.597	CB1	0.112
	Output 2	10.978	0.000	0.000	10.978	CB8	0.017
	Input 1	11.567	−0.059	0.000	11.508	CB16	0.871
CB10	Output 1	17.596	0.000	0.000	17.596	CB8	0.004
	Output 2	11.004	0.000	0.000	11.004	CB1	0.156
	Input 1	11.566	−0.073	0.000	11.493	CB6	0.839
CB11	Output 1	17.596	0.000	0.000	17.596	CB16	1.000
	Output 2	10.854	0.000	0.053	10.908	CB7	0.000
	Input 1	12.042	−0.574	0.000	11.468		
CB12	Output 1	17.596	0.000	0.000	17.596	CB1	0.425
	Output 2	11.168	0.000	0.000	11.168	CB16	0.575
	Input 1	11.565	−0.051	0.000	11.514	CB7	0.000
CB13	Output 1	17.596	0.000	0.000	17.596	CB16	1.000
	Output 2	10.828	0.000	0.080	10.908	CB7	0.000
	Input 1	11.499	−0.031	0.000	11.468		
CB14	Output 1	17.595	0.000	0.000	17.595	CB1	0.162
	Output 2	11.007	0.000	0.000	11.007	CB16	0.838
	Input 1	11.880	−0.395	0.000	11.485	CB7	0.001
CB15	Output 1	17.598	0.000	0.000	17.598	CB1	0.068
	Output 2	10.953	0.000	0.000	10.953	CB8	0.050
	Input 1	12.215	−0.657	0.000	11.558	CB16	0.882
CB16	Output 1	17.596	0.000	0.000	17.596	CB16	1.000
	Output 2	10.908	0.000	0.000	10.908		
	Input 1	11.468	0.000	0.000	11.468		
CB17	Output 1	17.596	0.000	0.000	17.596	CB16	1.000
	Output 2	10.865	0.000	0.043	10.908	CB7	0.000
	Input 1	12.257	−0.789	0.000	11.468		

(Continued)

Banks	Variable	Original Value	Radial Movement	Slack Movement	Projected Value	Listing of Peers	Lambda Weight
CB18	Output 1	17.596	0.000	0.000	17.596	CB16	1.000
	Output 2	10.828	0.000	0.080	10.908	CB7	0.000
	Input 1	11.565	−0.096	0.000	11.468		
CB19	Output 1	17.596	0.000	0.000	17.596	CB16	1.000
	Output 2	10.828	0.000	0.000	10.828	CB7	0.000
	Input 1	11.564	−0.096	0.080	11.468		
CB20	Output 1	17.596	0.000	0.000	17.596	CB16	1.000
	Output 2	10.828	0.000	0.000	10.908	CB7	0.000
	Input 1	11.619	−0.151	0.080	11.468		
CB21	Output 1	17.596	0.000	0.000	17.596	CB16	1.000
	Output 2	10.828	0.000	0.080	10.908	CB7	0.000
	Input 1	11.674	−0.205	0.000	11.468		

In Table 4.10, the seventh column shows the peers or benchmarking units for the corresponding DMUs. The weight of each peer is indicated in the eighth column. For instance, inefficient CB10 is peered by CB8, CB1 and CB6, which offer best reference composite benchmarks for DMU. As the summation of all lambda values (λ) in these three banks are equal to 1 (0.004, 0.156, 0.839), they are used as multiplier weights for the input levels of best banks' management practices. CB6 obtained the highest lambda value (0.839), which indicates that CB6 is the most influential benchmark.

In relation to Table 4.10, Table 4.11 shows the benchmark ranking of DMUs on the basis of frequency in reference set in 2007. Efficient DMUs are ranked according to their level of importance attributable to inefficient CB units that do not lie on the frontier. A detailed benchmarking of inefficient CBs is shown in Table 4.11. Each set is formed by the efficient CBs that are similar to the input and output levels of inefficient CBs. For example, CBs numbering 16, 7, 1, 8 and 6, appear 17, 13, 9, 6 and 1 times in the reference set, respectively. CB16 and CB7 are ranked as the two best benchmarking organisations. CB7 appear as the best frontier and to be referred to as the reference set for other inefficient CBs. Thus CB7 is considered as a superior bank as it is not only efficient but is also close to the input-output levels of inefficient DMUs in the group. Surprisingly, CB16, CB1, CB8 and CB6 were found to be inefficient with OTE scores of 0.957, 0.953, 0.838 and 0.949, respectively, while also being referred to as a reference set for other inefficient CBs. The results indicate that these CBs are adequate to be followed by other banks that wish to become efficient.

4.6.5 Slacks for inefficient commercial banks

Taking 2007 as the base year for analysis, Table 4.12 provides the input and output slacks derived from the Charnes-Cooper-Rhodes (CCR) model for

Table 4.11 Benchmark Ranking of DMUs on the Basis of Frequency in Reference Set in 2007

DMU (Banks)	OTE Score	Frequency in Reference Set	Benchmark Ranking
CB16	0.957	17	1
CB7	1.000	13	2
CB1	0.953	9	3
CB8	0.838	6	4
CB6	0.949	1	5
CB13	0.954	–	6
CB18	0.949	–	7
CB19	0.949	–	7
CB12	0.949	–	7
CB9	0.948	–	10
CB10	0.948	–	10
CB3	0.947	–	12
CB2	0.945	–	13
CB20	0.944	–	14
CB5	0.943	–	15
CB4	0.943	–	15
CB21	0.940	–	17
CB14	0.923	–	18
CB11	0.911	–	19
CB15	0.898	–	20
CB17	0.895	–	21

Note: CB18, CB19 and CB12 share the same benchmark ranking (rank 7th), CB9 and CB10 share the same benchmark ranking (rank 10th), and CB5 and CB4 share the same benchmark ranking (rank 15th). CB16, CB17 and CB1 are benchmarked in the top three rankings.

inefficient banks in order to find a solution that maximises the sum of input excesses and output shortfalls while keeping $\theta = \theta^*$. Here, the study observes that CB7 produces zero-slacks since its efficiency score is 1.000. However, slacks exist for the identified inefficient CBs found to have a shortage (missing) in output ($y1$) for CB1 and CB2, while having a shortage (missing) in output ($y2$) for the remaining inefficient CBs. These shortages are needed to push the CBs to the frontier (target).

For specific analysis, the results note that CB3 cannot reduce any inputs, but must augment the amount of customer deposits by approximately 35679. The study also observes that none is missing in input ($x1$) and output ($y1$) for inefficient CBs. However, despite a reduction in this output, the banks would not achieve efficiency. With regard to non-zero slacks for output variable ($y2$), it has been observed that 20 banks have non-zero slacks for customer deposits. This suggests that all inefficient CBs in the Asia-Pacific region need to increase customer deposits in order to show the positive impact of derivative usage and thus move on to the efficient frontier and effectiveness of interest rate swaps usage.

Table 4.12 Input-Oriented Slacks for Inefficient Banks

DMU	OTE Score	Excess (Surplus) Interest rate swap (x1)	Shortage Mortgages, corporate and commercial loans (y1)	Shortage Customer deposits (y2)
		S−(1)	S+(1)	S+(2)
CB1	0.953	0	0	20254.31
CB2	0.945	0	0	24000.16
CB3	0.947	0	0	35679.70
CB4	0.943	0	0	67691.07
CB5	0.943	0	0	61084.26
CB6	0.949	0	0	69487.29
CB7	1.000	0	0	0
CB8	0.838	0	0	67763.79
CB9	0.948	0	0	62466.56
CB10	0.948	0	0	60859.41
CB11	0.911	0	0	69165.64
CB12	0.949	0	0	50086.31
CB13	0.954	0	0	70539.85
CB14	0.923	0	0	60586.14
CB15	0.898	0	0	64084.20
CB16	0.957	0	0	66332.79
CB17	0.895	0	0	68613.63
CB18	0.949	0	0	70539.46
CB19	0.949	0	0	70536.81
CB20	0.944	0	0	70537.74
CB21	0.940	0	0	70538.45

Note: The OTE scores will determine the excess and/or shortage values.

4.6.6 *Dual weights sensitivity analysis*

Based on year 2007, CB7 was the only bank that achieved an efficient level. Thus, for undertaking a sensitivity analysis, this study explores the changes of parameters affecting the optimal solution – in this case the input efficiency results derived from the dual values provided by the efficient DMU. The projection settings for inefficient organisation projects are vital for guiding the management to improve performance (Cooper et al. 2006; Boussofiane et al. 1991).

Efficiency performance improvements were done by setting input-output projections through controlling the balancing of input utilisation with output produced. Projections for inefficient projects were calculated by using reference sets given by the DEA. For these projects, the reference set and its dual weight were given by DEA to improve efficiency scores. Dual weights were obtained from the dual model by using the *DEA-Solver* software, which runs as part of Microsoft Excel. The dual weights for input orientation DEA are shown in Table 4.13.

Table 4.13 Dual Weights for Input-Orientation DEA, 2007

Inefficient Bank	Efficient Bank
	CB7
CB1	1.046403
CB2	1.042956
CB3	1.041056
CB4	1.041014
CB5	1.041017
CB6	1.041009
CB8	1.043649
CB9	1.041061
CB10	1.04103
CB11	1.041009
CB12	1.041011
CB13	1.041009
CB14	1.040983
CB15	1.041145
CB16	1.04101
CB17	1.04101
CB18	1.041009
CB19	1.041009
CB20	1.041009
CB21	1.041009

From the reference sets given by DEA, projections for inefficient projects were measured for input orientation. The projection of CB1 for input of Interest Rate Swap in input orientation is discussed as follows. CB7 is the efficient bank that becomes a reference set for CB1 to improve its efficiency score. The mathematical formulation for the projection of any inefficient projects from the input-orientation is given as follows:

$$P = \sum_{j=1}^{n} W_{ij} X_{ij}$$

(4.14)

$$j = 1, 2, \ldots, n$$
$$i = 1, 2, \ldots, k$$

where:

P denotes the projection for input-orientation;
W_{ij} *denotes* the dual weight of inefficient project i for reference project j;
X_{ij} *denotes* the input of inefficient project i for reference project j;
n denotes the number of reference projects;
k denotes the number of inefficient projects.

To show the sensitivity analysis for CB1, the projection for input of Interest Rate Swap in the input-orientation is derived as follows:

$$= \text{(Dual Weight) CB7 (Interest Rate Swap) CB7}$$

$$= (1.046403)\ (10.5374318189242)$$

$$= 11.0264$$

The calculations of input-oriented projections for all banks are summarised in Table 4.14.

Table 4.14 Projection from Dual Weight Analysis, 2007

DMU	Score			
I/O	Data	Projection	Difference	%
CB1	0.952533			
Interest rate swap	11.57586	11.0264	−0.549469009	−4.75%
Mortgages, corporate and commercial loans	17.59652	17.68682	9.03E-02	0.51%
Customer deposits	11.52072	11.52072	0	0.00%
CB2	0.944883			
Interest rate swap	11.63115	10.99008	−0.641075363	−5.51%
Mortgages, corporate and commercial loans	17.59646	17.62857	3.21E-02	0.18%
Customer deposits	11.48277	11.48277	0	0.00%
CB3	0.94685			
Interest rate swap	11.58585	10.97006	−0.615792686	−5.32%
Mortgages, corporate and commercial loans	17.59646	17.59646	0	0.00%
Customer deposits	11.35452	11.46186	0.107343549	0.95%
CB4	0.942831			
Interest rate swap	11.63476	10.96961	−0.66514673	−5.72%
Mortgages, corporate and commercial loans	17.59574	17.59574	0	0.00%
Customer deposits	10.88277	11.46139	0.578614256	5.32%
CB5	0.943314			
Interest rate swap	11.62885	10.96965	−0.659194898	−5.67%
Mortgages, corporate and commercial loans	17.5958	17.5958	0	0.00%
Customer deposits	10.99986	11.46143	0.461569855	4.20%
CB6	0.948578			
Interest rate swap	11.56422	10.96956	−0.594660492	−5.14%
Mortgages, corporate and commercial loans	17.59566	17.59566	0	0.00%
Customer deposits	10.84828	11.46134	0.613056476	5.65%
CB7	1			
Interest rate swap	10.53743	10.53743	0	0.00%
Mortgages, corporate and commercial loans	16.90251	16.90251	0	0.00%
Customer deposits	11.00983	11.00983	0	0.00%

DMU	Score			
I/O	Data	Projection	Difference	%
CB8	0.837579			
Interest rate swap	13.12996	10.99738	−2.132578924	−16.24%
Mortgages, corporate and commercial loans	17.64028	17.64028	0	0.00%
Customer deposits	10.97998	11.4904	0.510424746	4.65%
CB9	0.948363			
Interest rate swap	11.56741	10.9701	−0.597305421	−5.16%
Mortgages, corporate and commercial loans	17.59653	17.59653	0	0.00%
Customer deposits	10.97801	11.4619	0.483899575	4.41%
CB10	0.948463			
Interest rate swap	11.56586	10.96978	−0.596073433	−5.15%
Mortgages, corporate and commercial loans	17.59602	17.59602	0	0.00%
Customer deposits	11.00403	11.46157	0.457533454	4.16%
CB11	0.910949			
Interest rate swap	12.0419	10.96956	−1.072338822	−8.91%
Mortgages, corporate and commercial loans	17.59566	17.59566	0	0.00%
Customer deposits	10.8545	11.46133	0.606835516	5.59%
CB12	0.948539			
Interest rate swap	11.56472	10.96958	−0.595133098	−5.15%
Mortgages, corporate and commercial loans	17.5957	17.5957	0	0.00%
Customer deposits	11.16833	11.46136	0.293029208	2.62%
CB13	0.953953			
Interest rate swap	11.49906	10.96956	−0.529499352	−4.60%
Mortgages, corporate and commercial loans	17.59565	17.59565	0	0.00%
Customer deposits	10.82759	11.46133	0.633745506	5.85%
CB14	0.923367			
Interest rate swap	11.87965	10.96928	−0.910368518	−7.66%
Mortgages, corporate and commercial loans	17.59521	17.59521	0	0.00%
Customer deposits	11.00696	11.46105	0.454082781	4.13%
CB15	0.898134			
Interest rate swap	12.21532	10.971	−1.244325378	−10.19%
Mortgages, corporate and commercial loans	17.59796	17.59796	0	0.00%
Customer deposits	10.95304	11.46284	0.509798344	4.65%
CB16	0.956509			
Interest rate swap	11.46834	10.96958	−0.498764237	−4.35%
Mortgages, corporate and commercial loans	17.59569	17.59569	0	0.00%
Customer deposits	10.90784	11.46135	0.553510859	5.07%
CB17	0.89493			
Interest rate swap	12.25747	10.96957	−1.287895206	−10.51%
Mortgages, corporate and commercial loans	17.59567	17.59567	0	0.00%
Customer deposits	10.86515	11.46135	0.59619704	5.49%

(Continued)

DMU		Score		
I/O	*Data*	*Projection*	*Difference*	*%*
CB18	0.948544			
Interest rate swap	11.56463	10.96956	−0.595074994	−5.15%
Mortgages, corporate and commercial loans	17.59565	17.59565	0	0.00%
Customer deposits	10.82759	11.46133	0.633737743	5.85%
CB19	0.948567			
Interest rate swap	11.56434	10.96956	−0.594783369	−5.14%
Mortgages, corporate and commercial loans	17.59565	17.59565	0	0.00%
Customer deposits	10.82765	11.46133	0.633684914	5.85%
CB20	0.94409			
Interest rate swap	11.61919	10.96956	−0.649629426	−5.59%
Mortgages, corporate and commercial loans	17.59565	17.59565	0	0.00%
Customer deposits	10.82763	11.46133	0.633703472	5.85%
CB21	0.939692			
Interest rate swap	11.67356	10.96956	−0.704003819	−6.03%
Mortgages, corporate and commercial loans	17.59565	17.59565	0	0.00%
Customer deposits	10.82761	11.46133	0.633717721	5.85%

The table above implies that the input reduction is achieved through the banks' improvement projections. Clearly, in principle, the above sensitivity analysis has provided an infinite number of improvement projections on the efficiency frontier line. The improvement projection of the original DEA models provides a practical solution, which is based on a uniform input reduction. In the context of risk management, all banks have to admit that CB7 had a strong risk management from the use of Interest Rate Swap. As discussed throughout the study, we understand that CB7 has strategised its risk management scope to ensure that the use of Interest Rate Swap plays a significant role in minimising risks as well as to maximise the firm's performance. Therefore, these projections serve as an important guide for all banks to further strategise themselves in achieving good risk management.

4.6.7 *Comparative efficiency results for banks in the developed and developing countries in the Asia-Pacific region*

Commercial banks in developing countries (Malaysia, the Philippines and Thailand) achieved higher mean scores than banks in developed countries (Australia, Hong Kong, Japan, New Zealand, Singapore and Taiwan) (see Table 4.15). These results revealed that the mean (average) OTE scores for banks in the developed countries were higher than those for banks in the developing countries in 2007, 2010 and 2012, while the means for banks

Table 4.15 Comparative Analysis based on OTE for Commercial Banks between the Developed and Developing Countries in the Asia-Pacific Region

	2007	2008	2009	2010	2011	2012
BANK/COUNTRY (DEVELOPED COUNTRIES)	*Efficiency Scores for Thirteen Banks in Developed Countries*					
Australia						
CB1	0.953	1.000	0.835	0.976	0.840	0.991
CB2	0.945	0.993	0.845	0.985	0.803	1.000
CB3	0.947	0.993	0.867	0.977	0.809	1.000
CB4	0.943	0.994	0.827	0.970	0.791	0.996
Hong Kong						
CB5	0.943	0.993	0.825	0.969	0.808	1.000
Japan						
CB6	0.949	0.960	0.827	0.970	0.799	0.994
CB7	1.000	1.000	0.843	1.000	0.836	0.974
CB8	0.838	0.890	0.813	0.954	0.757	0.994
New Zealand						
CB9	0.948	0.993	0.827	0.970	0.817	0.994
CB10	0.948	0.993	0.827	0.970	0.796	0.993
CB11	0.911	0.997	0.826	0.970	0.796	0.998
Singapore						
CB12	0.949	0.994	0.827	0.970	0.806	0.996
Taiwan						
CB13	0.954	0.995	0.822	0.969	0.783	0.984
Mean	**0.941**	**0.984**	**0.832**	**0.973**	**0.803**	**0.993**
BANK/COUNTRY (DEVELOPING COUNTRIES)	*Efficiency Scores for Eight Banks in Developing Countries*					
Malaysia						
CB14	0.923	0.988	1.000	0.969	1.000	0.974
CB15	0.898	0.970	0.854	0.970	0.781	0.969
CB16	0.957	0.990	0.825	0.970	0.803	0.969
CB17	0.895	1.000	0.824	0.970	0.803	0.986
Philippines						
CB18						
Thailand	0.949	0.993	0.827	0.970	0.795	0.993
CB19						
CB20						
CB21	0.949	0.993	0.827	0.970	0.794	0.994
Mean	0.932	0.990	0.851	0.970	0.821	0.984

in the developing countries were higher than those for banks in the developed countries in 2008, 2009 and 2011. Throughout this time, risk management efficiency of the 21 banks ranged from 0.757 to 1.000. In 2008, two banks (CB1 and CB7) from the developed countries were operating at the best practice or *efficient frontier* of technically efficiency (100%), where no wastage of inputs affected the quantity level of outputs. However, these two banks were unable to increase their mean scores in 2008 due to the lower efficiency scores of other banks in the same group. But, it is important to recognise that CB1 located in Australia and CB7 located in Japan experienced an advanced risk management strategy by using derivative instruments.

In 2007, on average, commercial banks in the developed countries had a higher TE of 0.941, compared to 0.932 for those in the developing countries. Again, CB7 contributed to the highest mean score for risk management efficiency ranking. These results were expected and further confirmed the findings in other cross-country studies (e.g. Eling and Luhnen 2010; Rai 1996). The results for 2010 and 2012 also indicate that banks in the developed countries yielded higher mean scores of 0.973 > 0.970 and 0.993 > 0.984, respectively, as compared to the banks in the developing countries in 2008, 2009 and 2011, when the mean scores were 0.990, 0.851 and 0.821, respectively.

Almost all banks in the developed and developing countries have shown a lower efficiency score in their risk management. This scenario might have been affected by the falling stock market in August 2011 when a sharp drop in overall stock market price was experienced right across the USA, Middle East, Asia and Europe. The fear of sovereign debt crises in Italy and Spain, and concerns over the slower economic growth in the USA have affected financial institutions' performances all over the world (Lane 2012). However, the results for 2007, 2008 and 2012 do not show that banks were still being affected by the global credit crunch beginning in August 2007. In fact, banks in Japan are indicated as being the most successful banks in managing risk during that period. Financial analysts believe that Japan is among the major economies that continued to pursue an aggressive monetary stimulus policy, with almost all banks being well capitalised under "crisis containment" aimed at buffering the impact of a global crisis (Nanto 2009). Their involvement in multilateral swap agreements in 2009 had sharpened their strategies for facing global financial crises. Cautious management and continuous monitoring improved their efficiency in providing the best value while managing interest rate risk. This result confirms the findings by Hahn (2008) that Japanese banks are significantly managerially efficient when compared to European and US banks.

Figure 4.4 shows that the mean efficiency of banks in the developed and developing countries falls on a narrow margin. Figure 4.4 reveals that in the developed countries with larger banks and more advanced technology, banks are not necessarily efficient in risk management. The results indicate that despite having smaller banks and less advanced technology, banks in developing countries are able to achieve TE and competency. Their efficiency

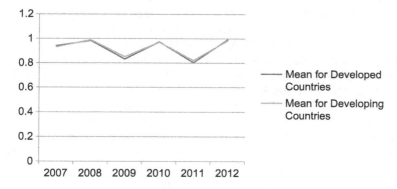

Figure 4.4 Mean OTE Score Comparison between Developed and Developing Countries in Asia-Pacific (2007–2012).

in risk management highlights the sufficiency of financial instruments in adjusting fair value changes affected by an interest rate volatility, which is attributable to both the risk being hedged and the offsetting of interest rate risk. Since 2007, the use of derivative instruments among banks in the developing countries has been playing a role as a risk management tool. Consequently, the use of technology and highly skilled personnel can be seen to be the main factors that contribute to the risk management of these banks, indicating that in both the developed and developing countries, the performances of banks are comparable, particularly for OTE. These findings are in contrast to the assumption that banks in developed countries are larger, and thereby more efficient than banks in developing countries, thus providing a different direction to the study by Drake and Hall (2003), which empirically found a strong relationship between bank size and TE.

In short, under OTE, PTE and SE assumptions, banks in developed and developing countries exhibit narrow margins of difference in levels of efficiency. Therefore, this study further determines that banks from the same population in the developed and developing countries have significant differences based on the country status and background.

4.6.8 *DEA-based test results (robustness)*

The results show that the development level and status of a country[6] affects the efficiency of risk management in banks (Section 4.6.6). From the DEA evaluation, it appears that banks in developed countries are more capable in financial structuring and play more effective roles when using derivatives, particularly in the banking sector. However, due to the growth of derivatives in developing countries (Njoroge et al. 2013; Mihaljek and Packer 2010) and the inconclusive evidence of relationships between the derivative market and economic growth in these countries (Haiss and Sammer 2010; Baluch and Ariff 2007), further tests need to be conducted. For this reason, the hypotheses H1, H2 and H3 are used to further strengthen and confirm previous evidence from the DEA results. Thus, a DEA-based test analysis is performed to provide evidence to support the third question of this study.

Following Ahmad and Rahman (2012), Havrylchyk (2006) and Isik and Hassan (2002), the DEA based analysis in this study performs a number of parametric (*t*-test) and non-parametric (Wilcoxon Rank-Sum, Kruskal–Wallis, and Kolmogorov–Smirnov) tests to confirm the null hypothesis that all banks come from the same population. The first main test aims at comparing the efficiency scores across 21 commercial banks in the Asia-Pacific region, with an emphasis on efficiency comparison between the developed and developing countries in the same region.

A probability of the *p*-value difference explains that a value lower than 0.05 ($p \leq 0.05$) indicates strong evidence for differences in group scores. The cut-off point of 0.05 is used as a level of significance, which is an acceptable percentage for determining whether the tests are statistically significant between both groups, with the first test of differences shown in Table 4.16 as (i) a parametric *t*-test and (ii) the non-parametric Mann–Whitney (Wilcoxon) and Kruskal–Wallis tests. Table 4.17 presents the Kolmogorov–Smirnov test in which each hypothesis is tested using panel regression to evaluate the following hypotheses:

Hypothesis 1:

$H_0 1$: The OTE of banks in developing countries is lower than or equal to that in developed countries.

$H_a 1$: The OTE of banks in developing countries is higher than that in developed countries.

Hypothesis 2:

$H_0 2$: The PTE of banks in developing countries is lower than or equal to that in developed countries.

$H_a 2$: The PTE of banks in developing countries is higher than that in developed countries.

Hypothesis 3:

$H_0 3$: The SE of banks in developing countries is lower than or equal to that in developed countries.

$H_a 3$: The SE of banks in developing countries is higher than that in developed countries.

4.6.8.1 *Mann–Whitney U-test result*

In Table 4.16, the Mann–Whitney test is used to evaluate the hypotheses in which the results indicate that based on OTE (64.56 > 61.78) and PTE (68.16 > 55.93), banks' ownership in the developed countries scores higher than banks in developing countries, but have lower mean ranks for SE (57.68 < 72.96). It appears that PTE does not significantly differ in both groups.

Table 4.16 Summary of Parametric and Non-Parametric Tests on Banks in the Developed and Developing Countries in the Asia-Pacific Region

	Parametric test		Non-Parametric Test			
Individual test	*t*-test		Mann–Whitney		Kruskal–Wallis	
Hypothesis			Median		Equality of Populations test	
Test statistics	$t(Prb > t)$		$z(Prb > z)$		$X^2(Prb > X^2)$	
	Mean	T	Mean Rank	z	Mean Rank	X^2
OTE						
Developed Countries	0.921	0.221	64.56	−0.415	64.56	0.172
Developing Countries	0.924		61.78		61.78	
PTE						
Developed Countries	0.948	−0.749	68.16	−1.834*	68.16	3.365*
Developing Countries	0.937		55.93		55.93	
SE						
Developed Countries	0.973	2.317**	57.68	−2.451**	57.68	6.006**
Developing Countries	0.987		72.96		72.96	

Notes:
i   Developed countries include 13 banks from six Asia-Pacific countries. Developing countries include eight banks from three Asia-Pacific countries.
ii $t = 2.317$ shows a significant difference because the value in the 'Sig. (2-tailed)' row is .022, which is less than 0.05.
iii   (***), (**) and (*) indicate significance at the 1%, 5% and 10% levels, respectively.

Here, there is sufficient evidence to reject the null hypothesis, which implies that banks in the developed countries do not efficiently utilise their resources in an exogenous environment. However, OTE does not show significant results nor provide evidence to support the claim that the ownership or country location influences the levels of risk management efficiency in banks. These efficiency levels are determined based on the performance of the banks. This can be seen by the SE mean rank for banks in the developing countries, which was found to be statistically significant and higher than for banks in the developed countries ($p = 0.014$). This result enhances the levels of understanding for guiding banks in both the developed and developing countries. Banks in both country types need to concentrate on their scale size in order to boost their levels of performance, particularly when incorporating derivative instruments in their risk management strategy.

4.6.8.2 t-Test

Table 4.16 shows the results for the parametric *t*-test and non-parametric Mann–Whitney (Wilcoxon) tests. Under the parametric test, banks in the developed countries have higher mean scores for OTE and PTE. Even though mean scores for banks in the developing countries are higher than those for banks in the developed countries in OTE, it is not significant. The same result was found for PTE, with higher mean scores for banks in the developing countries, but the differences are not significant. However, the result also shows that the mean value for banks in the developed countries in terms of SE is 0.973 which is lower than that for banks in the developing countries with a mean value of 0.987, showing a 1% level of significance. This result indicates that banks in the developing countries have significantly higher scales of efficiency, which implies that regardless of size, all the eight banks in the developing countries are operating at their optimal levels (MPSS). In relation to the risk management efficiency context, banks' sizes and strategies in risk management are currently competent to face market risk.

4.6.8.3 Kruskal–Wallis test result

The Kruskal–Wallis test yields the same results as the Mann–Whitney test, with statistically significant differences between the bank groups in the developed and developing countries. The results indicate that PTE is statistically not significant, which implies that the analysis provide sufficient evidence to reject the null hypothesis and claim that the PTE performances of banks in the developing countries are lower than those of the banks in the developed countries. On the contrary, banks in the developing countries have an SE average rank of 72.96, compared to 57.68 for banks in the developed countries, where the *p*-value of SE is less than the cut-off point (0.05). Since the results provide insufficient evidence, at $\alpha = 0.05$, the study rejects the null hypothesis (H_03). The SE result posits that distributions differ according to the geographical location of banks, which indicates that banks in the developing countries performed better than those in the developed countries.

As shown in Table 4.16, the PTE and SE tests of difference between banks in the developed and developing countries were found as not being consistent and not of the same order over the three types of differences. However, it was found that banks in the developing countries group are more efficient and outperformed their counterparts in the developed countries in SE scores with a statistical significance of a *p*-value at less than 0.05. These results do not support the stated assumption (no significant difference) that banks located in developed countries are more efficient than banks in developing countries.

Turning again to country type, this study assumed that banks in the developing countries that were said to be more scale efficient when they proved that their size of risk management operations is optimal. With the enhancement of regulatory power in their internal control and risk management, it indicates that their banks have a good coordination and control with regard to financial risks (e.g. Greuning and Bratanovic 1999). Indirectly, the results reveal that the optimal SE obtained by banks located in the developing countries can provide both resilience to withstand adverse events and the ability to take advantage of development opportunities. For example, banks in Thailand have found that the establishment in their financial risk management was contributed by the risk management's seven critical success factors, based on the Standards Australia and Standards New Zealand (2004). These success factors have contributed significantly to providing sound financial risk management strategies. A study by Ranong and Phuenngam (2009) confirmed that these critical success factors can be used to support the theory for effective risk management procedures in financial industries from the perspective of financial institutions in Thailand. This shows how critical success factors influence the risk management environment, as suggested by risk management theory. Based on this argument, the evidence shown in Table 4.16 supports both the stakeholder and finance theories, which renewed attention to the issue of maximising benefit for stakeholders, as well as supporting the model of financial risks. Moreover, *Bank Negara Malaysia* (the central bank of Malaysia) has encouraged financial institutions in Malaysia to establish a well-resourced independent risk management strategy and take pro-active measures to fully embrace all aspect of financial risks. These initiatives have created a robust risk management framework for Malaysian banks (e.g. Aziz 2016).

By showing the integration between the results and theoretical issues, it helps all investigated banks to refine their risk management framework as well as guide them on the amount of hedging activity undertaken. This will help risk management managers to highly consider advance risk management strategies and drive their efficiency improvements.

4.6.8.4 *Kolmogorov–Smirnov (K–S) test*

As an alternative to the Mann–Whitney and Kruskal–Wallis tests, a Kolmogorov–Smirnov (K–S) test is used to compare whether the two samples are sensitive to differences in both country locations. This study uses a significance level of 0.05, and because p-value is less than 0.05 ($p < 0.05$), the null hypothesis is rejected, which points to a significant difference between the developed and developing countries in the Asia-Pacific region.

Contrary to expectations, Table 4.17 reveals that OTE and SE scores are significant, and therefore the null hypothesis (H3) is rejected. This indicates that there is no difference between banks in the developed and developing countries in measuring risk management efficiency performance. The findings indicate that neither banks in the developing nor developed countries provide any significant impact in measuring TE and SE.

In Table 4.18, the *t*-test indicates that SE is significant; the Mann–Whitney test indicates that PTE and SE are significant; and the K–S test indicates that OTE and SE are significant. For SE, all tests imply the presence of scale inefficiency among banks in the developing countries in the Asia-Pacific region, indicating that the null hypothesis can be rejected – thus confirming the presence of a scale inefficiency that is not influenced by scales and country locations of the banks. Referring to H1 and H2 discussed above (see page 159), both OTE and PTE may support the common view that banks in the developing countries are lower in terms of risk management efficiency than banks in the developed countries. On the other hand, the testing has lead us to reject the null hypothesis (H3), thus proving the SE of banks in developing countries is lower than it is in developed countries.

Overall, the study accepted the proposition that SE levels of banks in the developing countries are higher than those in the developed countries. However, the findings show that there is no significant difference between the developing and developed countries in terms of OTE and PTE. However, both OTE and PTE scores are inconclusive. These results are in contrast with

Table 4.17 Kolmogorov–Smirnov (K–S) Test

Kolmogorov–Smirnov $$Z = max_j \lvert d_j \rvert \sqrt{\dfrac{n_{1,f} n_{2,f}}{n_{1,f} + n_{2,f}}}$$	OTE	PTE	SE
Exact Sig.	0.734	1.529	1.214
D (*prob > D*)	0.654**	0.019	0.105**

Note: (***), (**) and (*) denote significance at the 1%, 5% and 10% levels, respectively. Exact Sig. = exact *p*-value.

Table 4.18 A summary of Hypothesis Testing Results from the Parametric *t*-test and the Non-Parametric Mann–Whitney, Kruskal–Wallis and Kolmogorov–Smirnov Tests

Test	OTE	Hypothesis Test	PTE	Hypothesis Test	SE	Hypothesis Test
t-test	Not Significant	Fail to Reject	Not Significant	Fail to Reject	Significant	Reject
Mann–Whitney	Not Significant	Fail to Reject	Significant	Reject	Significant	Reject
Kruskal–Wallis	Not Significant	Fail to Reject	Significant	Reject	Significant	Reject
Kolmogorov–Smirnov	Significant	Reject	Not Significant	Fail to Reject	Significant	Reject

previous findings (e.g. Sufian 2007a; Havrylchyk 2006; Bonin et al. 2005) that compare efficiencies between domestic banks in developing countries and foreign banks from developed countries. As these studies found that foreign banks are more scale efficient than domestic banks in all tests, the findings of the present study must be seen as inconclusive. Furthermore, in measuring the relationships between bank size and efficiency levels, both theoretical and empirical studies have found them to be ambiguous (Beck 2008; Beck et al. 2006). Thus, in accordance with Zhang et al. (2009), a combination of parametric and non-parametric tests can provide robust efficiency differences in banks in both country types by adequately providing normality to the valuation biases of arguments.

Regression analysis as a robustness check

In order to gain more insights into assessing the differences between two different groups (of countries), this study follows Shawtari (2014) and Beck et al. (2013) by running a regression analysis. In the present study, this method is used to find robust differences between banks in the three developing and six developed countries to confirm the DEA-based test findings. This analysis is intended to harmonise the differences in banks of both the developed and developing countries. The following regression models are used to investigate the differences between these banks:

i $OTE_{it} = \alpha + \beta_1 DVed_{it} + \varepsilon$ (4.15)

where OTE is a measure of the overall technical efficiency of bank i in period t when $DVed$ is the dummy, taking $DVed$ for developed countries and ε as an error term for the variable.

ii $OTE_{it} = \alpha + \beta_1 DVing_{it} + \varepsilon$ (4.16)

where OTE is a measure of overall technical efficiency of bank i in period t when $DVing$ is the dummy, taking $DVing$ for developing countries and ε as an error term for the variable.

iii $PTE_{it} = \alpha + \beta_1 DVed_{it} + \varepsilon$ (4.17)

where PTE is a measure of the pure technical efficiency of bank i in period t when $DVed$ is the dummy, taking $DVed$ for developed countries and ε as an error term for the variable.

i $PTE_{it} = \alpha + \beta_1 DVing_{it} + \varepsilon$ (4.18)

where PTE is a measure of the pure technical efficiency of bank i in period t when $DVing$ is the dummy, taking $DVing$ for developing countries and ε as an error term for the variable.

Table 4.19 shows the coefficient results for banks in the developed countries, with an estimated standard error of 0.0143, t-statistic of -0.2212 and *p*-value of 0.8253. At a significant level $\alpha = .05$ as $p > 0.05$, it is therefore statistically not significant. This result confirms the previous findings reported in Tables 4.14 and 4.15 in which commercial banks in the developed countries are shown to underperform compared to banks in the developing countries in terms of OTE. As a result, this analysis rejects the null hypothesis of OTE (Section 4.6.7).

As presented in Table 4.20, the coefficient of X for banks in the developing countries has an estimated standard error of 0.0145, *t*-statistic of 0.7226 and *p*-value of 0.4713. At a significant level $\alpha = 0.05$ as $p > 0.05$, this result is also statistically not significant, confirming the previous findings reported in Tables 4.14 and 4.15 in which commercial banks in the developed countries are shown to underperform compared to banks in the developing countries in terms of PTE. These regression results make intuitive sense and are generally robust, in agreement with Shawtari (2014) and Beck et al. (2013). As a result, this analysis rejects the null hypothesis of PTE.

It is often assumed that banks in the developed countries are more competent in managing their risk due to their strengths in human resources, technologies and risk management systems. However, the above results provide evidence that some banks in the developed countries have weaker risk management efficiency levels due to interest rate derivative usage in achieving effective and efficient risk management strategies for hedging purposes. This could be the case with many banks in the developed countries including Singapore, New Zealand and Taiwan, where the hedging instrument has had little impact in achieving high risk management efficiency despite benefiting from high economic growth and better economic

Table 4.19 Results for Test of Statistical Significance (Regression Coefficient) on OTE

	Coeff.	Stand. Error	t Stat	P-value
Intercept	0.924541667	0.011274303	82.00433	6.960748709
Banks in Developed Countries	−0.003169872	0.014329389	−0.22121	0.825289105

Table 4.20 Results for Test of Statistical Significance (Regression Coefficient) on PTE

	Coeff.	Stand. Error	t Stat	P-value
Intercept	0.937125	0.011380355	82.34584907	4.19614232
Banks in Developing Countries	0.010451923	0.014464179	0.722607428	0.4712818

banking performance than banks in developing markets. For instance, greater economic growth can lead to enriched access to funding for banks. Due to their developed economic status, Singapore's, New Zealand's and Taiwan's banks have greater capacity to articulate a vision of their development, obtain solid commitment of their member countries to their mission and vision, and have the ability to mobilise external resources based on their institutional strengths, both financial and administrative. But, in the context of risk management, the results of this study indicate a less competitive financial derivative usage in providing positive impacts on risk management efficiency levels. However, the rationale for hedging and the impact of a hedging instrument on risk management does not represent the performances of all banks.

In short, OTE and PTE scores of the banks are not influenced by the country's economic status and background, except SE. It means that the success of risk management in banks depends on their strategies in handling market risk.

4.7 Verification and validation of the model

Confirming to the validation process in McCarl and Spreen (1997, 2011), the procedure in this study is validated according to the theory of efficiency measurements using non-parametric procedures. As explained in Section 4.4.2, the integrated model was developed based on the DEA and DOR approaches. Verification of the model was supported by Chen and McGinnis (2007) who endorsed that conventional ratio analysis based on a DEA approach can enhance conventional ratio analysis applied in the DOR method, particularly in establishing the input-output ratio performance gap.

Based on DEA efficiency results, the integration of DEA-DOR model is behaving satisfactorily. These sets of analyses are important in the decision-making by different parties including bankers, investors, managerial personnel, etc. Finally, in order to provide valid measurements, this study includes realistic input and output variables representing the risk management context within the derivatives usage framework. The relationship between interest rate swaps and hedged items shows the close relationship in managing risks. Other derivative instruments have been excluded since no solid relationship has been indicated. Therefore, a realistic constraint is employed to ensure that this study attempts to offer more accurate and reliable empirical results.

4.8 Implications

The results of this study help to shed light on several valuable conclusions, particularly that an integrated approach between a DOR of hedge effectiveness test and a DEA method using derivative based instrument is suitable for measuring banks' risk management efficiency.

Due to complexities in the implementation of hedge accounting and its measurements based on hedge effectiveness, the integrated model between a DOR and DEA provides the decision to support risk management efficiency measures and strategies. In helping banks to integrate derivative elements in their risk management policies, the outcomes of this study address the research problems by providing strategies that assist in minimising potential risks in an organisation. The implications of this study are important for areas that include (i) a theoretical and methodological approach in risk management efficiency measures, (ii) risk assessment embedded in supporting banks' risk management frameworks, (iii) derivative measures, (iv) hedge accounting policies and hedging size adjustments, (v) predictions on portfolio management and monitoring and (vi) regulatory policy reforms in cross-country operations. The following subsections elaborate on the expected advantages from adapting a DEA model to further justify its use for measuring the risk management efficiency of derivatives in this study.

4.8.1 Theoretical and methodological approaches in risk management efficiency measures

The literature (Section 4.3), with more than two decades of research and work with risk measurement in banks, has shown that there are a number of common risk factors in investigating banks' efficiency. However, the majority of efficiency studies have ignored the role played by using a risk management tool for measuring the efficiency of risk management. Even though companies have used many different strategies in risk management including insurance, derivatives and diversifications, the problem of whether the implementation of these strategies has been measured efficiently or not, has been neglected. Previous researchers have focussed on accounting ratio elements, without any concern for its risk management indication, while ignoring the derivative instrument indications. This can lead to confusion and misinterpretation of true measurements of performance levels. Therefore, this methodological implication shows the need to systematically incorporate a measurement approach in the context of risk management.

An important methodological implication of this study lies in the fact that it systematically incorporates the DOR and DEA measurement approaches in the context of risk management. This study expands the multidisciplinary boundaries within both hedge accounting and operational research for DEA by proposing financial derivatives usage as a means of risk management. By introducing the DEA approach, the DOR measurement analysis can be improved by the involvement of mathematical programming in order to organise the ratios into aggregate measures of efficiency. This can lead to a better measurement approach, which helps avoid incorrect judgements and misclassifications.

Although the DEA method used in this study is not new, this approach is synthesised in novel ways that have not been previously attempted.

In particular, the analysis started by identifying risk management efficiency measurements using the DEA model based on hedge accounting. The DEA optimisation model was then integrated with the traditional DOR, using an optimisation technique to secure the best possible hedging instrument design for bank's risk management decision-making. The DOR analysis was chosen for this purpose as its method of formulating derivatives as the hedging instrument for monitoring the hedged items, can complement the DEA approach. The DOR is also a significant tool for measuring the efficiency of risk management in banks. But given the limitations of this method, this study formulates a non-parametric approach to use as a powerful and robust technique for measuring the efficiency levels of risk management in banks (Grosskopf 1996; Asmild et al. 2007; Casu and Molyneux 2003).

4.8.2 Risk assessment embedded in supporting the banks' risk management framework

In contrast to the perception that derivatives usage increases risk exposure in banks, the impact of the volatility of interest rates is examined on hedged items (further discussed in Section 4.7.4) to capture an important message for supporting banks' risk management frameworks. This assessment provides a mechanism to show how the derivative instrument can be considered as an important factor in operational and strategic planning for risk management. As most finance studies have noted, these derivative instruments cannot be separated (Cebenoyan and Strahan 2004; McNeil et al. 2005). Analysis of the efficiency of risk management using these instruments has been prompted by the need to assess the extent to which banks are able to deal with the increasing complexity of the external risk environment. In these cases, cautious management and continuous monitoring can improve efficiency and best value for managing any interest rate risk (Ahmed et al. 1997; Berkman et al. 1997). Despite the wide choice of available instruments, the use of derivatives as an option for managing risk in this study has offered an important alternative for measuring how banks perform in managing risk and implementing strategic plans for risk treatment and control. Using derivatives in risk management efficiency, this study predicts that banks' risk management frameworks can gain respectable performances when they recognise the different implications of business outcomes and performance while driving value creation. Increasing the usage of interest rate swaps as one of the tools for continually reviewing banks' risk management is an important part of the process of ongoing monitoring and assessment. However, banks' risk management may vary with the usage of interest rate swap performance. When banks have achieved perfect efficiency levels (100%), they will portray and document that the derivatives have responded effectively in risk management, thus indirectly enhancing their output growth and economic well-being significantly.

The shift of risk management measurement in this study emphasises to some extent the role of banks as financial intermediaries (Allen and Santomero 1998; Cornett and Saunders 2003). Each bank that has successfully achieved risk management efficiency scores in this study has not only been efficient in using their financial derivative instruments, but has also been assured of reducing not only the effect of risk, but has also enhanced its international competitiveness and economic prosperity. For the remaining less efficient banks, they may face remarkable challenges in re-allocating their purchasing of hedging derivatives. Here, the process of risk management evaluation, particularly for measuring the efficiency levels of banks in the Asia-Pacific region, has provided a substantial number of re-evaluations for both efficient and less efficient banks. It is also worth noting here that the proper supervision of derivatives as risk management tools can enhance our understanding of the attitude of banks as financial intermediaries towards risk management. This is important for supporting a more efficient governance structure, enhancing efficiency of the operations carried out by specialist risk groups, and establishing clear reporting and monitoring frameworks. These results strongly indicate the need for better mechanisms to monitor the performance of the loan and interest rate movements in banks.

4.8.3 Derivative measures in the financial context

On the basis of the survey and evidence of the empirical results, hedging strategy using interest rate swaps can be a value-enhancing activity that matches the efficiency of risk management in commercial banks. This implication might offer another motivation where derivatives act as a reduction tool in lowering the volatility of taxable income (Smith and Stulz 1985), reducing underinvestment problem (Lin et al. 2008; Myers 1977; Bessembinder 1991) and avoiding unnecessary fluctuations either in external funding or in investment spending (Froot et al. 1993). In managing access to the company's capital, financial executives are becoming increasingly important for financial derivatives to reduce risk while minimising the cost of capital. Therefore, the interest rate swaps used in this study were tested very carefully using a DEA approach to ensure that its usage meets the goals of risk management and can be used as risk parameters in banks, especially when the funding decisions are made in the event of high market interest rates.

The integration of derivative instrument with risk management also helps banks in planning the amount of borrowed funds. There is also the profitability that banks would be affected if rises in interest rate result in lesser borrowing and investment. Banks typically have a lot of government bonds and other long-term assets (example: loans given to corporations) in their portfolio, while their liabilities are predominantly short-term (example: deposits made by individuals ranging from one to five years). Hence, in order to address the risk resulting from the asset-liability mismatch, they generally use interest rate financial instruments to hedge their exposure to interest rate volatility. As this study evaluates interest rate swap as a financial tool to investigate the risk management performance of commercial banks, it shows that hedging strategies are able to reduce financial volatilities in securing forecasted (long-term) financial positions. This method recognises that hedging strategy can determine future financial performance of firms and avoid potential threats to firms (Miller and Waller 2003), so it can be considered as an essential element in formulating a bank's financial risk management strategy. Therefore, when banks used derivatives to manage risks, these instruments result in more stable banking institutions.

As this study uses derivatives as an input for analysis, it provides an alternative solution and mechanism to investors (banks) that can help them in investment decision-making. The results from the efficiency analysis using a DEA approach are hopefully of help in directing hedging decisions to ensure that banks are able to avoid unnecessary fluctuations.

4.8.4 Hedge effectiveness in hedge accounting policies, and hedging size adjustment

As this study uses the intermediation approach to highlight its role in strategically managing the risk of interest rates, the management of the hedging instruments to manage the exposure of the interest rate and exchange rate risk must reflect the concept of risk management efficiency. The assistance provided to banks is not just in assisting in documentation, testing of hedge effectiveness, reporting and disclosure, and accounting techniques for future value and cash flow, but include the strategic perspective on how to use derivatives to reduce business risk. In other words, a bank's hedge accounting policy report should sufficiently consider risk control and monitoring functions, including the administration of interest rate risk management. These concerns have been addressed by Kawaller (2004) when he realised that one of the shortcomings in hedge accounting practice is when the analyst's assessment has not been influenced by risk management concepts. The variability of hedge effectiveness measurement distorts the reality when insufficient information on risk management elements of a firm leads to a less credible assessment, affecting the performance of the whole firm.

For hedging size adjustment, the results of this study also show that the overall derivative instrument has a huge impact on risk management in banks. In the sample period of 2007, commercial banks in Australia and Japan (developed countries) and in Malaysian banks (a developing country) have achieved significant impact on interest rate swap to hedged items. However, the results reveal that all banks have performed under the region of DRS. It means that for all periods the operating size of the hedging instrument is considered "big and grown largely" within established banks. However, since a study covering the entire activities of the banking institutions is beyond the scope of this study, the nature of RTS is only concentrated on the scope of hedging instrument. Banks are advised (if possible) to reduce their derivative usages in order to spur risk management efficiency levels (Table 4.12). This examination helps hedging strategies, both in relation to the scope of effectiveness and efficiency, which can be tested for hedge effectiveness either at the inception or during the actual effectiveness test, and assists in minimising ineffectiveness issues by offsetting the exposure to changes in the hedged item. Consequently, the potential downsize of interest rate risk changes would be addressed via the hedge accounting measurement.

Therefore, these banks, especially commercial banks in Thailand and the Philippines are advised to reduce their hedging size and firm value to boost their risk management efficiency level. This suggestion, is consistent with the intuition and increased confidence of Lin et al. (2012) and Guay and Kothari (2003) who strongly believed that the hedging amount has a positive relationship with firm size. With an increase in hedging size, banks will achieve better risk management, and consequently reduce the negative impact on the hedged items. Improving risk management in this manner will increase firm value by reducing the cost of financial distress or under-investment problem (Purnanandam 2008; Jin and Jorion 2007; Borokhovich et al. 2004). In addition, the DRS region may have also been affected by the global financial crisis in 2007. In a study by Zeitun and Banjelloun (2012) of banks in Jordan during the 2007 financial crisis, similar results have been found with the majority of banks operating under the region of DRS, where the financial crisis was found to have a significant impact on the banking performance. The claim also has been supported by Sufian (2010) where he also found that all banks in the sample did not perform well during the financial crisis in 1997.

4.8.5 Prediction on portfolio management and monitoring policies and actions

Based on the findings of this study, under the intermediation approach, on average, all commercial banks in Australia and Japan successfully manage the fluctuation of market risk. Performance efficiency is not threatened by interest rate uncertainty, especially for CB3 (Australia) and CB7 (Japan). Almost all OTE, PTE and SE achieved an absolute efficiency score (100%). On average, these commercial banks are scale-efficient, technically and holistically efficient. In the Australian context, these outstanding results were attributed to the core principles for effective banking supervision implemented in 2001 that provided for asset securitisations and derivative instruments effectiveness under its scope.

The involvement of Australian financial institutions in derivative trading with an unknown degree of risk has been a cause of concern for the government as it could cause sudden implosion within the Australian financial sector. For instance, as explained by the government regulations imposed in the Australian Prudential Regulation Authority (APRA) 2010, four main (largest) banks in Australia (National Australia Bank, Commonwealth Bank, Westpac, and Australia and New Zealand Banking Group) have to meet strict criteria of risk governance and risk modelling. APRA has prescribed the criteria for risk weights to assess the performances of banks based on direct observation of characteristics on each exposure, where the assessment is predominantly in the form of corporate credit commitments, interest rate and foreign exchange derivatives. As a result, all Australian banks that have been analysed in this study have proven that they have experienced rapid development in their estimates of exposure probability of default and loss given default. Given the selectivity of hedging activities that may reflect economically insignificant results, a combination of the dynamics of the market and innovation in banking, the usage of derivative instruments will certainly ensure risk management effectiveness. The results also indicate that there are good structures in place in the Australian banking sector for controlling interest rate risk and effectively dealing with associated risks. The study also finds that appropriate procedures and policies are established to control and limit interest rate risk. The portfolio management and monitoring initiatives are "intended to realise the organisation's strategy in order to maximise business benefits, and each is undertaken with a certain level of risks and constraints" (Rajegopal 2012, 67). Here, all the main banks in Australia have increased the ability of their management to control risk factors, increase their capital and have responded successfully to global changes. As a result, the total capital ratio in Australian financial institutions rose by 1.3% from 2008 to 2010. This study believes that apart from reducing the dependency on government control, the Australian banking sector has achieved high performance and growth by following the guidelines and strict governance criteria.

In the context of Japanese banks, on average, their risk management efficiency estimations have shown that they are worst among the developed countries. The results may be affected by various factors including high NPL ratios in the 1990s whereby the period has shown NPL (9.0%) in the peak time until the Japanese government had to be involved in capital injection of about 12 trillion yen. According to Lonien (2003), the issue of poor risk management estimations are far under-developed compared to Western principles. The abundance of bad loans and over-capacity issues in Japanese banks over the years has contributed to the under-development of the banking institutions in Japan. The situation even worsened with the lack of domestic depositors' confidence in their financial market. Therefore, in order to implement proper future asset and liability management, the supervisory authorities should stress the importance of risk management by actively promoting financial literacy and encouraging market innovation in risk management tools and techniques.

In contrast to Australian banks, Malaysian commercial banks are less efficient in their risk management. The implementation of macro hedging to reduce the impact of market interest rate on the' assets and liabilities on the entire balance sheet of banks are not significantly responsive. Hence, observations on risk management policy and practice in the Australian banking sector are needed to maintain the flexibility of financial derivatives and create strong preferences for mitigating the behaviour of interest rate risk. The same indications can also be applied in other developing countries like the Philippines and Thailand. Even though these two countries, including Malaysia have experienced major interest rate movements during the economic crisis (1999–2000), they have a great potential to succeed because of their capabilities of monitoring and managing their risk in a timely manner. As evidenced, with limited financial assistance from the government, they managed to resolve the financial hardship quite rapidly, and subsequently ironed out the impact of the financial crisis.

This integrated model provides a strategic direction to develop strong decision-making strategies for the commercial banks to enhance their actions and risk management policies. This model offers a platform for the commercial banks to react to the interest rate movements and assist in assembling a better risk management policy, particularly in reducing the impact of changes in the interest rate. In addition, as an organisation, the model hopes to contribute to good corporate governance with good organisational design (structure) specialising in monitoring action in achieving profitability and growth, particularly within the interest rate risk boundaries.

4.8.6 Regulatory policy reform in cross-country operations

Most of the banking efficiency studies (e.g. Sharma et al. 2013; Drake et al. 2006) address the issue of regulatory policies across countries. However, these studies generally investigate external regulatory factors to see their impact on the efficiency of banks. For example, building effective regulatory policy reforms for banks in the developing countries can be addressed by the issue of TE design. In this case, the DEA efficiency measurement assesses the efficiency of risk management modelling that not only impacts on the quality of hedging instrument in measuring risk management performance, but also refers to the governance issue as a cause for cross-country productivity. Indirectly, the DEA implementation involving derivative instrument differs from these previous studies as it concentrates on risk management efficiency and regulatory policy reforms across countries.

The evidence of comparative analysis of this study seems to point to the fact that the roles of derivatives in banks' risk management in developed countries, such as Australia and Japan are more effective compared to developing countries. Supported by a banking sector that counts among the most stable and sound financial system in the world (ranked 4th by the global competitiveness 2011–2012), Australia's regulatory and policy reform has succeeded in making the anticipated impact on successful risk management strategies, where the banking sector has experienced significant growth with continuing financial innovation and appetite for new financial instruments. The active responses to trading activities, market conditions, capital controls and trade executions have contributed to the significant impact of derivatives in the financial landscape in Australia. The influence of floating exchange rates has also stabilised the interest rate whereby both elements are translated into fiscal policy and economic activity. Indirectly, policymakers of financial institutions face unpredictable consequences.

This scenario was handled well by the Australian banking sector with the involvement of interest rate swaps through the progress of Australian banks in implementing the appropriate procedures and arrangements for Australian dollar denominated interest rate derivatives. This observation must also be considered by New Zealand banks since their hedging profile and behaviour are almost similar to the Australian practices. However, New Zealand banks' microstructure and relative institutional size may influence the performance of risk management, thus the banks may need to selectively identify their best strategies to reduce greater interest rate risk behaviour for better outcomes. Furthermore, in the context of open and not controlled markets like Hong Kong, the system may have a big impact on their banks' risk management performances. It creates a dramatic increase in the presence of foreign banks in this matured financial market. However, through an intermediation approach and overall mean score, banks in Hong Kong have proven their victory for refocussing on efficiency and customer management using new skills and better management capabilities and maintaining safety and soundness of the overall financial landscape.

In relation to the above scenarios in the Australian market, this suggests the need for a policy review of commercial banks in developing countries to enable them to compete in the global market. In this case, Malaysian banks have chosen to follow the example of banks in Thailand and the Philippines due to their good risk management efficiency. Over the past decade, *Bank Negara Malaysia* (Central Bank of Malaysia) is putting monetary and financial policy in place following the government's broader economic plan. There is no issue of lack of independence in Malaysian commercial banks. Malaysian commercial banks operate quite independently and, have experienced a robust development of the money market after 2010. For instance, financial firms have helped to channel short-term funds between financial institutions to meet their financing needs and portfolio adjustments. However, the development in the derivative contracts still depends on government policies and the Central Bank, leading to slow growth and reduced sensitivity in the market structure and financial market. Nevertheless, the foreign exchange market has witnessed an increase in transactions, including hedging transactions. Apart from being used as an instrument for hedging purposes, financial derivatives are also being used by Malaysian commercial banks to further magnify the diversity of their investment products. This can be seen from the fact that the notional value of OBS interest rate and foreign exchange-related financial derivatives contracts amounted to MYR1.1 trillion at the end of 2010. Hence, it would not be wrong to assume that when the regulatory structure has been improved in mitigating interest rate and foreign exchange risks, the performance level of banks will gradually improve, which may also influence their risk management efficiency level. Again, this can be seen from the results generated here in this study which show that all Malaysian commercial banks stand a significant chance of achieving an absolute efficiency score by using interest rate swaps in their operations. CB14 and CB17 have shown good results on the impact of derivative instrument usage and its implication for asset and liability management. The strategy of active involvement in trading activity and the impact of enhanced regulatory framework on their asset and liability management will be able to further manage the exposure on an item-by-item basis.

4.9 Conclusion

This chapter discusses the hedge effectiveness test by integrating the DOR with the non-parametric approach of DEA. As it has been argued that DOR is inadequate for the purpose of representing derivatives as a risk management tool, developing risk management policy, decision-making process and risk performance measurement, the DEA approach offers an alternative evaluation and measurement technique of the efficiency of derivatives for countering interest rate volatility. Indeed, the efficiency level of banks' risk management can be evaluated effectively when we synergise the DOR and efficient frontier from the perspective of a DEA. The scope of this method is quite vast in that it measures risk management efficiency in the context of the derivative instrument usage. This integrated approach compares the performance of commercial banks in the developing and developed countries in the Asia-Pacific region. The DEA approach can provide a better derivative and risk management accounting measurement in banks that can be applied in the risk management context to reduce financial risks resulting from interest rate volatility.

DEA is used as a performance measurement framework to generate the efficiency score of banks' risk management which measures the risk management efficiency level of the bank. In contrast to previous research, this study controls the efficiency score based on risk management indicators that linked the derivative instrument and its effect on the balance sheet and income statement items based on the hedged items and hedging instruments, and reflected on asset-liability management. Based on this mechanism, hedging instruments and the hedged item emerged as reliable predictors of risk management efficiency based on a DEA approach that will provide a fair comparison in both the developing and developed financial markets, and on the consistencies of characters in DOR analysis.

Here, the DEA method to hedge accounting effectiveness analysis for measuring risk management efficiencies has been a proven method to measure banks' risk management performance. This frontier analysis method can identify banks that are able to convert multiple inputs to produce a higher amount of a combination of outputs. These are called the efficient banks and their risk management efficiency is measured by the ratio of their combination of multiple outputs to their multiple inputs involving mathematical weights (Nyhan and Martin 1999; Allen et al. 1997). Banks which have the scope to further increase their outputs given their existing inputs are considered to be low on efficiency (Battese et al. 1998).

Notes

1 The process is divided into two stages, and the ten factors are expressed as inputs and outputs in each stage.
2 Sherman (1981) and Mante (1997) discuss these same issues.
3 The suggestion of a new range for hedge effectiveness is highlighted because of the debate among accountants regarding the issue of hedge effectiveness measurements and its recognition. Further discussions are highlighted by Coughland (2004).
4 Taylor (1990) has criticised the relationship measurement between variables using coefficient correlation. He suggests that researchers further analyse relationship variables using a coefficient of determination due to limitations and weaknesses in the correlation coefficient.
5 According to the East Asia Analytical Unit (1999), Malaysia's banking system was stronger than other countries in the region when their capital controls were introduced in 1998. Such controls were considered as a strong weapon to challenge the Asian financial crisis. More importantly, Malaysia's financial system continued to make good progress in recapitalising its financial structure.
6 Islam and Chowdhury (1997) have provided a survey on the emergence of an integrated Asia-Pacific economy which covers various issues including the financial reform and economic development of Korea, Taiwan, Hong Kong, Singapore, Indonesia, Malaysia, the Philippines and Thailand.

5 Risk management efficiency measurement and analysis under uncertainty

5.1 Introduction

The previous stage of this study showed that it was possible to generate an initial efficiency model of risk management efficiency measurement in banks, based on the usage of derivative instruments. The analysis showed how the Data Envelopment Analysis (DEA) approach with an integrated approach of hedge effectiveness test (dollar-offset ratio) in hedge accounting is able to consistently measure and estimate risk management efficiency levels by using a deterministic method for classifying decision-making units (DMUs). The analysis utilised a small sample to gain insights into the nature of interested conceptions. Results from the deterministic DEA, however, were preliminary and cannot be generalised easily. There are also many uncertainties in the business environment, modelling and analysis of risk management. Therefore, this chapter undertakes an analysis of risk management efficiency measures under uncertainty, using stochastic models to provide new insights into the effect of methodological choice on estimated efficiency using three stochastic modelling approaches to DEA that include studies in different areas under an uncertainty context: (i) errors and noises in data or parameters; (ii) the presence of general uncertainty to allow meaningful risk management numerical scores due to changes or development in business, finance, markets and policies; and (iii) the requirement of developing optimal decision rules based on the probability of outcomes from constraints in the models for uncertainty analysis.

In this chapter, Part A addresses a methodological lacuna in DEA approach that assumes no errors in the data. The deterministic DEA fails to account for noise in the data, whereas the error is considered as statistical noise in the stochastic model. Inaccessibility to gather complete data and information about the DMUs or small sample size of DMUs can obstruct measurement of the real efficient frontier, which leads to incorrect classifications that create errors in the sampling (Sadjadi and Omrani 2010). Since this study involves a small sample size problem, it is necessary to address this issue in the DEA in risk management efficiency analysis (Mojtahedi et al. 2009). To remedy these problems in deterministic DEA, this section follows the procedure of bootstrapped DEA (BDEA) proposed by Simar and Wilson (2000) to examine the efficiency of risk management in banks. For the extension of the analytical framework, this section moves from the deterministic approach to observe the effect of change in input and output variables used for the DEA study. The input/output variables in this DEA model are not only affected by the nature of parameters selected, but also by the variation of data that may occur due to uncertainty in the business environment.

Part B addresses uncertainty issues by adopting the approach of sensitivity analysis to calculate the impact of variations on different quantifiable parameters and components that can then help management to identify potential pitfalls for more effective risk measurement. The sensitivity analysis investigates components of a plan that, when changed even slightly in input and/or output parameters, will have a high impact on the efficiency of the banks. This analysis also investigates the sensitivity of risk management efficiency scores to perturbation and uncertainty in the data. By addressing these assumptions of variability in parameters and data, the sensitivity analysis aids the DEA model in analysing the robustness of the optimal solution in the face of uncertainty in business environments.

Part C further addresses the issue of parameter uncertainty in the context of use of derivatives in banking operations by modifying the DEA model itself. For this purpose, the study utilises a stochastic form of DEA called a chance-constrained DEA (CCDEA) approach to address the issue of uncertainty in banks while focussing on parameters of uncertainty. To complete the research circle, it is unreasonable to assume that data provided by regulators is necessarily free from error (Brown 2006). Based on this understanding, it is important to use a CCDEA approach to address the presence of specification and measurement error, and to consider the inherent variability in banking processes under probabilistic conditions.

Based on the issues that have been discussed, including highlighting the limitation in deterministic DEA estimation, this chapter seeks to address the following questions:

Research Question 5:

Does modelling risk (uncertainty or risk in modelling) in the measurement of risk management efficiency influence banks' risk management efficiency and its measurements? If yes, how and why?

The above research question with uncertainty consideration hopes to provide banks an efficient way to ensure that risk management efficiency model is stable and reliable. This will help banks to understand how the uncertainty of outcome (risk) of its activities affects their degree of risk management efficiency. Therefore, it will be trusted to answer how both deterministic and stochastic techniques in DEA influence banks' risk management in the Asia-Pacific, as stated in the following question:

Research Question 6:

How do deterministic and stochastic efficiency scores influence banks' risk management and derivative policies in developed and developing countries?

Part A: Bootstrapping analysis of data uncertainty

5.2 Bootstrapping DEA for risk efficiency measurement – context

5.2.1 Need to go beyond deterministic DEA estimation

Original DEA evaluation assumes that the input and output parameters used in the model estimation translate into perfect measurement of efficiency. DEA is a purely deterministic analytical method and does not contain a stochastic term in its optimised linear programming approach (Filippou and Zervopoulos 2011; Manzoni 2007). By highlighting the uncertainty issue in data, this chapter provides an alternative methodological approach realising that linear programming approach strongly pushes the analysis with a true situation which is never the same as the gathered data that has been addressed.

Many scholars (Simar and Wilson 2008; Sengupta 2000) stated that the DEA model of efficiency ignores the fact that all the input and output variables are not deterministic. Zhang and Bartels (1998) also found that the estimated mean value of the technical efficiencies was dependent on the parameter values. Banker (1993) verified weak consistency of the DEA estimation particularly when the measurement involves a single-input and single-output case. As a result, they stressed the need for a stochastic frontier analysis (SFA) to correct DEA's approach to efficiency measurement.

Further, Simar and Wilson (1998) and Cummins et al. (2003) believe that DEA can create bias efficiency estimation as it refers to upward bias in finite samples in its evaluation. When the relative measurement of the best practice is observed in the sample, it can create a biased estimator (Maghyereh and Awartani 2012). As the scores in DEA are calculated through an unknown Data-Generating Process (DGP) (Xue and Harker 1999) without any confidence interval in the estimation, the results will be dependent on each other, thus creating a dependency problem. The sampling distribution error along with the asymptotic bias, will affect the DEA estimation as the scores generated are less sensitive towards the sampling variation (Gijbels et al. 1999).

Verification test statistics are of no significance in small samples, very poor power in small samples, so it is not possible for a bank or its supervisor to verify the accuracy of the DEA approach in efficiency estimation unless performance data for several years is available. For instance, Zhang and Bartels (1998) investigate the sample size-bias effect on the mean productive efficiency of electricity distribution industries in Australia, New Zealand and Sweden. The results indicated that an increase in the number of firms reduced the mean of the overall technical efficiency (OTE) of the industry. Using a Monte Carlo simulation on the DEA, Zhang and Bartes confirm that when the number of observations was added to the sample, more structural inefficiency was observed. This obviously shows that sample size bias leads to potentially wrong interpretations (biased estimation of performance measurement and efficiency estimation).

This discussion highlights the weakness of the efficiency score obtained by a deterministic DEA approach. One particular model for accuracy under uncertainty is called a stochastic DEA model. The stochastic model in DEA is for the possibility of variations in input and output parameters where the efficiency measure of a DMU is defined via joint probabilistic comparisons of inputs and outputs with other DMUs (Huang and Li 2001). Under the stochastic model, Brázdik (2004) emphasises that the derivation of nearly 100% (1.000) confidence chance-constrained problem is revised. It is necessary to estimate the efficiency score effectively to enhance decision-making and benchmarking strategies (Moradi-Motlagh et al. 2014). However, DEA ignores the risk management context required to produce a trustworthy assessment of a firm's risk management efficiency model. The stochastic model is transformed to the DEA deterministic model which will become the basis for the theoretical development of this model. Bootstrapping is employed to provide an efficient way to ensure that the risk management efficiency model is stable and reliable.

5.2.2 *Bootstrapping for risk analysis and management*

Bootstrapping generally refers to the application of a historical precedent to guide decision-making, specifically the professional judgement of technical experts devising solutions. Bootstrapping a model consistently applies the expert's rules to test whether the decisions and predictions from the model are similar to those from the experts (Armstrong 2001). Even though Armstrong use judgemental bootstrapping model to evaluate experts' prediction, Allen and Fildes (2001) state that bootstrapping is an accepted procedure in the social sciences and econometrics to provide more realistic outcomes and solutions.

The bootstrapping procedure in statistical analysis is required to produce a reliable assessment of the accuracy of a risk management model in predicting the efficiency measurement of the firms. Zenti and Pallotta (2000) note that bootstrapping approach can provide satisfactory assessments of strategic risk. Whether decision-making can be determined as "accepted" or "tolerable" based on risk analysis, the decision must proceed by the accuracy of the assigning and assessing method.

In the banking sector, bootstrapping has been used alongside expert advice since the 1970s. Slovic et al. (1972) propose the bootstrapping approach to examine the security return performance based on specific risk, and Ebert and Kruse (1978) also revealed superior performance in the field of security analysis by developing bootstrapping models for five analysts who forecasted returns for 20 securities using information on 22 variables and its associated risks. Given that the models violated guidelines for developing bootstrapping models, it is surprising that the bootstrapping models were more accurate than analysts for 72% of the comparisons of management capabilities assessment.

Another study by Abdel-Khalik and El-Sheshai (1980) used the bootstrapping model to investigate actual default in loans in comparison with figures predicted by 28 commercial-bank lending officers. The results found that prediction model by bootstrapping models were as accurate as the prediction of all officers. This bootstrapping analysis before awarding loans helped the banks to evaluate the risk from potential defaults in order to reduce costs and the likelihood of bias in awarding loans.

Another risk element that has been discussed by Libby (1976) concerns the prediction of bankruptcy for 60 large industrial corporations. But this study in contrast to those illustrated earlier showed that bootstrapping model used in insolvency risk and its relation to firms' bankruptcy is less accurate compared to experts' opinion and decision. However, Goldberg (1976) questions the validity of Libby's results as the analysis suffered from severe skewness in the causal variables. He re-analysed the data and found that the percentage of times produced by the bootstrapping model beat the expert opinion and increased in its accuracy by 49% (from 23% to 72%). Hence, the bootstrapping model that has been applied to evaluate firms' bankruptcy due to related risk elements is more reliable for risk management evaluation and prediction.

In addition to these studies that are guided by conventional financial aspects of efficiency, Chortareas et al. (2013) construct an interesting application of bootstrapping technique in a more abstract matter of banking efficiency relating to economic freedom. They employed a robust bootstrap procedure to regress the first-stage efficiency scores on economic freedom indices in banks operating in 27 European Union member countries. The variable of economic freedom was proxied by six governance indicators representing government quality that were replicated by 2000 bootstrap replications. Extending bootstrapping to a new area of efficiency analyses, this study again highlights the superiority of bootstrapping in accurate measurement of efficiency in financial institutions.

The literature presented in this subsection indicates the ability of bootstrapping approach in the risk analysis context. Empirical results consistently show that bootstrapping models are associated with increased accuracy in measuring risk elements. The results from a bootstrapping model have always matched or proved to be more accurate than those of expert analysts. Though the relationship between bootstrapping and the risk management context has not been developed theoretically, empirical evidence has found that the principle of a bootstrapping model is able to deliver analyses of specific risks in the banking sector with reliability and accuracy.

5.2.3 Bootstrapping technique as an extension to the traditional DEA measurement

DEA measurement is to enhance the traditional measurement of firms' efficiency measurement. The study applies bootstrapping technique to simulated risk management efficiency which allows for reliable calculations. This method provides a flexible, robust, intuitive and comprehensive risk management efficiency evaluation within the context of derivatives usage as a hedging instrument and items being hedged.

To this extent, the focus has been on the relationship between risk management efficiency measures with bootstrapping technique. This study looks at the implications of using the derivative instrument and its impact on hedged items. It generates a financial scenario over the derivative activity horizon using the information based on hedge accounting, and hence shows the need for multivariate empirical analysis. The usage of normal bootstrapping extended from DEA traditional approach is suitable for the raw effect (hedged item) because the "volatility" condition on the hedge item is already measured by the hedge effectiveness test (dollar-offset ratio), unless "missing" volatility happens. Having examined the relationship between bootstrapping approach in risk management measurement, it is now necessary to consider the application of bootstrap to ensure reliability and accuracy of risk management efficiency results. This study believes that the choice of bootstrapping approach as a risk management efficiency evaluation in banks based on hedge effectiveness test model affect the risk management efficiency measurement in banks in a persuasive way.

5.2.4 Bootstrapping approach in risk management efficiency measurement

Having examined the relationship between the bootstrapping approach in risk management measurement, it is now necessary to consider the application of bootstrap to ensure reliability and accuracy of risk management efficiency results. To this point, the focus has been on the relationship between risk management efficiency measurements with the bootstrapping technique.

Most previous studies measure and manage different risk sources using parametric methods (Medova and Smith 2005; Gil and Polyakov 2003; Iscoe et al. 1999), whereas bootstrapping is able to measure specific risks. For instance, credit risk and default risk which dealt with Credit Metrics only depend on the rating category without any contribution from idiosyncratic components, and are seldom updated and are not sensitive to current market conditions. Marsala et al. (2004) strongly agree that bootstrapping technique constructs a respected measurement analysis for obtaining a precise description of the financial instrument usage in managing risk. Focussing on one or more types of risk management products, the financial instrument is modelled in a robust way with a filtered bootstrap approach. In their study, they have applied filtered bootstrap technique as they believe that this non-parametric approach is able to simulate the stochastic processes and modelling risk factors.

Hashemi et al. (2013) have evaluated the risk assessment process using a bootstrapping approach to solve the issue of non-accuracy in port projects. Using the bootstrap method, Hashemi et al. have structured risk management approach in three phases. Beginning with project risk planning to establish project's goals and outcomes, this first phase focussed on assessing risk issues, providing risk handling plans and monitoring process. The second phase involved project risk identification where risks are categorised into a specific structure. The last phase is project risk assessment where non-parametric bootstrap method (B = Mi) is used to obtain compromising final risk ranking. From the results, the study concludes that bootstrap confidence interval approach can be applied to risk assessment problems yielding reliable and meaningful results that cannot often be obtained by the traditional approach.

In a study that further extended the utility of bootstrapping in the risk management context, Huang et al. (2009) proved that bootstrapping technique can simulate the distribution of future movements in systemic risk, which can be used as a forecasting tool. This analysis showed remarkable ability of the bootstrapping approach which not only functions as a bias-corrected technique, but is also able to forecast future risk management strategies of the firm.

In short, the bootstrapping technique has several advantages. Prior to the methodological implications of integrating the bootstrap approach to DEA, this section has not only reviewed the limitations of DEA but has also established the relationship between the bootstrapping approach and the risk management context, which has been neglected in most studies until recently. All this has highlighted the need to bring bootstrapping into dialogue with traditional DEA employed in this study, as this study is concerned with generating accurate and reliable measurements of risk management efficiency from financial derivatives.

5.3 Bootstrapping technique for stochastic optimisation of DEA – theoretical approach

5.3.1 *Efficiency bias correction, confidence intervals construction and dependency issue incorporating noise in data and sampling error issue*

This study looks at the implication of using the derivative instrument and its impact on multiple items (hedged items). It generates a financial scenario over derivative activity horizon using the information based on hedge accounting, and hence shows the need for multivariate empirical analysis. The usage of normal bootstrapping extended from the DEA traditional approach is suitable for the raw effect (hedged item) because the "volatility" condition on the hedged item is already measured by hedge effectiveness test (dollar-offset ratio), unless there is "missing" volatility. This basic idea therefore drives the study to apply the BDEA formulations as stochastic amendments to the traditional DEA that is able to address the effect of noise in the data and the sampling error on efficiency estimation. This study believes that applying the bootstrapping approach to DEA provides an effective risk management efficiency evaluation as it employs both the deterministic and stochastic evaluations:

> Accuracy and reliability in risk management efficiency = Deterministic measurement (due to riskless or no error in data) + Stochastic measurement (due to risk evaluation in data)

BDEA overcomes a major weakness of DEA which is its failure to deal effectively with the stochastic element of efficiency estimation (Hawdon 2003). This is because the observed data (input and output) would normally be subjected to the measurement error that can create noise in the data due to omitted input or output variables. Also, there may be events that affect the level of input-output of some of the production units. As in SFA, specific assumptions are made in BDEA for evaluating the distribution of the inefficiency to isolate the noise from efficiency.

In addition, Mellenbergh et al. (2008) state that bootstrapping was strongly recommended when the theoretical distribution of the statistics of interest are complex or unknown. Bootstrapping the DEA allows for the estimation of the sample distribution of almost any statistic using a simple method (Kao and Liu 2014; Munisamy and Danxia 2013; Chernick 2008). Since this procedure is distribution-independent, it provides an indirect way of assessing both the actual distribution underlying the sample, and the extent of interest derived from this distribution. Thus, the DEA bootstrap can be applied to encounter the intrinsic problems of measurement error in the standard DEA in order to estimate the bias-corrected DEA efficiency scores (Halkos and Tzeremes 2013; Halkos et al. 2012; Biener and Eling 2011).

Maghyereh and Awartani (2012) state that the DEA estimator tends to become biased when it measures relative efficiency from the best practice observations in the sample. DEA does not provide any assumptions regarding the exogenous factors or measurement error, and does not allow confidence intervals. In this type of measurement, DEA may introduce an upward bias in measuring the efficiency scores as it depends on the best practice observations (Barros et al. 2014; Gutiérrez et al. 2014). In contrast, bootstrapping the DEA will correct the efficiencies for bias and estimate confidence intervals for them. This approach was chosen because it can be applied to the institutional efficiency measurement obtaining confidence intervals and bias-corrected efficiency.

In addition, Staat (2001) re-analysed the original DEA data from Banker and Morey (1986) to arrive at the conclusion that the results were significantly influenced by the number of observations and sample size effect. In an early study on this matter, Efron (1979) introduced a bootstrapping technique as an alternative method of conducting inference when the sample size is small. Following that, Banker (1993) also shows the utility of bootstrap techniques as an alternative method for conducting inferences, particularly with a sample.

DEA efficiency scores can also violate the inherent independence within the sample (Casu and Molyneux 2003). Xue and Harker (1999) were perhaps the first to address the problem of inherent dependency of efficiency scores when applied in the regression model. They explained that a number of studies used regression analysis (two-stage DEA) such as Tobit and Ordinary Least Square (OLS) to explain the variation of efficiency scores among different firms. The authors found that the efficiency results produced by the DEA approach were clearly dependent on each other and independent within the sample because of the fact that the DEA efficiency measured the relative efficiency index, not an absolute efficiency index. Bootstrapping DEA can solve dependency problems with the assumption that "the distances $Q_{DEA} - Q^*$ are distributed as the distances $Q - Q_{DEA}$" (Fried et al. 2008, 456).

Problems can also arise in sampling distributions that are analytically intractable (Alonso et al. 2006). Alonso et al. (2006) also agreed that the bootstrapping approach was able to solve sampling distributions that are hard to trace due to pretesting and nonlinearity. Hence, they proposed a "smoothed bootstrap" procedure to improve the estimation and avoid remarking problems. This study has followed Atkinson and Wilson (1995) and Simar and Wilson (2000) who apply a smoothed distribution of efficiency values to the generation.

Motivated by these issues that highlight the limitations of the traditional DEA approach, and previous studies that have made improvements on it, this study uses the bootstrap DEA proposed by Simar and Wilson (1998, 2000) as well as Sadjani and Omrani (2010) who developed a bootstrapping measurement for efficiency studies known as BDEA. Based on the literature, this study believes that the BDEA's integration approach will strengthen the DEA and yield more accurate efficiency scores by addressing the following issues:

1   BDEA can resolve the bias in the parameter estimates, thus, producing more reliable estimations for risk management efficiency (Assaf and Agbola 2011; Johnes 2006; Simar and Wilson 2000).

2   BDEA can produce more reliable results in measuring risk management efficiency in banks (Zakaria et al. 2014).

3   The bootstrap method can also be used to reasonably predict the future performance of the firm that generally improves both the precision and the reliability of predictions (Friedman and Friedman 2013; Johanson 2013).

4   Policy makers in banks will be provided with more trustworthy and dependable findings for them to strategise their risk management plan.

5.3.2 *Bootstrap DEA in banking efficiency studies*

In 1997, Ferrier and Hirschberg examined the efficiency of Italian banks with the application of the bootstrapping method. The authors adapted the bootstrap technique in the context of linear programming approach because of its computational power in measuring unknown values in true frontier production function. They showed how bootstrapping can be used to obtain a sampling distribution of the efficiency scores of individual banks from which confidence intervals and a measure of bias can then be constructed. Ferrier and Hirschberg believe that the results generated by bootstrapping approach allow the decision maker to consider the reliability of the calculated efficiency scores in a more rigorous manner.

In a later study, Tortosa-Ausina et al. (2008) explore productivity growth and productive efficiency for Spanish Deposits banks over the post-deregulation period of 1992–1998 using DEA and bootstrapping techniques. While mean efficiency had remained fairly constant over time due to the improvement in production possibilities, the bootstrapping approach of the study revealed that the disparities in the original efficiency scores of some firms were lessened to a great extent. Hence, this approach allows for a more careful analysis of what happens at the level of actual firm operations.

With a similar objective and methodology, Assaf et al. (2011b) evaluated the real values of technical efficiency (TE) in Saudi banks using the bootstrapping technique by resampling the original data. They found that the efficiency bias-corrected estimations for every observation were within the confidence interval. They consider the result derived from this analysis to be a statistical advantage over traditional DEA measurement as it used more rigorous criteria for evaluation. The same findings have been found by Zakaria et al. (2014) by comparing the efficiency of 12 Islamic banks in Malaysia. The BDEA approach has been employed to resolve the uncertainty issue of traditional DEA measurement practice. They believe that by adopting this approach, it is not only essential for a more precise efficiency measurement but also compatible with Islamic banking concepts that differ substantially in objectives and operations from those of conventional banks. The purpose of the BDEA approach to reduce uncertainties suits Islamic banking principles in order to reduce any uncertainties in their operations.

In a different study, Assaf et al. (2011a) applied the bootstrap Malmquist index to provide a quantitative measure of productivity (total factor of productivity – TFP) change in *Shinkin* banks operating in Japan. With further support to the Malmquist results, the study found that efficiency productivity growth based on market share on deposit (MSD), number of branches, return on asset (ROA), net interest margin (NIM) and deposit concentration ratio are statistically significant to the efficiency scores except NIM. Based on the comparative results of normal efficiency estimates, they conclude that the bootstrap approach was able to provide less biased scores by correcting the efficiency estimates sensitivity to random variations in the data.

Investigating Gulf Cooperation Council (GCC) banks, Maghyereh and Awartani (2012) highlighted the disadvantages of the DEA estimator approach and found that bootstrap measure produced relatively unbiased results compared to the original DEA measure. The results found that the mean corrected bootstrap scores are lower than the mean of DEA original scores, thus implying that DEA measure is likely to be biased and tends to overestimate efficiency scores. They advocate the harmonisation and integration of DEA and bootstrap DEA for efficiency measurements that are better able to provide accurate evidence to improve GCC banking system.

Halkos and Tzeremes (2013) also conducted an interesting efficiency assessment on banks using DEA and BDEA on short-run efficiency bank merger and acquisition (M&A) in Greek banks. Both approaches confirmed that M&A banks were unable to generate short-run operating efficiency gains. The BDEA approach determined that the efficiency scores of Greek banking institutions are almost identical in terms of their levels of operating efficiency. After considering uncertainty in data sample, the bias-corrected results obtained indicated that no banks achieved the most efficient score (1.000), while traditional DEA showed that ten banks are most efficient. This study again reiterates how DEA is prone to overestimation of efficiency, whereas BDEA is able to incorporate uncertainty in the data sample and derive a more realistic efficiency score.

5.4 Integrated deterministic DEA for risk management efficiency measurement in banks based on hedge effectiveness test with stochastic optimisation approach: methodological framework

5.4.1 Framework

As indicated in the introduction that focusses on the alternative approaches, this chapter had constructed the following extension of the analysis framework from deterministic efficiency measurement (traditional DEA) approach to stochastic efficiency measurement using BDEA. By considering noise in data and sampling error, this study sought to induce stochastic optimisation approach, thus ensuring accurate and reliable results. Prior to the methodological implication, the framework has established the need and relationship between the bootstrapping approach and the risk management context, which has been neglected until recently. The majority of studies in the efficiency literature has focussed on the effect of methodological and results implication.

In line with the research objective, this methodological framework (see Figure 5.1) describes the concept and impact of noise and sampling error (small sample) in risk management efficiency measurement, and how the extended analysis can improve the risk management policy and strategy

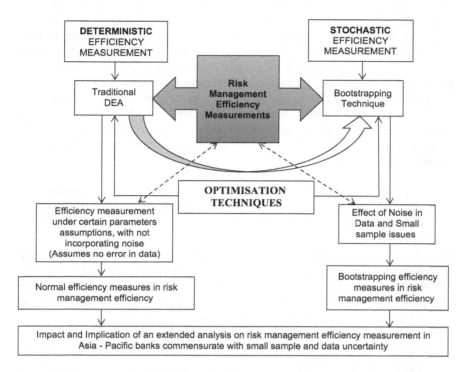

Figure 5.1 Bootstrapping Methodological Framework of DEA and BDEA Approaches.

development. The model is complementary to the DEA traditional efficiency measurements to produce reliable and robust results, and provides more trustworthy findings in strategising risk management plan and policies.

5.5 Bootstrap data envelopment analysis: model and formulation

This study addresses the limitation of DEA and obtains non-parametric envelopment estimator of the DEA efficiency score applying the bootstrapping approach developed by Simar (1992) and Simar and Wilson (1998, 2000) who were pioneers in using the bootstrap in frontier models. This approach basically estimates a true sampling distribution by mimicking the DGP by re-sampling the DEA data. The resampled data consists of original sample values using a selection of thousands of "pseudo samples" from the observed set of a sample data. Repeating this process enables us to build a good approximation of the true distribution.

However, Simar and Wilson (1998) retracted this method in the cases of non-parametric frontier estimation, arguing that "pseudo sample" provided an inconsistent bootstrap estimation of the confidence intervals (the so-called naive bootstrap) since the distance estimation values are close to unity when directly resampled from the set of original data. It shows that the consistent information of such confidence intervals is closely dependent on the consistent replication of a DGP. Besides, the DEA estimator may produce a large number of apparently efficient units with $\hat{\theta} = 1$ (the number of such units is likely to increase with p, the number of inputs). It will consequently influence $\hat{F}$ (density function), which will provide a poor estimation of F near the upper boundary. In particular, bootstrap estimates may be inconsistent if this issue is not raised. The bootstrap algorithm starts with some basic definitions:

1   A production set is defined as $\psi = \{(x,y) \ R_+^{p+q} | x \ can \ produce \ y\}$, where the amount of some p inputs x that can produce q output sy, while the set of inputs that make the output level y possible is defined as $X(y) = \{x \ R_+^{p+q} | (x,y) \ \psi\}$.

2   The efficient production limit can be defined as the subset of $X(y)$, such that $\partial X(y) = \{x | x \in X(y), \theta x \notin Xy \forall \theta \ (0,1)\}$ where it describes the possibility to obtain more outputs with a given level of input. The sets of $\psi, X(y), \theta_1$ and $\partial X(y)$ are unknown, meaning that if we assume that some DGP, P, generates a random sample $X = \{x_i y_i | i = 1,...,n\}$ of n homogenous organisations (firms).

3   Specifically, $\hat{\theta}_i$ can be obtained by DEA application, which indicates that the firm is completely technically efficient. Input orientation has been chosen and defined as $\theta_i = min\{\theta | \theta x_1 \in X(y)\}$, where it explains the DEA input-orientated efficiency measurements. $\hat{\theta}_i = 1$ indicates that the input and output unit (x_i, y_i) is fully efficient (100%).

Since DEA estimates a production frontier boundary, generating bootstrap samples is not a straightforward process. This approach is based on the DEA estimator by drawing replacement from the original estimates of theta, $\hat{\theta}_{DEA(x,y)}$ and then applying the reflection method proposed by Silverman (1986). As the efficiency measures being considered in this study are input-based measures, the bootstrap is performed over the original risk management efficiency scores. The steps for a smoothed bootstrap algorithm can be summarised as follows:

1   Compute the original DEA model to obtain efficiency scores $\hat{\theta}_1 ... \hat{\theta}_n$ by solving the linear programming models.

2   Use the smooth bootstrap that generates a random sample of size n from $\hat{\theta}_i = 1,...,n$.

3   Smooth the sampled values using the formula:

$$\tilde{\theta}_i^* = \{\theta_{Bi} + h \ i^* if \theta_{Bi} + h \ i^* \geq 1 \ or \ 2 - \theta_{Bi} - h \ i^* \ otherwise\} \tag{5.1}$$

4   Use the following formula to obtain the value of $\tilde{\theta}$ by adjusting the smoothed sample value as proposed by Farrell (1957).

$$\theta_i^* = \bar{B} + \frac{\tilde{\theta}_i^* - \bar{B}}{\left(1 + \left(\frac{h^2}{\hat{\sigma}_\theta^2}\right)\right)^{1/2}} \tag{5.2}$$

where:

$$\bar{B} = \left(\frac{1}{n}\right)\sum_{i=1}^{n} \theta_{Bi} \text{ and } \hat{\sigma}_\theta^2 = \left(\frac{1}{n}\right)\sum_{i=1}^{n}(\hat{\theta}_i - \hat{\bar{\theta}}) \tag{5.3}$$

5   Adjust the original input using the ratio $\hat{\theta}/\theta_i^*$.
6   Resolve the original DEA model using the adjusted input to obtain θ_{kb}^*.
7   Repeat step 2 to 6 B times to provide for B sets of estimations which are; samples generated for each bank.

In Equation 5.1, h is the smoothing parameter and ε is a randomly drawn error term. According to Walden (2006), the h value is the most difficult step in the procedure. This study uses an alternative procedure of "normal reference rule", where the h value is calculated using the following formula:

$$h = \left[4/(p+q+2)\left(\frac{1}{p}+q+4\right) * N^{\left(-\frac{1}{p}+q+4\right)}\right] \tag{5.4}$$

where p equals the number of inputs, q is the number of outputs and N refers to the number of observations in the sample. The bias of the original estimate of theta will be calculated once the number of desired samples is generated. The following formula will then be computed:

$$bias\hat{\theta}_k = B^{-1}\sum_{b=1}^{B}\hat{\theta}_{kb}^* - \hat{\theta}_{kb} \tag{5.5}$$

Then, a bias-corrected estimator of the true value of theta, $\theta(x,y), \hat{\theta}_k^*$, can be computed using the following formula developed by Simar and Wilson (2000).

$$\hat{\theta}_k^* = \hat{\theta}_k - bias\hat{\theta}_k$$
$$= 2 * \hat{\theta} - B^1\sum_{b=1}^{B}\hat{\theta}_{kb}^* \tag{5.6}$$

Given the debate about the sample size in the literature, this study realised that there might be a sampling error problem due to our small sample size. The number of sampled banks is limited because not all the commercial banks in the Asia-Pacific region are directly involved with derivative instruments in their risk management operations, particularly in relation to the interest rate swap for hedging purposes. There were also issues in accessing the data for the whole period from all the DMUs, so many eligible banks also had to be removed from the sample. The deficiencies in the sample may create hurdles for more holistic analyses, so this issue will be addressed by a BDEA approach to be performed on the Performance Improvement Management (PIM-DEA) Software, which was introduced by Emrouznejad (2010) to estimate TE. This approach provides an advanced alternative that can estimate confidence intervals on DEA efficiencies and incorporate bias correction factors. Thus, this study presents the bootstrap efficiency scores for individual banks in two major categories, namely the commercial banks in developed and developing Asia-Pacific countries.

5.6 Results and discussion

In this study, two stages of bootstrapping were performed. In the first stage (Section 5.6.1), bootstrapping DEA was used for efficiency bias estimations in pure technical efficiency (PTE) of the original DEA estimates, where the bootstrapping results are compared to PTE results using the following formula:

$$PTE_1 = (PTE_0 - Bias) \tag{5.7}$$

where:

PTE_1 denotes the new pure technical efficiency;
PTE_0 denotes the previous pure technical efficiency derived from original DEA estimates;
Bias denotes the bias derived from bootstrapping analysis.

In the second stage (Section 5.6.2), the bias estimates found in the first stage analysis will be subtracted from PTE_0 scores and times with scale efficiency (*SE*) scores. Therefore, the final efficiency results after bias correction are estimated. New efficiency scores are based on the following formula:

$$OTE_1 = PTE_1 x \ SE \tag{5.8}$$

where:

OTE_1 denotes the new overall technical efficiency;
PTE_1 denotes the new pure technical efficiency;
SE   denotes the scale efficiency.

This decomposition is unique and depicts the sources of inefficiency accurately, clarifying whether it is caused by inefficient operation PTE or by disadvantageous scale efficiency (SE) or by both. This study presents individual banks on a yearly basis (2007–2012), which presents the efficiency of PTE and bias-corrected estimates trend.

5.6.1 First stage of bootstrapping results: a comparison to pure technical efficiency

In the first stage, Table 5.1 summarises the annual mean efficiency in 21 Asia-Pacific banks over the period of 2007–2012. Column 2 lists the average (mean) of PTE from normal DEA estimated efficiency, and column 3 lists the bias corrected by bootstrapping for each year. Column 4 presents the average amount of bias by comparing estimated efficiency and bias-corrected estimates. Although the overall mean score indicates that all banks are inefficient over years, the whole banking industry risk management efficiency level improves over the period of 2007–2008. However, the efficiency level declines considerably in 2009 and 2011. In 2010, the efficiency scores almost achieve perfectly efficient status.

Based on the bootstrap estimates of 95% confidence interval in the last two columns in Table 5.1, the results reflect the relevance of the theory of confidence interval constructed by Simar and Wilson (1998) as the mean (average) of estimated efficiency lies to the right of the estimated confidence intervals. The inverse of the average bias-corrected Variable Return to Scale (VRS) efficiency score amounts to 93.6%. This indicates that based on average PTE, the banks in the Asia-Pacific region are managing their resources ineffectively under exogenous environment. This first stage of findings is quite different from other studies. A previous study by Arjomandi (2011) directly reported the mean of efficiency scores (OTE) for the Iranian banking industry, but he found inefficient results over all years of analysis although the industry efficiency level was found to be improving over this period.

Table 5.1 Annual Average PTE Estimates for Asia-Pacific Banks based on the Bootstrap Method (2007–2012)

Year	PTE Estimated Efficiency	Bias-Corrected	Bias	Bootstrap Lower Bound	Bootstrap Upper Bound
2007	0.985	0.984	0.001	0.982	0.986
2008	0.991	0.991	0.001	0.988	0.991
2009	0.862	0.843	0.018	0.779	0.862
2010	0.9996	0.9995	0.00005	0.9994	0.9995
2011	0.835	0.810	0.025	0.728	0.836
2012	0.990	0.989	0.001	0.987	0.990
Mean	0.944	0.936	0.008	0.911	0.944

Note: All efficiency scores are presented in three decimal places except in 2010 due to the close estimations.

In addition, the results show that the bias in DEA scores is quite small. All bias scores are less than 0.03, which indicates that the results from DEA efficiency scores are relatively stable. However, results from this table are relatively general. According to Arjomandi (2011), the annual average PTE does not help in making a fair comparison between the performances of individual banks.

Before detailed assessment of the findings, it is important to highlight that the stochastic approach takes the missing error portion in efficiency measurement into account. The bias measurement could be upward or downward, while upward bias in estimation applied in stochastic BDEA, downward bias (error is considered in measuring the efficiency score) is applied in traditional DEA. Hence, the efficiency results in bias-corrected analyses are definitely influenced by the error portion discarded. The estimation of bias-corrected efficiency may produce lower or higher scores compared to TE in DEA. Assaf and Matawie (2010) noted that due to the upward-bias in the original estimates and the bootstrap correction in the confidence interval (95%), the original estimates lie outside for every observation but close to the lower bound for the confidence interval, whereas the bias-corrected estimates for each observation lie within the confidence interval.

The results in Table 5.2 show that the estimated efficiency scores for all banks are within the confidence interval. Furthermore, Table 5.2 shows the bias difference between the estimated PTE and bias-corrected. The average estimated PTE is 0.985 and bias-corrected bootstrapped scores are 0.984; therefore, the average bias of banks is 0.001. The minor bias of VRS again implies that the results are relatively stable. Among developed countries, CB1 from Australia, appear to be relatively efficient, while two banks from Japan (CB7 and CB8) are relatively efficient. However, CB16 from Malaysia is the only bank that achieved the most efficient bank status among developing countries. CB17 showed the lowest efficiency score in 2007.

In Table 5.3, CB1 and CB7 are efficient in both periods (2007 and 2008), while CB3 is technically efficient compared to 2007. However, CB8 and CB16 efficiency level declined to 0.950 and 0.990, respectively. Average bias for both years shows similar results, indicating that there is a small amount of bias correction to the original PTE scores. Again, Australian banks ranked higher on the efficiency level compared to other banks.

Table 5.4 presents slightly different results. Due to some reason, almost all banks showed lower PTE estimations (the reason for this will be explored in the next section). However, CB3, CB8 and CB14 were located in the true efficiency threshold, where CB3 maintained their best risk management efficiency level. All other banks' PTE scores ranged from 0.824 to 0.902. In addition, the average bias results show 0.018, which is higher than those for 2007 and 2008. The gap in estimated efficiency after bias correction showed that original technical scores differed from the bias-corrected scores. For instance, among 21 commercial banks, CB2 becomes worse with 0.062 bias differences in 2009. The average of estimated confidence intervals showed relatively large difference in lower and upper bound (0.090).

Table 5.2 Individual PTE Estimates based on Estimation by the Bias-Corrected Bootstrap Method (2007)

Financial Institutions	Estimated PTE	Est. Efficiency Bias-Corrected (PTE1)	Bias	Bootstrap Lower Bound	Bootstrap Upper Bound
Banks in Developed Countries					
Australia					
CB1	1.000	1.000	0.000	1.000	1.000
CB2	0.995	0.991	0.004	0.989	0.995
CB3	0.997	0.995	0.002	0.994	0.997
CB4	0.986	0.984	0.002	0.982	0.986
Hong Kong					
CB5	0.988	0.986	0.002	0.984	0.988
Japan					
CB6	0.992	0.991	0.001	0.988	0.992
CB7	1.000	1.000	0.000	1.000	1.000
CB8	1.000	1.000	0.000	1.000	1.000
New Zealand					
CB9	0.995	0.993	0.002	0.991	0.995
CB10	0.994	0.992	0.002	0.990	0.994
CB11	0.952	0.951	0.001	0.949	0.953
Singapore					
CB12	0.996	0.994	0.002	0.991	0.996
Taiwan					
CB13	0.997	0.996	0.001	0.995	0.997
Banks in Developing Countries					
Malaysia					
CB14	0.967	0.965	0.002	0.963	0.967
CB15	0.946	0.944	0.002	0.941	0.947
CB16	1.000	1.000	0.000	1.000	1.000
CB17	0.936	0.934	0.002	0.932	0.936
Philippines					
CB18	0.992	0.991	0.001	0.988	0.992
Thailand					
CB19	0.992	0.991	0.001	0.989	0.992
CB20	0.987	0.986	0.001	0.984	0.987
CB21	0.982	0.981	0.001	0.979	0.982
Mean	0.985	0.984	0.001	0.982	0.986

Note: All estimated efficiency bias-corrected scores are lower than original efficiency estimates of DEA. Four banks (CB1, CB7, CB8 and CB16) perform most efficiently with 1.000, which are the same result with the traditional DEA score.

Table 5.3 Individual PTE Estimates based on Estimation by the Bias-Corrected Bootstrap Method (2008)

Financial Institutions	Estimated PTE	Est. Efficiency Bias-Corrected (PTE1)	Bias	Bootstrap Lower Bound	Bootstrap Upper Bound
Banks in Developed Countries					
Australia					
CB1	1.000	1.000	0.000	1.000	1.000
CB2	0.993	0.992	0.001	0.989	0.993
CB3	1.000	1.000	0.000	1.000	1.000
CB4	0.995	0.993	0.002	0.991	0.995
Hong Kong					
CB5	0.993	0.991	0.002	0.989	0.993
Japan					
CB6	0.994	0.993	0.001	0.990	0.994
CB7	1.000	1.000	0.000	1.000	1.000
CB8	0.950	0.948	0.002	0.945	0.950
New Zealand					
CB9	0.993	0.992	0.001	0.990	0.993
CB10	0.994	0.992	0.002	0.990	0.994
CB11	0.997	0.996	0.001	0.995	0.997
Singapore					
CB12	0.994	0.992	0.002	0.989	0.995
Taiwan					
CB13	0.995	0.994	0.001	0.992	0.995
Banks inDeveloping Countries					
Malaysia					
CB14	0.989	0.988	0.001	0.985	0.989
CB15	0.970	0.969	0.001	0.966	0.970
CB16	0.990	0.989	0.001	0.986	0.990
CB17	1.000	1.000	0.000	1.000	1.000
Philippines					
CB18	0.993	0.993	0.000	0.990	0.993
Thailand					
CB19	0.993	0.993	0.000	0.990	0.993
CB20	0.994	0.993	0.001	0.990	0.994
CB21	0.993	0.993	0.000	0.990	0.993
Mean	0.991	0.991	0.001	0.988	0.991

Note: All estimated efficiency bias-corrected scores are lower than the original efficiency estimates of DEA. Four banks (CB1, CB3, CB7 and CB17) perform most efficiently with 1.000, which are the same result with the traditional DEA score.

Table 5.4 Individual PTE Estimates based on Estimation by the Bias-Corrected Bootstrap Method (2009)

Financial Institutions	Estimated PTE	Est. Efficiency Bias-Corrected (PTE1)	Bias	Bootstrap Lower Bound	Bootstrap Upper Bound
Banks in Developed Countries					
Australia					
CB1	0.861	0.813	0.048	0.744	0.862
CB2	0.904	0.842	0.062	0.808	0.906
CB3	1.000	1.000	0.000	1.000	1.000
CB4	0.827	0.814	0.013	0.734	0.827
Hong Kong					
CB5	0.825	0.812	0.013	0.733	0.826
Japan					
CB6	0.827	0.812	0.015	0.733	0.827
CB7	0.902	0.842	0.060	0.805	0.903
CB8	1.000	1.000	0.000	1.000	1.000
New Zealand					
CB9	0.827	0.811	0.016	0.733	0.827
CB10	0.827	0.817	0.010	0.737	0.827
CB11	0.826	0.815	0.011	0.735	0.827
Singapore					
CB12	0.828	0.791	0.037	0.708	0.829
Taiwan					
CB13	0.822	0.812	0.010	0.733	0.823
Banks in Developing Countries					
Malaysia					
CB14	1.000	1.000	0.000	1.000	1.000
CB15	0.854	0.823	0.031	0.739	0.855
CB16	0.825	0.815	0.010	0.736	0.826
CB17	0.824	0.814	0.010	0.735	0.824
Philippines					
CB18	0.827	0.817	0.010	0.737	0.827
Thailand					
CB19	0.827	0.817	0.010	0.737	0.827
CB20	0.826	0.816	0.010	0.737	0.826
CB21	0.826	0.816	0.010	0.737	0.827
Mean	0.862	0.843	0.018	0.779	0.862

Note: All estimated efficiency bias-corrected scores are lower than the original efficiency estimates of DEA. Three banks (CB3, CB8 and CB14) perform most efficiently with 1.000, which are the same result with the traditional DEA score.

Table 5.5 shows a balance efficiency performance between banks in developed and developing countries. Two banks in developing countries (CB2 and CB7), and two banks in developing countries (CB15 and CB17) are fully efficient. Banks from Malaysia dominated the risk management efficiency scores, while the other two banks almost achieved an efficiency score. However, results in 2010 were different in comparison to other years when the average bias results are almost zero. This is considered to be a signal of excellent performance in those banks.

The situation in 2011 (Table 5.6) indicates that mean bias scores worsened in comparison to 2009. The mean bias is almost 0.03 with the difference at about 0.03. However, CB7 and CB14 are performed well with the highest efficiency scores (100%). CB15 performed the least efficient with 0.756, indicating that this bank is far below the most efficient level.

Lastly, Table 5.7 shows that there are also biases in efficiency estimations; however, the bias scores are quite small. Two banks from Australia are efficient (CB2 and CB3) and CB5 from Hong Kong also provides similar result. None of the banks in the developing countries achieve 100% efficiency scores.

Overall, Figure 5.2, summarising the detailed figures above in a graphic chart, shows the differences in average efficiency estimates from the comparison of the traditional PTE measurement in normal DEA and BDEA approaches. It shows the presence of a small bias average in the efficiency scores in the DEA as the BDEA produced a lower average of PTE for all periods. Similar to this study, Latruffe et al. (2008) also identified bias-corrected PTE in their research, but this was done through the estimation of bias in determinants of PTE. From their estimations, they believe that there is clear-cut evidence that bias is involved in investigating relative superiority among the samples investigated. In a nutshell, Latruffe et al. (2008) support the purpose of bias detection in PTE pursued in this study.

5.6.2 *Second stage of bootstrapping results: a comparison to OTE as a final bias efficiency analysis*

In employing the BDEA, Simar and Wilson (1998) advise that the relative comparisons of performance among firms on the basis of estimated efficiency scores should be made with caution. Continuing from the first stage (Section 5.6.1), this section discusses the observation of the second stage of BDEA results. In Table 5.8 for 2007, Column 2 lists the PTE scores after subtracting the bias efficiency results. It was apparent that all PTE scores were influenced by bias. As a result, the original OTE (OTE0 in column 4) estimations were directly affected, hence producing the new OTE (OTE1 in column 5). Although biases were detected on almost all of the CBs, the average (mean) was marginally small compared to traditional DEA estimations. No bias was detected in four CBs (CB1, CB7, CB8 and CB16). CB7 in Japan continued to operate in the Constant Returns to Scale (CRS) region.

Table 5.5 Individual PTE Estimates based on Estimation by the Bias-Corrected Bootstrap Method (2010)

Financial Institutions	Estimated PTE	Est. Efficiency Bias-Corrected (PTE1)	Bias	Bootstrap Lower Bound	Bootstrap Upper Bound
Banks in Developed Countries					
Australia					
CB1	0.9998	0.9997	0.0001	0.9997	0.9998
CB2	1.0000	1.0000	0.0000	1.0000	1.0000
CB3	0.9999	0.9998	0.0001	0.9998	0.9999
CB4	0.9995	0.9994	0.0001	0.9993	0.9995
Hong Kong					
CB5	0.9990	0.9989	0.0001	0.9988	0.9990
Japan					
CB6	0.9995	0.9994	0.0001	0.9993	0.9995
CB7	1.0000	1.0000	0.0000	1.0000	1.0000
CB8	0.9995	0.9994	0.0001	0.9992	0.9995
New Zealand					
CB9	0.9995	0.9994	0.0001	0.9993	0.9995
CB10	0.9995	0.9995	0.0000	0.9993	0.9995
CB11	0.9994	0.9994	0.0000	0.9992	0.9994
Singapore					
CB12	0.9996	0.9995	0.0001	0.9992	0.9996
Taiwan					
CB13	0.9992	0.9992	0.0000	0.9991	0.9992
Banks in Developing Countries					
Malaysia					
CB14	0.9987	0.9986	0.0001	0.9983	0.9987
CB15	1.0000	1.0000	0.0000	1.0000	1.0000
CB16	0.9995	0.9995	0.0000	0.9993	0.9995
CB17	1.0000	1.0000	0.0000	1.0000	1.0000
Philippines					
CB18	0.9995	0.9994	0.0001	0.9993	0.9995
Thailand					
CB19	0.9995	0.9994	0.0001	0.9993	0.9995
CB20	0.9993	0.9993	0.0000	0.9992	0.9993
CB21	0.9997	0.9997	0.0000	0.9996	0.9997
Mean	0.9996	0.9995	0.00005	0.9994	0.9995

Notes: (i) All estimated efficiency bias-corrected scores are lower than the original efficiency estimates of DEA. Four banks (CB2, CB7, CB15 and CB17) perform most efficiently with 1.000, which are the same result with the traditional DEA score. (ii) All efficiency results are reported in four decimal places due to their close efficiency scores between DMUs.

Table 5.6 Individual PTE Estimates based on Estimation by the Bias-Corrected Bootstrap Method (2011)

Financial Institutions	Estimated PTE	Est. Efficiency Bias-Corrected (PTE1)	Bias	Bootstrap Lower Bound	Bootstrap Upper Bound
Banks in Developed Countries					
Australia					
CB1	0.967	0.938	0.029	0.933	0.969
CB2	0.846	0.806	0.040	0.715	0.848
CB3	0.855	0.813	0.042	0.722	0.856
CB4	0.791	0.766	0.025	0.667	0.793
Hong Kong					
CB5	0.809	0.783	0.026	0.682	0.810
Japan					
CB6	0.808	0.782	0.026	0.683	0.809
CB7	1.000	1.000	0.000	1.000	1.000
CB8	0.776	0.750	0.026	0.657	0.777
New Zealand					
CB9	0.879	0.823	0.056	0.757	0.881
CB10	0.797	0.771	0.026	0.671	0.798
CB11	0.796	0.775	0.021	0.677	0.797
Singapore					
CB12	0.836	0.804	0.032	0.707	0.838
Taiwan					
CB13	0.783	0.764	0.019	0.668	0.784
Banks in Developing Countries					
Malaysia					
CB14	1.000	1.000	0.000	1.000	1.000
CB15	0.781	0.756	0.025	0.659	0.782
CB16	0.823	0.795	0.028	0.697	0.824
CB17	0.803	0.784	0.019	0.685	0.803
Philippines					
CB18	0.796	0.776	0.020	0.678	0.796
Thailand					
CB19	0.794	0.775	0.019	0.667	0.795
CB20	0.795	0.776	0.019	0.678	0.796
CB21	0.795	0.776	0.019	0.678	0.795
Mean	0.835	0.810	0.025	0.728	0.836

Note: All estimated efficiency bias-corrected scores are lower than the original efficiency estimates of DEA. Two banks (CB7 and CB14) perform most efficiently with 1.000, which are the same result with the traditional DEA score.

Table 5.7 Individual PTE Estimates based on Estimation by the Bias-Corrected Bootstrap Method (2012)

Financial Institutions	Estimated PTE	Est. Efficiency Bias-Corrected (PTE1)	Bias	Bootstrap Lower Bound	Bootstrap Upper Bound
Banks in Developed Countries					
Australia					
CB1	0.991	0.990	0.001	0.987	0.992
CB2	1.000	1.000	0.000	1.000	1.000
CB3	1.000	1.000	0.000	1.000	1.000
CB4	0.996	0.995	0.001	0.993	0.996
Hong Kong					
CB5	1.000	1.000	0.000	1.000	1.000
Japan					
CB6	0.994	0.992	0.002	0.990	0.994
CB7	0.974	0.971	0.003	0.966	0.974
CB8	0.994	0.993	0.001	0.990	0.994
New Zealand					
CB9	0.994	0.993	0.001	0.990	0.994
CB10	0.993	0.992	0.001	0.990	0.994
CB11	0.998	0.997	0.001	0.996	0.998
Singapore					
CB12	0.996	0.994	0.002	0.992	0.996
Taiwan					
CB13	0.984	0.983	0.001	0.981	0.984
Banks in Developing Countries					
Malaysia					
CB14	0.974	0.972	0.002	0.968	0.974
CB15	0.969	0.968	0.001	0.965	0.969
CB16	0.969	0.968	0.001	0.966	0.969
CB17	0.986	0.985	0.001	0.983	0.986
Philippines					
CB18	0.993	0.993	0.000	0.990	0.994
Thailand					
CB19	0.994	0.993	0.001	0.991	0.994
CB20	0.993	0.992	0.001	0.990	0.993
CB21	0.992	0.991	0.001	0.989	0.992
Mean	0.990	0.989	0.001	0.987	0.990

Note: All estimated efficiency bias-corrected scores are lower than the original efficiency estimates of DEA. Three banks (CB2, CB3 and CB5) perform most efficiently with 1.000, which are the same result with the traditional DEA score.

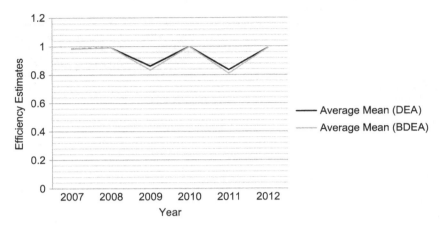

Figure 5.2 Comparative of PTE Results in Normal DEA and BDEA Estimation Models.

Table 5.8 OTE DEA Estimate and Bias-Corrected Efficiency Scores (2007)

Financial Institutions	*Est. PTE Bias-Corrected (PTE1)*	*SE from normal DEA Estimation*	*OTE0*	*OTE1*	*Bias*
Banks in Developed Countries					
Australia					
CB1	1.000	0.953	0.953	0.953	0.000
CB2	0.991	0.950	0.945	0.941	0.004
CB3	0.995	0.950	0.947	0.945	0.002
CB4	0.984	0.956	0.943	0.941	0.002
Hong Kong					
CB5	0.986	0.955	0.943	0.942	0.001
Japan					
CB6	0.991	0.957	0.949	0.948	0.001
CB7	1.000	1.000	1.000	1.000	0.000
CB8	1.000	0.838	0.838	0.838	0.000
New Zealand					
CB9	0.993	0.953	0.948	0.946	0.002
CB10	0.992	0.955	0.948	0.947	0.002
CB11	0.951	0.957	0.911	0.910	0.001
Singapore					
CB12	0.994	0.953	0.949	0.947	0.002

Financial Institutions	Est. PTE Bias-Corrected (PTE1)	SE from normal DEA Estimation	OTE0	OTE1	Bias
Taiwan					
CB13	0.996	0.957	0.954	0.953	0.001
Bank in Developing Countries					
Malaysia					
CB14	0.965	0.955	0.923	0.921	0.002
CB15	0.944	0.949	0.898	0.896	0.002
CB16	1.000	0.957	0.957	0.957	0.000
CB17	0.934	0.957	0.895	0.893	0.002
Philippines					
CB18	0.991	0.957	0.949	0.948	0.001
Thailand					
CB19	0.991	0.957	0.949	0.948	0.001
CB20	0.986	0.957	0.944	0.943	0.001
CB21	0.981	0.957	0.940	0.939	0.001
Mean	0.984	0.951	0.937	0.936	0.001

Note: OTE1 = PTE1 x SE, Bias = OTE1-OTE0.

For 2012, the mean difference of the two periods is better. Through a re-sampling process, the results show that all efficiency types (OTE, PTE and SE) are close to 1.000 with only 0.001 bias found. Four banks have zero bias (CB2, CB3, CB5 and CB18) with three banks (CB2, CB3 and CB5) appearing to be relatively efficient in 2012.

According to Tables 5.8 and 5.9, no banks showed similar efficiencies in both periods. On the other hand, banks that were efficient in normal TE measurement show similar efficiencies in TE for both periods. But all other inefficient banks become worse after bootstrapping analysis has been used. For instance, the score for CB7 decreased the most after the highest amount of bias correction (0.003) compared to other banks. The result indicates that CB7 is not consistently efficient over the two periods.

In conclusion, after the criticism of "deterministic" DEA efficiency estimation for lacking rigorous statistical foundations, the bootstrapping technique presented in this study was perceived as a useful method for constructing a stochastic DEA model for measuring risk management efficiency in banks with derivative instruments. Confidence intervals in the efficiency analysis developed in this approach provide a bank's risk management managers with more accurate information for better decision-making. The bootstrapping efficiency analysis has clearly indicated its ability to reduce bias and noise in data with better estimation than the normal DEA approach. Furthermore, with the small sample size of this study, BDEA has provided

Table 5.9 OTE DEA Estimate and Bias-Corrected Efficiency Scores (2012)

Financial Institutions	Est. PTE Bias-Corrected (PTE1)	SE from normal DEA Estimation	OTE0	**OTE1**	Bias
Banks in Developed Countries					
Australia					
CB1	0.990	1.000	0.991	0.990	0.001
CB2	1.000	1.000	1.000	1.000	0.000
CB3	1.000	1.000	1.000	1.000	0.000
CB4	0.995	1.000	0.996	0.995	0.001
Hong Kong					
CB5	1.000	1.000	1.000	1.000	0.000
Japan					
CB6	0.992	1.000	0.994	0.992	0.002
CB7	0.971	0.998	0.972	0.969	0.003
CB8	0.993	1.000	0.994	0.993	0.001
New Zealand					
CB9	0.993	0.999	0.994	0.992	0.002
CB10	0.992	1.000	0.993	0.992	0.001
CB11	0.997	1.000	0.998	0.997	0.001
Singapore					
CB12	0.994	1.000	0.996	0.994	0.002
Taiwan					
CB13	0.983	1.000	0.984	0.983	0.001
Bank in Developing Countries					
Malaysia					
CB14	0.972	1.000	0.974	0.972	0.002
CB15	0.968	1.000	0.969	0.968	0.001
CB16	0.968	1.000	0.969	0.968	0.001
CB17	0.985	1.000	0.986	0.985	0.001
Philippines					
CB18	0.993	1.000	0.993	0.993	0.000
Thailand					
CB19	0.993	1.000	0.994	0.993	0.001
CB20	0.992	1.000	0.993	0.992	0.001
CB21	0.991	1.000	0.992	0.991	0.001
Mean	0.989	0.9998	0.990	0.989	0.001

Note: OTE1 = PTE1 x SE, Bias = OTE1-OTE0

accurate and reliable results where all bias estimations for each observation lie within the confidence interval. In short, the bootstrapping results confirm that there is a bias in analysing efficiency measurement by showing a small fraction of the means.

5.6.3 *Efficiency difference tests*

Following Chen (2002), this study further examined the BDEA/DEA results by conducting efficiency difference tests between the sampled banks. To compare the efficiency difference test between deterministic efficiency scores of ordinary DEA and stochastic approach of BDEA, Welch's mean test and the Mann–Whitney test have been used to test for inefficiency differences. For Welch's mean test, the test statistic under the assumption of unequal variances is given by:

$$\bar{X}_a - \frac{\bar{X}_b}{\sqrt{\left(\frac{\sigma_a^2}{N_a}\right) + \left(\frac{\sigma_b^2}{N_b}\right)}} \tag{5.9}$$

which follows the t distribution of freedoms, where $\bar{X}_a$ and $\bar{X}_b$ are the sample means and σ_a^2 and σ_b^2 are the sample variances of the inefficiencies. This test does not assume that both methods have the same standard deviation (SD). As stated by Sawilowsky (2002), $\sigma_1^2 \neq \sigma_2^2$.

For the Mann–Whitney test, the test statistic z value is calculated by $Z = u - E(u)/\sqrt{V(u)}$, and u is the lower figure between the calculated magnitude of U_a and U_b:

$$U_a = N_a N_b + \frac{N_a(N_a+1)}{2} - W_a$$

$$U_b = N_a N_b + \frac{N_b(N_b+1)}{2} - W_b$$

$$E(\mu) = \frac{N_a N_b}{2}$$

$$V(\mu) = \frac{N_a N_b (N_a + N_b + 1)}{12} \tag{5.10}$$

In this study, one of N has large sample sizes ($N > 15$). The z value is generated and refers to the standardised normal distribution to test the null hypothesis. The hypotheses of the OTE, PTE and SE of banks based on BDEA approach are better than those that were evaluated for DEA efficiency measurement (Table 5.10).

Based on the result of Welch's test, the p-value for all types of efficiency are larger than the cut-off point (0.05). This indicates that the null hypotheses are to be rejected and to accept the alternative hypotheses. Therefore, the analysis concludes that the evidence is not enough to surmise that these

Table 5.10 Efficiency Difference between DEA and BDEA based on Welch's Test

Classification	Test Procedure	DEA vs. BDEA		
		TE	PTE	SE
Traditional efficiency tests	Welch's test	0.522	0.524	1.000

Note: ** indicates significance at the 5% level.

Table 5.11 Efficiency Difference between DEA and BDEA based on the Mann–Whitney Test

Classification	Test Procedure	DEA			BDEA		
		TE	PTE	SE	TE	PTE	SE
Traditional efficiency tests	Mann–Whitney test	131.84	130.90	126.50**	121.16	122.10	126.50**

Note: ** indicates significance at the 5% level.

two approaches means are different, even though the analysis assumed that the two method groups have different SDs. These results are supported by Chen (2002) who found no difference in measuring technical efficiencies based on DEA and CCDEA. However, measurements using both deterministic and stochastic approaches are important due to the intrinsic difficulty of prediction, particularly in the environment of the banking system.

In contrast, different results are presented in Table 5.11, where both DEA and BDEA approaches are found to be statistically significant for SE analysis ($p = 0.000$). This result implies that the use of BDEA approach provides similar results to those provided by the DEA measurements. The advanced setting of the bootstrapping mechanism has strengthened the DEA measurement. In addition, it does not change the instinctive differences between the traditional and advanced efficiency measurement.

Overall, the results of the efficiency measurement from the BDEA approach were consistent with major findings from the literature (see Section 5.3), except some dissimilarities from previous studies in risk management efficiency measurement contexts.

5.7 Implications

After both DEA and BDEA results have been contrasted, the study compares how BDEA has contributed significant theoretical knowledge and practical application in the context of risk efficiency measurement of derivatives in banking institutions in the Asia-Pacific region. The implications are collectively discussed from both the first and second stage of the BDEA results.

5.7.1 Theoretical implications

The first implication of this work relates to theoretical knowledge. This study has further strengthened and refined risk management efficiency measurement in banking sector for a viable model which allows for investigating the potential impact of derivative activities on risk management efficiency.

Although the DEA model from the previous stage met all of the relevant criteria for viability, the results were preliminary, and some parts were too vague and incoherent to be considered as a complete model that is representative of risk management efficiency measurement. The convergence of DEA with the bootstrapping approach has shown that it is possible to take a part of the previous DEA model and refine it with an extended approach. One of the major implications of the adoption of the bootstrapping approach is that the initial model can serve as an initial risk management efficiency measurement framework from which to study the accuracy and dependability of problem solving in more detail. With this connection, this study explicitly proved that the bootstrapping method is useful for refining and critiquing the model assessments.

This bootstrapping approach is introduced to strengthen the risk management concept and evaluation. The integrated methodology allows for a targeted analysis procedure that is more comprehensive in nature (Dong and Featherstone 2006; Casu and Molyneux 2003). Specifically, a bootstrap strategy has a significant impact in enhancing the reliability of risk management modelling. Although the BDEA method used in this study is not new, bootstrapping was combined with DEA in ways that have not been experimented upon in previous studies. In particular, the analysis method started with the identification of input and output variables derived from the formula given in the dollar-offset ratio in hedge effectiveness test of hedge accounting. From that, the derivative instrument as an input has been investigated using the DEA approach to examine the impact of the use of derivatives as hedging instruments for risk management efficiency in banks. Consequently, the hedge effectiveness through the measurement of the dollar-offset ratio has been enhanced with some advanced characteristics offered by the BDEA approach.

A non-parametric bootstrap also has the advantage of making it easy for the analysis of this study to estimate the precision metrics such as standard errors and confidence intervals for better risk management efficiency measurement that can be estimated from the sample data (Davison 1997; Efron and Tibshirani 1994). With bias reduction estimates, new ventures on efficiency measurement based on the derivatives usage exhibit higher effectiveness in reducing risk effects. Other than reducing sampling error issues, this approach led to the development of the traditional DEA measurement. It proved to be a fruitful analysis method that led to a refined traditional efficiency model describing small data. Overall, this non-parametric BDEA approach allows the study to interpret the resulting risk measure estimates

(Cotter and Dowd 2006) as potential estimates of risk management with derivatives requirements.

The method of breaking the analysis into non-bias reduction (DEA) and bias reduction (BDEA) has solved the risk management efficiency measurement with a realistic solution (Sadjadi and Omrani 2010; Xue and Harker 1999). The approach and interconnection to the classical efficiency measurement were easily contrasted for better problem-solving and decision-making where it merged the two measurement concepts. Again, the method provided transparent, more robust and more flexible ways to ensure the viability of the method.

5.7.2 *Practical implications*

Practically, banks are continually concerned with developing a better risk management efficiency measurement approach, which can guide their decision-making process with accuracy and reliability. Research has shown that an efficiency measurement framework can be an effective tool in the decision-making process related to risky undertakings (Wanke and Barros 2014; Chan et al. 2014; Kasman and Carvallo 2013; Chang and Chiu 2006; Laeven 1999). The BDEA approach developed in this study has provided such a tool with an explicit focus on bias-corrected estimates that improve upon efficiency measures derived from conventional DEA. This helps risk management teams to connect this knowledge that they may consider new in banking perspectives, to knowledge they may already have. Although this risk efficiency measurement in the banking sector study was done within the specific context of derivatives and the hedge effectiveness test, the results can nonetheless be related to research into decision-making and benchmarking described in Chapter 4.

The BDEA can also increase the potential scope for reporting and segregating the duties within banking organisations to intensify the role of financial derivatives as a tool in risk management. This "new" risk management perspective must treat derivatives as a solution to create more effective risk management strategies. Although previous studies have found that banks in the current markets have engaged quite extensively in derivative activities to reduce the probability of financial distress (Stulz 2015; Sinkey and Carter 2001; Whidbee and Wohar 1999), more reliable analyses are needed to specifically measure firm's risk management efficiency using derivatives.

5.8 Conclusion

After outlining some weaknesses of classical DEA, this chapter has introduced the utility of bootstrap in the risk management context to assist in the development of a BDEA approach. Previous studies were reviewed to show that BDEA is able to solve the issues of uncertainty of noise in the data and small sample size (sampling error) under a linear programming optimisation technique. This study provides a good solution through the accuracy of a prediction and estimation that is practical within perplexing environments and has reached a high-level efficient solution method that can solve real problems. The argument is that a combination of both DEA and BDEA on risk management efficiency in banks is now able to appropriately incorporate two complimentary approaches, hence providing a more sustainable efficiency measurement for institutions.

Part B: Sensitivity analysis

5.9 Introduction

Uncertainty in the business environment is one of the primary reasons why sensitivity analysis is important for any type of risk management (Saltelli et al. 2000a; Saltelli et al. 2000b; Pannell 1997). In linear programming, the sensitivity analysis can show any impacts on the model from changes in the environment. Testing the percentage of differences, it shows how the output of the model can change due to a slight difference in model input that finally affects the performance of the item. As the previous chapter has derived efficiency scores based on absolute values, the purpose of sensitivity analysis is to examine how the model operates with variable values in inputs.

In order to observe the impact of uncertainty on decision-making, the range of differences from the percentage of sensitivity adopted by Thompson et al. (1996) is generated to check the parameter values and assumptions of the efficiency model that are subject to change and error. In this approach, the value of a numerical parameter is set through the levels at which the percentage will be set. The sensitivity analysis will examine the impact of uncertainty in two conditions:

1   To vary input parameter for extreme efficient DMUs one at a time, leaving all other DMUs at standard or base values (Section 5.12.2); and
2   To examine combinations of changes in input and output for both efficient and inefficient DMUs (Section 5.12.3).

5.10 Need for including uncertainty in sensitivity analysis: context

Researchers have to be alert to sensitivity of the model to perturbation in the data while using the DEA method (Zhu 2009). There can be changes in parameters due to uncertainty in the environment in the banking sector, either internally or externally. Researchers need to conduct a sensitivity analysis in order to check if the calculated frontiers of DEA models are stable if the frontier DMUs remain in the same position after data changes are made. Furthermore, due partly to the lack of consideration of uncertainty elements on the trend to improve performance development to perform sensitivity analysis to cater for uncertainty issues, there is increasing pressure to undertake uncertainty analysis in various sectors. As stated by Frey (1992), uncertainty issues must be taken into account to help decision makers and analysts make dependable decisions. Therefore, the measurement of firm's risk management efficiency must critically evaluate to support more accurate policy making.

According to Zhu (2009), sensitivity analysis of DEA creates a super-efficiency model of DEA. This sensitivity analysis is able to determine the change in model's output values (changes in efficiency values) that result from uncertain changes in input values. Besides, one can often use the same set of model runs for sensitivity analyses. It is possible to carry out a sensitivity analysis of the model around a current solution, and then use it as part of a first-order uncertainty analysis. The sensitivity analysis may change the input and/or output to test the stability of the efficiency frontier in a DEA model. For instance, Ahn and Seiford (1993) examined the sensitivity analysis of DEA results to the variable and model selection. Similarly, Charnes et al. (1985) preserved the efficiency frontier with a more stable and determined impact by changing a single output variable as a test.

5.11 Sensitivity analysis: approach

This model has been applied in various efficiency studies, for example, Charnes et al. (1992) and Charnes et al. (1996). The sensitivity analysis allows for situations where simultaneous proportional change is assumed for all input and output parameters for a specific DMU under consideration. By incorporating this criterion, inputs or outputs can be changed individually to test the efficiency of DMU. Consequently, regions with stable enumerations can be identified and obtained (Charnes et al. 1992). However, the weakness of this approach is that this method is only applicable for testing efficient DMUs, with the data for the remaining (inefficient) DMUs is assumed as fixed. This approach is inadequate and unconvincing since possible data errors may occur in each DMU under observation. In addition, input and output data of inefficient DMUs are also prone to uncertainty. As a result, it is important that all DMUs be considered as operating under conditions of uncertainty that can create data variations.

Note that in the study by Thompson et al. (1996), sensitivity analysis was performed using a straightforward procedure by varying the data for the inputs and outputs simultaneously. They explored the sensitivity case using a simple illustrative scenario in which data was allowed to vary simultaneously for extremely efficient DMUs, but not for efficient DMUs. In the extremely efficient DMU_0, all outputs were decreased and all inputs were increased by a specified percentage. The same treatment was also applied to other efficient DMUs. On the contrary, the reserve adjustment in the other DMU_j has been made by increasing the proportion of all outputs and decreasing the proportion of all inputs by the same amount (or percentage). Thus, the DMU_0 will be reduced along with other extremely efficient DMUs (DMU_0) and the ratios for the other DMUs (DMU_j) will be increased. Continuing this treatment, the DMU_0 then progressively lost the status of being a fully efficient DMU and no longer remained a top ranker. In their study, a 5% increase was introduced in each input for extremely efficient DMUs, and a 5% decrease of inputs introduced for the other inefficient DMUs. Even though the 5% increase in portion of inputs was found to worsen DMU performance as efficiency scores fell, they managed to maintain their top-ranked status. Decreasing inputs by 5% indicated that the efficiency performances of DMUs were better and results were robust and more stable. These results further supported other efficiency studies which found these classifications of efficient and inefficient performers to be rigorous and dependable in DEA. However, even though the results show good indications for a sensitivity analysis, the proportional decreases and increases of inputs and outputs determined by Thompson et al. (1996) were not motivated and guided by the uncertain environment.

Sensitivity analysis has been discussed within a deterministic approach in order to increase the efficiency levels of a firm based on the projections of input and output suggested by duality sensitivity analysis. General methodological issues only show the impact on efficient and inefficient DMUs and do not review the impact of uncertainty on firm performances. In relation to the above discussion, this section is motivated to examine the impact of changes in parameters due to a stipulated percentage. In this case, Frey (1992) has strongly recommended that the sensitivity of results assuming different values and amounts of the decision variable(s) needs to be explored using a sensitivity analysis. This analysis is able to determine changes in a model's output values (changes in efficiency values) which result from uncertain changes in input values.

Seiford and Zhu (1998) developed a technique of sensitivity measurement whereby the efficiency of the efficient DMU was assumed to be deteriorating, while the efficiencies of the other DMUs were improving. Under their assumption, the maximum percentage of data change is set at the same figure while testing the efficient DMU and other DMUs, thus fulfilling the conditions for determining an extremely efficient DMU.

Therefore, in this section, the study focusses on a DEA sensitivity analysis based on the assumptions developed by Zhu (2009). Zhu who assumed that since an increase of any output or decrease of any input cannot worsen the efficiency of DMU, the proportional decreases in outputs or proportional increases in inputs are equated as follows:

$$\hat{x}_{i0} = \beta_i x_{i0} \beta_i \geq 1, i = 1, \ldots, m \tag{5.11}$$

$$\hat{y}_{r0} = \alpha_r y_{r0} \ 0 < \alpha_r \leq 1, r = 1, \ldots, s \tag{5.12}$$

where x_{i0} $(i = 1,2,...,m)$ and y_{r0} $(r = 1,2,...,s)$ are, respectively, the inputs and outputs for a specific extreme efficient $DMU_0 = DMU_{J0}$ among n DMUs.

5.12 Sensitivity model and the initial solutions: methodological framework

5.12.1 Steps to perform sensitivity analysis (parameters and sensitivity model)

This study has used the Risk Solver Platform software to perform the sensitivity analysis, which begins by reviewing parameters in the Task Pane. The input cell is defined as a parameter, selecting the cell by choosing the 'Parameter' and 'Sensitivity'. For instance, two parameters at C3 and D23 were defined. Parameters C3 until C23, and D3 until D23 were selected, and their properties were shown in the lower part of the Task Pane.

The next step is to enter a lower and upper limit on values for the parameter and insert the formula as =PsiSenParam (Lower,Upper,Base) to provide a different list of values which represent the variability of parameter value. The parameter then appears in the Task Pane Model.

The sensitivity analysis results can be solved, produced and confirmed by clicking on the "Auto Adjust Sensitivity Analysis" which appears at the top of the Task Pane. From there, a new solution appears with the message "Solver has converged to the current solution". All constraints are satisfied.

5.12.2 Sensitivity of the extreme efficient DMU

Since DMU7 (CB7) was determined as an extremely efficient DMU based on the ranking principle over other DMUs in 2007, 2008 and 2012, it is considered as the top-ranked DMU. Besides that, CB7 has also achieved efficient results based on the projection from Dual Weight Analysis in 2007. This section explores the changes of parameters in CB7 (in this case the input change or variance), leaving all other DMUs at standard or base values, in order to examine the impact on optimal solution on risk management efficiency results.

From the results, CB7 defined as the extreme efficient DMU achieves efficient frontier and mean OTE of the 21 sampled banks turned out to be 0.768 and 0.755 with increasing or input variation of ±5% and ±10%, respectively (see Table 5.12). This indicates that CB7 remains efficient in both cases of increasing or decreasing percentage of input. Following this, CB7 can still be considered as one of the most efficient DMU that can serve as benchmark for other banks. In contrast, there are many banks (e.g. CB3, CB11, CB16 and CB18) that showed a tremendous decrease in their level of efficiency when there was ±5% and ±10% change in CB7's input.

Table 5.12 Variation in Input for Extreme Efficient DMU with Stipulated
Percentage

DMU	Percentage (Δ%)	
	±5%	±10%
CB7	1.000	1.000
(Extreme Efficient)		
CB1	0.945	0.951
CB2	0.942	0.914
CB3	0.548	0.463
CB4	0.943	0.943
CB5	0.935	0.943
CB6	0.940	0.949
CB8	0.838	0.140
CB9	0.948	0.948
CB10	0.949	0.949
CB11	0.377	0.908
CB12	0.837	0.008
CB13	0.954	0.954
CB14	0.923	0.923
CB15	0.898	0.898
CB16	0.000	0.661
CB17	0.895	0.895
CB18	0.003	0.131
CB19	0.679	0.949
CB20	0.679	0.941
CB21	0.888	0.382
Mean OTE	0.768	0.755

Notes: (i) Weighted difference = Weighted Output − Weighted input, (ii) Projection amount refers to the sensitivity duality weight presented in Chapter 4.

5.12.3 Sensitivity analysis for examining combinations of changes in input and output for both efficient and inefficient DMUs

In order to investigate the sensitivity analyses gap between the top-ranked DMU (CB7) and other banks through the variation of input and output parameters, the percentage of projection from Table 4.14 (Section 4.6.6) is again referred to. As stated in that Table, most inefficient banks (except CB1 and CB2) need to change their input approximately by ±5% to ±10%, and output approximately by ±5% (except in CB8) in order to move up their efficient frontier. In that process, only interest rate swap (input) and customer deposits are involved in the analysis (output 2).

Comparatively, mixed results were found after varied percentage rates of change were imposed in the input and output parameters in this analysis. As shown in Table 5.13, nine banks (CB1, CB2, CB4, CB7, CB13, CB14, CB16, CB19 and CB21) perform on the same efficiency level after 4% changes were imposed. However, at the rate of 5% change, the impact is completely different as most banks showed reduction in their efficiency levels. For instance,

Table 5.13 Variation in Input and Output (Customer Deposits) for both Efficient and Inefficient DMUs with Stipulated Percentage

DMU	Percentage (Δ %) in Input and Output	
	±4%	±5%
Efficient CB7	1.000	1.000
Inefficient		
CB1	0.953	0.953
CB2	0.945	0.945
CB3	0.868	0.947
CB4	0.943	0.895
CB5	0.842	0.905
CB6	0.945	0.949
CB8	0.350	0.838
CB9	0.728	0.001
CB10	0.949	0.684
CB11	0.000	0.000
CB12	0.914	0.003
CB13	0.954	0.954
CB14	0.923	0.923
CB15	0.898	0.898
CB16	0.957	0.957
CB17	0.876	0.895
CB18	0.132	0.949
CB19	0.949	0.000
CB20	0.407	0.944
CB21	0.940	0.940
Mean OTE	0.784	0.742

Note: Percentage (Δ %) is the variation of percentage of input and output (customer deposits).

CB8 and CB20 have increased in their efficiency levels from 0.350 and 0.407 to 0.838 and 0.944, respectively. Twelve banks retained their efficiency levels, including CB1, CB2, CB3, CB7, CB13, CB14, CB15, CB16, CB17, CB18, CB20 and CB21. Moreover, CB7 maintained its position as the most efficient bank in Asia-Pacific region. In contrast, the analysis noticed that CB11 suffered the worst impact from the changes in parameters with the most inefficient results. In the presence of sensitivity analysis, the average for banks in developed countries (CB1–CB13) is ahead of banks in developing countries (CB14–CB21) by attaining 4% change in risk management efficiency (0.799 > 0.760), but lower average with 5% stipulated change (0.698 <0.813).

5.12.4 Verification and validation of the model

As discussed in Chapter 4, this study has taken several steps to check the model's construct or verify its validity. As this section has transformed the analysis using an Excel based data input system, the validity and verification requirements were rechecked using the Solver software available on the commercial Premium Solver Platform. This test is to check if the model is able to achieve satisfactory conditions to see an interrelationship between the input and output parameters in measuring the efficiency level of the banks. Steps taken are as follows:

1 Following the right procedure when developing the model.
2 Ensuring that the trial results indicate the model is working. Initially, the model experienced some problems such as unboundedness and infeasibility. However, the model was then remedied until it provided a satisfactory output.
3 Ensuring that constraints restricting the model to realistic solutions were imposed. In this step, the objective function and the constraints were developed from risk management efficiency in banking perspectives through the usage of derivative instrument and based on the hedge effectiveness theories and practices. Therefore, both objective functions and constraints were relevant for risk management efficiency and decision-making, and formulating risk management strategies.
4 Ensuring that the data is set up in a manner such that the data replicated real-life situations in practice. Data is specified based on risk management using financial derivative and hedge effectiveness perspectives. Data is collected from financial instruments and other secondary sources in derivative trading for hedging purposes. Therefore, the outcome of the model should be more informative for both financial analysts and risk management practitioners.

5.13 Comparative results

5.13.1 Increasing input for extreme efficient DMU (CB7) with stipulated percentage

In relation to Table 5.12 of the sensitivity analysis, assuming an increase in input for extremely efficient DMU (CB7) with a stipulated percentage, this study believes that when the input parameter of an efficient bank is changed, it will bring about significant change in the efficiency performance of other banks and the mean OTE. This is evident from the fact that the values of mean OTE obtained by changing the input of one efficient bank from the sample ranged between 0.768 and 0.755, which is very significantly different from 0.937 achieved in the mean OTE value of the deterministic DEA (see Table 5.14).

Table 5.14 Comparative Efficiency Results between Deterministic DEA and Sensitivity Analysis for the Extreme Efficient Bank (CB7)

	Deterministic DEA	Sensitivity Analysis	
	Assuming No Data Variation	±5%	±10%
Mean OTE	0.937	0.768	0.755

Table 5.15 Comparative Efficiency Results between Deterministic DEA and
Sensitivity Analysis for the Input and Output Variation in both
Efficient and Inefficient Banks in Asia-Pacific

	Deterministic DEA	*Sensitivity Analysis*	
	Assuming No Data Variation	±4%	±5%
Mean OTE	0.937	0.784	0.742

In short, by varying one input over a range in CB7, the efficiency level
of other banks also varies – the higher the variation, the bigger the difference to the original efficiency values. Therefore, the efficient frontier of the
Asia-Pacific banking industry has been proven to have changed as a result
of change in input parameters.

5.13.2 Sensitivity in examining the combinations of changes in input and output for both efficient and inefficient DMUs

As shown in Table 5.15, the variation in both input and output parameters
indicate that the mean OTE across the banks have changed tremendously.
With 4% and 5% changes, the OTE is reduced by 0.153 (0.937–0.784) and
0.195 (0.937–0.724), respectively.

Here, the changes are not attuned to the purpose of finding the best-
performing banks in Asia-Pacific, but are more focussed on how the overall efficiency patterns of banks vary when the element of uncertainty is
involved.

5.14 Implications

Banks do not make profits. On top of that, banks face uncertainties from
either internal or external environment. In this situation, besides demon-
strating the new efficiency scores for all banks in the sample, this study has
determined how the variation of the parameters (input and output) under an
uncertainty environment can affect the efficiency level in risk management
measurement in banks.

To discuss the implication of the sensitivity analysis, it is worth mention-
ing here that these combinations of input and output variables are uncom-
mon in the efficiency literature. The input used is a derivative instrument
that is then analysed for its impact on the risk management efficiency of
banks. Therefore, the sensitivity analysis takes account of uncertainty in
the environment that banks are unable to obviate and challenge the risk
management efficiency of banks.

Furthermore, the work done by scholars in measuring sensitivity analysis in efficiency studies so far has focussed on moving the efficiency levels from inefficient to efficient DMUs (Thompson et al. 1996; Ahn and Seiford 1993). But the results of this study add another dimension to the literature and practice by showing how situations of uncertainty in the organisation can be integrated into efficiency measurement frameworks in general and for the banking sectors in particular. The model is operational and can be used in real banking business scenarios, especially those that operate under uncertain environments.

It is also demonstrated that market volatility impacts risk management efficiency in banks especially when the interest rates vary. Here, the uncertainty environment certainly influences the usage of derivatives and its impact on the hedged items either for hedging or trading purposes. Indirectly, the analysis provides a calculation of general descriptions of uncertainty associated with risk management efficiency model predictions.

Therefore, the study has succeeded in developing a sensitivity analysis for efficiency measurement which is able to quantify the potential for efficiency improvement from capitalising on uncertainties in the banking world. As a result, policy decisions can be made more precisely in light of predicted levels of a bank's risk management performance in the event of the actualisation of any change in the environment.

5.15 Conclusion

This section has provided and elaborated a need for sensitivity analysis in the context of banking risk management efficiency and performance measurement of stochastic modelling. The approaches used for this purpose range from relatively simple deterministic sensitivity analysis (as what has been discussed in performing the target, reduction and increase for inefficient banks to reach 100% relative efficiency in Chapter 4) to more complex models that involve variations of percentage change in parameters. Here, Monte Carlo methods for uncertainty analysis may prove to be unattractive due to their complexity.

Banks operate under environments that are fraught with uncertainties where outcomes or events cannot be predicted with certainty; the sensitivity analysis varies the percentage of input and output in an attempt to obtain insights into their impact on efficiency levels of risk management in banks. This analysis hopes to achieve another way of checking the sensitivity of DEA efficiency of a DMU which will contribute to a reliable efficiency measurement of banks that incorporates the uncertainty and instability of real-life business environments.

In short, a sensitivity analysis can provide a systematic assessment of the impact of changes in parameter value. However, this study believes that no matter how much attention is given to quantifying and reducing uncertainties in modelling, uncertainties will still remain.

Part C: Chance-constrained stochastic variables (parameters uncertainty)

As more and more studies are conducted on DEA, researchers have felt the need to incorporate stochastic considerations into the model to accommodate the presence of measurement and specification errors. Under the condition that only a probability of or less (uncertainty), observed banks will do better than best-practice banks, how best to compare relative efficiency between Asia-Pacific banks from 2007 to 2012? Banks operate in services sectors which trade in complex and uncertain environments. Consequently, when examining the relationship between multiple simultaneous inputs and output range in environments that are not certain, a deterministic approach can lead to erroneous conclusions.

Furthermore, to estimate the "best-practice" frontier, the parametric has to assume restrictions on the frontier production function and the error term. Although organisational units can be efficient without being in the frontier due to randomness, strict restrictions or assumptions on the distributional form of the error term is the major drawback of this method. On the other hand, a non-parametric approach or DEA places fewer assumptions on the frontier. It, however, is deterministic and does not allow efficient units to be out of the frontier (Kasman and Turgutlu 2007).

To address this disadvantage of deterministic DEA, Land et al. (1993) have developed a new model for DEA, known as a CCDEA. The new model included uncertainty into its input and/or output parameters. This model overcomes the disadvantages of the deterministic DEA model, and is better able to contribute to risk management strategy and performance in situations of uncertainty. In addition, transformation of the traditional DEA model using CC programming (Sengupta 1987) has allowed the investigation of the effect of stochastic variations in input and output data on weighting schemes for efficiency measurement. This resulted in a shift in the focus of research from full efficiency (100%) evaluation under traditional DEA models to a less demanding objective of achieving a desired level of efficiency with a sufficiently high probability (Olesen and Petersen 1995). In this approach, the constraints involving random variables need to be satisfied with a certain level of probability of efficiency, which explain the diversity of criteria for optimising the stochastic objective functions. Therefore, the new model included uncertainty into its inputs and/or outputs to overcome the shortcoming of the non-stochastic (deterministic) DEA model.

Therefore, this study will utilise a CCDEA approach for measurement of risk management efficiency of Asia-Pacific banks from 2007 to 2012. It will then compare both CCDEA and non-stochastic (deterministic) DEA, and also compare CCDEA to other stochastic DEA (BDEA) to measure risk management efficiency differences between approaches of Asia-Pacific banking institutions.

5.16 Uncertainty issues in parameters: context

5.16.1 Uncertainty in banking operation and business and uncertainty issue in derivatives and, input and output variables

As noted in the previous chapters, uncertainty issues in the banking world can arise from a range of output parameters which can create uncertainty and cause financial crisis including mortgage loans and customer deposits. For instance, if banks have a ten-year fixed-rate loan funded by a three-year customer deposit term, the bank faces a risk of borrowing new deposits, or refinancing them at a higher rate for three years. In this way, interest rate increases would reduce net interest income and lead to lower profits. The bank would only benefit with higher net interest income if the rates fall due to the cost of renewing deposits decreasing and earning rates on assets not changing (Schlueter et al. 2015; Abedifar et al. 2013; Diamond and Dybvig 1986). In the case of mortgage loans, even though mortgage-backed securities (MBS) initially offer attractive rate of returns due to higher interest rate on the mortgages, lower credit capabilities can ultimately cause a higher propensity to default (Diamond and Rajan 2009). Moreover, the housing price also may stop rising and indeed start falling, in turn, creating mortgage defaults. Given this, mortgage lenders impose a default premium on the loans they originate to compensate for the possibility that borrowers will not make payments. Nowadays, risk studies have shown increasing evidence of defaulting behaviour from the average mortgage borrower, therefore, mortgage loans as a product category have become riskier (Demyanyk and Van Hemert 2009).

Given the seriousness of this issue, Krainer and LeRoy (2010) have developed a structural model that can be used to evaluate mortgage loan rates for all lenders' institutions. The model yields reasonable assumptions about the future path of house prices, where mortgage default is not treated as a random event precipitated by a life circumstance (e.g. job loss, illness, etc.). The payment default is considered to be a strategic event that occurs when a borrower agrees that the cost of continuing mortgage payments, less the value of housing services or rental income, exceeds the expected value of future capital gains.

An increasing body of empirical studies suggests that banks that rely more heavily on customer deposit funding performed better during the global financial crisis than those that were more dependent on other sources (Beltratti and Stulz 2012; Dagher and Kazimov 2012). Bank-depositor relationships mitigate runs, suggesting that the relationship with depositors help banks reduce fragility (Iyer and Puria 2012). The issue of risk and uncertainty has been addressed since 1972 when Kaufman empirically found that deposit variability affected bank holdings of cash and excess reserves, the distribution of total member bank reserves within the banking system, and thereby influenced the path and speed of monetary policy actions.

Moreover, deposit variability affects the mix of bank assets, as well as the availability of funds for loans and consequently the loan rate. Among the factors prominently identified as affecting deposit variability is bank size. In an uncertain environment, it is reasonable that large banks should have less variability in their deposits and loans (Co-Pierre 2013; Dewald and Dreese 1970). This is simply because their large-sized permits uncorrelated variability in individual deposits and loans to be offsetting. This is in contrast to Romer et al. (1990) who argued that bank size does not influence the amount of deposits taken from customers and loans given to the borrowers. Banks can raise large deposits to maintain loan growth, regardless of whether they are undercapitalised or overcapitalised. So, the policy of the banks must respond accordingly. But, Kishan and Opiela (2000) believe that deposits are more variable at small banks than at large banks, and its growth would not respond to the modifications in policy.

Realistically, one must be concerned with the systemic aspects of the business environment, such as GDP growth, the level of inflation rate, interest rate volatility, etc. All of these macroeconomic environments are considered as situations of uncertainty, which may have an influence on commercial banks and are crucial for evaluating the degree of influence on risk management efficiency of banks.

5.16.2 Stochastic approach on efficiency analysis

Conventional efficiency DEA models require the exact information of inputs or outputs, however, in many observations and real-world applications, this simple assumption does not hold. There needs to be a stochastic approach of efficiency analysis that is able to handle uncertainty in data. The DEA model's fundamental assumption of deterministic data has also contributed to difficulty in incorporating environmental influences (Saen and Azadi 2011). As a result, stochastic approaches were developed to solve the disadvantage of non-stochastic variation of inputs and outputs in the deterministic measurement of the DEA model. Accordingly, a number of researchers have employed and compared the efficiency ranking of the firms or institutions, using stochastic approach including CCDEA and deterministic efficiency approaches.

In assessing the efficiency of hotels, Shang et al. (2010) applied the stochastic DEA (SDEA) and compared the results with those from deterministic models. Following Land et al. (1993), they assume three different probabilities (0.5, 0.6 and 0.7) subject to two sets of constraints. The SDEA results showed that the SDEA efficiency measures are higher than deterministic DEA – the greater the stochastic variability of outputs, the closer the envelope moves to 1 in efficiency score. They concluded that the hotels in Taiwan performed better by the SDEA approach because the conventional DEA models do not allow stochastic variation in both input and output. The results were consistent with the efficiency score findings investigated by Huang and Li (1996).

Realising that many observations in reality are stochastic in nature, Kao and Liu (2009) avoided the issue in conventional DEA, where efficiency measurement in that approach always requires input or output data to be constant. A simulation technique was employed to investigate 25 Taiwanese commercial banks, with four simulations running 100, 500, 1000 and 2000 replications. One thousand replications produced more reliable efficiency results, compared to other simulation runs. However, the authors believe that conventional DEA proved a clear categorisation between efficient and inefficient DMUs, rather than less sharp categorisation produced by SDEA approach. But, by adopting the probabilistic type in the category, they agreed with Land et al. (1993) that psychologically it is more acceptable to the DMUs being evaluated because it leaves a greater chance for the DMU to be classified as efficient.

Riccardi and Toninelli (2011) and Toninelli (2011) were also concerned about output uncertainty in investigating the efficiency of the world cement industry. The studies showed that CCDEA is the most commonly used technique to include noise variations in data and solve DEA problems with data uncertainty. However, in determining the probability level (α), also known as tolerance level, in efficiency estimation, Wong et al. (2011) stated that the choice of α is important. Normally, a small chance $\alpha = 0.05$ of falling inside (less than) or outside (greater than) the frontier is used to locate an efficient frontier. An excessively high value of the threshold level will give an accurate efficiency result.

In 1998, an efficiency study estimating New Zealand fund managers was conducted by Premachandra et al. to select the most efficient portfolios. They found that the SDEA approach is necessary due to the chance elements in short-term (ST) portfolio management performance. Based on the spreadsheet numerical SDEA model, the SDEA approach is found to be well suited for the purpose of examining the portfolio ranking. Furthermore, Wen et al. (2014) also indicated that DDEA could not be used in cases where uncertainty and volatility exists in inputs and/or outputs due to high sensitivity of efficiency scores given the actual levels of inputs and outputs. The same approach of spreadsheet-based SDEA has also been used by Watson et al. (2011) to examine 22 Australian domestic equity managed funds and SDEA has significantly identified efficient or inefficient DMUs. They argued that using SDEA in spreadsheet creates a model that can be easily replicated as it can be created using an everyday spreadsheet package such as Excel.

In assessing the efficiency of Spanish wastewater treatment plants (WWTPs) in an uncertain environment, Sala-Garrido et al. (2012) employed a DEA with a tolerances approach. The statistical tolerance approach for both input and output variables is used to overcome the unavailability of information uncertainty estimates in DEA models. The results indicate that WWTP efficiency scores change when data modifications are incorporated, but not all WWTPs performed the same sensitivity with respect to changes in the parameters (input and output). Therefore, the combination of the traditional DEA approach with uncertainty imposts is shown to offer more reliable and robust results and conclusions, leading to an accurate future prediction in WWTPs.

Edirisinghe (2012) uncovered another insight when they assumed uncertainty in accounting data to measure the actual relative financial strengths (RFS) of the public firm in US market sectors. In the analysis, stochastic programming DEA (SPDEA) framework was developed to yield a robust performance metric for selected firms. A strong correlation between SPDEA and stock returns of the public firms demonstrated that SPDEA is more reliable in estimating firm's performance which is heavily based on the accounting data. On the contrary, traditional DEA approach overestimates the actual firms' strengths.

In Turkey, Gedik et al. (2014) used CCDEA to estimate the efficiency of Iron and Steel manufacturing sector. By incorporating the Banker, Charnes and Cooper (BCC) model under the assumption of VRS, with chance-constrained programming formulations, the study shows that the number of efficient DMUs increased from 32 (in deterministic DEA) to 36 when the probability level $\alpha = 0.05$ is applied. Thus, they conclude that efficient DMUs can be determined by a combination between deterministic DEA and constrained BCC-additive model. Recent evidence by Wong et al. (2014) further highlighted the importance of stochastic setting in measuring the financial performance of banks.

Based on the CAMELS (Capital, Adequacy, Assets, Management Capability, Earning, Liquidity and Sensitivity) factors, the Monte Carlo Simulations method was used to analyse the efficiency estimations, and a genetic algorithm was applied to refine the accuracy of the efficiency measures. This approach differed from the traditional deterministic efficiency model, as the deterministic approach is more suitable for determining the bank's future financial operations and improving the overall financial soundness of the financial institution.

5.17 CCDEA: approach

5.17.1 *Chance-constrained DEA*

Other than bootstrap DEA in addressing data uncertainty, chance-constrained programming is the most used technique to include noise variations and to solve DEA problems with uncertainty in data. Chance-constrained programming developed by Charnes and Cooper (1963) is an operations research approach for optimisation under uncertainty when some or all coefficients in a linear programme are random variables distributed in accordance with some probability law. Chance-constrained programming provides an approach for decomposition of the total variation in the data for each DMU into its two components of noise and inefficiency based upon an envelopment procedure of the confident regions. This kind of approach makes it possible to replace deterministic characterisations in DEA, such as "efficient" and "not efficient", with characterisations such as "probably efficient" and "probably not efficient". Indeed, it is possible to go still further into characterisations such as "sufficiently efficient", with associated probabilities of not being correct in making inferences about the performance of a DMU.

In CCDEA, Land et al. (1993) considered two sets of constraints. There was a set of chance constraints that the probability of efficient DMUs was only 0.05 or less. This assumption suits the banking business processes that usually expose systematic and unsystematic factors. Land et al. (1993) agreed that in reality, the production process usually contains uncontrollable factors, which involved the stochastic variation in outputs and/or inputs. In the banking system, customer deposits and loans can be affected by the customers' behaviour like crowd psychology, which is not fully captured.

Based on the literature, this study believes that a traditional DEA measurement has weaknesses. Therefore, the consideration of the CCDEA approach enhances the research credibility and dependability, and helps to strengthen the following issues:

1 CCDEA offers an approach for the decomposition of the total variation in data for each bank into its two mechanisms of inefficiency and noise (Olesen and Petersen 1995).
2 CCDEA allows a positive probability that one or more inequality restrictions will be violated at the optimal solution of the problem (Farzipoor and Azadi 2011; Ray 2004).
3 CCDEA can produce results that indicate the sensitivity of efficiency indices due to variations in data caused by stochastic noise.
4 CCDEA maintains the instinctive nature of the DEA measurement, and is able to help policy makers in banks by providing dependable findings (Chen 2002) for them to strategise better risk management plans.

5.17.2 Related studies using CCDEA in bank efficiency analysis

In assessing the performance of 575 banking institutions that became members of the Federal Reserve System's Functional Cost Analysis in 1984, Ferrier and Lovell (1990) have employed both the DEA and the econometrics approaches. In their analysis, they suggested that measurement error and lack of misspecification in the deterministic linear programming was a major drawback, given the fact that stochastic variation and inefficiency were considered to be the same in non-stochastic DEA. This highlights the necessity for incorporating stochastic constraints into a DEA application. Chen (2002) utilised both CCDEA and SFA approaches to measure the efficiency of 39 banks in Taiwan and to find any differentiations. Beginning with a traditional DEA, the study found the average efficiency scores of CCDEA to be equivalent to 0.932, which is higher than ordinary DEA (0.920). However, SFA results found it to be significantly lower than the results gained from

CCDEA approach, with the average efficiency score of 0.782. The difference in results between DEA, CCDEA and SFA were confirmed by four univariate tests – the banker's two asymptotic DEA tests, Welch's mean test and the Mann–Whitney test. All tests indicated that there is a significant difference (significant at the 0.05 level) among the average efficiency scores of the DEA vs. SFA, and CCDEA vs. SFA methods.

This noticeable distinction between the two methods was noted in a similar study done by Ferrier and Lovell (1990). Ferrier and Lovell believe that the use of different techniques will lead to dramatically different findings even if they are used inside the same methodological framework. Conducting another study in the same country, Chen (2005) used both deterministic DEA and CCDEA to make calculations of efficiency scores and productivity change for 46 banking institutions in Taiwan during the Asian financial crisis, from two different periods, 1994–1996 and 1998–2000. It showed that pure technological change mainly contributed to the improvement of productivity during the Asian financial crisis. Moreover, the efficiency score from CCDEA was slightly higher than the deterministic DEA efficiency score.

In the first empirical evidence of using the Stochastic DEA (SDEA) in the efficiency literature, Fethi et al. (2001) investigated the efficiency of 36 Turkish banks in 1999, and compared the results to the deterministic DEA results. The findings revealed that there were wide variations between the deterministic DEA and SDEA efficiency scores. The SDEA suggested huge variability to stochastic error in the sample that has been influenced by systematic (macroeconomic factors) and unsystematic risks (e.g. banking rules and regulations). As a result, Fethi et al. (2001) believe that the outliers' effect in the data has been reduced by the stochastic approach.

A recent study by Thao (2012) employed both deterministic DEA and CCDEA to measure the performance of 33 Vietnamese banks over the period from 2006 until 2010. Other than filling the gap of no comprehensive study which employed both methods in Vietnamese banks, three different models shown in the study produced distinctive efficiency results. Model A addressed deterministic DEA in efficiency measurement, and Model B employed CCDEA with the assumption that inputs are deterministic but outputs are uncertain. Model C included uncertainty (stochastic variation) in both inputs and outputs. Based on the comparison of results of the three models, a slight difference in efficiency scores was noticed between the models, with decreasing scores obtained from Model A to Model B, and then Model C. As a result, Thao (2012) extended the analysis using the test analysis conducted by Banker (1993) to compare the efficiencies between three models with a null hypothesis to negate these differences. The null hypothesis was accepted by the results indicating that there are no differences between efficiency results in the three models. This indicates that there is no difference in efficiency scores between deterministic DEA and CCDEA. The results were found to contradict previous studies (e.g. Chen 2005; Chen 2002; Fethi et al. 2001), which found disagreements between the results of the two approaches (Table 5.16).

Table 5.16 Summary of CCDEA in Banking Efficiency Studies

Author	Country	Year	Main conclusions
Ferrier and Lovell (1990)	USA	1984	It is important to develop a stochastic programming approach to frontier analysis in order to solve a serious problem in efficiency measurement confounding noise in data.
Chen (2002)	Taiwan	1994–2000	The comparative analysis between DEA and CCDEA, the advance setting of the CCDEA does not change the instinctive characteristics of the DEA measurement. In fact, CCDEA has strengthened the efficiency analysis with a slight difference in efficiency scores.
Chen (2005)	Taiwan	1994–1996 and 1998–2000	There is a slight difference between the CCDE efficiency scores and deterministic DEA, but not significantly higher than that of deterministic DEA scores.
Fethi et al. (2001)	Turkey	1999	There is a wide-ranging variation between the results produced by DEA and stochastic DEA. One of the major elements that contributes to the difference in results is the measurement error in the raw data that may be influenced by macroeconomic factors and changes in banking regulations.
Thao (2012)	Vietnam	2006–2010	A disagreement between the DEA and CCDEA, which indicates that there is no difference between them.

Source: As described above.

5.18 Stochastic optimisation approach using CCDEA to resolve parameters uncertainty in banks: methodological framework

CCDEA is used to address the probability scores for risk management efficiency for the 21 sampled banks from the Asia-Pacific region accommodating the uncertainty parameters (variables). Prior to the methodological implication, the framework has established the need for incorporating noise (uncertainty issues) in the banking environment, which has been ignored in the context of risk management. Thus, the analysis not only brings the methodological implications, but also gives a chance to all DMUs to achieve

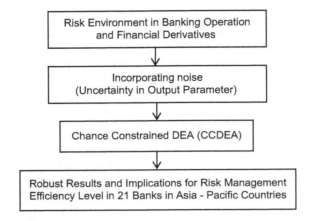

Figure 5.3 Risk Management Efficiency Measurements with CCDEA.

efficiency level in their risk management measurements. The CCDEA model is not for varieties, but as complementary to the assumption of the current environment in financial institutions' world (Figure 5.3).

5.18.1 CCDEA model with uncertainty in output variables

The procedure for DEA measurement based on TE is well known. The study takes one firm from the 21 banks in the Asia-Pacific region, in turn, and compares its performance with the reference set of the whole industry. This section follows the CCDEA model used by Thao (2012) and Chen et al. (2002), where it is assumed that the setting of the output variables is stochastic, while the inputs are certain (predetermined). The CCDEA allows the constraints to hold with the probability levels of efficiency.

Here, we incorporate the stochastic considerations of outputs into the deterministic DEA model to derive specifications and measurement errors. To do this, the study identifies the firm's θ value based on the firm's Farrell efficiency, where $0 \leq \theta \leq 1$. The values of $\theta = 1$ indicate that the firm is already one of those which define the frontier and is 100% efficient. Otherwise, the firm's inefficiency is $(1-\theta) \times 100\%$. In what follows it is necessary to examine particular output constraints that can be written in terms of k outputs: $y_{rj}, r = 1 \ldots k, j = 1 \ldots n$ for the n different producing units (banks), as follows:

r_{th} typical output constraint:

$$y_r' \lambda - y_{r0} \geq 0 \ i.e. \ \sum_{j=1}^{j=n} y_{rj} \lambda_j - y_{r0} \geq 0 \ r = 1, \ldots, k \qquad (5.13)$$

Before turning to the CCDEA problem, the study measures the producing unit's TE by calculating the following the linear programme for the firm:

$min\theta$

Subject to: $x_i'\lambda - x_{i0}\theta \leq 0$

$$y_i'\lambda - y_{i0}\theta \leq 0 \tag{5.14}$$

As described by Land et al. (1993), CCDEA allows the constraints to hold with the probability level α (0,1) to be sustainable, for which the higher this value is, the more likely is the satisfaction of these constraints. While the input constraint is retained, the output constraints are now modified corresponding to the chance-constrained efficiency measure as follows:

$min\theta$

Subject to: $Prob\left(y_r'\lambda - y_{r0} \geq 0\right) \geq \alpha\ r = 1,\dots,k$

$$\theta X_{jr0} - \sum_r x_{jr}\lambda_r \geq 0 \tag{5.15}$$

Charnes and Cooper (1963) have explained the idea of a modified certainty equivalent to transform this stochastic linear programming problem into deterministic non-linear programming. The difference between output and the reference weighted output of all the DMUs (firms) are treated as a random variable. Therefore, the constraints that contain random variables have to be written in the form of probabilistic or chance constraints.

When the study assumes the chance constraint, the rule does not allow the use of the algorithm straightaway. The chance constraint has to be converted into a deterministic equivalent. To construct the deterministic equivalent of the chance constraint, the constraint relating to the outputs makes the assumption that the random variable has a finite positive variance, so that the SD can be used as a divisor (Fethi et al. 2001), as follows:

$$SD = \left(var\left(y_r'\lambda - y_{r0}\right)\right)^{\frac{1}{2}} \tag{5.16}$$

Thus, the corresponding CCDEA measure is formulated as follows:

$min\theta$

$$Prob\left[y_{m,k}^t \leq \sum_{n=1}^{K} y_{m,n}^t \lambda_n^t\right] \geq 1 - \alpha\ m = 1,\dots,M$$

$$\sum_{n=1}^{K} x_{n,h}^t \leq \theta x_{n,h}^t \geq 1\ n = 1,\dots,N$$

$$\lambda_n^t \geq 0\ h = 1,\dots,K \tag{5.17}$$

The chance constraint of output: $Prob\left[y_{m,k}^t \leq \sum_{n=1}^{K} y_{m,n}^t \lambda_n^t \right] \geq 1 - \alpha$ indicates that the probability of the best practice output exceeding the observed output shall be at least at level α. This study assumes $\alpha = 0.95$, so that most DMUs (say, 5%) will be set as best performers. The value $\alpha = 0.95$ suits the 95% confident interval used in bootstrap DEA.

The numerical results of the CCDEA model for 21 Asia-Pacific banks utilises the optimiser stochastic approach which formulates the CCDEA model experiment. The optimisers used Risk Solver Platform Version 9.5 for Excel produced by Frontline Systems Incorporation, the developers of the Solver in Excel. Risk Solver Platform was chosen because:

1   It is the commercial edition of the regular Solver that comes free with Excel;
2   It has an interactive simulation approach that works well with "what if" scenarios under uncertain environments and provides quick insights;
3   It is helpful for the purpose of risk analysis and optimisation; and
4   It is visible and accessible for management accountants who are working on the decision planning with spreadsheet modelling in Excel.

5.18.2 CCDEA analysis using risk platform solver

5.18.2.1 The objective function

First, a normal distribution with mean and SD are calculated before defining the deterministic to stochastic function. The specification of objective function depends on uncertainties, and the deterministic objective function is then defined by selecting "Expected" from the Type dropdown list in the stochastic group.

5.18.2.2 Constraints: normal, chance, bound

•   In this case, input is defined as a certain parameter and a normal decision variable. It is "deterministic" and calls this as a **Normal constraint**.
•   Two outputs of this study are defined as uncertain variables. To define, the study has specified the **mean** for these constraints to be satisfied. This is called a **Chance constraint**, whereas it is specified that the constraints must be satisfied at 95% of the times (it can be violated at 5% of the time).Using a probability distribution of 95% chance, we denote such constraints as **VaR0.95**. Prior to that, the primitive uncertainties (output variables) are defined as uncertain variables with =PsiNormal (Mean, SD), while input remains as a normal variable.
•   **Bound constraint** is determined by the weighted difference which must be greater than or equal to 0. Noted that, the difference between the firm's output and the reference weighted outputs of all the firms are treated as a random variable.

5.19 Results and discussion

This study examines the efficiency of 21 Asia-Pacific banks from nine countries based on the impact of the usage of derivative instrument on the efficiency of their risk management.

Table 5.17 presents the efficiency estimated from CCDEA methods in 2007, while Table 5.18 presents the comparative efficiency results between Deterministic DEA and Stochastic DEA (BDEA and CCDEA) in 2007.

Table 5.17 Efficiency Estimated based on CCDEA Approach in 2007

	Stochastic Efficiency
DMU	CCDEA
Australia	
CB1	0.986
CB2	0.985
CB3	0.991
CB4	0.998
Hong Kong	
CB5	0.992
Japan	
CB6	0.974
CB7	0.977
CB8	0.900
New Zealand	
CB9	0.985
CB10	0.987
CB11	0.964
Singapore	
CB12	1.000
Taiwan	
CB13	0.945
Malaysia	
CB14	0.977
CB15	0.946
CB16	0.987
CB17	0.932
Philippines	
CB18	0.992
Thailand	
CB19	0.995
CB20	0.983
CB21	0.989

Table 5.18 Efficiency Estimated among DEA, BDEA and CCDEA in 2007

DMU	Deterministic Efficiency	Stochastic Efficiency	
	DEA	*BDEA*	*CCDEA*
Australia			
CB1	0.953	0.953	0.986
CB2	0.945	0.941	0.985
CB3	0.947	0.945	0.991
CB4	0.943	0.941	0.998
Hong Kong			
CB5	0.943	0.942	0.992
Japan			
CB6	0.949	0.948	0.974
CB7	1.000	1.000	0.977
CB8	0.838	0.838	0.900
New Zealand			
CB9	0.948	0.946	0.985
CB10	0.948	0.947	0.987
CB11	0.911	0.910	0.964
Singapore			
CB12	0.949	0.947	1.000
Taiwan			
CB13	0.954	0.953	0.945
Malaysia			
CB14	0.923	0.921	0.977
CB15	0.898	0.896	0.946
CB16	0.957	0.957	0.987
CB17	0.895	0.893	0.932
Philippines			
CB18	0.949	0.948	0.992
Thailand			
CB19	0.949	0.948	0.995
CB20	0.944	0.943	0.983
CB21	0.940	0.939	0.989
Mean	0.937	0.936	0.975

Table 5.19 Efficiency Difference of TE between DEA, BDEA and CCDEA in 2007 based on Welch's Test

Classification	Test Procedure	DEA vs. CCDEA	BDEA vs. CCDEA
Traditional efficiency tests	Welch's test	4.336**	4.476**

Note: ** indicates significance at the 5% level.

The mean ordinary DEA TE score is 0.937. Using the bootstrapping DEA approach, a small reduction in the mean value is found where the mean of the BDEA is 0.936. However, the study finds that the mean using the CCDEA approach is 0.975, higher than the deterministic DEA and BDEA. As mentioned by Chen (2002), the difference in results implies that the CCDEA frontier is naturally a "soft" frontier, at which the input observations of the banks are allowed to cross the envelope. This means that CCDEA can move closer to making any observation, in contrast to the deterministic DEA that posits a naturally "hard" frontier where the envelope is located far from the chance-constrained one.

Further evidence is shown in Table 5.18 that CB12 achieved an efficiency score of 0.949 based on the deterministic DEA, and 0.947 based on the BDEA evaluations, it registered a significantly higher score of 1.000 in the CCDEA result. Overall, even though almost all banks are still beneath the frontier (less than 100% or 1), all the banks have achieved over a 95% efficiency level, which indicates that the efficiency scores of these banks when calculated with CCDEA are higher than those calculated with the classical DEA.

To ensure robustness of these analyses, Welch's test, also called the Welch-Aspin test, is used to check the hypothesis whether the two approaches have equal means. Table 5.19 shows three comparisons of approaches between deterministic DEA and CCDEA, and, BDEA and CCDEA. Welch's test for the deterministic DEA vs. CCDEA, and BDEA vs. CCDEA, are significant enough to reject the null hypothesis. These indicate a difference when CCDEA is involved, thus indicating significant influence and impact on risk management efficiency measurement. The difference reported in the fourth column contrasted with the study by Chen (2002) who found no significant difference in a DEA vs. CCDEA.

5.20 Implications – CCDEA

The findings from the analysis enable us to evaluate the influence of uncertainty (risk) issues in the modelling measurement (DEA) of risk management efficiency. Collectively, the findings from the CCDEA approach have several significant implications in assessing the efficiency of risk management in banks. With huge variability attributable to stochastic error in the sample with measurement and specification errors, CCDEA helps to strategise risk management and ensure that banks appear relatively more efficient and can overcome disadvantage of deterministic DEA. Information on uncertainty can be communicated to assist decision makers in banks to determine the most efficient risk management in the presence of stochastic data. The uncertainty analysis in CCDEA helps decision makers decide on the implications for better risk management strategy based on the usage of derivative instruments and increase the responsiveness of a risk management system.

CCDEA is a superior methodology that is able to address realistic scenarios in banking operations particularly when it involves market and interest rate risks. Therefore, the probabilistic uncertainty analysis is an important step forward in the interpretation of uncertainty at the decision-making level (Hsu et al. 2012; Camerer and Weber 1992), as it provides a more unified methodology in contrast to deterministic approaches. Deterministic models alone are unrealistic in real-world applications as they are not flexible enough to measure a firm's performance objective and unable to handle imperfections in practical operations (Ringrose and Bentley 2015; Bruni et al. 2014; Mulvey and Vladimirou 1991). Therefore, the rebalancing decision is supported through the development of an integrated deterministic and stochastic framework where both models are jointly selected to determine the influence of hedging instrument in risk management of banks. Also, the decisions taken for risk management strategies in one period consequently affect subsequent periods. In addition, receptiveness to external environment in efficiency measurement is needed to cope with the influence of competitive markets (Hsu et al. 2012). The stakeholders need to be able to estimate stable financial consequences in banking actions and govern their investment activities across markets for high returns. Further, Udhayakumar et al. (2011) believe that investigating the efficiency using the CCDEA approach would be useful for policy makers to gauge the potential enhancement of inputs and/or outputs for efficient as well as inefficient banks.

5.21 Conclusion

In conclusion, this study can decisively argue that a stochastic analysis with a CCDEA approach has provided realistic and conclusive evidence for the measurement of risk management efficiency modelling. The analysis has made a contribution towards the development of an efficiency measurement system that incorporates uncertainty in the parameters to reflect real-life evaluations in the banking industry where the volatility of the financial markets can influence the outcome of banks. This section concludes that the CCDEA approach has been able to assess the risk management efficiency of banks in a more rigorous manner. This is the first study to use CCDEA for efficiency measurement in the context of risk management for banks with the aim of reducing uncertainty issues.

5.22 Implications of stochastic DEA analysis – modelling and risk management efficiency measurements

Stochastic techniques represent a superior approach to early attempts to measure uncertainty by including uncertainty elements in banking operations. This superiority arises from the possibility of using parameters in uncertain environments. As Cukierman and Gerlach (2003) and Devereux (1989) studied the impact of output growth uncertainty affected by inflation, the same situation occurred when uncertainty was associated with the usage of derivative instruments. The results have a significant reaction towards bank's risk management efficiency measurements. Even though mixed evidence is obtained from BDEA, sensitivity analysis and CCDEA, it highlights the gap in measuring risk management efficiency in banks by building a practical decision-making model for formulating sound risk management strategies. This result also has important implications for the development of risk management theory as it supports the recent emphasis in financial modelling on volatility forecasting for financial risk management. It means, this study offers an idea of integration of statistical ground and risk management aspects involving unpredictable financial market behaviour which are able to support risk management strategies in the financial area. Therefore, this study provides an extended understanding of how imperfect the financial environment is and hence how important it is to employ a variety of measurement tools with rigorous techniques that help inform the risk manager as well as the policy makers.

Based on earlier discussion, this study gives further insight into the issue of the accuracy of efficiency measurement. Thus, it supports the positive contribution of parameters uncertainty to input and output, as well as the efficiency scores obtained. This study posits the accuracy of the estimated performance measures subject to the use of appropriate and well-specified models, and the assumption of data under uncertainty environments. Therefore, the choice of appropriate models is an important methodological issue. Other than the quality of data (noise in data) and sampling error issues, the choices of multi-stochastic models in this study are based on the perspective taken, and the type and nature of organisations under investigation. Thus, realising that DEA approach is a non-parametric method that does not impose a functional form on the production frontier and ignores the stochastic elements, but stochastic approaches are trusted to be able to accommodate wide-ranging uncertainty, realistic market behaviour, reduce measurement errors and adopt a large degree of unexpected environments.

5.23 Concluding remarks

A summary of the integrated stochastic DEA has been presented in this chapter. First, by employing a BDEA approach, the analysis presented in Part A has provided reliable, encouraging and robust results. The plausibility was predicted on the measurement to solve the upward bias in finite samples of DEA estimations. Here, it was necessary to incorporate stochastic optimisation using BDEA to help estimate more plausible models for relative efficiency measurement of risk management in banks, and pinpoint structural weaknesses in the classical DEA model.

Furthermore, by realising that the linear programming approach strongly pushes the analysis by using a true situation, the sensitivity analysis with percentage variation in data provided a good solution that is practicable within a perplexing environment. This sensitivity analysis test is believed to strengthen the argument that banks work in uncertain environments. This part provided incontestable evidence that the analysis has provided more effective results when percentage differences were imposed.

Lastly, questioning the plausibility and validity of efficiency measurement under the stochastic environment, Part C has proven that CCDEA can perform advanced analyses in the presence of uncertainty issues. This is a new approach incorporating stochastic CCDEA for risk management efficiency measurement in banks and highlights its usefulness in the decision-making process which has never been considered before in the literature. Currently, there is no other study that addresses risk management efficiency measurements based on a derivative instrument that uses a CCDEA approach, as compared to deterministic DEA and BDEA results.

In a nutshell, through the development of a multi-approach using the stochastic programming model of BDEA, sensitivity analysis, and CCDEA, this study helps contribute to more robust and stable efficiency measurements for optimal risk management in banks. The insensitivity of the deterministic DEA to uncertainty in business conditions may cause inaccurate measurements of actual risk management efficiency levels and lead to misdirected policy formulation for derivative instrument usage in the banking sector. Incorporating these various forms of stochastic measures into the integrated DEA and dollar-offset ratio as a new measure makes the analyses more robust in its assessment of real-life scenarios that can create greater consensus in the activities between practitioners and researchers.

6   Research summary and conclusion

6.1 Introduction

In concluding this book, the discussion here summarises the main research findings and reflects on their implications for theory and practice in measuring risk management efficiency in banks. This study emphasises the development of a new approach for measuring risk management efficiency via the integration of two main elements: (1) dollar-offset ratio from the hedge effectiveness measurement test, and (2) Data Envelopment Analysis (DEA), both driven by a derivative instrument for determining input and output, applied to the banking sector of the Asia-Pacific region. The study began with risk and risk management issues, finding that no appropriate approach has previously been found for risk management efficiency measurements. However, this book argues that the dollar-offset ratio employed in a hedge effectiveness test is inadequate to account for risk management measures. Consequently, a DEA approach was found to be suitable for improving the hedge effectiveness test measurement as it can provide more insightful and systematic evidence in measuring risk management efficiency, as well as the effects of derivatives usage. This is followed by an overview of the way stochastic approaches have been integrated to enable the model to address uncertainty issues. Extending the rich tradition of sophisticated quantitative models in the field, this study has developed a range of improvements on integrated DEA and dollar-offset ratio including the bootstrapping, sensitivity analysis and chance constraints, that better gauge efficiency levels of risk management in banks. The ways in which the rigorous analysis of data from 21 banks in the Asia-Pacific region have been conducted to measure their risk management efficiency is presented. This chapter will also discuss theoretical and policy implications of the study. To conclude, limitations of this study are highlighted and recommendations proposed for further study.

6.2 Issues

The study was set out to propose new risk management efficiency measures by proving an argument in hedge effectiveness of the dollar-offset ratio in order to show the impact of derivatives through the input (hedging instrument) and output (hedge item) ratio to be adopted as a measure of risk management efficiency for banks. The study sought to propose a new approach on the measurement and analysis of risk management efficiency through the operationalisation of a DEA model based on hedge accounting (hedge effectiveness test), with an application to banking institutions. The general theoretical and practical literature on this subject and specifically in the context of risk management efficiency measurement is incomplete within the risk management discourse.

6.3 Models, results and implications

As theoretically and empirically discussed in previous chapters, this section summarises the main findings of this study and draws out their implications, particularly for risk management efficiency measures. It thereby aims to enrich our understanding of this new measurement and analysis in the context of the Asia-Pacific region.

6.3.1 Risk management efficiency measures by integrating DEA with dollar-offset ratio analysis

After pointing out the limitation of risk management efficiency measures and of the simple concept of ratio analysis applied in the dollar-offset ratio of hedge effectiveness, this study has proposed the integration of the DEA approach together with a hedge accounting effectiveness test (dollar-offset ratio) to form a rigorous model for analysing risk management performance. The DEA method was able to accomplish an advanced analysis for risk management efficiency, highlighting the impact of interest rate swap as a hedging instrument in the banking sector. Moreover, DEA was also able to make simultaneous comparisons of multiple dependent performance measures including outcome, quality and output, with a new principle for determining weights directly from the data (Pourjavad and Shirouyehzad 2014; Avkiran 2001; Mante 1997). This is different from the simple ratio concept applied in the dollar-offset ratio as DEA is able to take simultaneous accounts of all resources and outputs when assessing performance. Furthermore, based on the argument by Thanassoulis et al. (1996) that simple ratio needs to be integrated with more advanced ratio techniques, this study posits that the two methods can support each other if used jointly. An integrated approach between DEA and dollar-offset ratio was therefore applied to measure risk management efficiency using derivatives as the hedging strategy in selected banks from the Asia-Pacific region.

The results of DEA for 21 commercial banks in nine Asia-Pacific countries for 2007 indicate that commercial banks in the Asia-Pacific region were characterised with small asymmetry between banks, with only CB7 achieving best practice or efficient frontier results (1.000 or 100%). The remaining 20 banks had an overall technical efficiency (OTE) of less than 1.000, which means that they were not fully technically efficient. With respect to their OTE, their average scores ranged between DEAOTE = 83.8% (0.838) and DEAOTE = 100% (1.000). The average OTE was 93.7% (0.937). In terms of individual countries in the Asia-Pacific region from 2007 to 2012, findings show that banks in Malaysia (developing country) and Australia (developed country) were the most technically efficient, averaging efficiency scores of 92.9% and 92.8%, respectively. Overall, Malaysian banks were at par with other banks in developed and developing countries and even had the highest average OTE scores among developed and developing countries in the region. These unexpected results were supported by Mihaljek and Packer (2010), who showed that derivatives usage among developing countries had increased after 2001. Thus, this study believes that the management performance of Malaysian banks has been influenced by the increasing usage of derivatives. On the other hand, contrary to expectation, the analysis in this study showed that commercial banks in Japan were the worst performers compared to other countries, with average efficiency scores of only 91.1%. Throughout this period, Malaysian banks were able to operate close to 100% efficiency, which was more than banks in many developed countries. Potential and growth in using the derivative instrument as a risk management tool, in general, recorded a respectable positive trend in estimated risk management efficiency performance in banks in Malaysia. Australian commercial banks were also found to be among the best banks in developed countries in the region. The results of their risk management efficiency measurements reveal that Australian banks experienced a remarkable growth in both derivative activities and other financial sources.

Furthermore, as expected, the trend of risk management efficiency scores from the DEA approach reversed in 2007 and 2011, apparently due to the global economic crisis of 2007 that affected all banks. However, in these circumstances, although certain categories of derivatives had shrunk, the total market value of derivatives had not been reduced. As a result, after 2008 the performance measurement of all banks was able to grow again, and has continued to expand rapidly ever since. This scenario resulted in a significant rise in the average OTE in 2012 when the crisis abated, and the scores rebounded higher than in previous years. Nevertheless, despite these results, efficiency in risk management indicates that a majority of banks in Asia-Pacific region exhibit a low performance measurement, and thus, are considered to be under-performing. This clearly indicates that inefficient banks have substantial room for improvements to sustain their competitive edge in the risk management context. With the assumption that almost all banks in the Asia-Pacific region are inefficient, they are too large to take full advantage of scale. As Kumar and Gulati (2008) stated, most of these banks are included in the Decreasing Returns to Scale (DRS) region, which indicates a sub-optimum scale size. Thus, a reduction in scale of derivative instrument usage would necessitate an increase in levels of risk management efficiency. These inefficient banks can improve their risk management efficiency level by cutting costs (utilising resources) rather than focussing on the usage of financial derivatives. These elements may be inter-related and contribute to better risk management efficiency in banks. The results can be further associated with the modern banking theory, which focusses on the incentives and different approaches managers need to take in considering risk. Thus, efficiency analyses through derivative instruments can help in monitoring risk-taking elements for the protection of banks from costly episodes of financial distress (Hughes and Mester 2008).

Through integration of DEA and the dollar-offset ratio analyses of efficiency measurements, this study supports the proposal that DEA can reveal the effect of an entity's risk management activities. The less rigid ranges (between 0% and 100%) proposed by the DEA approach is more rational and flexible in assessing risk management efficiency compared to the range used in hedge effectiveness accounting which has not been accepted by some companies. This difference in the analysis may assist in reducing some of the concerns about how hedge accounting can work in risk management practices (Mann and Sephton 2010; Zhang 2009; Bodnar and Gebhardt 1999; Asay et al. 1981). Hedge effectiveness should focus not only on its levels of success, but also on the accessibility and flexibility of potential hedging instruments which would be able to clearly address the risk management objectives of institutions. As recommended in the exposure draft (ED) of International Swaps and Derivatives Association (ISDA), hedging relationships need to be driven by risk management activities. Measurements that do not correspond with risk management can only create more difficulties in the hedge accounting concept, especially in the case of institutions and their users. In other words, the integration model proposed in this study enhances the relationship between hedge accounting and risk management which makes it simpler for banks to apply hedge accounting in their risk management policies using derivative financial instruments, and consequently reduces the lack of clarity and consistency in how banks account for and reveal their derivatives use in financial reports as underlined by Bushman and Smith (2001). Furthermore, this study will improve shareholders' and investors' understandings of how banks can more effectively manage risk. In short, the integration of hedge effectiveness accounting and DEA encompasses both the measurements from hedge effectiveness tests and brief but rigorous operational DEA method demonstrations of risk management efficiency can further support the development of risk management in both banks and real-world settings.

6.3.2 Risk management with derivatives

The accuracy and stability of risk measurement tools play a critical role in the realisation of financial stability for banks in real-world settings. In this regard, Cebenoyan and Strahan (2004) have found that banks with advanced risk management strategies have greater credit availability, which consequently, give them better opportunities to increase productive assets and profit margins. The capability of strategising and allocating resources and expenditure through effective risk management, in turn, can facilitate the earnings of banks for their own growth and development. In line with finance and Stulz theory principles, results from the risk management efficiency measurement provide substantial support that the usage of derivatives for hedging purposes can directly increase a firm's value by reducing expected taxes, and certainly serve as a guide for better risk management (Deng et al. 2014; Christoffersen 2012; Stulz 2003; Wysocki 1998). However, these findings contradict classical finance theory which states that the use of financial derivatives does not influence firm value (Phan et al. 2014; Khediri and Folus 2010). The results from this study provide evidence that the use of derivatives can positively impact on risk management efficiency levels and lead to increases in firm value. The findings even enhance the analysis of Rivas et al. (2006), which verified that derivative usage has an impact on banking efficiency. Thus, the results of the present study have provided an understanding that derivatives can strongly impact on a bank's income statement, and are useful for hedging against financial risks arising from borrowing and lending activities.

In addition, this study provides an extended understanding of the governance role in risk management for banks (Lang and Jagtiani 2010; Masulis and Thomas 2009). As the management team plays an important role in risk reduction and achieving success in risk management strategies, these findings also indicate that the top management of banks may use derivative instruments to reduce risk. This could explain how agency theory can be related by managers to mitigate risk with the use of derivatives. This is supported by a previous study which found that division managers who are far removed from shareholders have incentives to use derivatives to reduce risk in measuring division performance (Kim et al. 2014; Wysocki 1998). Thus, it agrees with agency theory which states that top management may have incentives to use derivatives to reduce firm risk. Furthermore, in agreement with these findings connecting the use of derivative instruments and risk management, Panaretou et al. (2013) believe that information asymmetry can be reduced. Therefore, as in the study by DeMarzo and Duffie (1995), this study finds that hedging instrument disclosure is important for decision-making of risk managers in banks.

Although this idea has been suggested by hedge accounting theorists, this study also embeds the hedge effectiveness test of derivatives in the risk management context. As discussed in Chapter 3, the current practice of hedge accounting on the basis of fair value must be linked with risk management efficiency measurements and analyses based on risk exposures. The empirical illustration of this point is carried out using Australian and Malaysian banks to represent the scenarios of developed and developing countries that are actively involved in derivative activities in the Asia-Pacific region. In this way, the present study paves the way for rethinking financial derivatives in the management of financial institutions. It covers the nature and function of banks as financial intermediaries which use derivatives for risk management, consequently influencing the allocation of banking resources (Eakins and Mishkin 2012; Radoi 2012; Beets 2004).

In all, the results have led to the conclusion that the hedge effectiveness test of dollar-offset ratio needs to consider the simultaneous needs for the dimensions of accounting treatment and risk management. This will be helpful in enhancing the function of financial derivatives as a risk management tool, with significant advantages for hedging purposes, as well as helping firms in making financial risk management decisions. Finally, these results provide further support towards the theoretical model extension in supporting the predictions of financial economics theory for corporate hedging.

6.3.3 Managerial accounting practices and perspectives using dollar-offset ratio in hedge accounting

The first milestone of this study was marked by a criticism of the existing method of the hedge effectiveness test to justify the need for a new assessment model using DEA. As the dollar-offset ratio is the primary tool used for determining hedge effectiveness, its utility for risk management efficiency evaluation was examined. However, due to the risks involved in the business model of the banking sector, a reasonable question arose as to whether a dollar-offset ratio can be used to evaluate the use of derivatives as a hedging instrument in the improvement of levels of risk management efficiency. It was found that the ratio concept applied in the dollar-offset ratio does not make use of mathematical programming models to assimilate ratios into a single aggregate measure of efficiency. In other words, the dollar-offset ratio only applies a simple ratio concept, which does not strongly comply with performance measures theories (Mante 1997). Further, input variables in the ratio analysis depend on the preferences of policy makers in their assignment of weights, as pointed out by Manzoni and Islam (2009b), Nyhan and Martin (1999) and Allen et al. (1997). These studies have argued that this method is unsuitable as a performance measurement due to its decision rule.

Furthermore, the dollar-offset ratio, as an evaluative tool, is unable to provide the synchronous and historical comparisons of the performance of institutions over a period of time. Besides lacking the tools for quality assessment and effectiveness measurement, the hedge effectiveness approach is too complex to be able to collectively discuss the potential impact of derivatives, particularly in enhancing the safety and the soundness of risk management in financial institutions. In addition, Ramirez (2007) has raised the issue of the accepted effectiveness range of 80%–125% which may be unrealistically high. In this book, the empirical dollar-offset ratio analysis represented by eight banks shows that only one bank (CB4) technically achieved a level of high effectiveness and passed the effectiveness test (between 80% and 125%) with an effectiveness result of 116%. Meanwhile, seven banks were found to be ineffective in exploiting the derivative instrument for hedging purposes. However, these hypothetical results of effectiveness range are outside the scope of this study, as the most important thing to know is that, this range is probably the cause of conflict between practitioners choosing the methods for testing hedge effectiveness (Mann and Sephton 2010; Ramirez 2007). Some experts have even suggested eliminating the range altogether.[1] This issue has challenged corporations to develop risk management strategies that are reliable for both economic and accounting effectiveness. As a result, many firms ultimately find themselves having to implement an approach based on a blend of risk management objectives that address the ground rules of both economics and accounting, even though the assessment methods are inconclusive (Franzen 2010; Coughlan 2004). Thus, this theoretical argument implies that companies tend to make their decisions without proper rules and guidance.

Finally, the criticisms on the concept of a simple ratio applied in the dollar-offset ratio analysis and its inconsistencies in measuring the hedge effectiveness test have clearly justified the need for a wider assessment of banking institutions. It can be concluded that this concept has not been able to adequately capture the right purpose and measurement intuitions of risk management using derivative instruments. This study therefore concludes that these criticisms can be generalised to both financial and non-financial institutions which are involved in the use of derivatives for hedging purposes.

6.3.4 Risk management efficiency measurement for banks in the developing and developed countries in Asia-Pacific region

This section addresses the fourth objective of the study. Based on the first layer findings using parametric and non-parametric tests the analyses determined whether more advanced countries in the Asia-Pacific region are more efficient compared to banks in the developing countries. It was found that the efficiency levels of banks in the developing countries are higher than those in the developed countries.

DEA-based test (Section 4.6.7) has been performed to confirm the difference of bank risk management efficiency in the developed and developing countries in the Asia-Pacific region. In deterministic DEA, both parametric and non-parametric tests have shown a significant difference of scale efficiency (SE) between developed and developing countries with bank's risk management in developing countries better than banks in the developed countries (t-test = 2.317**, Mann–Whitney = −2.451** and Kruskal–Wallis = 6.006**). Kolmogorov–Smirnov has also shown that SE is significantly different for both country statuses with 0.105**. However, for the pure technical efficiency (PTE), significant values presented by Mann–Whitney and Kruskal–Wallis are significant only at 10% levels, respectively, which is less than the cut-off point (0.05). Based on these inconsistencies, the empirical findings have been ambiguous and inconclusive. The findings were also found to be contradicting previous studies that found that banks in developing countries are less efficient compared to banks from developed countries (e.g. Sathye 2005; Pastor et al. 1997).

As presented in Shawtari (2014), DEA analyses were followed by regression analysis for a robustness check. Both OTE and PTE showed insignificant results with p=0.8253 and p=0.4713, which indicates insignificant relationships between OTE and PTE to the country's status (developed or developing). This confirmed that OTE and PTE scores of the banks are not influenced by the level of country or regional status, background and competitiveness either in the developed or developing countries. The banks in developed countries were not necessarily more efficient and the banks in less developed countries were not necessarily inefficient. This means that successful risk management in banks depends on the bank's own strategies in handling market risk (Schlich and Jackson 2013). It appears that a bank's risk management efficiency depends on organisation-specific risk management practices in handling market risks rather than national background. Moreover, the evidence of the insignificant influence of background and economic status somehow opposes the assumption of dependency theories, for example, the Prebisch-Singer hypothesis in an economic theory concludes that economic and political powers are heavily dependent on, concentrating and centralised towards the industrialised (developed) countries. Even though banks are located in a so-called perceived economic "backwardness", the economic relations and globalisation influences have changed their perspectives in the scope of risk management. Unlike Wong and Zhou (2014) who found that developed countries such as the UK, China, and the USA have strong economic growth, the evidence from this study has shown that banks in developing countries can now be considered a significant part of the global financial system and are able to construct world-class risk management strategies. This is in line with the aggressive growth of the use of derivatives among developing countries (Aysun and Guldi 2011; Mihaljek and Packer 2010).

In a nutshell, banks in both developed and developing countries could protect their trading profit by hedging with derivative instruments from any undesirable risks, and hence achieve their risk management objective.

6.3.5 Stochastic efficiency analysis under uncertainty

The fourth objective of this study was to use stochastic efficiency DEA to evaluate and reduce the influence of uncertainty in the DEA modelling measurement of risk management efficiency. This was done for the purpose of using both deterministic and stochastic techniques in DEA to measure banks' risk management, as stated in the following two questions:

Research Question 5: (Section 1.1, Page 3)

Does modelling risk (uncertainty or risk in modelling) in the measurement of risk management efficiency influence banks' risk management efficiency and its measurements? If yes, how and why?

Research Question 6 (Section 1.1, Page 3)

How do deterministic and stochastic efficiency scores influence the risk management and derivative policies of banks in developed and developing countries?

This research indicates that bootstrap DEA (BDEA), the sensitivity analysis test and chance-constrained DEA (CCDEA) are progressive models of stochastic efficiency measurement, which can contribute to successful implementation of a decision model for risk management. Given the fact that financial markets are fraught with uncertainty, it is important to incorporate stochastic measurements which are able to analyse the existing information in light of these uncertainties (Sengupta 2005, 1987). BDEA (Assaf and Agbola 2011; Simar and Wilson 2000), sensitivity analysis (Zhu 2009; Thompson et al. 1996) and CCDEA (Riccardi and Toninelli 2011; Land et al. 1993) correct the flaws in the efficiency measurement approach proposed by DEA on risk management efficiency in banks. The weaknesses and limitations of DEA can be avoided with these stochastic approaches for an understandable and reliable analysis considering the context of uncertainty in markets.

With the BDEA, two stages of bootstrapping results suggest that the uncertainty in the data (noise in data) and sampling errors could occur in the deterministic measurement. Even though the results showed a small average bias (0.001) in 2007 and 2012, respectively, the efficiency measures calculated with the BDEA approach are robust in precision metrics, for instance, confidence intervals and standard errors. The results are similar to those found in an Iranian banking efficiency study by Arjomandi (2011), where efficiency measurements were improved with the BDEA approach even though by only a small margin in the differences. This also proves and simplifies that the BDEA approach can be used concurrently with a hedge effectiveness test in determining efficiency levels with respect to possible sampling and data errors.

In the sensitivity analysis method, the analysis was restricted to the case where the input parameter varied for extremely efficient decision-making units (DMUs), while other DMUs were kept at their current data or level, and combination of changes in input and output for both efficient and inefficient DMUs. The first sensitivity analysis created a significant change in the efficiency performance of banks and the mean OTE. The efficiency ranged between 0.768 and 0.755 with increasing or input variation of ±5% and ±10%, respectively, which is significantly different from 0.937 achieved in the mean OTE value of the deterministic DEA analysis. The second analysis assumed variation in both input and output parameters at 4% and 5% changes, and this changed the mean OTE across the banks tremendously. The OTE score is reduced by 15.3% and 19.5%, respectively with efficiency scores of 0.784 and 0.742. Thus, the initial scores from the deterministic DEA test were significantly lowered with the sensitivity analysis even when no data variation is assumed (0.937). Findings point out that overall risk management efficiency patterns in the banks in the Asia-Pacific region vary when an element of uncertainty is involved.

The study also found that the CCDEA approach features were important for enhancing the level of risk management efficiency in Asian-Pacific banks as it could address any specification or measurement errors. Following Thao (2012), output variables are assumed to be stochastic while the inputs are certain (predetermined) in the CCDEA analysis. By allowing the constraints to hold with probability levels and the existence of certain structural features, this method is quantitatively linked to different measures of efficiencies to maximise the function of derivatives as a risk management tool. In particular, the analysis did support the possibility theory[2] while evaluating the non-deterministic existences and evolving over time. The results of the CCDEA showed that risk management efficiency level of banks increased in 2007 and 2012. Compared to the deterministic DEA, this analysis indicated that efficiency scores were relatively high. With the condition that the constraints must be satisfied 95% (VaR0.95) of the time, only allowing violations for 5%, the results clearly indicate a mean of CCDEA (0.975), which is higher than the deterministic DEA efficiency scores (0.937). This implied that the CCDEA approach is not only able to benefit risk management measurement for banks, but also empowers banks and governments to make policies for their risk management strategies, as advocated by many efficiency studies (Thao 2012; Chen 2005, 2002; Fethi et al. 2001). More importantly, the results show that decision-making under uncertainty will necessarily take account of both the consequences of choice and the elements of probabilities (Fehr-Duda and Epper 2012; Starmer 1992).

The stochastic approaches were shown to provide more accurate and reliable measures of risk management with implications for efficiency levels leading to high profitability. This approach of incorporating stochastic measures into DEA refines the efficiency model to help policy makers and researchers, to arrive at a more accurate score for the efficiency level that considers elements of uncertainty and chance. This convergent DEA approach helps stem the limitation of deterministic DEA. In practical applications, these stochastic measurements assist in a more efficient allocation of financial risks that considers market uncertainties (Cukierman and Gerlach 2003; Devereux 1989).

6.3.6 *Efficiency difference between deterministic and*
stochastic approaches

Evidence from the experimental stochastic DEA approaches also illustrates the efficiency difference between the BDEA and the deterministic DEA. Welch's test result indicates that all efficiency types (OTE, PTE and SE) have insignificant differences with p-values more than 0.05. They are comparatively less vulnerable to the impact of efficiency differences in testing regardless of whether the country's status has influenced the performance of the bank's risk management. However, Mann–Whitney results found a statistically significant value for SE analysis (p=0.000). This result implies that the use of the BDEA approach can provide a better indicator in measuring the SE.

The difference between stochastic approaches (BDEA vs. CCDEA) was also checked using Welch's test (Table 5.19). Results between (i) DEA and CCDEA, and (ii) BDEA vs. CCDEA were both significant at 5% level (4.336** and 4.476**, respectively). These indicate efficiency differences when the CCDEA approach was involved, thus providing a significant influence and impact on risk management efficiency measurements. The results contradicted the study by Chen (2002), and indeed, this may be the first empirical evidence associating efficiency and stochastic measurement theories through the implementation of a CCDEA approach.

Here, findings illustrate that different efficiency measures calculated by Mann–Whitney are robust in addressing this issue. This is mainly due to its novelty and distinctive characteristics, which afford significant effect and influence on risk management efficiency measurement and analysis. Stochastic DEA approaches recognise the probabilistic behaviour of risk management in banking institutions, which are ultimately subjective in measurement and decision-making. The results prove that the stochastic DEA approaches are reliable techniques for measuring efficiency particularly in banks where environments are more complex and ambiguous.

6.3.7 Other implications: organisational design and corporate governance

The investigation towards risk management efficiency has a direct influence on the organisational design and the corporate governance context of the firm. The model of risk management analysis used in the conceptual phase of this study could also be used to assess attitude and skill levels for a firm in strategising their risk management. While most firms in the current study were familiar with the usage of derivatives as a risk management tool, the results show that this was relatively infrequent. In the situation where banks and other firms enjoy the usage of derivatives in mitigating risks (Rahman and Hassan 2011; Mihaljek and Packer 2010; Allayannis and Weston 2001), analyses has shown that their usage needs to be well-monitored. Banks need to ensure that derivatives are used properly. As suggested by Stulz (2004), firms need to have their well-planned risk management policies to understand the derivatives positions. By understanding how risk is managed and what role derivatives play, positive impacts from the usage of derivatives help make the firm more efficient. Thus, this study guides the firm on the emergence of the usage of financial derivative instruments as a product that legitimately helps risk management in firms. It also encourages managers to embrace change for their organisations.

However, there are some barriers which often obstruct the derivative performance. These include a low knowledge and skills base, as well as a lack of research and development (R&D) programmes. Thus, this combination of approaches helps to facilitate the assessment of the efficiency and effectiveness of the use of derivatives, and provides more coordination among risk management personnel from different areas and this leads to better decision-making. This argument again aligns with Stulz (2004) where he has suggested that those employees who are in charge of taking derivatives positions must have adequate training. In a broader context, Kleffner et al. (2003) have supported this argument whereas the risk management issues lie within the context of corporate governance and derivatives usage for risk management purposes, reflecting the behavioural agency model. As an example, the role played by board of directors (BODs), who act on behalf of the shareholders, is important to explain their initiatives in managerial risk-taking (Wiseman and Gomez-Mejia 1998). This theory assumes that BOD or executive personnel can decide to use financial strategies in order to achieve the firm's financial gains. This illustrates how the internal governance mechanism plays a role in corporate derivatives policy (Marsden and Prevost 2005) especially in evaluating a firm's performance and making a decision under conditions of risk. On the contrary, this scenario supports the argument by Madhumathi (2012), which states that shareholders may not practically engage in firms' hedging activities because they do not have the professional knowledge and the same access to hedging operations and information. Therefore, financial derivatives must be captured closely by the firm in either developed or emerging markets because the governance system and mechanism are important for risk management strategies as they can influence the managerial incentives as well as external monitoring of the decision to use derivatives (Hagelin et al. 2006; Whidbee and Wohar 1999).

While DEA was applied in investigating comparative analyses of risk management efficiencies between banks, this study has proven that CB7 was successful in three different efficiency tests (DEA, BDEA and the sensitivity analysis). It can be assumed that given the robust nature of these results, CB7 were successful in managing their risks. This bank can confidently extrapolate to the rest of the organisation. In addition to that, this study can reinforce the underlying contention that future studies can further apply an optimisation model to corporate governance (e.g. Zelenyuk and Zheka 2006; Belu 2009; Manzoni and Islam 2009a). Other inefficient banks can also set CB7 as their benchmark to boost their risk management efficiency levels. This is especially possible for banks in other newly industrialised countries such as Malaysia, Thailand and the Philippines.

In short, the analysis of risk management efficiency in the context of corporate governance in hedging policy and derivatives usage[3] can indirectly have a positive effect on the overall risk management strategic planning including setting risk management objectives, risk monitoring and assessing risk (Ameer 2010; Whidbee and Wohar 1999; Carter and Sinkey 1998; Weinberger et al. 1995).

6.4 Theoretical and policy implications

As discussed in Section 6.2, this study proves that the innovative approach of integrating dollar-offset ratio with DEA holds two implications in the context of risk efficiency of derivatives. First, with respect to its theoretical advance over other techniques available for risk management efficiency measurement in banks, and second, for suggesting policy recommendations to the banking sector in Asia-Pacific after quantitatively estimating risk management efficiency results, and comparing their efficiency ranking. Both of these are explained below in two subsections.

6.4.1 Theoretical implications

The research findings of this study have implications for academics and others involved in theory building. First, the review of risk management issues raised concerns about the development of a new approach to measure the efficiency of banks' risk management. By recognising the disclosure of financial derivatives in the treatment of hedge accounting, this study argued that an optimisation model must involve a function of financial risk modelling instead of using accounting perspectives alone. In the scope of hedge accounting, the use of derivatives for trading and hedging treatment remain unresolved. The hedge effectiveness measurement through various tests, with the dollar-offset ratio that was chosen in this study, was less indicated on firms' risk management perspectives (McCarroll and Khatri 2014; Ernst & Young 2011). This scenario has also been highlighted by the International Financial Reporting Standards (IFRS) on derivatives for corporate risk management (Panaretou et al. 2013). This research has been able to embed the use of derivatives in a sophisticated inter-disciplinary field incorporating both hedge accounting and risk management perspectives. It developed a methodology integrating the conventional dollar-offset ratio analysis with DEA which is better able to measure the efficiency of derivatives in hedging risks from market exposure. This integration thus adds valuable information for managerial accounting scope for better recognising and expressing its hedge effectiveness measurement. This is in agreement with Andrade and Nakaoa (2011) who stated that accounting information must be in line with the undertaking of measurement of economic facts. Thus, this study demonstrated how risk management concepts aligned with hedge accounting effectiveness can produce a system of integrated risk and management reporting, which, in turn, enables the firm to incorporate its risk appetite into its financial planning and budgeting. Exploiting this potential of derivatives as a tool for managing risk, DEA as a quantitative model provides a robust accounting risk management. The DEA efficiency analysis is able to strengthen the effectiveness of risk management measurement, particularly when it involves a mutual element in the measurements and solutions. This risk framework is capable of finding a simple rule to determine the impact of derivatives usage on the organisation's risk management, and becomes an alternative tool for quality assessment and effectiveness measurement. Further, by questioning the dollar-offset ratio analysis this study showed the limitations to the current method of hedge effectiveness measurement in hedge accounting. This is supported by Blidisel and Popa (2012) and Mante (1997) who argued that the performance of the units of analysis cannot be determined by the examination of the simple ratio concept unless the relative importance (weight) of each ratio is specified. Rather than employing a single accounting function, i.e. ratio analysis, the composite dollar-offset ratio and the DEA model are able to integrate important accounting functions within a linear programming approach to measure the effectiveness of derivatives usage. This integrated model can solve the problem of determining the performance of the banks better than analyses based on a simple concept.

Furthermore, the argument of financial derivative implications towards firms' performance shows that competing theoretical perspectives of derivatives usage provide contrasting impact strategies on organisations. As suggested above, there is no clear impact of the derivative use towards banks' risk management efficiency. Although leading researchers in financial risk management claim that derivative instruments are superior for firms' risk management performances, the findings of this study seem to suggest that they are less efficient in measuring the risk management efficiency of banks. This argument indicates that the performance of the majority of Asian-Pacific banks was less efficient when derivatives were used as a major indication to investigate their risk management efficiency levels. This finding is in contrast to Cummins et al. (2001) and Borokhovich et al. (2004), who stated that corporate risk management theory is useful when firms engage in derivatives for hedging purposes. This means that the applicability of the derivatives in measuring risk management efficiency may seem to depend on the purpose of its usages. Even though this study also investigates the efficiency from hedging perspectives, the involvement of banks in other activities (i.e. trading to increase income or speculating) may possibly influence the finding. As explained by Yong et al. (2009), the decision in altering the risk profile by the bank can directly affect the level of their risk management. Moreover, modern financial theory suggests that capital market imperfections provide wider alternatives for banks to use derivatives for hedging or other purposes. Thus, a challenge for this study and future research is to limit these contingent factors. However, the conflict and consensus perspectives are complementary to each other to understand the complex relationship between derivatives usage and its involvement in measuring banks' risk management efficiency.

Finally, the framework of this study was also built around a number of elements aimed at developing and analysing risk management indicators under uncertainty unlike traditional deterministic DEA models. The deterministic DEA approach was extended with stochastic techniques from different perspectives to improve the robustness of results considering uncertainty in the environment. The BDEA, the sensitivity analysis test and CCDEA were able to formulate evaluation models with stochastic analyses to create a holistic approach to risk management supervision in banks, as well as to reduce bias in risk management efficiency measurement. The current risk model was unable to quantify the potential impact of the translation of analytical outputs reported in the balance sheet, income statement or profit and loss (P&L) on a firm's financial report. In the conventional derivatives treatment in hedge accounting, risk managers might be unable to capture structural risk metrics on the impacts of derivatives on P&L or balance sheets. Thus, the integrated approach developed in this study aided with stochastic measurement techniques should be able to enhance managerial judgement to express the "uncertainty" and sensitivity of the P&L, balance sheet and income statement against emerging risk, particularly in relation to interest rate movement.

In short, this study has shown how modelling of risk can be accomplished using an integrated approach between a hedge effectiveness test and nonparametric approach (DEA). The empirical findings can now be used to develop and map strategies from the perspective of hedge accounting (risk management accounting) and efficiency measurement for the benefit of all stakeholders. The next subsection discusses the policy implications of this study.

6.4.2 Potential practical and policy implications

The objective of this study was to provide decision makers in commercial banks a means of modelling risk management efficiency measurement with derivatives usage. The study endeavoured to develop the model in a manner suited to real practice in banks. The framework holds great relevance in today's banking practice for decision-making in the financial world, particularly when derivative instruments are closely related to asset-liability management performance. This is in line with the Basel Committee on Banking Supervision that has aggressively promoted rules, guidance and guidelines on sound risk management of derivative activities that can be utilised by supervisory authorities and banking organisations. This study also contributes to further development in risk management policies for derivative usage and reassessment of the key elements of risks involved in derivatives. It helps to emphasise sound internal risk management for prudent operations of banks as well as promoting stability in the financial system as a whole, particularly in addressing market interest rates movement.

This new approach in the accounting field may have little impact on the ability of banks to avert losses; however, it does help to facilitate a risk management strategy for banks to derive the benefits of derivatives to hedge against market risks from interest rate volatility. As banks are intrinsically connected by a set of risk exposures, the integrated framework is able to bring the hedge accounting perspective to address risk management purposes and to ensure consistency in risk management decision-making. Pointing out flaws in popular approaches that are currently being used, the study shows that banks should not become complacent with their existing risk models. This study has proven that its integrated approach delivers reliable results, which can reduce the complexity of derivative activities and deliver a more direct assessment technique for banks to strategise their risk management. The integrated approach of this model is also able to predict banks' future performance by directly assessing the level of financial and institutional competitiveness. Apart from providing insights on structural risk from external environmental economic indicators, risk managers can strengthen their analysis with a predictive "forward-looking" approach based on reliable measurement. Based on these measurements, financial institutions that are not satisfied by their performance can shift to more effective methods, such as outsourcing services or obtaining outside financial experts, to improve their risk management level and productivity.

Moreover, the analysis also helps in improving corporate governance in banking organisations. This initiative can be considered to further enhance the corporate governance of the financial services sector, including the review and issuance of guidelines describing the general principles, minimum standards and specific requirements for corporate governance. In particular, this initiative improves performance, accounting standards and internal controls to enable benchmarking with international best practices. Continuous focus can be given to strengthening the capacity of the financial risk management of banks to support the implementation of a risk-based capital framework.

The results from the comparison between developed and developing countries in the Asia-Pacific region support the supervision of banks' derivatives operations. This study anticipates a framework as a basis for developing guidelines that allow fund managers to use derivatives in portfolio management. The high risk management efficiency scores shown in Malaysian and Australian banks in this study urge them to seriously consider derivatives as risk management tools and integrate a variety of strategies across different market segments. Therefore, an understanding of the different financial institutions and the characteristics of the system is crucial for policy makers to develop suitable policies for the country's financial systems. The results support the development of a capital market for improving the asset-liability management burden on investments as well as the liquidity and vitality of the derivatives market in the Asia-Pacific region. On the other hand, the efficiency results indicate that the majority of banks in the Asia-Pacific region exhibit low risk management efficiency. These inefficient banks have substantial room for improvement regarding risk management practices.

6.5 Limitations and areas of future research

As with any research effort, this study encountered some limitations owing to the specificity of its focus and methodology as well as some unforeseen circumstances in the research process. It must be acknowledged that a number of constraints were uncontrollable, and may have affected the outcomes and interpretations of the empirical analyses performed.

The first limitation was the issue of data availability. As the participating banks were under no obligation to report derivatives transactions (e.g. futures and options) in hedge accounting reporting systems, the involvement of most of the commercial banks in these areas was undisclosed. There were also significant variations in the type and extent of derivative instruments that created inconsistencies in data availability (e.g. only a few banks were involved in futures and swaps instruments for hedging purposes). The data limitation on this front prompted the researcher to exclude many commercial banks.

The second limitation focussed on the lack of data on input and output variables. Since the study has referred to the hedging activity in the banking sector, the usage of the derivative instrument and the hedged items must be matched. The input variables chosen must be well integrated with the items being hedged. These factors must be based on the definition of hedging instruments and the hedged items regulated in hedge accounting treatment that reflect asset-liability management in banks. This study avoids mixing variables in determining input and output parameters, as in most efficiency studies, preferring to derive a direct relationship between the hedging instrument and the hedged item. However, due to limited disclosure of these variables in financial reports of these banks, only one input and two outputs were able to be determined in this analysis.

This study has demonstrated the ability of DEA to create an integrated framework with a hedge effectiveness test for measuring the risk management efficiency based on the derivatives usage in banks. Further enhancing the argument for a superior hedge effectiveness measurement involving risk management aspects, certain areas which emerge from this research should be considered relevant for future studies. First, a future study should investigate and validate if other derivative instruments used for the purpose of hedging have the same impact on risk management efficiency in the Asia-Pacific banking sector. Future research should continue to look upon the development of knowledge about different financial derivative instruments for risk management in firms. This should focus on the specific derivative type as well as the integrated elements from the hedge accounting perspective to highlight the role played by that instrument, particularly to highlight the benefits from interest rate swap usage through more capabilities inherent in the debt ratio and exploit tax benefits (Yang et al. 2001). It will help to further understand the implications of tax incentives towards hedging. The application of hedge effectiveness tests in hedge accounting also needs to be explored further. Future studies may be undertaken to construct alternative measurement approaches to improve the hedge effectiveness measurement instead of the DEA method presented here. Other hedge effectiveness tests, such as short-cut method and critical terms match method, must be investigated by merely assigning the possibilities to the concept of efficiency analysis.

The effectiveness of measurement can also be evaluated using other measurement approaches. For instance, the fractional programming under the optimisation technique can be used as a method for investigation in order to analyse a better risk management strategy in the implementation of two or more financial derivative instruments simultaneously. Hence, this approach can serve as a useful alternative to the DEA approach. On the other hand, other parametric and non-parametric approaches such as stochastic frontier approach (SFA), distribution-free approach (DFA) and thick frontier approach (TFA) among others can also be used as performance measurement tools. In agreement with previous studies (Sufian 2007b; Asmild et al. 2004; Webb 2003), this study also suggests that DEA window analysis[4] should be developed further to reduce bias and small sample issues.

Due to uncertainty in derivative instrument trading and transactions, future research needs to explore specific uncertainty issues in the input (interest rate swaps) used under the hedging platform. Uncertainty from input and output data and model parameters needs to be treated separately, so that individual and collective impact of uncertainty over the output can be quantified clearly. To achieve that purpose, future research may use other stochastic formulation techniques, such as robust DEA (RDEA), Fuzzy DEA (FDEA) and other stochastic approaches, other than BDEA, the sensitivity analysis and CCDEA approaches used here, with the assumption that both input and/or output parameters are uncertain.

Finally, since the efficiency level of institutions was also related to corporate governance (Bozec and Dia 2007; Destefanis and Sena 2007; Zelenyuk and Zheka 2006), this study thus suggests a strategy for authorities seeking to improve governance in banking to further investigate the efficiency of banks by considering corporate governance elements. However, in the case of a risk management efficiency study, embarking on an agent's effort to suit the objective of principles in order to reduce agency costs or problems, it is essential to represent input and output parameters. These may seem different to previous studies which considered corporate governance indicators in the second stage analysis towards efficiency scores, however, without this step it is difficult to comprehend the true success of the corporate governance effort in determining the efficiency level of institutions.

6.6 Conclusion

This study had developed an integrated dollar-offset ratio/DEA approach to measure risk management efficiency involving a financial derivatives-based instrument. As shown, the functional structure in dollar-offset ratio of a hedge effectiveness test can be operationalised using the DEA approach. As financial derivatives have experienced accelerated growth in Asian-Pacific banks, this study had sought to measure the impact of derivatives on risk management efficiency measurement. This would contribute to a more competitive financial sector which would have a positive impact on the real economy. This study also developed a range of techniques, including BDEA, sensitivity analysis test and CCDEA approaches which consider the influence of data as well as uncertainty in the modelling measurement (DEA) of risk management efficiency, mainly in highly stressed settings.

The empirical findings of this study using the DEA approach in conjunction with non-parametric methods showed that banks in the Asia-Pacific sector have disparate levels of risk management efficiency. Moreover, this study found that the national background of the banks did not influence the performance of risk management efficiency. The developed and developing countries within the Asia-Pacific region seem to have similar efficiency scores when it comes to the relative impact of derivative instruments used as a hedging strategy. This new integrated method is not only highly accurate in establishing risk management efficiency rankings, but also identifies and promotes the benefits of derivatives usage as a risk management tool.

Despite all these, the methodology and results of this study were not without limitations as explained previously. However, the rigour of this study had been ensured with careful analysis of the data, thorough literature review and an innovative methodology with the purpose of ensuring the credibility and generalisability of this research.

Notes

1 Some articles written by the ISDA are well endorsed for their elimination of the effectiveness range (80%–125%). This includes several reasons such as reduction of bias in hedge effectiveness measurement, being less in line with firms' risk management strategies and less in allowing tolerance towards firms and institutions (www2.isda.org/).
2 The possibility theory is an alternative to the probability theory that had first been introduced by Professor Lotfi Zadeh in 1978. This theory had been developed as an extension of his fuzzy theory. For further understanding, see Negoita et al. (1978). In practice, Arenas et al. (1998) stated that the possibility (probability) theory might be more appropriate to be used to support best results in some banking decision-making problems.
3 Marsden and Prevost (2005) demonstrate that the role of corporate governance at both firm level and country level in derivatives usage and its relation to hedging policy is essential in explaining corporate governance measures and helping to avoid corporate failures that may be caused by huge derivative losses.
4 In a DEA window analysis, data on each bank is treated differently and this provides a better degree of freedom as it effectively increases the number of units (DMUs) for evaluations and hence the discriminatory power of the method which commonly uses small sample size to avoid the robustness-related problems (Shawtari 2014; Pjevčević et al. 2012; Halkos and Tzeremes 2009; Avkiran 2004). Basically a DEA window analysis calculates the average efficiency of CCR and BCC models, and is useful for detecting efficiency trends of DMU over time (Asmild et al. 2004; Charnes et al. 1994).

References

Abdel-Khalik, A. R. 2013. *Accounting for Risk, Hedging and Complex Contracts.* New York: Routledge.

Abdel-Khalik, A. R., and K. M. El-Sheshai. 1980. Information choice and utilization in an experiment on default prediction. *Journal of Accounting Research* 18 (2):325–342.

Abedifar, P., P. Molyneux, and A. Tarazi. 2013. Risk in Islamic banking. *Review of Finance* 17 (6):2035–2096.

Acar, O., and A. B. Acar. 2014. Modern risk management techniques in banking sector. In *Handbook of Research on Strategic Business Infrastructure Development and Contemporary Issues in Finance*, edited by N. Ray and K. Chakraborty. Hershey, PA: Business Science Reference, IGI Global, 186–206.

Acworth, W. 2011. Record volume 2010 (annual volume survey). *Futures Industry*, 12–29.

Adams, R., and H. Mehran. 2003. Is corporate governance different for bank holding companies? *Available at SSRN 387561.*

Adcock, C., X. Hua, K. Mazouz, and S. Yin, 2017. Derivative activities and Chinese banks' exposures to exchange rate and interest rate movements. *The European Journal of Finance* 23(7–9):727–751.

Adkins, L. C., D. A. Carter, and W. G. Simpson. 2007. Managerial incentives and the use of foreign exchange derivatives by banks. *Journal of Financial Research* 30 (3):399–413.

Adler, N., L. Friedman, and Z. Sinuany-Stern. 2002. Review of ranking methods in the data envelopment analysis context. *European Journal of Operational Research* 140 (2):249–265.

Ahmad, N., and B. Haris. 2012. Factors for using derivatives: Evidence from Malaysian non-financial companies. *Research Journal of Finance and Accounting* 3 (9):79–87.

Ahmad, S., and A. R. A. Rahman. 2012. The efficiency of Islamic and conventional commercial banks in Malaysia. *International Journal of Islamic and Middle Eastern Finance and Management* 5 (3):241–263.

Ahmed, A., A. Beatty, and C. Takeda. 1997. Evidence on interest rate risk management and derivatives usage by commercial banks. *Available at SSRN 33922.*

Ahn, J., M. Matic, and C. Vallence. 2012. Australian OTC derivatives markets: Insights from the BIS semiannual survey. In *RBA Bulletin*: Reserve Bank of Australia, 39–46.

Ahn, T., and L. M. Seiford. 1993. Sensitivity of DEA to models and variable sets in a hypothesis test setting: The efficiency of university operations. In *Creative and innovative Approaches to the Science of Management*, edited by Y. Ijiri. New York: Quorum Books, 6:191–208.

Aigner, D., C. Lovell, and P. Schmidt. 1977. Formulation and estimation of stochastic frontier production function models. *Journal of Econometrics* 6 (1):21–37.

Alam, N. 2012. Efficiency and risk-taking in dual banking system: Evidence from emerging markets. *International Review of Business Research Papers* 8 (4):94–111.

Alexander, K. 2006. Corporate governance and banks: The role of regulation in reducing the principal-agent problem. *Journal of Banking Regulation* 7 (1/2):17–40.

Ali, R., N. Ahmad, and S. F. Ho. 2006. *Introduction to Malaysian Derivatives*. University Publication Centre (UPENA), Universiti Teknologi MARA.

Alkebäck, P., and N. Hagelin. 1999. Derivative usage by nonfinancial firms in Sweden with an international comparison. *Journal of International Financial Management & Accounting* 10 (2):105–120.

Allayannis, G., G. W. Brown, and L. F. Klapper. 2003. Capital structure and financial risk: Evidence from foreign debt use in East Asia. *The Journal of Finance* 58 (6):2667–2710.

Allayannis, G., and J. P. Weston. 2001. The use of foreign currency derivatives and firm market value. *Review of Financial Studies* 14 (1):243–276.

Allen, F., and A. M. Santomero. 1998. The theory of financial intermediation. *Journal of Banking & Finance* 21 (11):1461–1485.

———. 2001. What do financial intermediaries do? *Journal of Banking & Finance* 25 (2):271–294.

Allen, P. G., and R. Fildes. 2001. Econometric Forecasting. In *Principles of Forecasting*, edited by J. Scott Armstrong. Boston, MA: Springer, 303–362. https://link.springer.com/book/10.1007/978-0-306-47630-3

Allen, R., A. Athanassopoulos, R. G. Dyson, and E. Thanassoulis. 1997. Weights restrictions and value judgements in data envelopment analysis: Evolution, development and future directions. *Annals of Operations Research* 73 (0):13–34.

Ally, Z. 2013. Efficiency analysis of commercial banks in Tanzania: An application of Data Envelopment Analysis (DEA) Approach: The case study of regional & small banks. *European Journal of Business and Management* 5 (31):193–203.

Alonso, A. M., D. Peña, and J. Romo. 2006. Introducing model uncertainty by moving blocks bootstrap. *Statistical Papers* 47 (2):167–179.

Althoff, J. M., and J. D. Finnerty. 2001. Testing hedge effectiveness. *Special Issues* 2001 (1):44–51.

Altunbas, Y., S. Carbo, E. P. Gardener, and P. Molyneux. 2007. Examining the relationships between capital, risk and efficiency in European banking. *European Financial Management* 13 (1):49–70.

Altunbas, Y., M.-H. Liu, P. Molyneux, and R. Seth. 2000. Efficiency and risk in Japanese banking. *Journal of Banking & Finance* 24 (10):1605–1628.

Ameer, R. 2010. Determinants of corporate hedging practices in Malaysia. *International Business Research* 3 (2):120–130.

Andrade, d. J. A. M. J., and S. H. Nakaoa. 2011. Intrinsic accounting uncertainty and risk: Toward a theory of accounting measurements. *Available at SSRN 2061856*.

Arenas, M. M., A. Bilbao, M. V. R. Uría, and M. Jimenez. 1998. A Theory of Possibility Approach to the Solution of a Fuzzy Linear Programming. In *Applied Decision Analysis*. Netherlands: Springer, Dordrecht, 147–157.

Arjomandi, A. 2011. Efficiency and Productivity in Iran's Financial Institutions. PhD, School of Economics, Faculty of Commerce, University of Wollongong.

Armstrong, J. S. 2001. Judgmental bootstrapping: Inferring experts' rules for forecasting. In *Principles of Forecasting*. Boston, MA: Springer, 171–192.

Asay, M. R., G. A. Gonzalez, and B. Wolkowitz. 1981. Financial futures, bank portfolio risk, and accounting. *Journal of Futures Markets* 1 (4):607–618.

Asmild, M., J. C. Paradi, V. Aggarwall, and C. Schaffnit. 2004. Combining DEA window analysis with the Malmquist index approach in a study of the Canadian banking industry. *Journal of Productivity Analysis* 21 (1):67–89.

Asmild, M., J. C. Paradi, D. N. Reese, and F. Tam. 2007. Measuring overall efficiency and effectiveness using DEA. *European Journal of Operational Research* 178 (1):305–321.

Assaf, A., and K. Matawie. 2010. Improving the accuracy of DEA efficiency analysis: A bootstrap application to the health care foodservice industry. *Applied Economics* 42 (27):3547–3558.

Assaf, A. G., and F. W. Agbola. 2011. Modelling the performance of Australian hotels: A DEA double bootstrap approach. *Tourism Economics* 17 (1):73–89.

Assaf, A. G., C. P. Barros, and R. Matousek. 2011a. Productivity and efficiency analysis of Shinkin banks: Evidence from bootstrap and bayesian approaches. *Journal of Banking & Finance* 35 (2):331–342.

———. 2011b. Technical efficiency in Saudi banks. *Expert Systems with Applications* 38 (5):5781–5786.

Ataullah, A., T. Cockerill, and H. Le. 2004. Financial liberalization and bank efficiency: A comparative analysis of India and Pakistan. *Applied Economics* 36 (17):1915–1924.

Ataullah, A., and H. Le. 2006. Economic reforms and bank efficiency in developing countries: The case of the Indian banking industry. *Applied Financial Economics* 16 (9):653–663.

Athanassopoulos, A. D., and S. P. Curram. 1996. A comparison of data envelopment analysis and artificial neural networks as tools for assessing the efficiency of decision making units. *Journal of the Operational Research Society* 47 (8):1000–1016.

Atkinson, S. E., and P. W. Wilson. 1995. Comparing mean efficiency and productivity scores from small samples: A bootstrap methodology. *Journal of Productivity Analysis* 6 (2):137–152.

Au Yong, H. H., R. Faff, and K. Chalmers. 2009. Derivative activities and Asia-Pacific banks' interest rate and exchange rate exposures. *Journal of International Financial Markets, Institutions and Money* 19 (1):16–32.

Australian Prudential Regulation Authority (APRA). 2012. *Australian OTC Derivatives Markets: Insights from the BIS Semiannual Survey*, edited by Jason Ahn. Reserve Bank of Australia, 39–46.

Avkiran, N. K. 1999a. An application reference for data envelopment analysis in branch banking: Helping the novice researcher. *International Journal of Bank Marketing* 17 (5):206–220.

Avkiran, N. K. 1999b. Decomposing the technical efficiency of trading banks in the deregulated period. Paper read at 12th Australasian Finance and Banking Conference, UNSW, Australia.

Avkiran, N. K. 1999c. The evidence on efficiency gains: The role of mergers and the benefits to the public. *Journal of Banking & Finance* 23 (7):991–1013.

234   *References*

Avkiran, N. K. 2000. Rising productivity of Australian trading banks under deregulation 1986–1995. *Journal of Economics and Finance* 24 (2):122–140.

———. 2001. Investigating technical and scale efficiencies of Australian universities through data envelopment analysis. *Socio-Economic Planning Sciences* 35 (1):57–80.

———. 2004. Decomposing technical efficiency and window analysis. *Studies in Economics and Finance* 22 (1):61–91.

Aysun, U., and M. Guldi. 2011. Derivatives market activity in emerging markets and exchange rate exposure. *Emerging Markets Finance and Trade* 47 (6):46–67.

Aziz, R. A. 2016. Managing operational risks in a bank: Applied research in Malaysia. *Asia-Pacific Management Accounting Journal* 3(1); 47–65.

Bajo, E., M. Barbi, and S. Romagnoli. 2014. Optimal corporate hedging using options with basis and production risk. *The North American Journal of Economics and Finance* 30:56–71.

Balakrishnan, C. 2009. On the Determinants of Interest Rate Swap Usage by Indian Banks. Paper read at Refereed International Conference Proceedings of the World Congress on Engineering.

Baluch, A., and M. Ariff. 2007. Derivative markets and economic growth: Is there a relationship? Bond University.

Banaeian, N., M. Omid, and H. Ahmadi. 2011. Application of data envelopment analysis to evaluate efficiency of commercial greenhouse strawberry. *Research Journal of Applied Sciences, Engineering and Technology* 3 (3):185–193.

Bank for International Settlements (BIS). 2003. Sound practices for the management and supervision of operational risk. In *Risk Management Group of the Basel Committee on Banking Supervision*, edited by B. C. o. B. Supervision. Switzerland: Basel, 1.

———. 2012. OTC Derivatives Market Activity in the First Half of 2012. In *November*.

Bank Negara Malaysia. 2004. Governor's keynote address at the 4th banking and financial law school seminar. Renaissance Hotel, Kuala Lumpur: Bank Negara Malaysia.

Banker, R. D. 1984. Estimating most productive scale size using data envelopment analysis. *European Journal of Operational Research* 17 (1):35–44.

Banker, R. D. 1993. Maximum likelihood, consistency and data envelopment analysis: A statistical foundation. *Management Science* 39 (10):1265–1273.

Banker, R. D., A. Charnes, and W. W. Cooper. 1984. Some models for estimating technical and scale inefficiencies in data envelopment analysis. *Management Science* 30 (9):1078–1092.

Banker, R. D., and R. C. Morey. 1986. The use of categorical variables in data envelopment analysis. *Management Science* 32 (12):1613–1627.

Banker, R. D., and R. Natarajan. 2011. Statistical tests based on DEA efficiency scores. In *Handbook on Data Envelopment Analysis*, edited by W. W. Cooper, L. M. Seiford, and J. Zhu. Boston, MA: Springer, 273–295. https://link.springer.com/book/10.1007/978-1-4419-6151-8

Banker, R. D., Z. E. Zheng, and R. Natarajan. 2010. DEA-based hypothesis tests for comparing two groups of decision making units. *European Journal of Operational Research* 206 (1):231–238.

Barrieu, P., and G. Scandolo. 2015. Assessing financial model risk. *European Journal of Operational Research* 242 (2):546–556.

Barros, C. P., S. Dumbo, and P. Wanke. 2014. Efficiency determinants and capacity issues in Angolan Insurance Companies. *South African Journal of Economics* 82 (3):455–467.

Barros, C. P., S. Managi, and R. Matousek. 2012. The technical efficiency of the Japanese banks: Non-radial directional performance measurement with undesirable output. *Omega* 40 (1):1–8.

Bartesaghi, M., S. H. Grey, and S. Gibson. 2012. Defining (the concept of) risk. *An Interdisciplinary Journal of Rhetorical Analysis and Invention* 8 (1):6.

Barth, J. R., G. Caprio, and R. Levine. 2001. *The Regulation and Supervision of Banks Around the World: A New Database.* Washington, DC: World Bank Publications.

Bartram, S. M., G. W. Brown, and F. R. Fehle. 2003. International evidence on financial derivatives usage. *Financial Management* 38 (1):185–206.

———. 2009. International evidence on financial derivatives usage. *Financial Management* 38 (1):185–206.

Batten, J. A., and S. Hettihewa. 2007. Risk management and derivatives use in Australian firms. *Journal of Asia Business Studies* 1 (2):37–44.

Battese, G. E., T. Coelli, and D. Rao. 1998. *An Introduction to Efficiency and Productivity analysis.* London: Kluwer Academic Publisher.

Battilossi, S. 2008. Did governance fail universal banks? Moral hazard, risk taking, and banking crises in interwar Italy. *The Economic History Review* 62 (s1):101–134.

Beatty, A. 1999. Assessing the use of derivatives as part of a risk-management strategy. *Journal of Accounting and Economics* 26 (1):353–357.

Beccalli, E., B. Casu, and C. Girardone. 2006. Efficiency and stock performance in European banking. *Journal of Business Finance & Accounting* 33 (1–2):245–262.

Beck, T. 2008. Bank competition and financial stability: Friends or foes? In *World Bank Policy Research Working Paper 4656.*

Beck, T., A. Demirgüç-Kunt, and R. Levine. 2006. Bank concentration, competition, and crises: First results. *Journal of Banking & Finance* 30 (5):1581–1603.

Beck, T., A. Demirgüç-Kunt, and O. Merrouche. 2013. Islamic vs. conventional banking: Business model, efficiency and stability. *Journal of Banking & Finance* 37 (2):433–447.

Beets, S. 2004. The use of derivatives to manage interest rate risk in commercial banks. *Investment Management and Financial Innovations* 2:60–74.

Beltratti, A., and R. M. Stulz. 2012. The credit crisis around the globe: Why did some banks perform better? *Journal of Financial Economics* 105 (1):1–17.

Bergendahl, G., and S. Sjögren. 2013. The management of Foreign exchange exposures. In *Bank Stability, Sovereign Debt and Derivatives*, edited by F. Joseph, and M. Philip. New York: Palgrave Macmillan, 203–251.

Berger, A. N., and D. B. Humphrey. 1997. Efficiency of financial institutions: International survey and directions for future research. *European Journal of Operational Research* 98 (2):175–212.

Berger, A. N., D. Hancock, and D. B. Humphrey. 1993. Bank efficiency derived from the profit function. *Journal of Banking & Finance* 17 (2):317–347.

Berger, A. N., and D. B. Humphrey. 1991. The dominance of inefficiencies over scale and product mix economies in banking. *Journal of Monetary Economics* 28 (1):117–148.

———. 1997. Efficiency of financial institutions: International survey and directions for future research. *European Journal of Operational Research* 98 (2):175–212.

Berger, A. N., and G. F. Udell. 2004. The institutional memory hypothesis and the procyclicality of bank lending behavior. *Journal of Financial Intermediation* 13 (4):458–495.

Berkman, H., and M. E. Bradbury. 1996. Empirical evidence on the corporate use of derivatives. *Financial Management* 25 (2):5–13.

Berkman, H., M. E. Bradbury, and S. Magan. 1997. An international comparison of derivatives use. *Financial Management* 26 (4):69–73.

Bernhardt, T., D. Erlinger, and L. Unterrainer. 2014. IFRS 9: The new rules for hedge accounting from the risk management's perspective. *ACRN Journal of Finance and Risk Perspectives* 3 (3):53–66.

Besley, S., and E. F. Brigham. 2007. *Essentials of Managerial Finance*. Cincinnati, OH: South-Western Pub.

Bessembinder, H. 1991. Forward contracts and firm value: Investment incentive and contracting effects. *Journal of Financial and Quantitative Analysis* 26 (04):519–532.

Bessis, J. 2002. *Risk Management in Banking*. 2nd ed. West Sussex, England: John Wiley & Sons.

———. 2011. *Risk Management in Banking*. West Sussex, England: John Wiley & Sons.

Bicksler, J., and A. H. Chen. 1986. An economic analysis of interest rate swaps. *The Journal of Finance* 41 (3):645–655.

Bicksler, J., and A. H. Chen. 2012. An economic analysis of interest rate swaps. *The Journal of Finance* 41 (3):645–655.

Biener, C., and M. Eling. 2011. The performance of microinsurance programs: A data envelopment analysis. *Journal of Risk and Insurance* 78 (1):83–115.

Blidisel, R. G., and A. S. Popa. 2012. Traditional ratio versus data envelopment analysis in Romanian public higher education. Paper read at 1st International Conference Accounting and Auditing Perspectives November 29–30, 2012, at Romania.

Bodnar, G. M., and G. Gebhardt. 1999. Derivatives usage in risk management by US and German non-financial firms: A comparative survey. *Journal of International Financial Management & Accounting* 10 (3):153–187.

Bogetoft, P. 2012. *Performance Benchmarking: Measuring and Managing Performance*. New York: Springer Science & Business Media.

Bonin, J. P., I. Hasan, and P. Wachtel. 2005. Bank performance, efficiency and ownership in transition countries. *Journal of Banking & Finance* 29 (1):31–53.

Borokhovich, K. A., K. R. Brunarski, C. E. Crutchley, and B. J. Simkins. 2004. Board composition and corporate use of interest rate derivatives. *Journal of Financial Research* 27 (2):199–216.

Boukrami, L. 2002. The use of interest rate swaps by commercial banks. *SSRN 373482*.

Boussofiane, A., R. G. Dyson, and E. Thanassoulis. 1991. Applied data envelopment analysis. *European Journal of Operational Research* 52 (1):1–15.

Boyd, J. H., and M. Gertler. 1995. Are banks dead? Or are the reports greatly exaggerated? In *NBER Working Paper*: National Bureau of Economic Research, 1–33.

Bozec, R., and M. Dia. 2007. Board structure and firm technical efficiency: Evidence from Canadian state-owned enterprises. *European Journal of Operational Research* 177 (3):1734–1750.

Brázdik, F. 2004. *Stochastic Data Envelopment Analysis: Oriented and Linearized Models*. Working paper series. Charles University. Center for Economic Research and Graduate Education, Charles University, Prague, and the Economics Institute of the Academy of Sciences of the Czech Republic.

Breeden, D., and S. Viswanathan. 1998. Why do firms hedge? An asymmetric information model. *Fuqua School of Business Working Paper.*

Brewer, E., S. Deshmukh, and T. P. Opiela. 2014. Interest-rate uncertainty, derivatives usage, and loan growth in Bank Holding Companies. *Journal of Financial Stability* 15 (2014):230–240.

Brewer, E., W. E. Jackson, and J. T. Moser. 2001. The value of using interest rate derivatives to manage risk at US banking organizations. *Economic Perspectives-Federal Reserve Bank of Chicago* 25 (3):49–65.

Brewer, E., and M. R. Saidenberg. 1996. Franchise value, ownership structure, and risk at savings institutions. Federal Reserve Bank of New York.

Brewer, E. I., B. A. Minton, and J. T. Moser. 2000. Interest-rate derivatives and bank lending. *Journal of Banking & Finance* 24 (3):353–379.

Brigham, E., and M. Ehrhardt. 2013. *Financial Management: Theory & Practice.* San Francisco, CA: Cengage Learning.

Brown, G. W., P. R. Crabb, and D. Haushalter. 2006. Are firms successful at selective hedging? *The Journal of Business* 79 (6):2925–2949.

Brown, G. W., and A. M. Mood. 1951. On median tests for linear hypotheses. Paper read at *Proceedings of the Second Berkeley Symposium on Mathematical Statistics and Probability*, Berkeley: University of California Press, 159–166.

Brown, K. C., and D. J. Smith. 1988. Recent innovations in interest rate risk management and the reintermediation of commercial banking. *Financial Management* 17 (4):45–58.

Brown, R. 2006. Mismanagement or mismeasurement? Pitfalls and protocols for DEA studies in the financial services sector. *European Journal of Operational Research* 174 (2):1100–1116.

Bruni, M., P. Beraldi, and G. Iazzolino. 2014. Lending decisions under uncertainty: A DEA approach. *International Journal of Production Research* 52 (3):766–775.

Bunea-Bontaş, C. 2012. The assessment of hedge effectiveness. *Annals of the University Dunarea de Jos of Galati: FascicleI, Economics & Applied Informatics* 18 (1):57–62.

Bunea-Bontaş, C. A. 2009. Basic principles of hedge accounting. *Munich Personal RePEc Archive (MPRA)* 17072 (August 2009):1–14.

Bunea-Bontas, C. A., M. C. Petre, and G. Culita. 2009. Issues on hedge effectiveness testing. *SSRN 1494015.*

Bushman, R. M., and A. J. Smith. 2001. Financial accounting information and corporate governance. *Journal of Accounting and Economics* 32 (1):237–333.

Butler, C. 2009. *Accounting for Financial Instruments.* Chichester: Wiley.

Cabilio, P., and J. Masaro. 1996. A simple test of symmetry about an unknown median. *Canadian Journal of Statistics* 24 (3):349–361.

Camerer, C., and M. Weber. 1992. Recent developments in modeling preferences: Uncertainty and ambiguity. *Journal of Risk and Uncertainty* 5 (4):325–370.

Carter, D. A., and J. F. Sinkey. 1998. The use of interest rate derivatives by end-users: The case of large community banks. *Journal of Financial Services Research* 14 (1):17–34.

Carver, R. P. 1978. The case against statistical significance testing. *Harvard Educational Review* 48 (3):378–399.

Castelino, M. G. 1992. Hedge effectiveness: Basis risk and minimum-variance hedging. *Journal of Futures Markets* 12 (2):187–201.

———. 2000. Hedge effectiveness: Basis risk and minimum-variance hedging. *Journal of Futures Markets* 20 (1):89–103.

Casu, B., C. Girardone, and P. Molyneux. 2004. Productivity change in European banking: A comparison of parametric and non-parametric approaches. *Journal of Banking & Finance* 28 (10):2521–2540.

Casu, B., and P. Molyneux. 2003. A comparative study of efficiency in European banking. *Applied Economics* 35 (17):1865–1876.

Cavallo, M., and G. Majnoni. 2002. *Do Banks Provision for Bad Loans in Good Times? Empirical Evidence and Policy Implications.* Boston, MA: Springer.

Cebenoyan, A. S., and P. E. Strahan. 2004. Risk management, capital structure and lending at banks. *Journal of Banking & Finance* 28 (1):19–43.

Chamberlain, S., J. S. Howe, and H. Popper. 1997. The exchange rate exposure of US and Japanese banking institutions. *Journal of Banking & Finance* 21 (6):871–892.

Chan, S. G., M. Z. A. Karim, B. Burton, and B. Aktan. 2014. Efficiency and risk in commercial banking: Empirical evidence from East Asian countries. *The European Journal of Finance* 20 (12):1114–1132.

Chan, Y., and R. P. Walmsley. 1997. Learning and understanding the Kruskal-Wallis one-way analysis-of-variance-by-ranks test for differences among three or more independent groups. *Physical Therapy* 77 (12):1755–1761.

Chance, D., and R. Brooks. 2015. *Introduction to Derivatives and Risk Management.* Boston, MA: Cengage Learning.

Chance, D. M., and R. Brooks. 2009. *Introduction to Derivatives and Risk Management.* Mason, OH: South-Western Pub.

Chance, D. M., and R. E. Brooks. 2010. *An Introduction to Derivatives and Risk Management.* Mason, OH: South-Western Cengana Learning.

Chang, C.-C. 1999. The nonparametric risk-adjusted efficiency measurement: an application to Taiwan's major rural financial intermediaries. *American Journal of Agricultural Economics* 81 (4):902–913.

Chang, T.-C., and Y.-H. Chiu. 2006. Affecting factors on risk-adjusted efficiency in Taiwan's banking industry. *Contemporary Economic Policy* 24 (4):634–648.

Charnes, A., and W. W. Cooper. 1963. Deterministic equivalents for optimizing and satisfying under chance-constraints. *Operations Research* 11:18–39.

Charnes, A., W. W. Cooper, Z. M. Huang, and D. Sun. 1990. Polyhedral cone-ratio DEA models with an illustrative application to large commercial banks. *Journal of Econometrics* 46 (1):73–91.

Charnes, A., W. Cooper, A. Y. Lewin, R. C. Morey, and J. Rousseau. 1985. Sensitivity and stability analysis in DEA. *Annals of Operations Research* 2 (1):139–156.

Charnes, A., W. W. Cooper, A. Y. Lewin, and L. M. Seiford. 1994. *Data Envelopment Analysis: Theory, Methodology, and Applications.* Dordrecht, Netherlands: Springer.

Charnes, A., W. W. Cooper, and E. Rhodes. 1978. Measuring the efficiency of decision making units. *European Journal of Operational Research* 2 (6):429–444.

Charnes, A., S. Haag, P. Jaska, and J. Semple. 1992. Sensitivity of efficiency classifications in the additive model of data envelopment analysis. *International Journal of Systems Science* 23 (5):789–798.

Charnes, A., J. J. Rousseau, and J. H. Semple. 1996. Sensitivity and stability of efficiency classifications in data envelopment analysis. *Journal of Productivity Analysis* 7 (1):5–18.

Charnes, J. M., P. Koch, and H. Berkman. 2003. Measuring hedge effectiveness for FAS 133 compliance. *Journal of Applied Corporate Finance* 15 (4):95–103.

Chaudhry, M. K., R. Christie-David, T. W. Koch, and A. K. Reichert. 2000. The risk of foreign currency contingent claims at US commercial banks. *Journal of Banking & Finance* 24 (9):1399–1417.

Chen, K.-H. 2012. Incorporating risk input into the analysis of bank productivity: Application to the Taiwanese banking industry. *Journal of Banking & Finance* 36 (7):1911–1927.

Chen, T.-y. 2002. A comparison of chance-constrained DEA and stochastic frontier analysis: Bank efficiency in Taiwan. *Journal of the Operational Research Society* 53 (5):492–500.

Chen, T. 2005. A measurement of Taiwan's bank efficiency and productivity change during the Asian financial crisis. *International Journal of Services Technology and Management* 6 (6):525–543.

Chen, W.-C., and L. F. McGinnis. 2007. Reconciling ratio analysis and DEA as performance assessment tools. *European Journal of Operational Research* 178 (1):277–291.

Chen, Y. Q., H. Lu, W. Lu, and N. Zhang. 2010. Analysis of project delivery systems in Chinese construction industry with data envelopment analysis (DEA). *Engineering, Construction and Architectural Management* 17 (6):598–614.

Chernenko, S., and M. Faulkender. 2008. A panel data analysis of interest rate risk management. Evanston, IL: Finance Department, Kellogg School of Management.

Chernenko, S., and M. Faulkender. 2012. The two sides of derivatives usage: Hedging and speculating with interest rate swaps. *Journal of Financial and Quantitative Analysis* 46 (06):1727–1754.

Chernick, M. R. 2008. *Bootstrap Methods: A Guide for Practitioners and Researchers*. Vol. 619: Wiley. com.

Cho, M. H. 1998. Ownership structure, investment, and the corporate value: An empirical analysis. *Journal of Financial Economics* 47 (1):103–121.

Choi, F. D. 2003. *International Finance and Accounting Handbook*. Hoboken, NJ: John Wiley & Sons, Inc.

Chortareas, G. E., C. Girardone, and A. Ventouri. 2013. Financial freedom and bank efficiency: Evidence from the European Union. *Journal of Banking & Finance* 37 (4):1223–1231.

Christoffersen, P. F. 2012. *Elements of Financial Risk Management*. Waltham, MA: Academic Press.

Chung, K., and R. L. Smith. 1987. Product quality, nonsalvageable capital investment and the cost of financial leverage. *Modern Finance and Industrial Economics: Papers in Honor of J. Fred Weston*. New York: Basil Blackwell, 146–167.

Clark, J. A. 1996. Economic cost, scale efficiency, and competitive viability in banking. *Journal of Money, Credit and Banking* 28 (3):342–364.

Clark, J. A., and T. Siems. 2002. X-efficiency in banking: Looking beyond the balance sheet. *Journal of Money, Credit, and Banking* 34 (4):987–1013.

Clarke, C. J., and S. Varma. 1999. Strategic risk management: The new competitive edge. *Long Range Planning* 32 (4):414–424.

Clemente, A. D. 2015. Hedge accounting and risk management: An advanced prospective model for testing hedge effectiveness. *Economic Notes* 44 (1):29–55.

Co-Pierre, G. 2013. The effect of the interbank network structure on contagion and common shocks. *Journal of Banking & Finance* 37 (7):2216–2228.

Coelli, D. S. P. Rao, C. J. O'Donnell, and G. E. Battese. 2005a. *An Introduction to Efficiency and Productivity Analysis*. New York: Springer.

Coelli, T. 1996. A guide to DEAP version 2.1: a data envelopment analysis (computer) program. Armidale: University of New Engaland, 1996. 49p: CEPA Working Papers 08/96.

Coelli, T., and S. Perelman. 1999. A comparison of parametric and non-parametric distance functions: With application to European railways. *European Journal of Operational Research* 117 (2):326–339.

Coelli, T., D. Rao, and G. Battese. 1998. *An introduction to efficiency and productivity analysis*: Kulwar Academic Publishers, Massachusetts, USA.

Coelli, T. J., D. S. P. Rao, C. J. O'Donnell, and G. E. Battese. 2005b. *An introduction to efficiency and productivity analysis*. New York: Springer Science & Business Media.

Collier, P. M. M. 2009. *Fundamentals of Risk Management for Accountants and Managers*. New York: Routledge.

Collier, P. M. M., A. Berry, and G. T. T. Burke. 2006. *Risk and Management Accounting: Best Practice Guidelines for Enterprise-wide Internal Control Procedures*. Burlington, MA: CIMA Publishing.

Collins, B. M., and F. J. Fabozzi. 1999. Derivatives and risk management. *The Journal of Portfolio Management* 25 (5):16–27.

Commission, E. 1997. Credit institution and banking, The single market review. In *Subseries 2*.

Conrow, E. H. 2003. *Effective Risk Management: Some Keys to Success*. AIAA (American Institute of Aeronautics & Astronautics).

Cooper, W. W., L. M. Seiford, and K. Tone. 2006. *Data Envelopment Analysis: A Comprehensive Text with Models, Applications, References and DEA-solver Software*. 2nd ed. New York: Springer Science + Business Media, LLC.

Cooper, W. W., L. M. Seiford, and J. Zhu. 2011. *Data Envelopment Analysis: History, Models, and Interpretations*. New York: Springer.

Cornell, B., and A. C. Shapiro. 1987. Corporate stakeholders and corporate finance. *Financial Management* 16 (1):5–14.

Cornett, M. M., and A. Saunders. 2003. *Financial Institutions Management: A Risk Management Approach*. New York: McGraw-Hill/Irwin.

Corvoisier, S., and R. Gropp. 2002. Bank concentration and retail interest rates. *Journal of Banking & Finance* 26 (11):2155–2189.

Cotter, J., and K. Dowd. 2006. Estimating financial risk measures for futures positions: A non-parametric approach. *SSRN 994523*.

Coughlan, G. 2004. *Corporate Risk Management in an IAS 39 Framework*. London: Incisive Media Plc.

Cukierman, A., and S. Gerlach. 2003. The inflation bias revisited: Theory and some international evidence. *The Manchester School* 71 (5):541–565.

Cummins, J. D. 1999. Efficiency in the US life insurance industry: Are insurers minimizing costs and maximizing revenues? In *Changes in the Life Insurance Industry: Efficiency, Technology and Risk Management*, edited by J.D. Cummins, and A.M. Santomero. Boston, MA: Springer, 75–115.

Cummins, J. D., R. D. Phillips, and S. D. Smith. 2001. Derivatives and corporate risk management: Participation and volume decisions in the insurance industry. *Journal of Risk and Insurance* 68 (1):51–92.

Cummins, J. D., M. A. Weiss, and H. Zi. 1999. Organizational form and efficiency: The coexistence of stock and mutual property-liability insurers. *Management Science* 45 (9):1254–1269.

———. 2003. Economies of scope in financial services: A DEA bootstrapping analysis of the US insurance industry. *Unpublished Manuscript, The Wharton School*, Philadelphia, PA.

DaDalt, P., G. D. Gay, and J. Nam. 2002. Asymmetric information and corporate derivatives use. *Journal of Futures Markets* 22 (3):241–267.

Dagher, J., and K. Kazimov. 2012. Banks' Liability structure and mortgage lending during the financial crisis. *SSRN 2045029.*

Daniel, W. 1990. Procedures that utilize data from two independent samples. In *Applied Nonparametric Statistic*, edited by Wayne W. Daniel. Boston, MA: PWS-Kent Publishing Co., 82–143.

Daraio, C., and L. Simar. 2007. *Advanced Robust and Nonparametric Methods in Efficiency Analysis: Methodology and Applications.* Vol. 4. New York: Springer Science & Business Media.

Davison, A. C. 1997. *Bootstrap Methods and Their Application.* New York: Cambridge University Press.

De Jong, A., M. Verbeek, and P. Verwijmeren. 2011. Firms' debt–equity decisions when the static tradeoff theory and the pecking order theory disagree. *Journal of Banking & Finance* 35 (5):1303–1314.

Deegan, C., and J. Unerman. 2006. *Financial Accounting Theory: European Edition.* London: McGraw-Hill Maidenhead.

Deesomsak, R., K. Paudyal, and G. Pescetto. 2004. The determinants of capital structure: Evidence from the Asia Pacific region. *Journal of Multinational Financial Management* 14 (4):387–405.

Dekle, R., and M. Lee. 2015. Do foreign bank affiliates cut their lending more than the domestic banks in a financial crisis? *Journal of International Money and Finance* 50 (2015):16–32.

DeLancer, P. 1996. Public productivity and data envelopment analysis (DEA): How compatible are they? Paper read at annual meeting of the American Society for Public Administration, Atlanta, GA.

Delis, M. D., and G. P. Kouretas. 2011. Interest rates and bank risk-taking. *Journal of Banking & Finance* 35 (4):840–855.

DeMarzo, P. M., and D. Duffie. 1995. Corporate incentives for hedging and hedge accounting. *Review of Financial Studies* 8 (3):743–771.

Demsetz, M. Saidenberg, and P. Strahan. 1997. Agency problems and risk taking at banks. *FRB of New York Staff Report* September 1997 (29).

Demsetz, H., and B. Villalonga. 2001. Ownership structure and corporate performance. *Journal of Corporate Finance* 7 (3):209–233.

Demyanyk, Y., and O. Van Hemert. 2009. Understanding the subprime mortgage crisis. *Review of Financial Studies* 24 (6):1848–1880.

Deng, S., E. Elyasiani, and C. X. Mao. 2014. Derivatives hedging, risk shifting and cost of debt: Evidence from bank holding companies. *Risk Shifting and Cost of Debt: Evidence from Bank Holding Companies* (March 26, 2014).

Denis, D. J. 2011. Financial flexibility and corporate liquidity. *Journal of Corporate Finance* 17 (3):667–674.

Deprins, D., L. Simar, and H. Tulkens. 1984. Measuring Labor-efficiency in Post Offices. In *Public Goods, Environmental Externalities and Fiscal Competition*, edited by M. Marchand, P. Pestieau, and H. Tulkens. Boston, MA: Springer, 285–309.

Destefanis, S., and V. Sena. 2007. Patterns of corporate governance and technical efficiency in Italian manufacturing. *Managerial and Decision Economics* 28 (1):27–40.

Devereux, M. 1989. A positive theory of inflation and inflation variance. *Economic Inquiry* 27 (1):105–116.

Dewald, W. G., and G. R. Dreese. 1970. Bank behavior with respect to deposit variability. *The Journal of Finance* 25 (4):869–879.

DeYoung, R. 2010. Banking in the United States. In *The Oxford Handbook of Banking*, edited by R. De Young. New York: Oxford University Press, 777–806.

Dhanani, A., S.G.M. Fifield, C.V. Helliar, and L.A. Stevenson. 2005. Interest rate risk management – An investigation into the management of interest rate risk in UK companies: CIMA, 1–6.

Diamond, D. W. 1984. Financial intermediation and delegated monitoring. *The Review of Economic Studies* 51 (3):393–414.

Diamond, D. W., and P. H. Dybvig. 1986. Banking theory, deposit insurance, and bank regulation. *Journal of Business* 59 (1):55–68.

Diamond, D. W., and R. Rajan. 2009. The credit crisis: Conjectures about causes and remedies. National Bureau of Economic Research.

Do, Q.-T., and A. A. Levchenko. 2007. Comparative advantage, demand for external finance, and financial development. *Journal of Financial Economics* 86 (3):796–834.

Dong, F., and A. M. Featherstone. 2006. Technical and scale efficiencies for chinese rural credit cooperatives: A bootstrapping approach in data envelopment analysis. *Journal of Chinese Economic and Business Studies* 4 (1):57–75.

Dong, Y. 2010. Cost efficiency in the Chinese banking sector: A comparison of parametric and non-parametric methodologies, Business School, Loughborough University, Leicestershire, UK.

Drake, L. 2001. Efficiency and productivity change in UK banking. *Applied Financial Economics* 11 (5):557–571.

Drake, L., and M. J. Hall. 2003. Efficiency in Japanese banking: An empirical analysis. *Journal of Banking & Finance* 27 (5):891–917.

Drake, L., M. J. Hall, and R. Simper. 2006. The impact of macroeconomic and regulatory factors on bank efficiency: A non-parametric analysis of Hong Kong's banking system. *Journal of Banking & Finance* 30 (5):1443–1466.

———. 2009. Bank modelling methodologies: A comparative non-parametric analysis of efficiency in the Japanese banking sector. *Journal of International Financial Markets, Institutions and Money* 19 (1):1–15.

Drehmann, M., S. Sorensen, and M. Stringa. 2008. The integrated impact of credit and interest rate risk on banks: An economic value and capital adequacy perspective. *Available at SSRN*.

Dyson, R. G., R. Allen, A. S. Camanho, V. V. Podinovski, C. S. Sarrico, and E. A. Shale. 2001. Pitfalls and protocols in DEA. *European Journal of Operational Research* 132 (2):245–259.

Eakins, G., and S. Mishkin. 2012. *Financial Markets and Institutions*: Boston, MA: Prentice Hall.

East Asia Analytical Unit. 1999. *Asia's Financial Markets: Capitalising on Reform*. Barton: National Library of Australia.

Ebert, R. J., and T. E. Kruse. 1978. Bootstrapping the security analyst. *Journal of Applied Psychology* 63 (1):110.

Ederington, L. H. 1979. The hedging performance of the new futures markets. *The Journal of Finance* 34 (1):157–170.

Edirisinghe, N. 2012. Stochastic Programming DEA Model of Fundamental Analysis of Public Firms for Portfolio Selection. In *Operations Research Proceedings 2011*: Berlin, Heidelberg: Springer, 539–544.

Edward, F. R. 1984. *Strategic Management: A Stakeholder Approach*. Boston: Pitman.

Efron, B. 1979. Bootstrap methods: Another look at the jackknife. *The Annals of Statistics* 7 (1):1–26.

Efron, B., and R. J. Tibshirani. 1994. *An Introduction to the Bootstrap.* Florida: Chapman & Hall/CRC.

Ehrhardt, M. C., and E. F. Brigham. 2011. *Financial Management: Theory and Practice*: Mason, OH: South-Western Cengage Learning.

El-Masry, A. A. 2003. A survey of derivatives use by UK nonfinancial companies. Manchester, England: Manchester Business School, 455–403.

Eling, M., and M. Luhnen. 2010. Efficiency in the international insurance industry: A cross-country comparison. *Journal of Banking & Finance* 34 (7):1497–1509.

Ellis, P. D. 2010. *The Essential Guide to Effect Sizes: Statistical Power, Meta-analysis, and the Interpretation of Research Results.* Cambridge: Cambridge University Press.

Elsinger, H., A. Lehar, and M. Summer. 2006. Risk assessment for banking systems. *Management Science* 52 (9):1301–1314.

Elzinga, K. G., and D. E. Mills. 2011. The Lerner index of monopoly power: Origins and uses. *The American Economic Review* 101 (3):558–564.

Emrouznejad, A., R. Banker, A. L. Miranda Lopes, and M. Rodrigues de Almeida. 2014. Data envelopment analysis in the public sector. *Socio-Economic Planning Sciences* 48 (1):2–3.

Emrouznejad, A., and E. Thanassoulis. 2010. *Performance Improvement Management Software (PIMsoft): A User Guide.*

Ernst & Young's International Financial Reporting Standards Group. 2011. Hedge accounting under IFRS 9 — a closer look at the changes and challenges: Ernst & Young's International, 1–45.

Fabozzi, F. J., and S. V. Mann. 2005. *The Handbook of Fixed Income Securities.* Vol. 6. New York: McGraw-Hill.

Fadzlan, S. 2010. The impact of the Asian financial crisis on bank efficiency: The 1997 experience of Malaysia and Thailand. *Journal of International Development* 22 (7):866–889.

Fama, E. F. 1980. Agency problems and the theory of the firm. *The Journal of Political Economy* 88 (2):288–307.

Fama, E. F., and K. R. French. 2002. Testing trade-off and pecking order predictions about dividends and debt. *Review of Financial Studies* 15 (1):1–33.

Fan, H. 2009. Hedging and trading activities of bank holding companies: Analysis of foreign exchange derivatives accounts, University of Saskatchewan Saskatoon.

Farrell, M. J. 1957. The measurement of productive efficiency. *Journal of the Royal Statistical Society. Series A (General)* 120 (3):253–290.

Farzipoor, R. S., and M. Azadi. 2011. A chance-constrained data envelopment analysis approach for strategy selection. *Journal of Modelling in Management* 6 (2):200–214.

Fatemi, A., and M. Glaum. 2000. Risk management practices of German firms. *Managerial Finance* 26 (3):1–17.

Fehle, F., and S. Tsyplakov. 2005. Dynamic risk management: Theory and evidence. *Journal of Financial Economics* 78 (1):3–47.

Fehr-Duda, H., and T. Epper. 2012. Probability and risk: Foundations and economic implications of probability-dependent risk preferences. *Annual Review of Economics* 4 (1):567–593.

Fernando, J. R., and P. Nimal. 2014. Does risk management affect on bank efficiency? An analysis of Sri Lankan banking sector. *International Journal of Management and Sustainability* 3 (2):97–110.

Feroz, E. H., S. Kim, and R. L. Raab. 2003. Financial statement analysis: A data envelopment analysis approach. *Journal of the Operational Research Society* 54 (1):48–58.

Ferrier, G. D., and C. Lovell. 1990. Measuring cost efficiency in banking: Econometric and linear programming evidence. *Journal of Econometrics* 46 (1):229–245.

Feruś, A. 2014. The application of data envelopment analysis method in managing companies' credit risk. *Business and Economic Horizons* 10 (1):60–69.

Fethi, M. D., P. M. Jackson, and T. G. Weyman-Jones. 2001. *An Empirical Study of Stochastic DEA and Financial Performance in the Case of the Turkish Commercial Banking Industry*. University of Leicester, Management Centre.

Fethi, M. D., and F. Pasiouras. 2010. Assessing bank efficiency and performance with operational research and artificial intelligence techniques: A survey. *European Journal of Operational Research* 204 (2):189–198.

Fiechter, P. 2011. The effects of the fair value option under IAS 39 on the volatility of bank earnings. *Journal of International Accounting Research* 10 (1):85–108.

Filippou, M., and P. Zervopoulos. 2011. Developing a short-term comparative optimization forecasting model for operational units' strategic planning. Greece: Panteion University of Athens, 14.

Finnerty, J. D., and D. Grant. 2003. Testing hedge effectiveness under SFAS 133. *CPA Journal* 73 (4):40–47.

Fite, D., and P. Pfleiderer. 1995. *Should Firms Use Derivatives to Manage Risk?* New York: McGraw Hill.

Fok, R. C. W., C. Carroll, and M. C. Chiou. 1997. Determinants of corporate hedging and derivatives: A revisit. *Journal of Economics and Business* 49 (6):569–585.

Fong, K., D. R. Gallagher, and A. Ng. 2005. The use of derivatives by investment managers and implications for portfolio performance and risk. *International Review of Finance* 5 (1–2):1–29.

Frank, M., and V. Goyal. 2007. Trade-off and pecking order theories of debt. *Available at SSRN 670543*.

Franzen, D. 2010. Managing investment risk in defined benefit pension funds. In *OECD Working Papers on Insurance and Private Pension*, 1–65.

Fraser, D. R., J. Madura, and R. A. Weigand. 2002. Sources of bank interest rate risk. *Financial Review* 37 (3):351–367.

Fratzscher, O. 2006. Emerging derivative market in Asia. *EAP Flagship on Asian Financial Market and Development*. World Bank Report (March 23).

Freeman, R. E. 1984. *Strategic Management: A Stakeholder Approach*. Boston, MA: Pitman.

Freeman, R. E. 1994. The politics of stakeholder theory: Some future directions. *Business Ethics Quarterly* 4 (04):409–421.

Freeman, R. E., A. C. Wicks, and B. Parmar. 2004. Stakeholder theory and "the corporate objective revisited". *Organization Science* 15 (3):364–369.

Freixas, X., and J.-C. Rochet. 1997. *Microeconomics of Banking*. London: MIT press Cambridge.

Frey, H. C. 1992. Quantitative analysis of uncertainty and variability in environmental policy making. *Fellowship Program for Environmental Science and Engineering, American Association for the Advancement of Science*, Washington, DC.

Fried, H. O., C. Knox Lovell, and P. V. Eeckaut. 1993. Evaluating the performance of US credit unions. *Journal of Banking & Finance* 17 (2):251–265.

Fried, H. O., C. K. Lovell, and S. S. Schmidt. 2008. *The Measurement of Productive Efficiency and Productivity Growth*. New York: Oxford University Press.

Friedman, L. W., and H. H. Friedman. 2013. Bootstrapping: Resampling methodology. In *Encyclopedia of Operations Research and Management Science*, edited by S. I. Gass, and M. C. Fu. Boston, MA: Springer, 127–130. https://link.springer.com/referenceworkentry/10.1007%2F978-1-4419-1153-7_84#howtocite

Froot, K. A., D. S. Scharfstein, and J. C. Stein. 1993. Risk managements coordinating corporate investment and financing policies. *The Journal of Finance* 48 (5):1629–1658.

Froot, K. A., D. S. Scharfstein, and J. C. Stein. 1994. A framework for risk management. *Journal of Applied Corporate Finance* 7 (3):22–33.

Fu, X. M., Y. R. Lin, and P. Molyneux. 2014. Bank competition and financial stability in Asia Pacific. *Journal of Banking & Finance* 38:64–77.

García-Marco, T., and M. D. Robles-Fernández. 2008. Risk-taking behaviour and ownership in the banking industry: The Spanish evidence. *Journal of Economics and Business* 60 (4):332–354.

Géczy, C., B. A. Minton, and C. Schrand. 1997. Why firms use currency derivatives. *The Journal of Finance* 52 (4):1323–1354.

Géczy, C. C., B. A. Minton, and C. M. Schrand. 2007. Taking a view: Corporate speculation, governance, and compensation. *The Journal of Finance* 62 (5):2405–2443.

Gedik, H., H. Bal, and M. İzciler. 2014. Chance constrained data envelopment analysis for efficiency analysis: An application to Turkish manufacture of iron and steel sector. *Mathematical and Computational Applications* 19 (1):1–11.

Genay, H. 1998. Assessing the condition of Japanese banks: How informative are accounting earnings? *Economic Perspectives* 22:12–34.

Gibbons, J. D. 1985. *Nonparametric Statistical Inference*. 2nd ed. New York and Basel: McGraw-Hill Inc.

Gijbels, I., E. Mammen, B. U. Park, and L. Simar. 1999. On estimation of monotone and concave frontier functions. *Journal of the American Statistical Association* 94 (445):220–228.

Gil, A., and Y. Polyakov. 2003. Integrating Market and Credit Risk in Fixed Income Portfolios. In *Advances in Portfolio Construction and Implementation*, edited by S. Satchell, and A. Scowcroft. Oxford, UK: Butterworth- Heinemann. 215–242. https://www.sciencedirect.com/book/9780750654487/advances-in-portfolio-construction-and-implementation#book-info

Giovanis, E. 2013. Application of stationary wavelet support vector machines for the prediction of economic recessions. *International Journal of Mathematical Models and Methods in Applied Sciences* 3 (7):226–237.

Girardone, C., P. Molyneux, and E. P. Gardener. 2004. Analysing the determinants of bank efficiency: The case of Italian banks. *Applied Economics* 36 (3):215–227.

Goldberg, L. R. 1976. Man versus model of man: Just how conflicting is that evidence? *Organizational Behavior and Human Performance* 16 (1):13–22.

Gorton, G., and R. Rosen. 1995. Banks and derivatives. In *NBER Macroeconomics Annual 1995*, edited by M. Eichenbaum, E. Hurst, and J. A. Parker. Vol. 10. Cambridge, MA: MIT Press, 299–349.

Graham, J. R., and D. A. Rogers. 2002. Do firms hedge in response to tax incentives? *The Journal of Finance* 57 (2):815–839.

Grant, K., and A. P. Marshall. 1997. Large UK companies and derivatives. *European Financial Management* 3 (2):191–208.

Gregoriou, G. N., K. Sedzro, and J. Zhu. 2005. Hedge fund performance appraisal using data envelopment analysis. *European Journal of Operational Research* 164 (2):555–571.

Greuning, H., and S. B. Bratanovic. 1999. *Analyzing Banking Risk: A Framework for Assessing Corporate Governance and Financial Risk Management*. Washington, DC: The World Bank.

Grigorian, D. A., and V. Manole. 2002. Determinants of commercial bank performance in transition: An application of data envelopment analysis. *World Bank Policy Research Working Paper* (2850).

Grosskopf, S. 1996. Statistical inference and nonparametric efficiency: A selective survey. *Journal of Productivity Analysis* 7 (2–3):161–176.

Grote, G. 2015. Promoting safety by increasing uncertainty–Implications for risk management. *Safety Science* 71 (2015):71–79.

Guay, S. Kothari, and Y. Loktionov. 2008. *Accounting for Derivatives in Emerging Market Economies*. Cambridge: MIT Sloan School of Management.

Guay, W. and S. P. Kothari. 2003. How much do firms hedge with derivatives? *Journal of Financial Economics* 70 (3):423–461.

Guay, W. R. 1999. The impact of derivatives on firm risk: An empirical examination of new derivative users. *Journal of Accounting and Economics* 26 (1):319–351.

Gulati, R. 2011. Evaluation of technical, pure technical and scale efficiencies of Indian banks: An analysis from cross-sectional perspective. Paper read at 13th Annual Conference on Money and Finance.

Gup, B. E., and J. W. Kolari. 2005. *Commercial Banking: The Management of Risk*. 3rd ed. Hoboken, NJ: John Wiley & Sons.

Gutiérrez, E., S. Lozano, and S. Furió. 2014. Evaluating efficiency of international container shipping lines: A bootstrap DEA approach. *Maritime Economics & Logistics* 16 (1):55–71.

Gyntelberg, J., and C. Upper. 2013. The OTC interest rate derivatives market in 2013. *BIS Quarterly Review* 69.

Hagelin, N., M. Holmen, and B. Pramborg. 2006. Family ownership, dual-class shares, and risk management. *Global Finance Journal* 16 (3):283–301.

Hahn, F. R. 2008. Efficiency of regional banks in Europe, Japan and the USA. A best-practice analysis. *WIFO Monatsberichte (monthly reports)* 81 (3):191–201.

Hailer, A. C., and S. M. Rump. 2005. Evaluation of hedge effectiveness tests. *Journal of Derivatives Accounting* 2 (1):31.

Hair, J. F. 2009. *Multivariate Data Analysis*. 7th ed. Upper Saddle River: Prentice Hall.

Haiss, P. R., and B. Sammer. 2010. The impact of derivatives markets on financial integration, risk, and economic growth. *Risk, and Economic Growth*. Working Paper August 2010.

Halkos, G., and N. Tzeremes. 2010. Performance evaluation using bootstrapping DEA techniques: Evidence from industry ratio analysis. *MPRA Paper No. 25072* 25072.

Halkos, G., N. G. Tzeremes, and S. A. Kourtzidis. 2012. Measuring public owned university departments' efficiency: A bootstrapped DEA approach. *Journal of Economics and Econometrics* 55 (2):1–24.

Halkos, G. E., and D. S. Salamouris. 2004. Efficiency measurement of the Greek commercial banks with the use of financial ratios: A data envelopment analysis approach. *Management Accounting Research* 15 (2):201–224.

Halkos, G. E., and N. G. Tzeremes. 2009. Exploring the existence of Kuznets curve in countries' environmental efficiency using DEA window analysis. *Ecological Economics* 68 (7):2168–2176.

Halkos, G. E., and N. G. Tzeremes. 2013. Estimating the degree of operating efficiency gains from a potential bank merger and acquisition: A DEA bootstrapped approach. *Journal of Banking & Finance* 37 (5):1658–1668.

Hariri, A., and P. Roberts. 2015. Adoption of innovation within universities: Proposing and testing an initial model. *Creative Education* 6 (02):186.

Harker, P. T., and S. A. Zenios. 2000. *Performance of Financial Institutions: Efficiency, Innovation, Regulation.* Cambridge: Cambridge University Press.

Harper, J. T., and J. R. Wingender. 2000. An empirical test of agency cost reduction using interest rate swaps. *Journal of Banking & Finance* 24 (9):1419–1431.

Hashemi, H., S. M. Mousavi, R. Tavakkoli-Moghaddam, and Y. Gholipour. 2013. Compromise ranking approach with bootstrap confidence intervals for risk assessment in port management projects. *Journal of Management in Engineering* 29 (4):334–344.

Hassan, M. K., and A.-H. M. Bashir. 2003. Determinants of Islamic banking profitability. Paper read at 10th ERF Annual Conference, Morocco.

Havrylchyk, O. 2006. Efficiency of the polish banking industry: Foreign versus domestic banks. *Journal of Banking & Finance* 30 (7):1975–1996.

Hawdon, D. 2003. Efficiency, performance and regulation of the international gas industry—a bootstrap DEA approach. *Energy Policy* 31 (11):1167–1178.

Healy, P. M., and K. G. Palepu. 2001. Information asymmetry, corporate disclosure, and the capital markets: A review of the empirical disclosure literature. *Journal of Accounting and Economics* 31 (1):405–440.

Hellmann, T. F., K. C. Murdock, and J. E. Stiglitz. 2000. Liberalization, moral hazard in banking, and prudential regulation: Are capital requirements enough? *The American Economic Review* 90 (1):147–165.

Hentschel, L., and S. P. Kothari. 2001. Are corporations reducing or taking risks with derivatives? *Journal of Financial and Quantitative Analysis* 36 (01):93–118.

Herbst, A. F., D. D. Kare, and J. F. Marshall. 1985. A time varying, convergence adjusted, minimum risk futures hedge ratio. *Advances in Futures and Options Research* 6:137–155.

Herring, R. J. 1998. Banking disasters: Causes and preventative measures, lessons derived from the US experience. In *Preventing Bank Crises–Lessons from Recent Global Bank Failures*, edited by Gerard Caprio, Jr., William C. Hunter, George G. Kaufman, and Danny M. Leipziger. Washington, D.C.: The World Bank, 209–236.

Heston, S., and S. Nandi. 2000. Derivatives on Volatility: Some Simple Solutions based on Observables. In *Federal Reserve Bank of Atlanta WP*. Atlantan: Federal Reserve Bank of Atlanta 1–19.

Hirst, D. E., and P. E. Hopkins. 1998. Comprehensive income reporting and analysts' valuation judgments. *Journal of Accounting Research* 36:47–75.

Hirtle, B. J. 1997. Derivatives, portfolio composition, and bank holding company interest rate risk exposure. *Journal of Financial Services Research* 12 (2–3):243–266.

Holod, D., and H. F. Lewis. 2011. Resolving the deposit dilemma: A new DEA bank efficiency model. *Journal of Banking & Finance* 35 (11):2801–2810.

Homburg, C., O. Jensen, and A. Hahn. 2012. How to organize pricing? Vertical delegation and horizontal dispersion of pricing authority. *Journal of Marketing* 76 (5):49–69.

Hong Kong Monetary Authority (HKMA). 2010. The foreign-exchange and derivatives markets in Hong Kong, 1–9.

Hsu, W.-K., C.-P. Tseng, W.-L. Chiang, and C.-W. Chen. 2012. Risk and uncertainty analysis in the planning stages of a risk decision-making process. *Natural Hazards* 61 (3):1355–1365.

Huang, G., and F. M. Song. 2006. The determinants of capital structure: Evidence from China. *China Economic Review* 17 (1):14–36.

Huang, R., and J. R. Ritter. 2009. Testing theories of capital structure and estimating the speed of adjustment. *Journal of Financial and Quantitative Analysis* 44 (02):237–271.

Huang, X., H. Zhou, and H. Zhu. 2009. A framework for assessing the systemic risk of major financial institutions. *Journal of Banking & Finance* 33 (11):2036–2049.

Huang, Z., and S. X. Li. 1996. Dominance stochastic models in data envelopment analysis. *European Journal of Operational Research* 95 (2):390–403.

———. 2001. Stochastic DEA models with different types of input-output disturbances. *Journal of Productivity Analysis* 15 (2):95–113.

Hubbard, R. G., K. N. Kuttner, and D. N. Palia. 2002. Are there bank effects in borrowers' costs of funds? evidence from a matched sample of borrowers and banks. *The Journal of Business* 75 (4):559–581.

Hughes, J., and L. Mester. 2008. Efficiency in banking: Theory, practice, and evidence.

Hughes, J. P., and L. J. Mester. 1993. A quality and risk-adjusted cost function for banks: Evidence on the "too-big-to-fail" doctrine. *Journal of Productivity Analysis* 4 (3):293–315.

Hull, J. 2009. *Options, Futures, and Other Derivatives.* 7th ed. Upper Saddle River, NJ: Pearson.

———. 2012. *Risk Management and Financial Institutions.* 3rd ed. Hoboken, NJ: John Wiley & Sons.

Inman, O. L. 2004. Technology forecasting using data envelopment analysis, Portland State University, Portland, USA.

Institute of Bankers Malaysia (IBBM). 2012. Asian-Pacific Association of Banking Institutes (APABI) regional conference on global challenges, local opportunities. *The Journal of the Institute of Bankers Malaysia* (139):1–47.

Institute of Risk Management. 2002. *A Risk Management Standard.* London: Institute of Risk Management.

Iscoe, I., A. Kreinin, and D. Rosen. 1999. An integrated market and credit risk portfolio model. *Algo Research Quarterly* 2 (3):21–38.

Isik, I., and M. K. Hassan. 2002. Technical, scale and allocative efficiencies of Turkish banking industry. *Journal of Banking & Finance* 26 (4):719–766.

Islam, I., and A. Chowdhury. 1997. *Asia-Pacific Economies: A Survey.* New York: Psychology Press.

Iyer, R., and M. Puria. 2012. Understanding bank runs: The importance of depositor-bank relationships and networks. *The American Economic Review* 102 (4):1414–1445.

Jackson, P. M., and M. D. Fethi. 2000. Evaluating the technical efficiency of Turkish commercial banks: An Application of DEA and Tobit Analysis. Paper read at International DEA Symposium, University of Queensland, Brisbane, Australia.

Jagtiani, J. 1996. Characteristics of banks that are more active in the swap market. *Journal of Financial Services Research* 10 (2):131–141.

Jahanzeb, A. 2013. Trade-off theory, pecking order theory and market timing theory: A comprehensive review of capital structure theories. *Economics Bulletin* 33 (1):11–18.

Jalilvand, A., J. Switzer, and C. Tang. 2000. A global perspective on the use of derivatives for corporate risk management decisions. *Managerial Finance* 26 (3):29–38.

Japan, B. o. 2003. Results of Regular Derivatives Market Statistics in Japan.

Jemriæ, I., and B. Vujèiæ. 2002. Efficiency of banks in Croatia: A DEA approach. *IFC Bulletin*, 106.

Jensen, M. 1986. Agency cost of free cash flow, corporate finance, and takeovers. *American Economic Review* 76 (2):1–14.

Jensen, M. C., and W. H. Meckling. 1976. Theory of the firm: Managerial behavior, agency costs and ownership structure. *Journal of Financial Economics* 3 (4):305–360.

Jin, Y., and P. Jorion. 2006. Firm value and hedging: Evidence from US oil and gas producers. *The Journal of Finance* 61 (2):893–919.

———. 2007. Does hedging increase firm value? Evidence from the gold mining industry: Working paper, University of California at Irvine.

Johanson, B. L. 2013. Deterministic and Stochastic Analyses to Quantify the Reliability of Uncertainty Estimates in Production Decline Modeling of Shale Gas Reservoirs, Degree's Thesis, Colorado School of Mines, Texas A&M University.

Johnes, J. 2006. Data envelopment analysis and its application to the measurement of efficiency in higher education. *Economics of Education Review* 25 (3):273–288.

Jondrow, J., C. Knox Lovell, I. S. Materov, and P. Schmidt. 1982. On the estimation of technical inefficiency in the stochastic frontier production function model. *Journal of Econometrics* 19 (2):233–238.

Jones, M. 2014. Seeking diversification through efficient portfolio construction using cash-based and derivative instruments. *British Actuarial Journal* 19 (02):468–498.

Jorion, P. 1995. Predicting volatility in the foreign exchange market. *The Journal of Finance* 50 (2):507–528.

———. 2003. *Financial Risk Manager Handbook*. 2nd ed. Hoboken, NJ: John Wiley & Sons.

Joro, T., and P. J. Korhonen. 2015. Data Envelopment Analysis. In *Extension of Data Envelopment Analysis with Preference Information*. Boston, MA: Springer, 15–26.

Judge, A. 2006. Why and how UK firms hedge. *European Financial Management* 12 (3):407–441.

Kablan, S. 2007. Measuring bank efficiency in developing countries: The case of WAEMU (West African Economic Monetary Union). *African Economic Research Consortium*.

Kalotay, A., and L. Abreo. 2001. Testing hedge effectiveness for FAS 133: The volatility reduction measure. *Journal of Applied Corporate Finance* 13 (4):93–99.

Kao, C., and S.-T. Liu. 2009. Stochastic data envelopment analysis in measuring the efficiency of Taiwan commercial banks. *European Journal of Operational Research* 196 (1):312–322.

———. 2014. Measuring performance improvement of Taiwanese commercial banks under uncertainty. *European Journal of Operational Research* 235 (3):755–764.

Kaplan, S., and B. J. Garrick. 1981. On the quantitative definition of risk. *Risk analysis* 1 (1):11–27.

Kashyap, A. K., R. Rajan, and J. C. Stein. 2002. Banks as liquidity providers: An explanation for the coexistence of lending and deposit-taking. *The Journal of Finance* 57 (1):33–73.

Kasman, A. 2012. Cost efficiency, scale economies, and technological progress in Turkish banking. *Central Bank Review* 2 (1):1–20.

Kasman, A., and O. Carvallo. 2013. Efficiency and risk in Latin American banking: Explaining resilience. *Emerging Markets Finance and Trade* 49 (2):105–130.

Kasman, S., and E. Turgutlu. 2007. A comparison of chance-constrained DEA and stochastic frontier analysis: an application to the Turkish life insurance industry. Paper read at 8 Congreso Turco de Econometríay Estadística, Malaysia.

Kassi, D. F., D. N. Rathnayake, P. A. Louembe, and N. Ding. 2019. Market risk and financial performance of non-financial companies listed on the Moroccan stock exchange. *Risks* 7 (1):20.

Kawaller, I. G. 2002. Hedge Effectiveness Testing using Regression Analysis. Kawaller & Company, LLC: Association for Financial Professionals (AFP).

Kawaller, I. G. 2004. What analysts need to know about accounting for derivatives. *Financial Analysts Journal* 60 (2):24–30.

———. 2007. Interest rate swaps: Accounting vs. economics. *Financial Analysts Journal* 63:15–18.

Kearney, C. 2012. Emerging markets research: Trends, issues and future directions. *Emerging Markets Review* 13(2):159–183.

Kempf, A., C. Merkle, and A. Niessen-Ruenzi. 2014. Low risk and high return–affective attitudes and stock market expectations. *European Financial Management* 20 (5):995–1030.

Kent, C., and G. Debelle. 1999. *Trends in the Australian Banking System: Implications for Financial System Stability and Monetary Policy*. Economic Research Department, Reserve Bank of Australia.

Khediri, K. B., and D. Folus. 2010. Does hedging increase firm value? Evidence from French firms. *Applied Economics Letters* 17 (10):995–998.

Khor, H. E. 2001. Derivatives and Macroeconomic Management in Post-Crisis Asia. Singapore: Monetary Authority of Singapore.

Khoury, S. J., and K. H. Chanf. 1993. Hedging foreign exchange risk: Selecting the optimal tool. *International Financial Management* 5 (1993):134–155.

Kim, C., C. Pantzalis, and J. C. Park. 2014. Do family owners use firm hedging policy to hedge personal undiversified wealth risk? *Financial Management* 43 (2):415–444.

Kim, S. H., and G. Koppenhaver. 1992. An empirical analysis of bank interest rate swaps. *Journal of Financial Services Research* 7 (1):57–72.

Kim, W. C., P. Hwang, and W. P. Burgers. 1993. Multinationals' diversification and the risk-return trade-off. *Strategic Management Journal* 14 (4):275–286.

Kirkwood, J., and D. Nahm. 2006. Australian banking efficiency and its relation to stock returns. *Economic Record* 82 (258):253–267.

Kishan, R. P., and T. P. Opiela. 2000. Bank size, bank capital, and the bank lending channel. *Journal of Money, Credit and Banking* 32 (1):121–141.

Kleffner, A. E., R. B. Lee, and B. McGannon. 2003. The effect of corporate governance on the use of enterprise risk management: Evidence from Canada. *Risk Management and Insurance Review* 6 (1):53–73.

Klimczak, K. 2007. Risk management theory: A comprehensive empirical assessment. *Available at SSRN*.

Klimczak, K. M. 2008. Corporate hedging and risk management theory: Evidence from Polish listed companies. *The Journal of Risk Finance* 9 (1):20–39.

Knill, A., K. Minnick, and A. Nejadmalayeri. 2006. Selective hedging, information asymmetry, and futures prices. *The Journal of Business* 79 (3):1475–1501.

Kocon, M. J. 2007. Hedge Accounting in Banks in the Light of the International Financial Reporting Standards. Master's Thesis Aarhus School of Business Aarhus University.

Kohn, D. L. 2010. Focusing on bank interest rate risk exposure. Virginia: Federal Reserve System, 2010.

Kotrlik, J., and C. Higgins. 2001. Organizational research: Determining appropriate sample size in survey research appropriate sample size in survey research. *Information Technology, Learning, and Performance Journal* 19 (1):43.

Krainer, J., and S. LeRoy. 2010. Underwater mortgages. In *FRBSF Economic Letter*, edited by S. Zuckerman and A. Todd. San Francisco, CA: Federal Reserve Bank of San Francisco, 31–35.

Kumar, S., and R. Gulati. 2008. An examination of technical, pure technical, and scale efficiencies in Indian public sector banks using data envelopment analysis. *Eurasian Journal of Business and Economics* 1 (2):33–69.

Kupper, E. F. 2000. Risk management in banking. In *Crisis*. Australia: ASX.

Kwan, C.-H. 1994. *Economic Interdependence in the Asia-Pacific Region: Towards a Yen Bloc*. USA and Canada: Psychology Press.

Kwan, S. H. 2006. The X-efficiency of commercial banks in Hong Kong. *Journal of Banking & Finance* 30 (4):1127–1147.

Laeven, L. 1999. Risk and efficiency in East Asian banks. *World Bank Policy Research Working Paper* (2255).

Lam, J. 2014. *Enterprise Risk Management: From Incentives to Controls*. 2nd ed. Hoboken, NJ: John Wiley & Sons.

Lambert, R. A. 2001. Contracting theory and accounting. *Journal of Accounting and Economics* 32 (1):3–87.

Land, K. C., C. Lovell, and S. Thore. 1993. Chance-constrained data envelopment analysis. *Managerial and Decision Economics* 14 (6):541–554.

Landsman, W. 2006. Fair value accounting for financial instruments: Some implications for bank regulation.BIS Working Papers No 209. Monetary and Economic Department, Basel, Switzerland.

Lane, P. R. 2012. The European sovereign debt crisis. *The Journal of Economic Perspectives* 26 (3):49–67.

Lang, W. W., and J. A. Jagtiani. 2010. The mortgage and financial crises: The role of credit risk management and corporate governance. *Atlantic Economic Journal* 38 (3):295–316.

Lange, H. P. 2007. *Financial Institutions Management*. McGraw-Hill Higher Education.

Laplume, A. O., K. Sonpar, and R. A. Litz. 2008. Stakeholder theory: Reviewing a theory that moves us. *Journal of Management* 34 (6):1152–1189.

Latruffe, L., S. Davidova, and K. Balcombe. 2008. Application of a double bootstrap to investigation of determinants of technical efficiency of farms in Central Europe. *Journal of Productivity Analysis* 29 (2):183–191.

Lauterbach, B., and A. Vaninsky. 1999. Ownership structure and firm performance: Evidence from Israel. *Journal of Management and Governance* 3 (2):189–201.

Léautier, T. O. 2007. *Corporate Risk Management for Value Creation: A Guide to Real-Life Applications*. London: Risk Books.

Leightner, J. E., and C. Lovell. 1998. The impact of financial liberalization on the performance of Thai banks. *Journal of Economics and Business* 50 (2):115–131.

Levine, R. 2005. Finance and growth: Theory and evidence. *Handbook of Economic Growth* 1:865–934.

Li, L., and Z. Yu. 2010. The impact of derivatives activity on commercial banks: Evidence from US Bank Holding Companies. *Asia-Pacific Financial Markets* 17 (3):303–322.

Li, Q., K. Wang, and S. Cross. 2013. Evaluation of warm mix asphalt (WMA): A case study. In *Airfield and Highway Pavement*, edited by Imad L. Al-Qadi and Scott Murrell. Los Angeles, CA: American Society of Civil Engineers, 118–127.

Li, S., and M. Marinč. 2014. The use of financial derivatives and risks of US bank holding companies. *International Review of Financial Analysis* 35 (2014):46–71.

Libby, R. 1976. Man versus model of man: the need for a nonlinear model. *Organizational Behavior and Human Performance* 16 (1):23–26.

Lien, D., and M. Zhang. 2008. A survey of emerging derivatives markets. *Emerging Markets Finance and Trade* 44 (2):39–69.

Lin, C.-H., C.-H. Lin, and Y.-Y. Wang. 2012. The impacts of firm size on the interactions between investment, financing and hedging decisions. *Journal of Statistics and Management Systems* 15 (6):663–683.

Lin, C.-M., R. D. Phillips, and S. D. Smith. 2008. Hedging, financing, and investment decisions: Theory and empirical tests. *Journal of Banking & Finance* 32 (8):1566–1582.

Lintner, J. 1965. The valuation of risk assets and the selection of risky investments in stock portfolios and capital budgets. *The Review of Economics and Statistics* 47 (1):13–37.

Lioui, A., and P. Poncet. 2005. *Dynamic Asset Allocation with Forwards and Futures*. New York: Springer Science & Business Media.

Loftus, J., L. Ken, P. Ruth, W. Victoria, and C. Kerry. 2013. *Understanding Australian Accounting Standards*. Australia: John Wiley & Sons.

Lonien, C. 2003. *The Japanese Economic and Social System: From a Rocky Past to an Uncertain Future*. Amsterdam: IOS Press.

López de Silanes, F., R. La Porta, and A. Shleifer. 1999. Corporate ownership around the world. *Journal of Finance* 54 (2):471–517.

Ludwin, W. G., and T. L. Guthrie. 1989. Assessing productivity with data envelopment analysis. *Public Productivity Review* 12 (4):361–372.

Luptacik, M. 2010. *Mathematical Optimization and Economic Analysis*. New York: Springer.

Lynch, D. 1996. Measuring financial sector development: A study of selected Asia-Pacific countries. *The Developing Economies* 34 (1):1–27.

Maddaloni, A., and J.-L. Peydró. 2011. Bank risk-taking, securitization, supervision, and low interest rates: Evidence from the Euro-area and the US lending standards. *Review of Financial Studies* 24 (6):2121–2165.

Madhumathi, R. 2012. *Derivatives and Risk Management*. New Delhi, India: Pearson Education India.

Madura, J., and E. R. Zarruk. 1995. Bank exposure to interest rate risk: A global perspective. *Journal of Financial Research* 18 (1):1–13.

Maghyereh, A. I., and B. Awartani. 2012. Financial integration of GCC banking markets: A non-parametric bootstrap DEA estimation approach. *Research in International Business and Finance* 26 (2):181–195.

Mai, S. 2008. *The Global Derivatives Market*. Germany: Deutsche Börse Group, 1–42.

Maines, L. A., and L. S. McDaniel. 2000. Effects of comprehensive-income characteristics on nonprofessional investors' judgments: The role of financial-statement presentation format. *The Accounting Review* 75 (2):179–207.

Malana, N. M., and H. M. Malano. 2006. Benchmarking productive efficiency of selected wheat areas in Pakistan and India using data envelopment analysis. *Irrigation and Drainage* 55 (4):383–394.

Mallin, C., K. Ow-Yong, and M. Reynolds. 2001. Derivatives usage in UK non-financial listed companies. *The European Journal of Finance* 7 (1):63–91.

Mann, J., and P. Sephton. 2010. A comparison of hedging strategies and effectiveness for storable and non-storable commodities. Paper read at Proceedings of the NCCC-134 Conference on Applied Commodity Price Analysis, Forecasting, and Market Risk Management. St. Louis, MO.

Mante, B. D. 1997. A Study to Model Secondary School Efficiency. PhD Thesis, School of Business, Faculty of Law and Management, La Trobe University.

Manzoni, A. 2007. A New Approach to Performance Measurement using Data Envelopment Analysis: Implications for Organisation Behaviour, Corporate Governance and Supply Chain Management, Faculty of Business and Law, Victoria University, Melbourne.

Manzoni, A., and S. M. Islam. 2009a. The best exponents of corporate social responsibility and organisation behaviour. Paper read at Industrial Engineering and Engineering Management (IEEE), 8–11 December 2009, at Hong Kong.

———. 2009b. *Performance Measurement in Corporate Governance: DEA Modelling and Implications for Organisational Behaviour and Supply Chain Management.* Heidelberg: Springer Science & Business Media.

Marsala, C., M. Pallotta, and R. Zenti. 2004. Integrated risk management with a filtered bootstrap approach. *Economic Notes* 33 (3):375–398.

Marsden, A., and A. K. Prevost. 2005. Derivatives use, corporate governance, and legislative change: An empirical analysis of New Zealand listed companies. *Journal of Business Finance & Accounting* 32 (1–2):255–295.

Marshall, A. P. 2000. Foreign exchange risk management in UK, USA and Asia Pacific multinational companies. *Journal of Multinational Financial Management* 10 (2):185–211.

Marshall, J. F., and V. K. Bansal. 1992. *Financial Engineering: A Complete Guide to Financial Innovation.* New York: New York Institute of Finance.

Masulis, R. W., and R. S. Thomas. 2009. Does private equity create wealth? The effects of private equity and derivatives on corporate governance. *The University of Chicago Law Review* 76 (Finance Working Paper No: 253/209):219–259.

Maudos, J. n., and J. Fernandez de Guevara. 2004. Factors explaining the interest margin in the banking sectors of the European Union. *Journal of Banking & Finance* 28 (9):2259–2281.

McAllister, P. H., and D. McManus. 1993. Resolving the scale efficiency puzzle in banking. *Journal of Banking & Finance* 17 (2):389–405.

McCarl, B. A., and T. H. Spreen. 1997. Applied mathematical programming using algebraic systems. Cambridge: Massachusetts Institute of Technology (MIT).

———. 2011. Applied mathematical programming using algebraic systems. Texas A&M University.

McCarroll, J., and G. R. Khatri. 2014. Aligning hedge accounting with risk management. *Financial Reporting-Accountancy Ireland* 46 (2):36–38.

McConnell, P. 2014. New hedge accounting model will improve investor understanding of risk management. *Investor Perspectives* June 2014: 1–5.

McNeil, A. J., R. Frey, and P. Embrechts. 2005. *Quantitative Risk Management: Concepts, Techniques, and Tools*. Princeton, NJ: Princeton university press.

McNeil, A. J., R. Frey, and P. Embrechts. 2010. *Quantitative Risk Management: Concepts, Techniques, and Tools*. Princeton, NJ: Princeton university press.

Medova, E. A., and R. G. Smith. 2005. A framework to measure integrated risk. *Quantitative Finance* 5 (1):105–121.

Mellenbergh, G., H. Ader, and D. Hand. 2008. *Advising on Research Methods: A Consultant's Companion*. Huizen, Netherlands: Johannes van Kessel Publishing.

Merton, R. C., and A. Perold. 1993. Theory of risk capital in financial firms. *Journal of Applied Corporate Finance* 6 (3):16–32.

Mester, L. J. 1996. A study of bank efficiency taking into account risk-preferences. *Journal of Banking & Finance* 20 (6):1025–1045.

Mihaljek, D., and F. Packer. 2010. Derivatives in emerging markets. *BIS Quarterly Review* (December 2010):16.

Miller, K. D., and H. G. Waller. 2003. Scenarios, real options and integrated risk management. *Long Range Planning* 36 (1):93–107.

Miller, S. M., and A. G. Noulas. 1996. The technical efficiency of large bank production. *Journal of Banking & Finance* 20 (3):495–509.

Milos Sprcic, D. 2007. The derivatives as financial risk management instruments: The case of Croatian and Slovenian non-financial companies. *Financial Theory and Practice* 31 (4):395–420.

Miltersen, K. R., K. Sandmann, and D. Sondermann. 2012. Closed form solutions for term structure derivatives with log-normal interest rates. *The Journal of Finance* 52 (1):409–430.

Minh, N. K., P. Van Khanh, and P. A. Tuan. 2012. A new approach for ranking efficient units in data envelopment analysis and application to a sample of Vietnamese agricultural bank branches. *American Journal of Operations Research* 2 (1):126–136.

Minton, B. A., R. Stulz, and R. Williamson. 2009. How much do banks use credit derivatives to hedge loans? *Journal of Financial Services Research* 35 (1):1–31.

Modigliani, F., and M. H. Miller. 1958. The cost of capital, corporation finance and the theory of investment. *The American Economic Review* 48 (3):261–297.

———. 1963. Corporate income taxes and the cost of capital: A correction. *The American Economic Review* 53 (3):433–443.

Mojtahedi, S., S. Mousavi, and A. Aminian. 2009. A non-parametric statistical approach for analyzing risk factor data in risk management process. *Journal of Applied Sciences* 9 (1):113–120.

Mokhtar, H. S. A., S. M. AlHabshi, and N. Abdullah. 2006. A conceptual framework for and survey of banking efficiency study. *UniTAR e-Journal* 2 (2):1–19.

Moradi-Motlagh, A., A. Valadkhani, and A. S. Saleh. 2014. Rising efficiency and cost saving in Australian banks: A bootstrap approach. *Applied Economics Letters*, 22(3):189–194. (ahead-of-print):1–6.

Morgan, G. 2008. Market formation and governance in international financial markets: The case of OTC derivatives. *Human Relations* 61 (5):637–660.

Morgan, M. G., and M. Small. 1992. *Uncertainty: A Guide to Dealing with Uncertainty in Quantitative Risk and Policy Analysis*. Cambridge: Cambridge University Press.

Morita, H., and N. K. Avkiran. 2009. Selecting inputs and outputs in data envelopment analysis by designing statistical experiments. *Journal of the Operations Research Society of Japan* 52 (2):163.

Mulugetta, A., and H. Hadjinikolov. 2004. Derivatives and risk management in the banking industry. *The International Journal of Banking and Finance* 2 (1):4.

Mulvey, J. M., and H. Vladimirou. 1991. Solving multistage stochastic networks: An application of scenario aggregation. *Networks* 21 (6):619–643.

Munisamy, S., and W. Danxia. 2013. Ranking efficiency of Asian container ports: A bootstrapped frontier approach. *International Journal of Shipping and Transport Logistics* 5 (6):668–690.

Murinde, V., and T. Zhao. 2009. Bank competition, risk taking and productive efficiency: Evidence from Nigeria's banking reform experiments. University of Stirling, Division of Economics.

Myers, D., and C. W. J. Smith. 1987. Corporate insurance and the underinvestment problem. *Journal of Risk and Insurance* 54 (1):45–54.

Myers, S. C. 1977. Determinants of corporate borrowing. *Journal of Financial Economics* 5 (2):147–175.

———. 1984. Capital structure puzzle. Cambridge, MA: National Bureau of Economic Research.

Myers, S. C., and N. S. Majluf. 1984. Corporate financing and investment decisions when firms have information that investors do not have. *Journal of Financial Economics* 13 (2):187–221.

Na Ranong, P., and W. Phuenngam. 2009. Critical Success Factors for Effective Risk Management Procedures in Financial Industries: A Study from the Perspectives of the Financial Institutions in Thailand. Master Thesis, Umea School of Business, Umea University, Sweden.

Nanto, D. K. 2009. *The Global Financial Crisis: Analysis and Policy Implications.* London: DIANE Publishing.

Neal, P. 2004. X-efficiency and productivity change in Australian Banking. *Australian Economic Papers* 43 (2):174–191.

Negoita, C., L. Zadeh, and H. Zimmermann. 1978. Fuzzy sets as a basis for a theory of possibility. *Fuzzy Sets and Systems* 1:3–28.

Nguyen, H., and R. Faff. 2002. On the determinants of derivative usage by Australian companies. *Australian Journal of Management* 27 (1):1–24.

Njoroge, N. N., N. G. Matumo, and K. E. Maina. 2013. Factors influencing development of financial derivatives markets: A survey of listed companies in Kenya. *Global Advanced Research Journals* 25 (5):258–267.

Nyhan, R. C. 2002. Benchmarking tools: An application to juvenile justice facility performance. *The Prison Journal* 82 (4):423–439.

Nyhan, R. C., and L. L. Martin. 1999. Comparative performance measurement: A primer on data envelopment analysis. *Public Productivity & Management Review* 22 (3):348–364.

Okochi, J. 2007. The death of the short-cut method & challenges with hedging future debt issuance. New York: Reval, 1–6.

Olesen, O. B., and N. Petersen. 1995. Chance constrained efficiency evaluation. *Management Science* 41 (3):442–457.

Omar, C., K. Jawad, L. Cindy, N. Alfonso, and T. Ozgur. 2014. Risk in emerging markets: The way forward for leading banks. Australia: McKinsey & Company.

Ong, M. K. 2006. *Risk Management: A Modern Perspective.* Burlington, MA: Elsevier Academic Press.

Otieno, C. O. 2013. The effect of foreign exchange risk management strategies on the financial performance of forex bureaus in Nairobi county, School of Business, University of Narobi, Kenya.

Ozcan, Y. A. 2008. *Health Care Benchmarking and Performance Evaluation: An Assessment using Data Envelopment Analysis (DEA).* Berlin: Springer.

———. 2014. Advanced DEA models. In *Health Care Benchmarking and Performance Evaluation,* edited by Yasar A. Ozcan. Boston, MA: Springer, 121–137.

Panaretou, A., M. B. Shackleton, and P. A. Taylor. 2013. Corporate risk management and hedge accounting. *Contemporary Accounting Research* 30 (1):116–139.

Pannell, D. J. 1997. *Introduction to Practical Linear Programming.* New York: Wiley-Interscience.

Paradi, J. C., S. Rouatt, and H. Zhu. 2011. Two-stage evaluation of bank branch efficiency using data envelopment analysis. *Omega* 39 (1):99–109.

Pasiouras, F. 2008. Estimating the technical and scale efficiency of Greek commercial banks: The impact of credit risk, off-balance sheet activities, and international operations. *Research in International Business and Finance* 22 (3):301–318.

Pastor, J. 1995. Improving the new DEA-efficiency measure of Tone. In *Working paper.* Alicante, Spain: University of Alicante.

Pastor, J., F. Pérez, and J. Quesada. 1997. Efficiency analysis in banking firms: An international comparison. *European Journal of Operational Research* 98 (2):395–407.

Pastor, J. M. 1998. *Efficiency and Risk Management in Banking Firms: A Method to Decompose Risk.* Instituto Valenciano de Investigaciones Económicas.

Pastor, J. M. 1999. Efficiency and risk management in Spanish banking: A method to decompose risk. *Applied Financial Economics* 9 (4):371–384.

Paul, S., and K. Kourouche. 2008. Regulatory policy and the efficiency of the banking sector in Australia. *Australian Economic Review* 41 (3):260–271.

Phan, D., H. Nguyen, and R. Faff. 2014. Uncovering the asymmetric linkage between financial derivatives and firm value—The case of oil and gas exploration and production companies. *Energy Economics* 45:340–352.

Phillips, A. L. 1995. 1995 derivatives practices and instruments survey. *Financial Management* 24 (2):115–125.

Phillips, R., A. S. Simsek, and G. van Ryzin. 2015. The effectiveness of field price discretion: Empirical evidence from auto lending. *Forthcoming in Management Science.*

Pjevčević, D., A. Radonjić, Z. Hrle, and V. Čolić. 2012. DEA window analysis for measuring port efficiencies in Serbia. *PROMET-Traffic&Transportation* 24 (1):63–72.

Pourjavad, E., and H. Shirouyehzad. 2014. A data envelopment analysis approach for measuring the efficiency in continuous manufacturing lines: A case study. *International Journal of Services and Operations Management* 18 (2):142–158.

Power, M. 2004. The risk management of everything. *The Journal of Risk Finance* 5 (3):58–65.

Pramborg, B. 2005. Foreign exchange risk management by Swedish and Korean nonfinancial firms: A comparative survey. *Pacific-Basin Finance Journal* 13 (3):343–366.

Prevost, A. K., L. C. Rose, and G. Miller. 2000. Derivatives usage and financial risk management in large and small economies: A comparative analysis. *Journal of Business Finance & Accounting* 27 (5–6):733–759.

Purnanandam, A. 2007. Interest rate derivatives at commercial banks: An empirical investigation. *Journal of Monetary Economics* 54 (6):1769–1808.

———. 2008. Financial distress and corporate risk management: Theory and evidence. *Journal of Financial Economics* 87 (3):706–739.

Raab, R. L., and R. W. Lichty. 2002. Identifying subareas that comprise a greater metropolitan area: The criterion of county relative efficiency. *Journal of Regional Science* 42 (3):579–594.

Radic, N., F. Fiordelisi, and C. Girardone. 2011. Efficiency and risk-taking in pre-crisis investment banks. *Journal of Financial Services Research* 41(1–2):81–101.

Radoi, M. 2012. Controversies in using derivatives in the context of the financial crisis. *African Journal of Business Management* 6 (12):4406–4412.

Ragsdale, C. 2010. *Spreadsheet Modeling & Decision Analysis: A Practical Introduction to Management Science*. Mason, OH: Cengage Learning.

Rahman, S., and M. K. Hassan. 2011. The potential of derivatives market in Bangladesh. *Journal of Economic Cooperation and Development* 32 (4):97–144.

Rajegopal, S. 2012. *Portfolio Management: How to Innovate and Invest in Successful Projects*. Basingstoke: Palgrave Macmillan.

Rajendran, M. 2007. Derivative use by banks in India. *Academy of Banking Studies Journal* 6 (1–2):27.

Ramanathan, R. 2003. *An Introduction to Data Envelopment Analysis: A Tool for Performance Measurement*. New Delhi: Sage.

Ramirez, J. 2007. *Accounting for Derivatives: Advanced Hedging Under IFRS*. Hoboken, NJ: John Wiley & Sons.

———. 2008. *Accounting for Derivatives: Advanced Hedging under IFRS*. West Sussex, England: John Wiley & Sons.

Rao, G. S. 2012. Derivatives in risk management. *International Journal of Advanced Research in Management and Social Sciences* 1 (4):55–60.

Ray, S. C. 2004. *Data Envelopment Analysis: Theory and Techniques for Economics and Operations Research*. Cambridge: Cambridge University Press.

Riccardi, R., and R. Toninelli. 2011. Data envelopment analysis with outputs uncertainty. *Journal of Information and Optimization Sciences* 32 (6):1289–1314.

Ringrose, P., and M. Bentley. 2015. Handling model uncertainty. In *Reservoir Model Design*, edited by P. Ringrose and M. Bentley. New York: Springer, 151–172.

Ritdumrongkul, A. 2011. Derivative Activities and the Thai Banks' Interest Rate and Exchange Rate Exposures, Faculty of Commerce and Accountancy Thammasat University, Bangkok, Thailand.

Rivas, A., T. Ozuna, and F. Policastro. 2006. Does the use of derivatives increase bank efficiency? Evidence from Latin American banks. *International Business and Economics Research Journal (IBER)* 5 (11):47–56.

Rizvi, S. F. A., and A. H. Khan. 2001. Post-liberalisation efficiency and productivity of the banking sector in Pakistan *The Pakistan Development Review* 40 (4):605–632.

Robinson, K. J. 2014. Banking recovery could be vulnerable to interest rate increases. *Southwest Economy* (2):10–13.

Romer, C. D., D. H. Romer, S. M. Goldfeld, and B. M. Friedman. 1990. New evidence on the monetary transmission mechanism. *Brookings Papers on Economic Activity* 1990 (1):149–213.

Rosmaini, K. 2002. Mengukur Kecekapan Relatif Operasi Loji Air BBA Kedah Dengan Menggunakan Kaedah Analisis Penyampulan Data, Universiti Utara Malaysia.

Rubinstein, M. 1999. *Rubinstein on Derivatives*. London: Risk Books.

Sadjadi, S., and H. Omrani. 2010. A bootstrapped robust data envelopment analysis model for efficiency estimating of telecommunication companies in Iran. *Telecommunications Policy* 34 (4):221–232.

Saen, R. F., and M. Azadi. 2011. A chance-constrained data envelopment analysis approach for strategy selection. *Journal of Modelling in Management* 6 (2):200–214.

Saka, A. N. A., A. Q. Aboagye, and A. Gemegah. 2012. Technical efficiency of the Ghanaian banking industry and the effects of the entry of foreign banks. *Journal of African Business* 13 (3):232–243.

Sala-Garrido, R., F. Hernández-Sancho, and M. Molinos-Senante. 2012. Assessing the efficiency of wastewater treatment plants in an uncertain context: A DEA with tolerances approach. *Environmental Science & Policy* 18:34–44.

Saltelli, A., K. Chan, and E. M. Scott. 2000a. *Sensitivity Analysis*. New York: Wiley.

Saltelli, A., S. Tarantola, and F. Campolongo. 2000b. Sensitivity analysis as an ingredient of modeling. *Statistical Science* 15 (4):377–395.

Samant, A. 1996. An empirical study of interest rate swap usage by nonfinancial corporate business. *Journal of Financial Services Research* 10 (1):43–57.

Sangha, B. S. 1995. Financial derivatives: Applications and policy issues. *Business Economics* 30 (1):46–52.

Sarkar, J., and S. Sarkar. 2003. Large shareholder activism in corporate governance in developing countries: Evidence from India. *International Review of Finance* 1 (3):161–194.

Sathye, M. 2001. X-efficiency in Australian banking: An empirical investigation. *Journal of Banking & Finance* 25 (3):613–630.

———. 2002. Measuring productivity changes in Australian banking: An application of Malmquist indices. *Managerial Finance* 28 (9):48–59.

———. 2005. Technical efficiency of large bank production in Asia and the Pacific. *Multinational Finance Journal* 9 (1&2):1–22.

Saunders, A., and M. M. Cornett. 2007. *Financial Markets and Institutions: An Introduction to the Risk Management Approach*. Irwin: McGraw-Hill.

Saunders, A., and L. Schumacher. 2000. The determinants of bank interest rate margins: An international study. *Journal of international Money and Finance* 19 (6):813–832.

Sawilowsky, S. S. 2002. Fermat, Schubert, Einstein, and Behrens-Fisher: The probable difference between two Means when $\sigma1^2 \neq \sigma2^2$. *Journal of Modern Applied Statistical Methods* 1 (2):461–472.

Saxena, S., and A. Villar. 2008. Hedging instruments in emerging market economies. In *Financial Globalisation and Emerging Market Capital Flows*: Bank for International Settlements (BIS), 71–87.

Scannella, E., and D. Bennardo. 2013. Interest rate risk in banking: A theoretical and empirical investigation through a systemic approach (asset & liability management). *Business Systems Review* 2 (1):59–79.

Schlich, B., and P. Jackson. 2013. Remaking financial services: Risk management five years after the crisis. New York: EY's Global Banking & Capital Markets Center, 1–80.

Schlueter, T., S. Sievers, and T. Hartmann-Wendels. 2015. Bank funding stability, pricing strategies and the guidance of depositors. *Journal of Banking & Finance* 51 (February 2015):43–61.

Scholtens, B., and D. Van Wensveen. 2000. A critique on the theory of financial intermediation. *Journal of Banking & Finance* 24 (8):1243–1251.

Schroeck, G. 2002. *Risk Management and Value Creation in Financial Institutions.* Hoboken: John Wiley & Sons.

Sealey, C. W., and J. T. Lindley. 1977. Inputs, outputs, and a theory of production and cost at depository financial institutions. *The Journal of Finance* 32 (4):1251–1266.

Seerden, H. 2010. Comment letter on the exposure draft Hedge Accounting. Luxembourg.

Seifert, B., H. Gonenc, and J. Wright. 2005. The international evidence on performance and equity ownership by insiders, blockholders, and institutions. *Journal of Multinational Financial Management* 15 (2):171–191.

Seiford, L. M., and J. Zhu. 1998. Sensitivity analysis of DEA models for simultaneous changes in all the data. *Journal of the Operational Research Society* 49 (10):1060–1071.

Sengupta, J. 2000. *Dynamic and Stochastic Efficiency Analysis: Economics of Data Envelopment Analysis.* Singapore: World Scientific.

Sengupta, J. K. 1987. Data envelopment analysis for efficiency measurement in the stochastic case. *Computers & Operations Research* 14 (2):117–129.

———. 2005. Nonparametric efficiency analysis under uncertainty using data envelopment analysis. *International Journal of Production Economics* 95 (1):39–49.

Servaes, H., A. Tamayo, and P. Tufano. 2009. The theory and practice of corporate risk management. *Journal of Applied Corporate Finance* 21 (4):60–78.

Shamsher, M., and H. Taufiq. 2007. Asian derivative markets: Research issues. *International Journal of Banking and Finance* 5 (1):1.

Shang, J.-K., F.-C. Wang, and W.-T. Hung. 2010. A stochastic DEA study of hotel efficiency. *Applied Economics* 42 (19):2505–2518.

Shanker, L. 1996. Derivatives usage and interest rate risk of large banking firms. *Journal of Futures Markets* 16 (4):459–474.

Sharma, D., A. K. Sharma, and M. K. Barua. 2013. Efficiency and productivity of banking sector: A critical analysis of literature and design of conceptual model. *Qualitative Research in Financial Markets* 5 (2):195–224.

Sharpe, W. F. 1964. Capital asset prices: A theory of market equilibrium under conditions of risk. *The Journal of Finance* 19 (3):425–442.

Shawtari, F. A. M. 2014. Efficiency Determinants and Impacts on Bank Margins and Discretionary Accruals: A Comparative Analysis of Islamic and Conventional Banks in Yemen. PhD Thesis, International Centre for Education in Islamic Finance (INCEIF).

Sheedy, E. 1997. Marketing derivatives: A question of trust. *International Journal of Bank Marketing* 15 (1):22–31.

Sheedy, E., and S. McCracken. 1997. *Derivatives: The Risks that Remain.* Allen & Unwin.

Sherman, D. H. 1981. Measurement of Hospital Technical Efficiency: A Comparative Evaluation of Data Envelopment Analysis, Graduate School of Business, Harvard University, Cambridge, MA.

Sherman, H. D., and F. Gold. 1985. Bank branch operating efficiency: Evaluation with data envelopment analysis. *Journal of Banking & Finance* 9 (2):297–315.

Shimshak, D. G., M. L. Lenard, and R. K. Klimberg. 2009. Incorporating quality into data envelopment analysis of nursing home performance: A case study. *Omega* 37 (3):672–685.

Shiu, Y. M., and P. Moles. 2010. What motivates banks to use derivatives: Evidence from Taiwan. *The Journal of Derivatives* 17 (4):67–78.

Shunko, M., L. Debo, L. Nan, and N. Secomandi. 2010. Optimal Managerial Compensation and Financial Hedging in Commodity Procurement. Pittsburgh, USA: Carnegie Mellon University.

Silverman, B. W. 1986. *Density Estimation for Statistics and Data Analysis*. New York: CRC Press.

Simar, L. 1992. Estimating efficiencies from frontier models with panel data: A comparison of parametric, non-parametric and semi-parametric methods with bootstrapping. *Journal of Productivity Analysis* 3 (1–2):171–203.

Simar, L., I. Van Keilegom, and V. Zelenyuk. 2014. Nonparametric least squares methods for stochastic frontier models: School of Economics, University of Queensland, Australia.

Simar, L., and P. W. Wilson. 1998. Sensitivity analysis of efficiency scores: How to bootstrap in nonparametric frontier models. *Management Science* 44 (1):49–61.

———. 2000. A general methodology for bootstrapping in non-parametric frontier models. *Journal of Applied Statistics* 27 (6):779–802.

———. 2008. Statistical inference in nonparametric frontier models: Recent developments and perspectives. In *The Measurement of Productive Efficiency and Productivity Growth*, edited by Harold O. Fried, C.A. Knox Lovell, and Shelton S. Schmidt. New York: Oxford University Press, 421–521.

Singh, S. 2010. Discussant remarks: Development of financial markets in Asia and the Pacific. *BIS Papers Chapters* 52:211–214.

Sinkey, J. F., and D. Carter. 1997. Derivatives in US banking: Theory, practice, and empirical evidence. *Advances in Finance, Investment and Banking: Derivatives, Regulation and Banking*, edited by J. F. Sinkey and D. Carter. New York: Elsevier Science BV: 41–78.

Sinkey, J. F., and D. A. Carter. 2000. Evidence on the financial characteristics of banks that do and do not use derivatives. *The Quarterly Review of Economics and Finance* 40 (4):431–449.

———. 2001. Evidence on the financial characteristics of banks that do and do not use derivatives. *The Quarterly Review of Economics and Finance* 40 (4):431–449.

Siregar, R. Y., V. Lim, and V. Pontines. 2011. *Post Global Financial Crisis: Issues and Challenges For Central Banks of Emerging Markets*. South East Asian Central Banks (SEACEN) Research and Training Centre.

Slovic, P., D. Fleissner, and W. S. Bauman. 1972. Analyzing the use of information in investment decision making: A methodological proposal. *The Journal of Business* 45 (2):283–301.

Smirnov, N. 1948. Table for estimating the goodness of fit of empirical distributions. *The Annals of Mathematical Statistics* 19:279–281.

Smith Jr, C. W., C. W. Smithson, and L. M. Wakeman. 1988. The market for interest rate swaps. *Financial Management* 17 (4):34–44.

Smith, C. W., and R. M. Stulz. 1985. The determinants of firms' hedging policies. *Journal of Financial and Quantitative Analysis* 20 (4):391–405.

Smith, P. 1990. Data envelopment analysis applied to financial statements. *Omega* 18 (2):131–138.

Soedarmono, W., A. Tarazi, A. Agusman, G. Monroe, and D. Gasbarro. 2012. Loan Loss Provisions and Lending Behaviour of Banks: Asian Evidence During 1992–2009. *Available at SSRN 2131583.*

Soin, K. 2005. Risk, regulation and the role of management accounting and control in UK financial services. In *Critical Perspectives in Accounting.* New York.

Sprčić, D. M. 2008. The derivatives as financial risk management instruments: The case of Croatian and Slovenian non-financial companies. *Financial Theory and Practice* 31 (4):395–420.

Staat, M. 2001. The effect of sample size on the mean efficiency in DEA: Comment. *Journal of Productivity Analysis* 15 (2):129–137.

Standards Australia and Standards New Zealand 2004. Australia/ New Zealand Standard Risk Management AS/NZS 4360:2004, Standards Australia, Sydney/Standards New Zealand, Auckland. Retrieved 30 March 2009, from www.saiglobal.com.

Starmer, C. 1992. Testing new theories of choice under uncertainty using the common consequence effect. *The Review of Economic Studies* 59 (4):813–830.

Stulz, R. 1990. Managerial discretion and optimal financing policies. *Journal of Financial Economics* 26 (1):3–27.

Stulz, R. M. 2003. *Risk Management & Derivatives.* South-Western Pub.

Stulz, R. M. 2004. Should we fear derivatives? Massachusetts National Bureau of Economic Research.

Stulz, R. M. 2008. Risk management failures: What are they and when do they happen? *Journal of Applied Corporate Finance* 20 (4):39–48.

Stulz, R. M. 2015. Risk-taking and risk management by banks. *Journal of Applied Corporate Finance* 27 (1):8–18.

Sufian, F. 2007a. The efficiency of Islamic banking industry in Malaysia: Foreign vs domestic banks. *Humanomics* 23 (3):174–192.

———. 2007b. Trends in the efficiency of Singapore's commercial banking groups: A non-stochastic frontier DEA window analysis approach. *International Journal of Productivity and Performance Management* 56 (2):99–136.

———. 2010. The impact of the Asian financial crisis on bank efficiency: The 1997 experience of Malaysia and Thailand. *Journal of International Development* 22 (7):866–889.

Sufian, F., and R. Haron. 2009. On the efficiency of the Malaysian banking sector: A risk-return perspective. *International Journal of Commerce and Management* 19 (3):222–232.

Sufian, F., and M.-Z. A. Majid. 2007. Deregulation, consolidation and banks efficiency in Singapore: Evidence from event study window approach and Tobit analysis. *International Review of Economics* 54 (2):261–283.

Sun, L., and T.-P. Chang. 2011. A comprehensive analysis of the effects of risk measures on bank efficiency: Evidence from emerging Asian countries. *Journal of Banking & Finance* 35 (7):1727–1735.

Sundaram, R. K. 2013. Derivatives in financial market development. *International Growth Centre.*

Swad, S. M. 1995. Accounting and disclosures for derivatives. In *1995 Twenty-Second Annual National Conference on Current SEC Developments.* Washington, DC: Office of the Chief Accountant, U.S. Securities and Exchange Commission.

Tahir, I. M., and N. M. A. Bakar. 2009. Evaluating efficiency of Malaysian banks using data envelopment analysis. *International Journal of Business and Management* 4 (8):P96.

Taylor, R. 1990. Interpretation of the correlation coefficient: A basic review. *Journal of Diagnostic Medical Sonography* 6 (1):35–39.

Thanassoulis, E., A. Boussofiane, and R. Dyson. 1996. A comparison of data envelopment analysis and ratio analysis as tools for performance assessment. *Omega* 24 (3):229–244.

Thao, N. H. 2012. A chance-constrained data envelopment analysis approach to the measurement of Vietnam's bank efficiency and productivity from 2006 to 2010, National Economics University.

Thompson, R. G., P. S. Dharmapala, J. Díaz, M. Gonzalez-Lima, and R. M. Thrall. 1996. DEA multiplier analytic center sensitivity with an illustrative application to independent oil companies. *Annals of Operations Research* 66 (2):163–177.

Titman, S. 1984. The effect of capital structure on a firm's liquidation decision. *Journal of Financial Economics* 13 (1):137–151.

Tone, K. 1993. An ε-free DEA and a new measure of efficiency. *Journal of the Operations Research Society of Japan* 36 (3):167–174.

———. 2001. A slack-based measure of efficiency in data envelopment analysis. *European Journal of Operational Research* 130:498–509.

Toninelli, R. 2011. Data envelopment analysis: Uncertainty, undesirable outputs and an application to world cement industry, Leonardo Fibonacci School, University of Pisa.

Tortosa-Ausina, E., E. Grifell-Tatjé, C. Armero, and D. Conesa. 2008. Sensitivity analysis of efficiency and Malmquist productivity indices: An application to Spanish savings banks. *European Journal of Operational Research* 184 (3):1062–1084.

Triantis, A. J. 2000. Real options and corporate risk management. *Journal of Applied Corporate Finance* 13 (2):64–73.

Trombley, M. A. 2003. *Accounting for Derivatives and Hedging*. New York: Irwin Professional Pub.

Troutt, M., A. Rai, and A. Zhang. 1996. The potential use of DEA for credit applicant acceptance systems. *Computers & Operations Research* 23 (4):405–408.

Tufano, P. 1996. Who manages risk? An empirical examination of risk management practices in the gold mining industry. *The Journal of Finance* 51 (4):1097–1137.

Türel, A., and A. Türel. 2014. The effect of derivatives on the financial positions of banks in Turkey and in EU: A comparative analysis. *International Journal of Critical Accounting* 6 (2):166–186.

Udhayakumar, A., V. Charles, and M. Kumar. 2011. Stochastic simulation based genetic algorithm for chance constrained data envelopment analysis problems. *Omega* 39 (4):387–397.

Ueda, T., and Y. Hoshiai. 1997. Application of principal component analysis for parsimonious summarization of DEA inputs and/or outputs. *Journal of the Operations Research Society of Japan-Keiei Kagaku* 40 (4):466–487.

Uzzi, B. 1999. Embeddedness in the making of financial capital: How social relations and networks benefit firms seeking financing. *American Sociological Review* 64 (4):481–505.

Velasco, L. G. 2014. Factors influencing derivatives usage by selected listed companies in the Philippines. *Philippine Management Review* 21:1–12.

Viceira, L. M. 2012. Bond risk, bond return volatility, and the term structure of interest rates. *International Journal of Forecasting* 28 (1):97–117.

Vincová, K. 2005. Using DEA models to measure efficiency. *Biatec* 13 (8):24–28.

Walden, J. B. 2006. Estimating vessel efficiency using a bootstrapped data envelopment analysis model. *Marine resource economics* 21 (2):181.

Wall, L. D. 1989. Interest rate swaps in an agency theoretic model with uncertain interest rates. *Journal of Banking & Finance* 13 (2):261–270.

Wallace, J. B. 2003. Derivative accounting and hedging under FAS 133. In *The Handbook of International Finance & Accounting*, edited by J. B. Wallace. New York: John Wiley, 1–6.

Wallenstein, S., C. L. Zucker, and J. L. Fleiss. 1980. Some statistical methods useful in circulation research. *Circulation Research* 47 (1):1–9.

Wang, Y. D. 2015. Convertibility restriction in China's foreign exchange market and its impact on forward pricing. *Journal of Banking & Finance* 50 (2015):616–631.

Wang, Y.-M., and Y.-X. Lan. 2013. Estimating most productive scale size with double frontiers data envelopment analysis. *Economic Modelling* 33:182–186.

Wanke, P., and C. Barros. 2014. Two-stage DEA: An application to major Brazilian banks. *Expert Systems with Applications* 41 (5):2337–2344.

Watson, J., J. Wickramanayke, and I. Premachandra. 2011. The value of Morningstar ratings: Evidence using stochastic data envelopment analysis. *Managerial Finance* 37 (2):94–116.

Webb, R. 2003. Levels of efficiency in UK retail banks: A DEA window analysis. *International Journal of the Economics of Business* 10 (3):305–322.

Weinberger, D., P. Tufano, C. Francis, A. Sodhani, D. Yeres, J. T. Smith, P. J. Isaac, and B. Becker. 1995. Using derivatives: What senior managers must know. *Harvard Business Review* 73 (1):33–41.

Wen, M., L. Guo, R. Kang, and Y. Yang. 2014. Data envelopment analysis with uncertain inputs and outputs. *Journal of Applied Mathematics*, Vol. 2014, Article ID 307108, 7: 1–8. http://dx.doi.org/10.1155/2014/307108.

Weston, J. F., and T. E. Copeland. 1992. *Financial Theory and Corporate Policy*. California: Addison Wesley.

Whidbee, D. A., and M. Wohar. 1999. Derivative activities and managerial incentives in the banking industry. *Journal of Corporate Finance* 5 (3):251–276.

Wilary, D. W. a. F. 2014. *Accounting for Interest Rate Derivatives*, edited by W. W. R. M. LLC.

Wiseman, R. M., and L. R. Gomez-Mejia. 1998. A behavioral agency model of managerial risk taking. *Academy of Management Review* 23 (1):133–153.

Wong, A., and X. Zhou. 2014. Development of financial market and economic growth: Review of Hong Kong, China, Japan, the United States and the United Kingdom. *International Journal of Economics and Finance* 3 (2):p111.

Wong, W.-P., Q. Deng, M.-L. Tseng, L.-H. Lee, and C.-W. Hooy. 2014. A stochastic setting to bank financial performance for refining effficiency estimates. *Intelligent Systems in Accounting, Finance and Management* 21 (4):225–245.

Wong, W. P., W. Jaruphongsa, and L. H. Lee. 2011. Budget allocation for effective data collection in predicting an accurate DEA efficiency score. *Automatic Control, IEEE Transactions on* 56 (6):1235–1246.

Woods, M., and D. E. Marginson. 2004. Accounting for derivatives: An evaluation of reporting practice by UK banks. *European Accounting Review* 13 (2):373–390.

Wysocki, P. D. 1998. Managerial motives and corporate use of derivatives: Some evidence. *Simon School of Business, University of Rochester Working Paper*.

Xue, M., and P. T. Harker. 1999. Overcoming the inherent dependency of DEA efficiency scores: A bootstrap approach. *Unpublished Working Paper*, Wharton Financial Institutions Center, University of Pennsylvania.

Yang, J., G. C. Davis, and D. J. Leatham. 2001. Impact of interest rate swaps on corporate capital structure: An empirical investigation. *Applied Financial Economics* 11 (1):75–81.

Yong, H. H. A., R. Faff, and K. Chalmers. 2009. Derivative activities and Asia-Pacific banks' interest rate and exchange rate exposures. *Journal of International Financial Markets, Institutions and Money* 19 (1):16–32.

———. 2014. Determinants of the extent of Asia-Pacific banks' derivative activities. *Accounting and Management Information Systems* 13 (3):430–448.

Young, S., D. Choi, J. Seade, and S. Shirai. 2009. *Competition among Financial Centres in Asia-Pacific: Prospects, Benefits, Risks and Policy Challenges*. Singapore: Institute of Southeast Asian Studies.

Zakaria, S., M. Salleh, and S. Hassan. 2014. A Bootstrap Data Envelopment Analysis (BDEA) approach in Islamic banking sector: A method to strengthen efficiency measurement. Paper read at Industrial Engineering and Engineering Management (IEEM) 2014.

Zeitun, R., and H. Banjelloun. 2012. The efficiency of banks and financial crisis in a developing economy: The case of Jordan. *International Review of Accounting, Banking and Finance* 4 (22):28–60.

Zelenyuk, V., and V. Zheka. 2006. Corporate governance and firm's efficiency: The case of a transitional country, Ukraine. *Journal of Productivity Analysis* 25 (1–2):143–157.

Zenios, S. A. 2007. *Practical Financial Optimization: Decision Making for Financial Engineers*. Cambridge: Blackwell Publishing Ltd.

Zenti, R., and M. Pallotta. 2000. Risk analysis for asset managers: Historical simulation, the bootstrap approach and value at risk calculation. Paper read at EFMA 2001 Lugano Meetings.

Zhang, H. 2009. Effect of derivative accounting rules on corporate risk-management behavior. *Journal of Accounting and Economics* 47 (3):244–264.

Zhang, Y., and R. Bartels. 1998. The effect of sample size on the mean efficiency in DEA with an application to electricity distribution in Australia, Sweden and New Zealand. *Journal of Productivity Analysis* 9 (3):187–204.

Zhang, Y., A. Yang, C. Xiong, T. Wang, and Z. Zhang. 2014. Feature selection using data envelopment analysis. *Knowledge-Based Systems* 64 (July 2014):70–80.

Zhao, F., and J. Moser. 2009. Use of derivatives and bank holding companies' interest rate risk. *Banking and Finance Review* 1 (1):51.

Zhu, J. 2009. Quantitative Models for Performance Evaluation and Benchmarking: DEA with Spreadsheets. Boston: Springer.

Zhu, J., and Z.-H. Shen. 1995. A discussion of testing DMUs' returns to scale. *European Journal of Operational Research* 81 (3):590–596.

Index

Note: **Bold** page numbers refer to tables; *italic* page numbers refer to figures and page numbers followed by "n" denote endnotes.